Learning To Discern God's Voice

180 Day Devotional for Walking in the Spirit

By Philip Allan Turner

Copyright 2014
Philip Allan Turner

All rights reserved. In accordance with the U.S. Copyright Act of 1976, the scanning, uploading, and electronic sharing of any part of this book without the permission of the publisher is unlawful piracy and theft of the author's intellectual property except by a reviewer who may quote brief passages in a review or brief passages used by churches, study groups or individuals who use it to build a closer relationship with God. In all cases, attribution is required.

ISBN-13: 978-0692335475

ISBN-10: 0692335471

I wish to dedicate this book to my parents whose guidance through it all has helped me to become a better man; a man closer to who God intended me to be. My hope is that this book glorifies God!

Table of Contents

Introduction
Day 1 Awaking your passion
Day 2 Writing your vision
Day 3 Prayer
Day 4 Choosing happy
Day 5 Love
Day 6 Being led by the Spirit
Day 7 Manifesting
Day 8 Power in us
Day 9 Numbering your days
Day 10 Faith
Day 11 Committing to God
Day 12 Restructuring
Day 13 Great Purpose
Day 14 Greatest Commandment
Day 15 A Receptive Heart
Day 16 A Godly Attitude
Day 17 Pleasing God
Day 18 An Abundant Life
Day 19 Our thoughts
Day 20 Love is the Path
Day 21 Internal Transformation
Day 22 Old Views
Day 23 The Great Motivator
Day 24 Gratitude
Day 25 Deeper Prayer
Day 26 I AM WHO I AM
Day 27 Kingdom of God
Day 28 What're you thinking about
Day 29 Readjusting our Aim
Day 30 Giving our best to God
Day 31 Letting God use you
Day 32 Internal Housekeeping
Day 33 Right Perspective
Day 34 Your Mission
Day 35 Our Heart
Day 36 Understanding
Day 37 The Journey
Day 38 Receiving the Gift
Day 39 The Big Picture
Day 40 Light and the Heart
Day 41 Deep Recesses of the Heart
Day 42 The Great Commission
Day 43 Promises of Psalms

Day 44 God's System
Day 45 Hope
Day 46 A Godly Mind
Day 47 The Inner Strength
Day 48 Purpose
Day 49 Eyes of your Heart
Day 50 A Radical Love
Day 51 Promises of God
Day 52 Trusting God
Day 53 Living in Love
Day 54 Loving in Godly Ways
Day 55 Transforming our Lives
Day 56 Right Believing
Day 57 God's Goodness
Day 58 Being Committed
Day 59 The Church
Day 60 Striving for God
Day 61 Spirit of Truth
Day 62 Our Walk
Day 63 Serving God
Day 64 Not Wavering
Day 65 Spiritual Maturity
Day 66 God as our Guide
Day 67 A Blessing
Day 68 Our Full Attention
Day 69 Being Spiritually Absorbed
Day 70 Personal Growth
Day 71 Inspiration
Day 72 Pleasing God
Day 73 Strength for the Journey
Day 74 Opening our Eyes
Day 75 Motivation
Day 76 Deepening our Spiritual Practice
Day 77 Letting Go
Day 78 New Beginnings
Day 79 Encouragement
Day 80 The Plank
Day 81 Pursuit of Happiness
Day 82 Living Fully Today
Day 83 Full Commitment
Day 84 The Inner Person
Day 85 Our Best
Day 86 Godly Positivity
Day 87 Impressing God
Day 88 Thriving
Day 89 Godly Dreams

Day 90 Giving Up is not an Option
Day 91 Our Thoughts
Day 92 Serving the Lord
Day 93 Good Success
Day 94 Changing our Perspective
Day 95 What is Happiness
Day 96 Forgiveness
Day 97 A Framework to Connect to God
Day 98 Sin
Day 99 His Holy Angels
Day 100 Staying Teachable
Day 101 Godly Perseverance
Day 102 Renewing Our Minds
Day 103 A God Consciousness
Day 104 A Christ-like Attitude
Day 105 Walking in the Light
Day 106 Being of Good Courage
Day 107 Living a Godly Life
Day 108 Rejoicing in the Lord
Day 109 The Christ-like Believer
Day 110 What is Faith
Day 111 God's Perfect Timing
Day 112 The Holy Spirit
Day 113 Walls between us and God
Day 114 Building Godly Character
Day 115 Living a Spiritually Radical Life
Day 116 God's Grace
Day 117 Pleasing God
Day 118 Serving God
Day 119 Going Deeper into the Word
Day 120 Understanding the enemy
Day 121 Repentance
Day 122 Abandoning mental bondage
Day 123 Eradicating limiting thoughts
Day 124 Building a deeper Godly Relationship
Day 125 Spiritual Diligence
Day 126 The Narrow Way
Day 127 Right Relationships
Day 128 Spiritual Priorities
Day 129 Genuine Belief
Day 130 Allowing Christ to Find You
Day 131 Developing a Thirst
Day 132 Strengthening our inner person
Day 133 Defining what Jesus Means to You
Day 134 God's Mercy
Day 135 Godly Encouragement

Day 136 Our Divine Nature
Day 137 Godly Guidance
Day 138 Spiritual Awareness
Day 139 Inner Rebirth
Day 140 Standing Out
Day 141 Love, Love, Love
Day 142 Fully Engaged with Christ
Day 143 Taking Care of Your Spirit
Day 144 Spiritual Absolutes
Day 145 Being Reconciled with Christ
Day 146 Being an Inheritor
Day 147 Expanding our Vision
Day 148 Seeker of God's Heart
Day 149 Saving Faith
Day 150 Purity
Day 151 Living within God's Will
Day 152 Is Jesus Enough
Day 153 Building ourselves up
Day 154 Being wonderfully made
Day 155 Spiritual Faithfulness
Day 156 Advancing in Faith
Day 157 What does it mean to be saved
Day 158 Radical Faith
Day 159 Seeking the Right Things
Day 160 Humility
Day 161 Obedience
Day 162 Praise
Day 163 The anointing on us
Day 164 What is acceptable
Day 165 Spiritual Excellence
Day 166 Looking for something real
Day 167 Our Thought Life
Day 168 The Beautiful Struggle Forward
Day 169 Choosing whom we will serve
Day 170 Combat a wavering faith
Day 171 Godly Self-Correction
Day 172 Creative Power of Words
Day 173 Accepting God's Mighty Grace
Day 174 Living with gratitude
Day 175 The God Effect
Day 176 Genuineness of our Faith
Day 177 Worshipping the Lord
Day 178 Smiling as Praise
Day 179 Truth and Honesty
Day 180 Fulfilling Our Ministry

Introduction

My goal of writing this daily devotional was to help me be more devoted to Christ Jesus, and I hope it helps you in the same manner. I want to motivate and inspire you to be all that God created you to be. I invite you to start a 180 day journey with me to walk in the Spirit. These motivational/inspirational tips are meant to inspire and refresh the spirit. Although each daily study builds on the previous lesson, feel free to pick and choose to read certain subjects when the Spirit moves you. This work is different than your average daily devotional; it's a study in how to discern God's voice in your everyday life. I want to ignite that fire within you to live passionately for God! This six-month devotional can change your life if you allow God's word to go deeply into your heart.

The process of writing this work helped me to walk in the Spirit each day. When a person is Spirit-led, they can achieve amazing things. I know what it feels like to be depressed and without hope but we can learn to discern God's voice which results in achieving an abundant life. By God's grace, I made a conscious decision to move forward and allow God into my heart. I lost my job and my life as I knew it but God had a cure for me. Since those dark days of depression, I have lived in victory with inner joy and happiness regardless of what is going on around me. My heart learned to trust God. I learned through it all that my purpose is to glorify the Lord with my life.

"Don't let your circumstances define or defeat you, let them motivate you."

My story, like many of yours, is not what I lost but what I found through Jesus Christ. I am not the man I used to be and with the grace of God I will eventually be the man that God intended me to be. Compassion and love are key components of my life now. I serve a God who has taught me more wisdom and understanding than I ever learned in the world. I realized that God wants to teach all of us to love, as we are loved by Him.

"There is no path to love, love is the path."

The man who I was no longer exists as I am a new creation in Christ. My goals are different, and my feet are no longer quick to run towards ungodly things. I have developed a God-consciousness which directs my steps. I decided that perhaps the lessons I learned in life could help others. I used to focus on the destination but I came to understand that it's about the journey. I was always so stressed out and anxious about reaching that next destination, not enjoying the moment but I missed the beauty along the way. The Apostle Paul stated from a Roman prison, "I have learned to be content, whatever the circumstances may be (Philippians 4:11)." When I finally surrendered, I felt God and heard Him speak to my heart. And it was then that it hit me, God was always with me but I couldn't hear His small still voice when I put so many other things before Him.

As Paul wrote, I look upon everything as loss compared with the overwhelming gain of knowing Christ Jesus my Lord...Philippians 3:8)." If it wasn't for my calamity or life quake as I call it where I lost my job, my relationship and reputation, I would've never come to know Christ, the greatest gift of my life. I was forced to challenge my old beliefs and attitudes so that I could reorder my priorities. God put so many things on my heart; one of the most powerful messages I received was that it's my choice how I want to live. God's not going to force us to love Him.

In Deuteronomy 30:19, God stated, "I call heaven and earth as witnesses today against you, that I have set before you life and death, blessing and cursing; therefore choose life, that both you and your descendants may live." I wouldn't have understood what this meant before my eyes were opened but today I know that God gives us free will to take any path we choose.

Choose life!

I wrote these motivational/inspirational tips to inspire and refresh the spirit. This project started out as a way to let me be mindful of God each day but it grew into something larger, a way to discern the voice of God. Further, I came to understand the power within myself through Christ, especially when I found myself depressed or worried about some big issue.

"C.S. Lewis referred to human suffering as God's megaphone. Sometimes God has to do something dramatic to get our attention. We need to hear Him as He clearly says, 'Don't do that anymore.' God loves us so (Jim Wood, The Life of Prayer, Embracing His Will book three pages 97-98.)"

I call the first 70 days, motivational tips, because I discovered that at times when my faith wavered, it was a motivational issue. When I wasn't motivated, it was easier for the devil to attack my spirit. I changed the name of these daily devotionals to "inspirational" tips for days 71-100 because I learned that as long as I poured in good, pure and Godly things into my spirit each day, I was in-spirited (in the Spirit). The last 80 days are called 'Spiritual Refreshers'. I was led by the Spirit to write this work and I hope it glorifies the Lord.

I'm not defective, and neither are you, we are all fully equipped. "And we know that all things work together for good to those who love God, to those who are called according to His purpose (Romans 8:28)." Many people wallow in a pool of self-pity and live a 'less-than' life but God created us to be 'more than conquerors'. We are God's greatest masterpiece! "For God has not given us the spirit of fear; but of power, and of love, and of a sound mind (2 Timothy 1:7)." The power is in us, we just have to stir up the gifts within us. I want everyone to understand the great love that God has for us. God sent His son, Jesus Christ, to save us so that we may have an abundant life!

Too many people learn about God from secondary sources, and not from the Bible. I urge and encourage everyone to read the Bible for themselves. See the great love, Jesus spoke about in the Gospels for yourself. Jesus taught a revolutionary type of love. I understand love now from reading God's words with an open heart. There are 66 love letters (books) in the Bible to help us get back into right relationship with God. When I opened my heart, God spoke clearly to me.

God is so good and faithful, I love Him so much! I want this daily devotional to help others stay uplifted, focused, and encouraged. Today, I look to fill my inner spiritual cup each day. My father, who is a minister, told me that if I over-filled my spiritual cup each day, then there would be no room for anything else to get in that wasn't 'of God'. He was right and I found that it kept me focused on the good and upright. We have all have the conditions for our own happiness right now. My perspective changed from a worldly view to a Godly view.

I still have faith failures and fall short but I am on target and understand who I am in Christ. The walk of faith is not an easy one in a world where things are becoming more unGodly each day. I struggle at times and my thought life wavers also. Joshua, one of my heroes from the Bible, is told several times by God, "Be strong and of good courage." I think that all believers have times when doubts enter but I believe the key is to not linger on these thoughts and to take action to refocus back on the Lord.

"Jesus is always victorious. We only have to get into the right relationship with Him and we shall see His power being demonstrated in our hearts and lives and service. And His victorious life will fill us and overflow through us to others. This is revival in its essence (Roy Hession)."

Who am I to speak about Jesus? I'm just a man who was lost but is now found. I was broken and depressed but I was healed through the power of the Holy Spirit. The Apostle Paul wrote that, "Christ Jesus came into the world to save sinners...(1 Timothy 1:15)." That is me, a sinner, but I now know my Redeemer lives. There are some people out here who may have been like me and looking for cures in all the wrong places. I tell people now, that all you need is more Jesus.

What God has taught me:

--Failure is not final and God can use me even now to bring others to Christ.
--God provides for all my needs because once my perspective changed, my needs changed.
--God taught me that a clean and merry heart can heal a multitude of diseases, even a disease of the soul.
--The tests which comes in our lives, only makes us stronger.
--Change always comes but hope is eternal.
--No one is beyond redemption, even the hardest of hearts can be touched by the love of God.
--If we are intentional and purposeful, we can learn to discern the voice of God and walk in the Spirit each day.

I started the first 100 tips with the phrase, "Stop what you are doing right now" and then modified it for the last 80 day to say, "Take this time to spiritually reflect on this point" because sometimes in life, we are so busy just existing, we don't take enough time to spend time with God.

I had to fully eject the baggage, shame and sorrow from the past to completely embrace a new way, to recalibrate my heart and mind along spiritual lines. There are two verses of scripture which affected me deeply in this regard. The first is: "My brothers, I do not consider myself to have grasped it fully even now. But I do concentrate on this: I forget all that lies behind me and with hands outstretched to whatever lies ahead I go straight for the goal, my reward the honor of my high calling by God in Christ Jesus (Philippians 3:13-14)." There are many different translations related to this verse and they're all focused on serving God in the present.

The second verse is related to the first: "And do not be conformed to this world, but be transformed by the renewing of your mind, that you may prove what is that good and acceptable perfect will of God (Romans 12:2)." I decided that I had to do everything in my life radically different, which could only happen by aligning my mind to an infallible system like the Bible.

They say a changed life should testify to what you believe in. When I started walking in faith, I became empowered and my fear started to fade. The fear told me that I was worthless and that my life was over. My fear told me that God didn't love me. My fear told me that God could never use me. Fear and doubt told me that I couldn't change but Jesus showed me the way, the truth and gave me life, a new life. I want to share parts of my journey so that it may be able to help others find their way. Jesus came for sinners, like me and you; and that knowledge gives me comfort.

Today, I strive to show others that God is awesome because I am free on the inside. I wrote this work to show others who are still in mental bondage that we can be free in spirit regardless of external circumstances.

My life message today is based on these three main points: Pray Big, Hope Big and Love Big; and do all three Boldly!

Religion should make us better, more loving people. Prayer is about faith in something bigger or greater than ourselves, trusting God to do for us even when we don't see it. Hope is centered on eternal life through Christ; hope in a better world by being a light to others; and having expectant hope in a better tomorrow. Love is the glue which holds these principles together. Love is the "how" in the life question of "how should we live". There are many Christians today without the love of God in them. I didn't have the love of God in me. Love strengthens, livens and carries us each day. With love in our hearts, we can share that love with others so that they may come to know Christ. The Gospel of Jesus isn't just something we read or hear but it's a framework in which we pattern our lives around.

"If we live in the Spirit, let us also walk in the Spirit (Galatians 5:25)." I want to share what God put on my heart so that others may not go through the self created problems I put myself through. One thing I now realize is that I am responsible for the hardships which came into my life. God's law will stand forever and I understand that God will always love us but that doesn't change his basic law, we reap what we sow. "Do not be deceived, God is not to be mocked; for whatever a man sows, that he will also reap (Galatians 6:7)." Whether some call it karma or 'reaping what we sow', it matters how we live. God wants us to serve Him willingly because we love Him, not because of some dogmatic obligation.

God told Solomon, "If my people who are called by My name will humble themselves, and pray and seek My face, and turn from their wicked ways, then I will hear from heaven, and will forgive their sin and heal their land (2 Chronicles 7:14)."

God loves us unconditionally and when we model our love based on His model, we live a more abundant life. The greatest truth that God ever put on my heart was that the Lord always loved me, the difference now is that I love Him.

Today Jesus is my life coach; make Him yours and watch God work in your life!

Sending you love, light and abundant amounts of positive energy!

This is the first in a series of 180 devotionals. I invite you to take this journey with me. Each of these first hundred tips begins with the phrase, "Stop what you are doing right now."

Motivational Tip for Day #1

Stop doing what you are doing right now.

It's time to wake up and start living the life that God intended you to live. Many people have been sleepwalking through life for too many years. The Lord wants us to be fully engaged in life so that we can honor and glorify Him. The devil wants us to stay asleep and continue to drift through life. But Jesus came so that we may have life, and have it more abundantly (John 10:10)." Be encouraged because it's never too late to be the person who God intended you to be!

Follow your passion right now. We each have dreams on our hearts which God has placed there. This is the day to start working towards that dream. Believe in something strongly enough to pursue it, right now for five minutes. Take this time to invest in your future. It's time to brainstorm or make a general outline or make that call to research the dream. Do something right now to turn your passion into a reality.

Love yourself enough to start the process. Life isn't about the destination but it's about the journey. Being intentional is the start of the journey because an abundant life unfolds through a series of planned small steps or actions.

Einstein said that, "nothing happens until an action occurs." Take action right now to start the process of realizing your dream.

Today is the day to turn that inner switch on; and to move towards that dream.

"Awake, you who sleep, Arise from the dead, and Christ will give you light (Ephesians 5:14)."

Motivational Tip for Day #2

Stop what you are doing right now.

"Write the vision and make it plain..." Habakkuk 2:2 New King James Version of the Bible.

The Bible describes visionaries who were given God inspired dreams. These great men and women trusted God and were able to see their dreams fulfilled because of their faith. 1 John 4:4 says that "You are of God, little children, and have overcome them: because greater is He that is in you than he that is in the world." We were created not only to dream but to have our dreams realized.

Take five minutes and write a detailed description of your dream. Write as many pieces of the dream that you can think of. Make it measurable but don't worry about how you will get there. Step out on faith, be audacious and bold! Make your dream as clear as possible and then keep it in front of you every day.

Each day after this day, schedule at least five minutes to continue moving the ball forward towards that goal. A journey of a thousand miles begins with one step.

Life unfolds abundantly through a series of small steps or actions.

"Faith and fear both require people to believe in something they can't see. Why not empower yourself and believe in the positive force that will lift you up and make your dreams come true: faith."

Motivational Tip for Day #3

Stop what you are doing now.

This tip is focused on prayer. Please read the following verses of scripture.

"Let us therefore come boldly to the throne of grace, that we may obtain mercy and find grace to help in the time of need." (Hebrews 4:16).

"...The effective, fervent prayer of a righteous man avails much." (James 5:16)

"Draw near to God and He shall draw near to you." (James 4:8).

Before you start to pray, I want to highlight one last verse directly relayed by Jesus: "Therefore I say to you, whatever things you ask when you pray, believe that you receive them, and you will have them." (Mark 11:24)

Get ready to pray, be bold in your prayers! Once you pray and leave it at God's throne of grace, you must do you part and believe. There can be no doubt or anxiety on your part. Unwavering faith on your part activates God's blessings in your life!

For the next several minutes, connect with God and pray!

Close your eyes and center yourself through deep breathing from the abdomen. Picture love and start to envelop yourself in the great love God has for you. Picture a light above you (that light is God) and move your essence towards it.

"There are times when God is not going to change our circumstances but instead wants to change us on the inside so our circumstances will no longer bother us anymore."

Motivational Tip for Day #4

Stop what you are doing. Please read the below sentence.

"...You shall be very happy, and it shall be well with you (Psalm 128:2)."

These are God's words. So today, you will choose to be happy because it is what God wants for you. This tip is about trusting God more.

I want you to repeat God's words right now using the first person. "I shall be very happy, and it shall be well with me." I want you to repeat this phrase 10 times now. Smile each time you say this phrase.

Place your hand in God's hand today by repeating this phrase throughout the day.

Remember what the Apostle Paul said from a Roman prison, "...For I have learned in whatever state I am, to be content." (Philippians 4:11)."

"Gray skies are gonna clear up, put on a happy face. Brush off the clouds and cheer up. Put on a happy face. Take off the gloomy mask of tragedy, it's not your style. You're look so good that you've decided to smile. Pick out a pleasant outlook, stick out that noble chin, wipe off that full of doubt look. Slap on a happy grin and spread sunshine all over the place. Just put on a happy face." Dick van Dyke and Elliot Lawrence, Greatest Hits of Broadway.

Motivational Tip for Day #5

Stop what you are doing right now.

Today's tip is focused on love. Love is the greatest power of the universe. Jesus Christ's mission on this earth was centered on love. Love will empower you and infuse your body with strength.

"Beloved, let us love one another, for love is of God; and everyone who loves is born of God and knows God. He who does not love does not know God, for God is love." 1 John 4:7

"My little children, let us not love in word or in tongue, but in deed and truth." 1 John 3:16

Love with your whole heart today. Love sees people not just as they are but as how God sees them. Today take the love that God has given you and give it to others.

Be love today. If there is anyone who you have a grudge against, reach out to them and give them a God inspired gift, love. Take five minutes and write a note or an email to those people who your heart has been closed off to lately. Offer that person or persons love with an open heart. In Mathew 5:8 Jesus said, "Blessed are the pure in heart, for they shall see God." Let us all strive to see God.

"Create in me a clean heart, O God." Psalm 51:10

The goal of the Gospel of Jesus Christ is to improve us. The Gospel is about love. Complete whole and healthy love will free you and inspire you in other areas of your life.

Motivational Tip for Day # 6

Stop what you are doing right now.

The purpose of this tip is to discuss how to be led by the Spirit. Further, I wanted to discuss how to hear the Holy Spirit and how to live by the Spirit.

The Holy Spirit is one of the greatest gifts that Jesus Christ left us with. The Holy Spirit empowers, guides and leads us in all things. The Holy Spirit is the special manifestation of God's divine Presence. The Holy Spirit is the Spirit of Truth and the Spirit of the Lord. Our inner spirit is that part of a person's being thought of as the center of life, the will, thinking, feeling; that part of man that survives death. Our goal is to connect our inner spirit to the divine Holy Spirit which indwells us.

"The very Spirit of Jesus Christ is in the believer's spirit (Galatians 4:6)."

How to hear the Holy Spirit: The Holy Spirit speaks to us, not with loud cymbals or a booming voice, but with a little nudge. That nudge or initial prompting which tugs on our heart to do the right thing is the influence of the Holy Spirit. So many believes are living in confusion and inner chaos. Too many believers try to refashion God to what we want Him to be for us. This is why its' important to listen to that nudge or initial prompting for the Holy Spirit.

For example, perhaps you got in an augment with your spouse or family member, there is that initial prompting which says 'apologize' or 'show compassion', that is from the Holy Spirit. That seed of God is what nudges you to do the right thing. When that initial prompting comes, usually the devil tries to convince us that we should harden our hearts, find faults, be right, be prideful and strive to get back at that person. Now the devil will not announce himself but his nudge touches our flesh which wants to rebel, so we do. The initial prompting of the Holy Spirit is trying to get our inner spirit to touch the Holy Spirit.

How to test whether that nudge is from above (the light) or from below (the darkness). I have a four point test:

1) Is it 'of God'? Does it line up with God's word? Is it what the Lord has asked us to do in the Bible?
2) Is it good (from a pure heart, with honest intentions)?
3) Is it loving? God is love and Jesus commands us to love others. Does that inner voice point in the direction of love (which is from God) or in the direction of strife, envy, jealousy, hate, anger, unforgiveness, bitterness or resentment (which is from the devil)?
4) Does the initial prompting further the kingdom of heaven? Does that nudge (initial prompting) serve God's plan; does it glorify God. Mathew 6:33 states that we should seek first the kingdom of heaven and then all things will be added to us.

If the initial inner promptings passes the above test then it's from God. Our flesh wants to rebel and follow our earthly desires but Jesus wishes us to follow Him in spirit and in truth. Galatians 5:16-18 provides further insight, "So I say, live by the Spirit, and you will not gratify the desires of the sinful nature. For the sinful nature desires what is contrary to the Spirit, and the Spirit is contrary to the sinful nature. They are in conflict with each other, so that you do not do what you want. But if you are led by the Spirit, you are not under the law."

When we follow the initial promptings of the Holy Spirit, it may hurt or feel uncomfortable because we will be struggling against the flesh or the sinful nature. This is one of the ways to know that we did the right thing because it may feel painful. The right thing often is painful because it pushes us out of our comfort zone. Walking in the light and in love can feel like being tortured because our flesh tells us, "why do I have to be the one to be the peacemakers?" Well, Jesus stated in His greatest sermon in Mathew 5 in verse 9, "Blessed are the peacemakers for they are the sons of God."

The world is not our friend and strives to keep us connected or aligned with the devil. Satan rules the earth and walks around seeking to steal, kill and destroy but Jesus came so that we may have life, and life more abundantly (John 10:10). This temporal world is the devil's playground. We are to be Ambassadors for Christ (2 Corinthians 5:20) by not adding more chaos in this world. God wants us to show others the way, not take others off the path of truth and love. Too many Christians live a life which leads people away from the church. Too few Christians refuse to view others as God' children too.

Our flesh will always want to do, what it wants. The flesh wants to act out, and behave like a child if given the opportunity. In Romans 8:5-8, we learn, "For those who live according to the flesh set their minds on the things of the flesh, but those who live according to the Spirit, the things of the Spirit. For to be carnally minded (living by the flesh) is death, but to be spiritually minded is life and peace. Because the carnal mind is enmity against God; for it is not subject to the law of God, nor indeed can be. So then, those who are in the flesh cannot please God." Romans 8:11 states, "...His Spirit who dwells in you." The Holy Spirit is in us, seeking to show us the way but too many believers have a closed mind and unreceptive heart where their pride and ego is allowed to get in the way of hearing the Spirit of Truth.

There have been times when I have gotten in an argument with someone, and that little voice said, "Just do your job; love them and apologize because it doesn't matter who's right or wrong, it's about serving Me." I felt that little nudge and fought against it at times, making inward excuses of why I can't forgive them or say I'm sorry because my pride (one of the devil's greatest tool) was trying to override the Godly choice. I now strive to act when the Holy Spirit speaks to me to do the right thing by apologizing or being kind to that person. Sometimes, I reach that person and other times, I just get an angry response but the reward is that I am serving God and furthering His kingdom. I have trained myself to now listen to these inner promptings. I now know that the sooner I follow the inner promptings or nudges, the easier it is. The longer I wait to follow the Holy Spirit, the harder it is. The devil loves procrastination because it makes his job easier. I still fall short at times but now I understand how to live by the Spirit and I strive to consistently do it.

God will never make us do the right thing, the Godly thing. God stated in Deuteronomy 30:15-20, that He has given us a choice between life and death, but desires that we choose life. In Romans 1:24-26, the Apostle Paul explains that, "God also gave them up to uncleanness, in the lusts of their hearts, to dishonor their bodies among themselves, who exchanged the truth of God for the lie, and worshipped and served the creature rather than the Creator, who is blessed forever. Amen. For this reason, God gave them up to vile passions..." This passage in Romans explains how God gave us 'free will' whereby we can choose. We must reprogram ourselves to listen to the small, still voice of God.

Be encouraged and motivated because "The Spirit of God Himself dwells in you (1 Corinthians 3:16)." We must always remember that He (the Spirit) is already in us. "His Spirit is in your heart (2 Corinthians 1:22)." One philosopher stated that "Man is done or undone by his desires." We can be better, and live an abundant life, when we stop rebelling and start following the Lord without question.

Ephesians 6:10 states, "Finally my brethren, be strong in the Lord and in the power of His might." I love this verse because it gives us hope. God gives us all that we need to live a fulfilling and abundant life. We must raise our expectancy level. We must seek out that small, still voice expecting to hear it. We must expect to feel the Holy Spirit nudge us to make the right choices. Then, we must do the difficult thing, which struggles against our earthly nature, and align our actions with our divine nature. Our divine nature comes from the indwelling of the Holy Spirit, and it will always lead us into the right Godly directions.

Do you feel powerful or powerless? The Holy Spirit empowers us and can show us the Godly (and righteous) path so we are not driven by what we see and feel in the natural. In John 14:26, we learn that the Holy Spirit will teach us all things. The Holy Spirit testifies that "with our spirit that we are children of God (Romans 8:16)." The small, still voice will always speak to us but we must be cognizant of it, seeking to hear to it.

The desires of the flesh wars against will of God. We can't be who God wants us to be without the Holy Spirit. The Holy Spirit is called the Spirit of Truth because it convicts us when we are tempted to do the wrong thing. Walking in the Spirit is a part of listening for the initial prompting or looking for that nudge. Walking in the Spirit is to live moment by moment with leaning on, trusting in and depending on God to show us the way. We seek out His voice and strive to obey it. In order to live a Godly life, we must live a life led by the Holy Spirit. The Spirit of God speaks to our spirit but we must set our mind to God's frequency.

We must reprogram ourselves to listen for and obey that initial prompting. We have been programmed to believe that we must be slaves to our feelings but our feelings are connected to the flesh and doesn't help us to walk in the Spirit. Mathew 9:29 states, "According to your faith, be it done." Many believers aren't enjoying the level of Godly favor in their lives that they desire because they fail to listen to Holy Spirit in their daily lives.

If we do the difficult, God will do the impossible. The difficult part is forgiving, loving, showing compassion and kindness, and being a light in the world despite what's going on with us. Our goal should be to help others who are still lost get to heaven.

Too many people are still stuck on fault-finding instead of looking for the Godliness in others. Judging and pointing fingers at others have reached a level of crisis in the church today. There are some believers who focus more on pointing out the 'hypocrisy' of their neighbors instead of loving their neighbors as Jesus commands. We need to stop finding faults in others, and start finding Jesus. We should stop fault finding, and start soul searching and heart cleansing. If we are all praising God then we won't have time to find faults in others or judge others. Some people only want to talk about how bad others are or how they were wronged by others. God commands us to love. Focus on hearing the voice of the Holy Spirit.

Life today is about many believers "speaking" about how much they love God instead of showing, through their actions, how much they love God. Isaiah 29:13 states, "The people honor me with their lips, but their heart is far from me."

Too many people block their own blessings because of the conditions of our hearts. It starts with listening to that small, still voice and then obeying without question, even if it's painful. God tells Joshua that He will be with Him when he is about to cross over the Jordan. Joshua had to trust God and order the people to put their foot in the Jordan River first. We must commit to God with our complete heart and spirit. God acts when we fully commit to Him. Tell God today, "Dear heavenly Father, I'm going to make a total commitment to you and listen to the Holy Spirit when it nudges me or prompts me to do something." If you want God to move in your life, move first for God.

"Today is a new day where I will no longer let the baggage of the past direct my steps. Today, I will live my life in such a way that says I still believe there are infinite opportunities for me to be the person that God intended me to be." Stop what you are doing." Philip Allan Turner

Motivational Tip for Day #7

Stop what you are doing right now.

Today will be focused on manifesting the type of life you want to live. We will focus on practicing unswerving intent.

"Jesus said to him, 'If you can believe, all things are possible to him who believes (Mark 9:23)."

Take five minutes. The goal will be to visualize the type of life you want to live, being as specific as possible. You are working in your imagination for this exercise. I want you to visualize that life with the people you want in it, that job or that dream fulfilled. What does it look like in your mind's eye? I want you to walk into that dream house, into that whole and healthy relationship or see that hobby you have a passion for become a lucrative endeavor.

Before you start the exercise, I want you to close your eyes and start breathing deeply into your abdomen. Put your hand on you abdomen while you breathe. Count to four while you inhale and do the same when you exhale. (Do not breathe in your chest). Now, go! Dream big and be a specific as possible in your mind's eye. Do this at least twice each day and watch signs and wonders appear in your life.

"What one can dream, one can achieve"

Motivational Tip for Day # 8

Stop what you are doing right now.

Today's tip will be focused on understanding the power each of us has within us.

"Do you not know that you are the temple of God and that the Spirit of God dwells in you (1 Corinthians 3:16)."

God has given each of us talents and gifts.

In 1 Corinthians 12:4-11 it states, "There are diversities of gifts, but the same Spirit. There are differences of ministries, but the same Lord. And there are diversities of activities, but it is the same God who works all in all. But the manifestation of the Spirit is given to each one for the profit of all: for to one is given the word of wisdom through the Spirit, to another the word of knowledge through the same Spirit, to another faith by the same Spirit, to another gifts of healings by the same Spirit, to another the working of miracles, to another prophecy, to another discerning of spirits, to another different kinds of tongues, to another interpretation of tongues, But one and the same Spirit works all these things, distributing to each one individually as He wills."

Right now, take five minutes and write a list of your talents. Which one are you not utilizing? Too many people's natural talents are going untapped. From the list, identify the one gift that you will start nurturing and using today. Make a detailed plan.

So go for it! Schedule that class, paint that work of art, write that novel, start that business, volunteer with that group, give that sermon, become a big brother/sister, get that certification and teach! You can do it!

It all starts with finding out where your strengths lie. I am including a simple formula below:

Your talent/strengths + investment of time = fulfilling your God inspired mission and purpose in life!

"Somewhere out there is the greatest violin player in the world whose talent was never realized. Don't let that be you. Live you purpose today!"

Motivational Tip for Day #9

Stop what you are doing right now.

It is a scientific fact that 1 out of every 1 human will die. I say this to motivate you so you will consider how you use your time each day.

The Psalmist asked God, "Teach us to number our days, that we may gain a heart of wisdom (Psalm 90:12)."

During this last week of December, many magazines and TV shows devote special editions to the "year in review." Today's tip is focused on doing an internal "year in review." In order to have an abundant life, we must all continue to grow and move closer to God.

The internal year in review is based on asking yourself, "What do I need to do differently to make this coming year a better year where I am making striving to get closer to God?"

Using spiritual principles, we can be better in each day. And when we get better, our lives will get better.

I provide this short verse of scripture as a guide:

"Therefore, as the elect of God, holy and beloved, put on tender mercies, kindness, humility, meekness, longsuffering; bearing with one another, forgiving one another, if anyone has a complaint against one another; even as Christ forgave you, so you also must do.

But above all these things put on LOVE, which is the bond of perfection. And let the peace of God rule in your hearts, to which also you were called in one body; and be thankful.

Let the word of the Christ dwell in you richly in all wisdom, teaching and admonishing one another in psalms and hymns and spiritual songs, singing with grace in your hearts to the Lord. And whatever you do in word or deed, do all in the name of the Lord Jesus, giving thank to God the Father through Him (Colossians 3:12-17)."

These are such beautiful words and is like a GPS, a God Positioning System, which can lead us to God allowing us to live an abundant life!

Socrates said, "The unexamined life is not worth living."

"Through the examination of ourselves, we can grow to become the people God intended us to become." Philip Allan Turner

Motivational Tip for Day #10

Stop what you are doing right now.

Today's tip is focused on faith, because without faith it's impossible to please the Lord.

"But without faith it is impossible to please Him, for he who comes to God must believe that He is, and that He is a rewarder of those who diligently seek Him (Hebrews 11:6)."

I also want to include another verse from James 4:8, "Draw near to God and he will draw near to you..."

Wherever your spiritual practice is today, it's time to do something extra for God. Too many Christians settle for too less in life when God has promised us so much.

2 Chronicles 16:9 states, "For the eyes of the Lord run to and fro throughout the whole earth, to show Himself strong on behalf of those whose heart is loyal to Him."

God is looking for a vessel to use and to bless. God needs people to see Him in a new way. Stop putting God in a box and see Him in a new light. See God from a different perspective and you will be seen in a different light by God.

Each day, we should all strive to seek to know God more. There is more of God to have, and He wants you to have that what He has promised you. We can experience more of God if we strive to dive deeper in his word in order to have a more meaningful relationship with Him.

Do you want to know the mind of God? This can only happen if you spend more time with Him and his word.

Today's tip is focused on communicating more with God each day. Take a few minutes right now and talk to God. Talk to Him conversationally about who you are, who you want to be and what you desire in your life. Tell God where you fall short and where you need help. Ask God for His help to know Him better, more deeply. If you draw nearer to God each day by spending more time with him, you will start to see signs and wonders come to pass in your life.

"Once you start to see God from a new vantage point, hungering to know Him more, you will begin to move along that specific path of what God wants you to be."

Motivational Tip for Day #11

Stop what you are doing right now.

Today's tip is to help you move forward by making a commitment to yourself!

The Apostle Paul stated in 1 Corinthians 15:58, "Therefore, my dear brothers and sisters, stand firm. Let nothing move you. Always give yourselves fully to the work of the Lord, because you know that your labor in the Lord is not in vain."

Sometimes we grow weary but if we are steadfast then we will be rewarded. Everything you do for the Lord will reap great benefits. God will reward those who strive for Him by bestowing a great blessing on them. Everyday strive to please God in all that you do and He will reward you.

The most important commitment you can make as you prepare to move forward, is give your life completely over to Christ.

As you look to make new commitments and fully engage with life, remember what the Apostle Paul said in Philippians 4:13, "I can do all things through Christ, who strengthens me." See yourself in a different light this new day. See yourself as God sees you, "more than a conqueror." You can do it! Stay steadfast; believe it and it will come to pass.

Make a commitment to a new life!

Jim Rohn stated, "*Your life does not get better by chance, it gets better by change.*"

Motivational Tip for Day #12

Stop what you are doing right now.

"With every new day; come new, exciting possibilities."

Today's tip is focused on restructuring our minds. We have the power to create our inner world as we want because we can choose the following:

1) How to react to every situation which confronts us;
2) What meaning we want to attach to those situations.

Nehemiah 8:10 says, "Do not be grieved, for the joy of the Lord is your strength."

Inside of us is the power to choose how we want to feel. Joy is a destination we can all reach. God gives us a choice.

"The Lord says, "You are precious and honored in My sight." God wants us to serve Him and to do His will. Part of doing God's will is seeing ourselves as God sees us. 1 Peter 2:9 says, "But you are a chosen generation, a royal priesthood, a holy nation; His own special people, that you may proclaim the praises of Him who called you out of darkness into His marvelous light." God sees us a special and He loves us without conditions. Sometimes it's so hard to look up when you've been down for so long but remember it's a new day which is leading into a new year. Restructure how you see the world and yourself today.

Whatever evil spirit has bound you up in the past; say right now out loud, "In the name of God, I rebuke any evil spirit that has ever been spoken over me. Abundance will now enter my life. I have the power to choose. I choose light and love, and Inner joy is mine for the taking."

The philosopher Rene Descartes stated, "Cognito ergo sum," Latin for 'I think therefore I am'. Gautama Buddha said, "We are what we think."

Proverbs 23:7 says, "So as a man thinks in his heart, so is he." All of these traditions are saying the same thing; all that arises in our life, starts with our thoughts. We have the power to remake the world in a way we want by maintaining unswerving positive intention each day!

"What time is it? It's time to stop letting your past control your destiny. Honor God by believing and accepting the promises He has in store for you."

Motivational Tip for Day #13

Stop what you are doing right now.

George Eliot stated that, "It's never too late to be who you might have become."

As we start on this journey, I ask you this one question: "What is your great purpose in life?"

We may not can choose our circumstances but we can choose our thoughts. In life, there are certain laws which govern us. "What a man sows, that shall also he reap (Galatians 6:7). Our thoughts are our seeds. That seed in our thoughts may be tiny, a grudge or resentment held against some friend or family member, but it will take root until it is manifested in some negative way in your life. The laws of God will operate whether we are aware of them or not.

This year, focus on controlling your thought life. Control over your thoughts can draw into your life what you want to reap. The more you practice controlling your thoughts, the better you will become at it. The goal is to not think of anything that you do not want to come into your life. Focusing on how you want your life to be instead of the fears, anxieties or worries.

Psalm 37:4 states, "Delight yourself in the Lord, and He shall give you the desires of your heart." God is delighted when we believe in Him and His promises.

Many people hire life coaches but the best life coach one can follow is Jesus Christ! Let Jesus Christ become your example.

How do you begin to change how you think? Get a small notebook and start to list how you want to think that day, such as:
"Today I will focus only on loving thoughts, forgiving thoughts, beautiful thoughts, uplifting thought, edifying thoughts and pure thoughts which are pleasing to God."

Align your thoughts with your great purpose. Move forward each day to make your great purpose come to fruition.

Satan wants us to live in the land of "oh no." The adversary wants us to say, "Oh no, I can't do that" or "Oh no, I need to work on that." This year, focus on living in the land of "oh yes" and serving the God of "oh yes! Oh yes, I can do that because I serve an all powerful, all mighty God.

Mathew 7:7 states, "Ask, and it will be given to you; seek and you will find; knock, and it will be opened to you." We need to ask God while diligently seeking to do His will and then take action by knocking on the door even if the door seems impossible to open.

Each of us can used as an instrument of God. We must do our part by analyzing our thoughts, words and actions to ensure that it is pleasing to God.

Accomplishing your great purpose happens when we align our lives with what God wants for us. Scientists have stated that we only use a small portion of our brain capacity. We do not know all the mysteries of the universe but faith tells us that we serve the God of the possible. What's impossible with man, is possible with God. The creative forces inside of us are immense and waiting for you to tap into.

Jesus says in John 10:10, "that He has come so that we may have life and have it more abundantly." With Jesus as your life coach, the only direction you can go, is up!

"Your vision will become clear only when you can look into your own heart...who looks outside dreams; who looks inside, awakes." Carl Jung.

Motivational Tip for Day #14

Stop what you are doing right now.

God loves you unconditionally! This means that God loves you without conditions. He loves you today as much as He ever will. There is nothing you can do to make God love you more. That said, we can certainly do things that God pleases God or displeases Him. We cannot earn our way to Heaven by doing good works. We earn our way to heaven through God's grace. Please read the below passage.
"Teacher which is the greatest commandment in the law?
Jesus said to them, "You shall love the Lord your God with all your heart, with all your soul, and with all your mind." This is the first and greatest commandment. And the second is like it, You shall love your neighbor as yourself (Mathew 22:36-39)."
So if we love God with everything, we should want to please Him and do good works. If we love God then we will desire to love, forgive and bless others because it pleases God. If our actions are aligned with the mind of God, then God will bless us.
Joel 2:25 says, "So I will restore to you the years that the swarming locust has eaten." It you have fallen down or failed, know that you can reap your blessings in due time because God is faithful.
In Isaiah 54:17, we learned what the Lord can do, "No weapon formed against you shall prosper, and every tongue which rises against you in judgment, you shall condemn. This is the heritage of the servants of the Lord, And their righteousness is from Me," says the Lord.

True servants of the Lord will live an abundant life. By putting God first and obeying Him, we have a promised heritage from God. It's time to take back what belongs to you. You must always remember that God has already fully equipped you with what you need to be successful. Satan wants to keep you in the darkness, but it's time to proclaim who you really are: God's beloved!

Today's tip is about seeing yourself in a different light! Psalm 96:1 says, "Oh sing to the Lord a new song! Sing to the Lord, all the earth." Sing and speak into existence only what you want to come true. Stop saying anything negative about yourself or your circumstances. Start now speaking only exactly what you desire.

"God has put a new song in my mouth--Praise to our God (Psalm 40:3)." Let only positive thoughts and words come from you because of your love of God and the desire to please Him.

"Today is a new day, treat it as such."

Motivational Tip for Day #15

Stop what you are doing right now.

Be uplifted because God is for us! Today's tip is focused on making sure our hearts are receptive and our minds are alert to what God is trying to tell us.
Psalm 46:10 says, "Be still and know that I am God."

We must understand that God created us to be overcomers and our attitude towards our problems affects the outcome of those problems. As the beloved child of God, we have certain rights and privileges but we need to put God first.

Thomas a Kempis stated in "The Imitation of Christ that we can find out union with God through the exploration of one's own soul, which derives it's very being from God. Kempis' book is about finding the way to the "land of everlasting clearness." Kempis was a monk who lived in the late 14th and early 15th century. I love the way Kempis puts it when he says, "Blessed are those eyes that are closed to outward things and attend to inward things." This tip is about taking care of our side of the street. Kempis went on to say that, "Blissful are they that take heed to God and cast themselves out from all impediments of the world."

God loves us so much that, "He desires everyone to be saved and to come to the knowledge of the truth (1 Timothy 2:4). In John 8:31-32 we learn that, "Then Jesus said to those Jews who believed Him. 'If you abide in My word, you are my disciples indeed. And you shall know the truth and the truth shall make you free." The truth is the light.

As Kempis stated, "we can find a union with God by exploring our soul". Some questions to consider:

Are you free today? Is your heart receptive? Who do your actions say you follow? Do your actions say you are a believer in the one true God? Does your attitude say that you are leaning on God? Are you seeking God with all your heart and soul? Do your actions say that you are putting God first?

These are some of the questions that I ask myself each day. I have learned that I need to value time spent with God more than anything else in the world. God wants us to have a blessed life, full of abundance! In Hebrews 11:6, the Bible says that, "He rewards those who earnestly seek Him." If you seek Him today, you will find Him. God is looking for people to bless and fill their lives with signs and wonders.
Proverbs 4:23 states, "Be careful how you think; your life is shaped by your thoughts."
We all need to think abundance always, see abundance everywhere, feel abundance daily and believe that abundance will come into your life each day. Harness the power inside of yourself. Make it and create it. Chaos on the inside will always create chaos on the outside.

Let the joy of the Lord be your strength today! Be encouraged because with belief comes blessings.

"Life can be very easy when love is your way of life," Don Miguel Ruiz in The Four Agreements.

Motivational Tip for Day #16

Stop what you are doing right now.

Today's tip is focused on attitude.

I will be working from the epistle of the Apostle Paul to the Philippians.
In the first chapter, verse 3 stated, "I thank God upon every remembrance of You. Always in every prayer of mine making request for you all with joy." Later in 1:12 Paul explained, "But I want you to know brethren, that the things which happened to me have actually turned out for the furtherance of the Gospel."

"Do all things with complaining and disputing (2:14)."

"Yet indeed I also count all things loss for the excellence of the knowledge of Christ Jesus my Lord... (3:8)."

"Not that I have already attained, or am already perfected but I press on, that I may lay hole of that which Christ Jesus has also laid hold of me. Brethren, I do not count myself to have apprehended; but on things I do , forgetting those things which are behind and reaching forward to those things which are ahead. I press toward the goal for the prize of the upward call of God in Christ Jesus (3:12-14)."

"Rejoice in the Lord always. Again I say, rejoice! (4:4)."

"Be anxious for nothing, but in everything by prayer and supplication, with thanksgiving, let your requests be made known to God. And the peace of God which surpasses all understanding will guard your hearts and minds through Christ Jesus (4:6-7)."

"Finally, brethren whatever things are true, whatever things are noble, whatever things are just, whatever things are of pure, whatever things are lovely, whatever things are of good report, if there is any virtue and if there is anything praiseworthy--meditate on these things (4:8)."

"Not that I speak in regard to need, for I have learned in whatever state I am, to be content (4:11)."

"I can do all things through Christ who strengthens me (4:13)." This last verse is one of my life verses.

Paul wrote this letter from a Roman prison. Paul's joy comes through clearly. If Paul could be content, so could I.

I wrote this tip with joy in my heart, with my soul afire for God wanting to spread His message. I am content and happy today because the joy of the Lord is my strength.

Where ever you are to your journey, you can wake up each morning with enthusiasm and a passion for life because of the power of Christ Jesus. You can decide to choose a different path: a light and love filled path.

I try each day too be a light in the world and you can be the light where you work and live too. Let the Christ show through all you do!

Paul was on fire for God and Philippians is a clear indication of how one should live. Are you wondering why you are not seeing more blessings in your life? Are you still worrying about things in which you have given to God? Are you pressing forward this day? Are you seeking to know God more each day?

Take a few minutes right now and read the complete chapter of Philippians (don't worry is very short). Before you start, ask God to show your areas where you can press forward. Ask God to give you wisdom and discernment as Paul asked from prison. After you finished reading this chapter, write down the areas where you wish to improve in your life. Ask God to help you and you will see more abundance enter into your life.

One wise person once said, "Pain is inevitable but misery is a choice."

Motivational Tip for Day #17

Stop what you are doing right now.

Today's tip will be focused on hope!

One of my favorite quotes is: "Strength for today and bright hope for tomorrow."

We need to be bold in our hope for a bright tomorrow. We live in the present but we must plan for success by hoping in the right manner. Hope is so important in life. Too many people walk around in defeat expecting every bad thing to come into their life. Hope is about joyful expectation; expecting the best from others and from ourselves, the expectation of miracles in coming into our lives. When we expect miracles and blessings, we are practicing hope. Hope never disappoints according to the Bible.

The Apostle Paul wrote about hope in Romans 8:25, "For in hope we have been saved, but hope is seen is not hope; for who hopes for what he has already sees? But if we hope for what we do not see, with perseverance we eagerly await for it."
We must always stay alert to use the tools that God has given us for good. Hope is one of the greatest tools God have given us. Do not fall victim to dark or defeated thoughts because this is not what God wants for us. Hope boldly!

I leave you with the following scriptures on hope.

"Be joyful in hope, patient in affliction, faithful in prayer (Romans 12:12)."

"Our hope is in the living God, who is the Savior of all people, and particularly those who believe (1 Timothy 4:10)."

"So be strong and take courage, all you who put your hope in the Lord (Psalm 31:24)."

"The Lord is good to those who hope is in Him, to the one who seeks Him (Lamentations 3:25)."

"For everything that was written in the past was written to teach us, so that through endurance and encouragement of the Scriptures we might have hope (Romans 15:4)."

"Praise God, the Father of our Lord Jesus Christ. God is so good, and by raising Jesus from death, He has given us a new life and a hope that lives on (1 Peter 1:3)."

"For I know the plans I have for you," declared the Lord, "plans to prosper you and not to harm you, plans to give you hope and a future (Jeremiah 29:11)."

We must be bold in our faith. Today I ask you to hope boldly!

Mother Teresa said, "Where there is love, there is God." I want to modify this by saying, "Where there is hope, there is God."

Motivational Tip for Day #18

Stop what you are doing right now.

Today we will be going a little deeper starting with this quote: "I am not a victim of my circumstances, my circumstances are a victim of me."

I know how it feels to hurt, feel lost, be depressed and have no hope. That said, I have been transformed and live in an entirely different world today. I live in a world of joy and of infinite possibilities! I no longer ride on the roller coaster of life because I totally surrendered to God. This is what I mean when I say I gave my life completely to God.

God knows us and sees our heart. 1 Samuel 16:7 states, "...For the Lord does not see as man sees, for man looks at the outward appearance, but the Lord looks at the heart."

Two major points I want to bring out with this verse.

#1: The Lord knows us, our weaknesses, warts, failures, problem areas and other issues. We can't hide from what He knows about us because He created us. We must start to be self-aware in order to move forward. This first point is about knowing your own internal environment. It's okay to acknowledge your faults because that is the only way to move forward.

#2: God knows that within each of us there are infinite possibilities to become the person He wants us to be. We can grow into what God has planned for us to be. We each have a God inspired purpose that many people are not realizing. God knows our hearts and what we can be. In order to get that breakthrough, you will have to intentionally move forward each day knowing that God wants more for you.

How do you get there? How do you work towards having a more abundant life?

I offer the following suggestion based from Mathew 7:7 which says, "Ask and it will be given to you; seek, and you will find; knock and it will be opened to you." There are three actions which the above verse mentions.

1) We have to ask ourselves what it will take to obtain the desired result. This first part involves asking the right questions, asking insightful questions of ourselves based on truth. The Lord already knows so let's get on the same page as God. Major point #1 is used in this step.

2) We have to ask ourselves what has kept us from an abundant life in the past, and seek to diligently follow a new path. This second point is based on honestly and diligently seeking the knowledge to move us in the direction our dreams. [Hosea 4:6 states that, My people are destroyed for lack of knowledge.] We should align the image of ourselves with how God sees us from major point #2--we were created with the infinite ability to

grow and change. We were created by an all-powerful God of light who sent his son, Jesus Christ, so that we should have life and have it more abundantly (John 10:10).

3) We have to work and strive towards creating the conditions which will allow our dreams to become a reality. Knocking involves taking actions and executing the solutions to gain the result we desire. God has plans for us, plans to prosper us. When we align our images, our actions with what God wants for our lives, we will then reap a beautiful harvest into our lives.

The Apostle Paul said in 1 Corinthians 11:1, "Imitate me, just as I imitate Christ." This is my goal today. Make it your too!

Martin Luther King said, "Faith is taking the first step even when you don't see the whole staircase."

Motivational Tip for Day #19

Stop what you are doing right now.

Today we will be working on winning the internal battle. Winston Churchill stated, "You create your own universe as you go along."

The Buddha stated, "All wrong doing arises because of the mind. If the mind is transformed can wrong doing remain."

In 1 Corinthians 3:16, we learn, "Do you not know that you are the temple of God and that the Spirit of God dwells within you."

Our thoughts can limit us or free us. The world has conditioned or programmed us since childhood. Today I want you to take the limits off your imagination. Take the limits off the amount of love in your heart. Free yourself by loving yourself fully!

The world is one of infinite and limitless possibilities but you must believe this point, fully and completely. The Gospel of Mark states, "Whatever things you desire, when you pray, believe that you have received them and you shall have them." We just have to believe.

"Now to Him that is able to do exceedingly abundantly above all that we ask or think, according to the power that worketh in us (Ephesians 3:20)." Wow! God is so good and wants so much for us. There is great power in us, waiting to be tapped. This beautiful declaration of truth from God tells us that we have an unlimited ability within us. God wants us to have an abundant life. Align your thoughts with what God wants for your life.

You life is as wonderful or as broken as you believe it is.

Today start to imagine how you want your life to be. Eliminate any negative thoughts or words from your spirit. Believe and have faith in all you do!

Be steadfast in loving yourself. Love starts with how you see yourself and what you say about yourself. When we see ourselves as God sees us, with a boundless spirit of power, an abundant life is the result!

"There is no limit to the amount of love the human heart can hold."

"A man is happy so long as he chooses to be happy." A. Solzhenitsyn

Motivational Tip for Day #20

Stop what you are doing right now.

Today's tip is focused on love!

One of my motto's is "There is no path to love, love is the path."

"God is love (1 John 4:8)." Since God is love, when we align ourselves with love, we are drawing near the mind of God. Every act of love rendered for His sake is noted and has eternal positive consequences.

The most important concept about being a Christian is doing everything based on love. Love is the very nature of God. When we make love our a centering principle inside of us, we empower ourselves. Love fulfills the law and helps us to become the person who God intended us to be. Make your life story, a love story. Focus today on loving with your whole heart, eradicate all other negative feelings to include unforgiveness and hatred. Love God first, then love your neighbor as yourself as Jesus commanded us.

Mother Teresa said that, "love was faith in action."

Oliver Wendell Holmes stated, "love is the master key that opens the gates of happiness."

Once you start loving with your whole heart, without limits, you will see more abundance enter into your life. Love is powerful in ways that we cannot understand or fathom. Love is a life force which produces its own curative energies.

The Apostle Paul said in Ephesians 5:1-2, "Therefore be imitators of God as dear children, and walk in love, as Christ also has loved us and given Himself for us, and offering and a sacrifice to God for a sweet smelling aroma."

1 Corinthians 13 is called the chapter of love as composed so beautifully by the Apostle Paul. Read it today!

"Let us love one another, for love comes from God." (1 John 4:7).

God is love, thus our nature is love as well, but through conditioning, many have forgotten that very nature. We have been taken off the path of love so we need to relearn how to love in a whole and healthy manner.

To ignite that fire within, we just have to do our job regardless of what others do--our job is to love others unconditionally. When we love other, we sow seeds of positive energy into world.

"Love draws forth love." Saint Teresa of Areila

Motivational Tip for Day #21

Stop what you are doing right now.

Prepare for the process of internal transformation to be mentally and physically exhausting. This is why too few people commit to living a higher life.

You can live a life of abundance by following your passion. Don't be lukewarm in what you do, whether it's at work or in life.

Live your day by having a passion for God throughout the day. "The Lord says: 'These people come near to m with their mouth and honor me with their lips, but their hearts are far from me. Their worship of me is made up only of rules taught by men." (Isaiah 29:13).

This step is focused on living with an inner fire. Living your passion will transform your life.

2 Timothy 1:6 states, "Therefore I remind you to stir up the gift of God which is in you through the laying on of My hands. For God has not given us a spirit of fear, but of power and of love and of a sound mind." God has already given us the power but we must passionately use the gifts that God has given us to the fullest.

If you have a passion for God, you will see amazing benefits unfold throughout your life. If we love God then we would happily do what pleases God. Some people say they love God but continually do things that God hates. We can elevate our life by first passionately loving God every moment of every day. Next we should love ourselves and our day passionately. Stir up that fire inside.

Get excited about life. God is excited about you! Love you so passionately that He wants the best for you. When life tries to beat you down, you can easily tap into that God given power inside to stir up yourself.

When I wake up each morning:

First, I thank God for giving me another day to be better than the day before.

Next I say, "Thank you God for being with me, giving me the power and loving me. I will use this day in a way which will glorify You and use the gifts you have given me to the maximum."

Third, I envision that I have switches inside of me. These are how some of the switches are marked inside of me: "inner joy", "excitement for life", "unlimited energy" and "love of my neighbors". All I have to do when I get up is to hit these switches and I feel differently immediately. Create your own internal switches and believe that by turning those switches on, you will get the power that is mentioned in the above verse in Timothy. What do you tell yourself when you get up each morning?

Because of God's power and faithfulness, we can attempt great things for God and expect great things from God. It's called life because it's meant to be lived!

"Living your dreams will heal any past hurt and living with passion each day helps us to live a life of meaning."

Motivational Tip for Day #22

Stop what you are doing right now.

There is a quote from the Zen Buddhist tradition which speaks of letting go of old views:

"Do not think the knowledge you presently possess is changeless, absolute truth. Avoid being narrow-minded and bound to present views. Learn to practice non-attachment with views in order to be open to receive other's viewpoints."
Seeking to know more of God each day allows us to grow and become the people God wants us to become. The philosopher Wang Yang Ming stated years ago, "To know and yet not do, is in fact, not to know."

In Proverbs 1:5, we learn, "Let the wise listen and add to their learning."

William Blake stated in "Jerusalem", "I must create a system, or be enslaved by another man's; I will not reason and compare: my business is to create." I love this statement because we are all looking for meaning and purpose in life but we must each create a system to acquire it.

Today's tip is about creating a system that helps us to become more perceptive. Everyone should understand that it's because of the past failures and hurts that one becomes open to doing things in a different way. In the Gnostic Gospel of Thomas, Jesus says, "Blessed is the one who has suffered and has found life." Out of my suffering, I have learned that my job is to strive for real internal change with my thoughts, words and actions. From the past, I have learned how to love in truth and deed.

An old African proverb says, "A closed mouth cannot eat." And I say that a closed heart cannot love. Strive today to open every part of your heart this day.
James 2:20 stated, "...faith without works is dead." Those who love is 'of God' and those who do not love, do not know God according to the Bible. Many people continue to stay in the muck, darkness, depression, unforgiveness or sadness because they do not understand who they are or the power they have on the inside. The Gospel of Luke states, "...For the Kingdom of God is within you."

You are boundless and have great power inside of you! An old saying states that, "we perceive things not as they are but as we are."

Today perceive that you are loved unconditionally by God, and are composed of love. Endeavor today to emanate love in all that you do. A deeper understanding of love leads to a new way of viewing the world. Use love to create a new whole and healthy system to view the world around you. Plato said, "He whom love touches, walks not in darkness."
Love will free you and empower you! Be uplifted and encouraged today because God is for you! Tell yourself today, "God has given me all I need each day, if I don't have it then I don't need."

Motivational Tip for Day #23

Stop what you are doing right now.

Today we will be focusing on the great motivator, God, and the fruits of the Spirit! God gave us 66 books in the Bible. I call these 66 love letters from God because they written to help us become better people.

I want to use 2nd Peter 1:5-11 today as the guide:

"But also for this very reason, giving all diligence, add to your faith virtue, to virtue knowledge, to knowledge self control, to self control perseverance, to perseverance godliness, to godliness brotherly kindness, and to brotherly kindness love. For these things are yours and abound, you will be neither barren nor unfruitful in the knowledge of our Lord Jesus Christ. For he who lacks these things is shortsighted, even to blindness, and has forgotten that he was cleansed from his old sins. Therefore, brethren, be even more diligent to make your call and election sure, for if you do these things you will be never stumble; for so an entrance will be supplied to you abundantly into the everlasting kingdom of our Lord and Savior Jesus Christ."

Growing spiritually is a lifelong process and leads to having an abundant life. Our job is to let the scriptures move us and change us for the inside out. Our daily goal should be to increase our understanding of God and what He wants for our life.

2nd Peter 3:18 states, "but grow in the grace and the knowledge of our Lord and Savior Jesus Christ." Make sure your Spiritual journey is taking you to new higher places and on positive paths each day.

2nd Peter 3:11 provide a great question for us all: "Therefore, since all these things will be dissolved, what manner of persons ought you to be in holy conduct and godliness." Wow! An excellent call to action for all of us!

If we serve God, He will make our way easier and reward us.

Today focus and strive to make your heart be in tune with God. Call on God to motivate you knowing that it's His plan for you to live abundantly. God will show you the path, if you lean on Him.

God's great love for you is detailed in so many beautiful ways in His 66 love letters! The scripture in 2nd Peter is a great guide to live a life pleasing to God.

Remember: "Pray Big, Love Big and Hope Big!"

Motivational Tip for Day #24

Stop what you are doing right now.

Today's tip is focused on gratitude, being thankful for all the things that come into our lives, good and bad. Having a loving heart includes having a thankful heart. Gratitude opens up the doors of infinite power in your life.

Do you want to open up a wave of positive energy in your life? If the answer is yes, then count your blessings each day; at the start of the day, during the day and before you go to bed.

1 Thessalonians 5:18 states, "In everything give thanks."
Why does the Bible, the Torah and the Qur'an all place great emphasis on being thankful at all times? I believe this is because God knows that it's easy for us living in the natural world to fall for the illusions and delusions of life.

Psalm 30:11-12 said, "You (God) have turned my mourning into dancing; You have put off my sackcloth and cloth me with gladness, to the end that my glory may sing to You and not be silent. O Lord, my God, I will give thanks to You forever."
I love this verse because I love God so much, with a crazy passionate love that He deserves. My love for God can hardly be put into speech because it's written on my heart. When our mind is on gratitude then it's on God, which leaves no room to complain or seek to please our lower nature.

Gratitude is part of our higher self, our God nature. When we are being thankful, we are aligning our soul and spirit with that of God. This tip is focused on being grateful at all time, at all times, not just the good times but I praise God when something bad happens in my life.

I quote Charles Spurgeon, an early spiritual thinker, who said:

"I bear witness that owe more to the fire, and the hammer, and the file, than to anything else in my Lord's workshop. I sometimes question whether I have ever learned anything except through the rod. When my school room is darkened, I see the most."

When my school room is darkened, I thank God the most because I know that joy comes in the morning. I know understand that I must praise God during all times especially the hard times. The hard times are for my benefit! I just have to trust God and maintain faith.

The opposite of gratitude is complaining. Complaining is not 'of God' while being thankful is 'of God'. In Joshua 1:9, God tells his people, "Have I not commanded you? Be strong and of good courage; do not be afraid, nor be dismayed, for the Lord your God is with you wherever you go." We shall be known by our actions as James, Jesus' half brother wrote in the Epistle which bears his name. Do your actions say you are thankful and trust God or does it say you are distrustful of God?

In the Qur'an it stated in 7:144, "So hold that which I have given you and be of the grateful."

Gratitude channels positive energy into the universe which is returned to you. Gratitude is one of the higher levels of energy which empowers you.
Gratitude is a powerful, positive feeling that should be felt throughout the body. It's all an open secret that God has laid out a plan for our lives, a plan to have an abundant life, and being grateful is about doing our part.

I end this section with a general thanksgiving prayer from the Book of Common Prayer:

"Almighty God, Father of all mercies, we, Your unworthy servants, give you humble thanks for all Your goodness and loving-kindness to us and to all men. We bless You for our creation, preservation, and all the blessings of this life; but above all for Your incomparable love in redemption of the world by our Lord Jesus Christ; for the means of grace, and for hope of glory. And, we pray, give us such awareness of Your mercies, that with truly thankful hearts we may make known Your praise, not only with our lips, but in our lives, by giving up ourselves to Your service, and by walking before You in holiness and righteousness all our days through Jesus Christ our Lord, to whom, with You and the Holy Spirit, be the honor and glory through the ages, Amen."

Say this prayer out loud and say thank you to God 100 times each day which will help you to have an abundant life!

Motivational Tip for Day #25

Stop what you are doing right now.

Today's tip is focused on learning how to pray in deeper ways.

The Bible says that we should pray incessantly in 1 Thessalonians 4:17, "Pray without ceasing."

James 5:16 states, "The effective, fervent prayer of a righteous man avails much."
Is your prayer life 'fervent'?

Most people do not have a deep and daily spiritual practice. It's difficult to have a deep spiritual life without a deep prayer life. Prayer allows us to align our lower self with our higher self. We hold great creative power inside of us but it we are living a broken or defeated lifestyle then it's difficult to tap into this power.

Therapists talk about the importance of cognitively restructuring our thoughts in order to transform our lives. Prayer is central to this change.

The urge to pray is universal because it orients our spiritual life towards God. Life has such great meaning and our purpose is to discover that meaning. Life today strives to keep us bound to illusions and delusions. Finding our true self is the goal. Prayer and meditation helps us to find our true God nature, to become closer to the divine nature in each of us.

Prayer is pure energy and right prayer leads to an abundant life. How does one pray in the right manner? I found eight principles which have helped me to deepen my prayer life.

1-Expressing thanks for our faith and for the change which knowing God has produced has produced in our lives. My life was changed through knowing God. (Asking God to help us develop a God conscious view of the world, God-consciousness).
2-Asking God to help us know what He wants to do for Him (Purpose).
3-Asking God to help us deepen our spiritual understanding (Wisdom).
4-Asking God to help us live for Him (Meaning).
5-Asking God to give us more knowledge of His nature and His mind (Seeking the right things).
6-Asking God to give us strength to endure (Endurance to live in this fallen world without being conformed, being steadfast).
7-Asking God to fill us with joy, strength and thankfulness each day (Being a light for others).
8-Asking God to share the above gifts with other (Our mission).

When reading the Bible, ask God to speak to you. When you meditate and pray throughout the day, ask God to provide you wisdom and ask God to show you how to help others. Prayer is all about coming into God's presence. We all have a deep inner desire to know God.

Jesus' disciples asked Him, "Lord, teach us to pray (Luke 11:1)." The disciples wanted to learn how they could draw closer to God and feel His presence in a deeper way. Are you trying to become closer to God each day through effective fervent prayer? In order to live an abundant life, one must seek to deepen their prayer life.

Remember what James, Jesus' half brother, wrote, "Draw near to God and He will draw near to you (James 4:8)."

Motivational Tip for Day #26

Stop what you are doing right now.

Today's tip is focused on God!

Some people do not realize that God is all-knowing, having infinite awareness, understanding and insight (omniscient), all-powerful and almighty (omnipotent) and all present, being present in all places at all times (omnipresent). I serve a God so all encompassing that it staggers me to imagine Him and all His glory. But because of God's grace, his unmerited favor-He is our God and we are His people.

God wants us to put Him first. All we do should glorify this great God!
In Exodus 3:14, God tells Moses that his name is, "I AM WHO I AM." God tells Moses to tell the children of Israel that "I AM" has sent Moses to them. God describes Himself as "I AM". This is because He is.

"Everyone who love is born of God, and knows God. He who does not love, does not know God, for God is love (1 John 4:8)." "And we have known and believed the love that God has for us. God is love, and he who abides in love abides in God, and God in him (1 John 4:16)." A close and intimate relationship with God creates the conditions for an abundant life.

God is what it's all about. I will break down this down in two simple points: 1) the big picture; and 2) the details of the little picture.

1: Big Picture is about God and His great love He has for us. Feel empowered because He loves us with a love that the human mind cannot comprehend. The depth of God's love is unfathomable because simple human love cannot compare. God wants you to have a joy-filled and abundant life (John 10:10). We must have a passion for God. Love is God so this means that we must love with our whole heart. The center of Christian faith is love. The first and greatest commandment that Jesus said in Mathew 22:37, "You shall love Lord your God with all your heart, with all your soul and with all your mind..." So the big picture is about loving God.

2: The details of the little picture are about the second part of what Jesus said in Mathew 22:37, "and the second great commandment is like the first, 'You shall love your neighbor as yourself." This second part is about HOW we live. It matter how you live each moment of each day. Your worship should show that as a believer, you understand the big picture and live a life where the little details matter. Do everything each day with love at its core. The little details are about striving to ensure our thoughts, words and deeds align with these two points. If we love God then we would happily do what pleases Him. The Christian walk is in the little details such as how we treat others including those who hate us or hurt us.

Life is about perspective and as we get older, God willing I pray that we all gain more perspective. The Bible is the greatest tool available to help anyone gain wisdom and perspective.

He is _____
I am _____

Today fill out the rest of the above sentence on a 3 x 5 note card. For example: God is my Creator, and I am His created. God is the Great Encourager, and I am his encouraged. God is love, and I am love. God is the Great Healer, and I am healed. God is my Great Life Coach, and I am his most precious, guided child. God is my strength, and I am empowered.

We are of God according to 1 John 4:6 and the Great "I AM" is invested in us. God knows our names!

Today, ask God to help you gain a new perspective. See God for what He is and how much He loves you.

God's love is agape, a self-giving love expressed freely without expecting anything in return. Having an intimate relationship with God helps one through the tough times and makes the good times even better.

Ask yourself today, do my actions show that I am a child of God. Do my actions glorify God? Faith is about the little details.

Tell yourself, "I'm not the person who I used to be; but with the grace of God, I'll eventually be the person that God wants me to be."

Motivational Tip for Day #27

Stop what you are doing right now.

Jesus said in Luke 17:21, "...For the Kingdom of God is within you."
If the kingdom of God is within us and we are 'of God' then the possibilities are infinite for us to develop and grow. What is you great purpose? What inspires you? Are you sharing your passion with others?

My passion is focused on serving God and sharing the gift that God gave me to others. I used to be broken and depressed but through God, I was healed. The redemptive power of God's love can heal anyone.

1 Corinthians 13:8a says that, "Love never fails."
Are you loving completely each day? God has given us all we need but our job is to fully utilize the gifts, tools and skills He has given us.

"Let all that you do be done with love (1 Corinthians 16:13-14)."

God is looking for a few spiritual warriors, people who are looking to stand up and stand out for Him by being unique in today's society. Romans 12:2 stated that, "we should not be conformed to this world but be transformed by the renewing of our minds that we may prove what is good and acceptable and the perfect will of God."
Many people routinely allow society to move them away from God each day. For example, people get hurt by someone and want to hurt those people in return, but God says that we should love our enemies and that we should repay evil with good. Too many people in society are conformed and giving to others the same thing they receive. But our job is to love and share God's message.

We can't share God's message if we are still acting like we have done in the past. If we can break out of the conditioning and programming of the past and strive to obey God in every facet of our life then we will have all that God promised for us, an abundant life!

Live today as if you believe that the Kingdom of God is within you!

"Our job is to examine ourselves constantly in order to get closer to God."

"Life can be very easy when love is your way of life," (Don Miguel Ruiz in The Four Agreements)

Motivational Tip for Day #28

Stop what you are doing right now.

Today's tip is focused on 'focusing what you think about.'

Don't leave any mental space for unbelief or negative feelings. Each day is another opportunity to think differently, and better in more whole and healthy ways. Today, be inspired! In-spirit-ed, leaning on power of the Holy Spirit inside.

Today listen, learn, absorb, embrace and internalize the love that God has for you! Joy is a destination we can all be arrive at. Today tell yourself that, "I will give birth to everything God has put on my heart."

See abundance entering your life in your mind's eye. Go from believing to expecting. Then go beyond expecting, act as if it's already here. "Be patient as you wait with expectancy, (James 5:7)."

We have to put the right thoughts and actions behind our faith. Mentally expect good things throughout the day. Stay hopeful and positive despite what's going on around you. Show the evil one, satan, the devil, the adversary that you will not fall for his mental tricks anymore.

This is your life, you write the script. Today focus on your thoughts and thinking in a way that is pleasing to God. God wants us to have an abundant life, so have faith in what God is wanting for your life. Faith unlocks the power of the Lord. God wants us to be faithful, to live holy and righteously and then he will bless us. By faith, we can love and forgive.

Inside there is an internal GPS device, a God positioning device which is waiting for you to put in the coordinates of a joy filled life. To activate the great power in ourselves, we must walk in the Spirit and be Christ-like daily.

Today, focus on your thoughts being about positive uplifting matters. Discipline your mind today to have pure and honest intentions. Philippians 4:6 states, "Don't fret or have anxiety about anything, but in every circumstance and in everything by prayer and petition, with thanksgiving, continue to make your wants known to God."

Aristotle said, "we cannot learn without pain." Only remember your pain so that you will not go back that same mental location. Appreciate the lessons.

"..And without the negative feedback of our pain that God allows in our lives, we would miss many of life's most important lessons," Tony Dungy

And remember, "don't lose heart because in due time, we shall all reap."

You have more power inside you than you ever imagined. God created you in His own image so we could glorify Him, align your mind with the mind of God and you will flourish in ways you could never have dreamed of!

"Without my pain, I would not have known God the way I do. I have no regrets, only experiences which allow me to move in healthier God-conscious ways."

Motivational Tip for Day #29

Stop what you are doing right now.

Everyone has the possibility to be more than they are. The concept of being "more than we are" is a part of our DNA. We are capable of such greatness but we each must change our vision from a 'natural' influenced vision to a 'God conscious' vision. Each time you decide to limit yourself and what God has put in your heart, you are rejecting God's plan for your life.

"Therefore we make it our aim, whether present or absent, to be well pleasing to Him (2 Corinthians 5:9)."

Today's tip is focused on readjusting our aim.

The above verse discusses how we should strive to be pleasing to God. It matters to God how we live our lives. Our aim should be to see ourselves as God sees us and then modify our behavior so it aligns with God's aim for our lives.
When we readjust our aim using a God conscious lens, we can then reach our full potential. God intended us to be 'more than conquerors'. We will always hit what we aim for, what we put our sights on. Most people aim too low. It's your aim; you can visualize anything you want to. Aim high! Aim straight! Aim for God! Aim God! Aim true!

Don't listen to the dream stealers, but instead listen to that small still voice inside of yourself. Listen to your heart.

Aim for wisdom! Aim to recognize God's hand moving in your life. God is always present and at work in our lives, it's just how we perceive Him each day that changes.

God is seeking to bless you in a mighty way, align your aiming mechanism to that of God's.

Today tell yourself, "This is my life. I am the star of my own life. This is the life God has given to me, and He wants me to succeed. My purpose is to do God's will and to believe in the promises He has for my life. I must stay on script, God's script for my life. If I am not on the script now, I can change the script right now by leaning on God because Jesus is the Director/Writer/Producer of all that's good, true and beautiful.

Ten steps on how to change your aim:

1) Think deeply about your life
2) Make a list of your dreams/goals and the places where your heart is trying to take you.
3) Take action - just do it. Execute the little, daily details to move you closer to your goal.
4) Never stop learning. Train your mind, retrain the inner seeker. Start reading more each day.

5) Be persistent and work hard. Do not be swayed when obstacles come in your path.
6) Learn to analyze the details and facts of your current situation.
7) Focus your time and money. Be focused with your limited resources (time and money).
8) Don't be afraid to change. Change is what will allow you to achieve your dreams. Embrace change. Love change.
9) Deal with, and communicate with people more effectively. Communicate with yourself and with others in deeper ways.
10) Be honest and dependable. Take responsibility for your life. It's your life! It's meant to lived fully! God wants you to choose life!

Motivational Tip for Day #30

Stop what you are doing right now.

"People should think less about what they ought to do, and more about what they ought to be," Meister Eckhart, a medieval German mystic.

Gandhi read Eckhart and thought only about what he should be and everything he did shone with beauty.

Today's tip is about being the best we can be for God.

"And we know that all things work together for good to those who love God, to those who are called according to His purpose (Romans 8:28)." If we focus on striving for God like King David, who would become known as "a man after God's own heart (Acts 13:22)," then we will have an abundant life.

We all have been infused with the Holy Spirit which has empowered us and guides us. Life in Christ involves consistently seeking God's purpose for our lives. Jude, the brother of James, wrote a beautiful short letter before Revelations. "But you, beloved, building yourselves up on your most holy faith, praying in the Holy Spirit. Keep yourselves in the love of God, looking for the mercy of our Lord Jesus Christ unto eternal life. And some have compassion, making a distinction; but others save with fear, pulling them out of the fire, hating even the garment defiled by the flesh. Now to Him who is able to keep you from stumbling, and to present you faultless before the presence of His glory with exceeding joy, To God our Savior, Who alone is wise, Be glory and majesty, Dominion and power, Both now and forever. Amen."

The Holy Spirit empowers us and having a deep intimate love of God will enable you to live a full life. Tapping into the Holy Spirit which already indwells within you, will help you from stumbling. We can be better today but it requires focus and determination because no one can gain the glory without striving.

Ask yourself today: "Is God satisfied with how I live my life?" Challenge yourself to be better. When we get better, our lives will be better.

God has given you all you need to achieve greatness today for His glory!

Motivational Tip for Day #31

Stop what you're doing right now.

Today, focus on letting God use you in new and different ways.

Is it a stumbling block or a stepping stone? Perception is reality and how you perceive your life differentiates the person living with a God consciousness or not.

"God hath sent forth the Spirit of His Son into your hearts (Galatians 4:6) so that "Christ may dwell in your hearts by faith (Ephesians 3:17)."

Faith unlocks the Power of the Lord. Our faith must be anchored in the Lord.
God wants us to live a fruitful life. By faith, we can forgive and love through the Holy Spirit which dwells within us. Faith is about understanding how out of every crisis comes opportunity. We must live our Christ nature each day. There are many different paths one can choose, and too many of us choose pain and then decide to reside there in defeat. Faith is about understanding that life is an experiment with infinite outcomes. We must be mindful that we always have the opportunity to change in more positive directions, learning from our failures.

Are you unhappy, unfulfilled at times? You don't have to be. If you want more, then you must demand more of yourself and open your heart to new radical notions of love.

How do you motivate yourself to live a God inspired life where love is at the center? Have a passion for God! Some people believe that motivation is difficult but it's easy because it's all in how you see the world and what you decide to focus on.

Five simple tips to help improve your level of motivation:

1) Start with the right attitude and the right inner dialogue. The anchor verse for this concept is Psalm 51:10 which say, "Create in me a clean heart, O God, and renew a steadfast spirit within me."
2) Seek, long for and have a hunger to do God's will and to serve Him. The anchor verse for this concept is Proverbs 8:17 which says, "I (God) love those who love me, and those who seek me diligently will find me."
3) Bring everything to God in prayer; talk to God throughout the day, discussing your thoughts, plans, fears and other issues. The anchor verse for this concept is 1 Thessalonians 5:17 which say, "Pray without ceasing."
4) Trust (and have faith) that God has a plan for your life whether good or bad things are happening in it. There are two anchor verses for this concept: Jeremiah 29:11 says, "I alone know the plans I have for you, plans to bring you prosperity and not disaster, plans to bring about the future you hope for." Isaiah 41:10 says, "Fear not, for I am with you; Be not dismayed, for I am your God. I will strengthen you, Yes, I will help you, I will uphold you with My righteous right hand.

5) Learn and train yourself to listen for that small still voice inside. Hunger to hear God's voice. The anchor verse for this concept is Psalm 46:10 which says, "Be still and know that I am God."

"The biggest human temptation is to settle for too little." Thomas Merton

Motivational Tip for Day #32

Stop what you are doing right now.

Today's tip is focused on a little internal housekeeping. Does your life say you live for Christ? This is a question I ask myself each day. Do people know through my words and actions that I serve God?

Motivation is acquired in many different ways. I believe that God is the Great Motivator and we learn how to be motivated by practically applying spiritual principles to our lives.

Enlightenment is a very personal thing, it's on each of us to move forward if we want. As we slowly gain a better understanding of our own mind, our perception and sense of the outside world grows. Too many people only know the results of learned misery and suffering. Our value systems have been distorted. We were born to value God's system but through time and conditioning throughout environments, we begin to value the things of this natural world. God's divine system is based on love, and we must come to value love and light more than any other thing in this world.

The verse for today is in Hebrews 10:22-25, "Let us draw near with a true heart in full assurance of faith, having our hearts sprinkled from an evil conscience and our bodies washed in pure water. Let us hold fast the confession of our hope without wavering for He who promised is faithful. And let us consider one another in order to stir up love and good works, not forsaking the assembling of ourselves together as is the manner of some, but exhorting one another, and so much more as you see the Day approaching."

Leave no room for mental doubt. Lack of faith is mental doubt.

Throughout the today, lift your arms above your head and cheer for yourself. Know that God wants you to soar. Accomplish great things for God today, attempt great things for God today!

Today's anchor verse is from Luke 18:27, "But Jesus said, 'The things which are impossible with men as possible with God." Repeat this verse today and know that God is your greatest supporter and encourager. God wants you to have an abundant life!

"Make an impact for God today!"

Motivational Tip for Day #33

Stop what you are doing right now.

"Cling to the thought that, in God's hands, the dark past is the greatest possession you have - the key to life and happiness for others. With it, you can avert death and misery from them." Alcoholics Anonymous Big Book p. 124

"No longer is my past an autobiography, it is a reference book to be taken down, opened and shared. All my past will this day be a part of me, because it is the key, not the lock."

The two verses above both come from AA and show us how the past is not a stumbling block but steps to a new and better life. Stop hauling that garbage of the past around with you. Shrug off the past, don't stress about the future but instead focus on living fully today. The Bible says that we will have trials and tribulations.

Romans 5:3-5 stated, "...but we also glory in tribulations, knowing that tribulation produces perseverance; and perseverance, character; and character, hope. Now hope does not disappoint, because the love of God has been poured out in our hearts by the Holy Spirit who was given to us."

"For I consider that the suffering of this present time are not worthy to be compared with the glory which shall be revealed in us (Romans 8:18)."

"My Brethren, count it all joy when you fall into various trials, knowing that the testing of your faith produces patience. But let patience have it's perfect work, that you may be perfect and complete, lacking nothing. If any of you lacks wisdom, let him ask God, who gives to all liberally and without reproach, and it will be given to him. But let him ask in faith, without no doubting for he who doubts is like a wave of the seas driven and tossed by the wind (James 1:2-6)."

True wisdom is having the right perspective. God knows you will go through trouble but He will be with you through it. Today, work on changing your perspective because without changing how you view the world, faith turns into doubt. Our trials are important because it helps to mold us. Have faith in the process, God's process to make us better people.

Tap into the power of God's love which is already inside of you. Free yourself from the bonds of the past. There is a song by the group Mary Mary called 'Shackles' which ask God to take the shackles off my feet so I can dance, because I just want to praise you. Many people walk around with shackles on their soul, spirit and mind. Ask God to free you today, asks God to help you change your perspective to align it with His view, to perceive the world as God sees it.

Rejoice, God is for you!!! "What then shall we say to these things? If God is for us, who can be against us? (Romans 8:31).

Motivational Tip for Day #34

Stop what you are doing right now.

Everyone has a mission to fulfill in life. Colossians 4:17 states, "...Take heed to the ministry which you have received in the Lord, that you may fulfill it."

Just as our physical bodies need food for healthy, our spirit needs the Word of God for spiritual health. We can't serve God the way we want to serve God and expect to be blessed. When we keep our minds on spiritual things (things on high), we are able to say connected to God. The real battle for each believer is the inner battle to stay focused on God and serving him, and not serving our lower nature.

I strive to know the mind of God each day by and the more I do this, the more inner peace I have. Loving God is curative for the soul. The life of a believer is not always easy because of our pride, ego and disobedient nature. We struggle against God's commands each day until we completely surrender. In our society, surrender and obedience are words which are displeasing to hear. This is a lie that Satan has successfully made many believe. The life of a believer is marked by the pursuit of perfection, to be Christ-like. The life of the believer is strengthened by the Holy Spirit and the evidence of the Holy Spirit is through a changed life. It's about listening to the right inner voice.

Many people want to be faithful in their Christian walk but their lifestyle does not line up with God's commands. Unless we change our inner nature, we will continue to go astray.

I started this tip discussing the fulfillment of our ministry. We can only do this by striving to live a virtuous life. Christian virtues are faith, hope, charity, love and forgiveness. The seven deadly sins are pride, covetousness, lust, anger, gluttony, envy and sloth (laziness). These sins keep us from God and his blessings as mentioned in Isaiah 59:2, "...your iniquities have separated you from your God; and your sins have hidden His face from you."

But living a higher life, striving to listen each day to what God is telling us, living for God and looking for radical ways to love everyone, we will be blessed. "Instead of your shame, you shall have double honor, and instead of confusion they shall rejoice in their portion. Therefore in their land they shall possess double; everlasting joy shall be theirs (Isaiah 61:7)."

God loves us with in ways that we can't imagine. God is looking for ways to bless you today! You can fulfill your purpose when you lean on God!

"And we know that all things work together for good to those who love God, to those who are called according to His purpose (Romans 8:28)."

"I almost gave up, the devil really had me bound but God's mercy kept me sound, so I wouldn't let go. I am here today because God kept me." An old spiritual song.

"There are two great days in a person's life -- the day we are born and the day we discover why." William Barclay

Motivational Tip for Day #35

Stop what you are doing right now.

Today, we will focus on the heart viewing other religious traditions, which have parallel ideals, to better understand the Christian walk.

In Buddhism there is a principle called the Four Noble Truths:

1) All life entails suffering. (Jesus said in John 16:33, "These things I have spoken to you, that in Me you may have peace. In this world, you will have tribulation, but be of good cheers, I have overcome the world.")
2) Suffering is caused by desire. (Jesus said in Luke 12:15, "Take heed and beware of covetousness, for one's life does not consist in the abundance of the things he possesses.")
3) Desire can be overcome; (Jesus stated in John 10:10, "The thief does not come except to steal, and to kill, and to destroy. I have come that they may have life, and that they may have it more abundantly.")
4) The means to overcome desire is the Noble Eightfold Path:
a-Right Views
b-Right Intentions
c-Right Speech
d-Right conduct
e-Right Work
f-Right Effort
g-Right meditation
h-Right Contemplation

The term right can be interpreted as 'true' or 'correct'. Jesus explained in Mathew 6:19-20, "Do not lay up for yourselves treasures on earth, where moth and rust destroy and where thieves break in and steal; but lay up for yourselves treasures in heaven, where neither moth nor rust destroys and where thieves do not break in and steal. For where your treasure is, there your heart will be also."

We must maintain a positive inner vision. We are already one with God and each day we should be aware of our connection to a loving God. Our inner world is the architect for our outer world.

Scientists have recently been writing about how the heart has 60,000 specialized neurons within it. The heart is the only part of the body, except for the brain, which contains neurons. Our heart is the center of our being, with the brain following what's in the heart. Proverbs 23:7 states, "So as a man thinks in his heart, so as he is." The cardiovascular neurons in our heart act as a highway from the heart to the brain. When children are formed in the womb, the heartbeat occurs before the brain is fully formed. I mention this as it relates to the eightfold noble path above. If we maintain any negative feelings in our hearts, it takes up root and produce negativity in our lives.

"A good man obtains favor from the Lord, But a man of wicked intentions He will condemn (Proverbs 12:2)."

Proverbs 16:9 stated, "A man's heart plans his way, But the Lord directs his steps." The heart is the center of our being. If we strive to keep our hearts pure, clean and without hatred, unforgiveness and other negative feelings each day, blessings and favor will be our reward.

Love can't flow from a closed heart or even a partially closed heart. Take charge of your inner world. Challenge yourself every moment of the day to act and think in only positive ways, the ways you know that only pleases God.

Make Jesus the center of your joy each day. When a person truly has Jesus on the inside, there is something to smile about.

Motivational Tip for Day #36

Stop what you are doing right now.

Today's tip is focused on understanding what we are. We are a tripartite being composed of three parts: Spirit, Soul and Body.

I am Spirit, I have a Soul and I live in a Body.

The Spirit is the high part where God deals with us. This is the part that God dwells in. "That He would grant you, according to the riches of His glory, to be strengthened with might through His Spirit in the inner man, that Christ may dwell in your hearts through faith; that you, being rooted and grounded in love, may be able to comprehend with all the saints what is the width and length and depth and height -- to know the love of Christ which passes knowledge; that you may be filled with all the fullness of God. Now to Him who is able to do exceedingly abundantly above all that we ask or think, according to the power that works in us (Ephesians 3:16-20)."

The soul is where the battle takes place. The soul is composed of mind, emotion and will. This is where we each decide whether we want to live according to God's will or the devil's will. "Set your mind on things above, not on things on the earth (Colossians 3:2)." The soul connects the body to the Spirit.

The body is the lowest part of our being. This is the part without God. The body only knows thirst, hunger, desires and other base urges. The body will act as it was created to act. The body reacts stupidly when given the opportunity or allowed to lead us. In 2 Timothy 3:2-7 we learn how the body leads us astray, "For men with be lovers of themselves, lovers of money, boasters, proud, blasphemers, disobedient to parents, unthankful, unholy, unloving, unforgiving, slanderers, without self-control, brutal, despisers of good, traitors, headstrong, haughty, lovers of pleasure rather than lovers of God, having a form of godliness but denying it's power. And from such people turn away! ...Always learning and never able to come to the knowledge of the truth." The body does all these things, desires all these things and seeks after these things instead of God.

We were meant to live for so much more! We have a choice each day as to which part we wish to feed. When we read the Bible, attend church, love others and act in ways pleasing to God rather than pleasing to the body, we nourish the Spirit. When we succumb to addictions, hatred, unforgiveness, and other negative emotions then we are giving in to the body. The devil loves our fleshly body; this is where the devil has the greatest influence.

When we chase the things in the world, we are nourishing the body. We can never find God when we are chasing things of this world. Each day we vote with our feet. There are times when we want our heart and soul to move closer to God but it's impossible when our feet is moving away from God by our choices in life.

God wants us to be blessed, blessed means happy. When we strive to fulfill the body, we will never be satisfied. The body always wants more. The body wants to master us. The soul was created for God, to serve God and it can't be satisfied through the pursuit of other things, except God.

God has put eternity in your heart! We were meant to live a higher, more abundant life!

You are the master of your internal world.

"For God gives wisdom and knowledge and joy to a man who is good in His sight (Ecclesiastes 2:26)."

Motivational Tip for Day #37

Stop what you are doing right now.

Today will be focused on the journey. The journey is from this world, to heaven. How do you plan to get there? Do you have a plan for victory? What does your daily plan for victory look like?

"Therefore I remind you to stir up the gift of God which is in you through the laying on of my hands. For God has not given us a spirit of fear, but of power and of love and of a sound mind (2 Timothy 1:6-7)." God has already fully equipped us for every good work, but we have to understand how to operate ourselves and utilize our tools.

Being fully conscious in the present moment can get us to where we want to go. Being aware during every moment of our life so that we do not let the evil one gain an internal foothold. Knowing the nature of our minds and inner characteristics will allow one to self-correct instead of having the world self-correct us. Knowing one's mind and how it works is critical to living an abundant life.

Faith will allow you to get to your ultimate destination. The Bible tells us that we shall be known by the fruits of our labor. The fruits are made up of our thoughts, words, and actions. Faith is something which can be practiced through our thoughts, words and actions. The Bible provides a blueprint how one should live.

The Bible does not impose limitations on what you can do because God has promised that you shall have life, and have it more abundantly. God will do what He says He will do.

A suggested plan on how we can get there?

1) Loving and forgiving. Loving completely, seeing the God in every one. Forgiving means acting like the offense never happened.
2) Thinking radically differently. See yourself as God sees you every moment. We need the power of Christ in our mind.
3) Finding meaning and purpose through serving God and being His child.
4) Participate in your own rescue, act now to move forward.
5) Having steadfast faith, belief in a loving God who knows the plans he has for your life. Eliminating doubt, and live in faith. Don't be double-minded or unstable in your ways as James describes in James 1:6-8.
6) Examining ourselves deeply and critically based on God's word.
The journey is meant to be instructive which means hardships at times, but they are for our benefit. God will not put more on us then we can bear. God has promised that He will never leave us. We must keep our hand in the Lord's hand in every moment.

"You will keep him (us) in perfect peace, whose mind is stayed on You, because he (us) trusts in You. Trust in the Lord forever, For in Yah (God), the Lord is everlasting strength (Isaiah 26:3-4). God will keep us grounded and in balance as long as we keep our minds on Him.

"Go confidently in the direction of your dreams." Henry David Thoreau

Motivational Tip for Day #38

Stop what you are doing right now.

Today's tip is focused on receiving the gift that God is trying to give you: abundance and abundant joy!

Ask God today to blow your mind!

"Be strong and of good courage; be not afraid, neither be you dismayed; for the Lord your God is with you wheresoever you go (Joshua 1:9)."

God wants an intimate relationship with you. God wants to be first in your life. In John 16:24 Jesus states, "Until now you have asked nothing in My name. Ask and you will receive, that your joy may be full."

Today, strive to want for yourself that which God wants for you. Do not give place to the devil but walk instead with God. Ask God to show Himself to you. God wants to show Himself to those who diligently seek Him. God wants you to know more about Him each day as described in Luke 8:10, "Unto you is given to know the mysteries of the kingdom of God...."

Ask the Lord to help you to remember Him throughout the day, not just when you pray. God says in His word that the man who hears His word and does them, loves Him. Being a Christian is a 24 hours a day job and entails living a Christ-like life every moment. God gives us all we need and reminds us above in Joshua that he is with us wherever we go.

Jesus said that if we love Him, then we'll hear his words and keep His commandments. Jesus wants to walk with us each day and has told us that if we seek Him, we will find Him.

Proverbs 14:12 states that, "There is a way that seems right to a man, But in the end is the way of death." Our way only leads to death. Our stubbornness to completely surrender to God only leads us to an unfulfilled life, where misery abounds. The above verse in proverbs says that there is a way that seems right to a man but Jesus offers another way. Jesus explained in John 14:6 that, "I am the way, the truth and the life. No one comes to the Father except through Me." There is another, better, higher path which will enable us to live an abundant life.

Spiritual question for today:

The Bible states that you'll know a tree by the fruit it bears. What fruit are you baring each day? If we focus on working on our inner self each day, striving to be more Christ-like and let God be God, and then abundance will come into our lives.

There is section in Isaiah 55:1-13 subtitled, "An invitation to an abundant life." I will just include a few verses here.

"Why do you spend money for what is not bread, and your wages for what does not satisfy? Listen carefully to Me, and eat what is good, And let your soul delight itself in abundance. Incline your ear, and come to Me. Hear, and your soul shall live; and I will make an everlasting covenant with you--- the sure mercies of David (Isaiah 55:2-3)."

"Seek the Lord while He may be found, Call upon Him while He is near. Let the wicked forsake his way, and the unrighteous man his thoughts; let him return to the Lord, And He will have mercy on him; and to our God, for He will abundantly pardon. 'For my thoughts are not your thoughts, nor are your ways My ways,' says the Lord. (Isaiah 55:6-8)"

Abundance comes from aligning our thoughts with that of God's. As a true Christian, we need to live a transformed life, a life different from the past with different attitudes, thoughts and believes. Ask God today to transform your thoughts so that your will be known by your fruits.

"No problem can be solved by the same consciousness that caused the problem in the first place." Albert Einstein

Motivational Tip for Day #39

Stop what you are doing right now.

Today's tip is focused on seeing the big picture.

"Whatever you do, do it for the glory of God (1 Corinthians 10:31)."
Life is not hard, it's only as hard as we make it. God has given us a choice in life, we can believe in His promises or we can believe the lies of the devil. We have amazing power inside of us and we will hit the target we are aiming for, whether we realize we are aiming or not. This is why it's so important to keep a firm hand on our thoughts. Never allow your mind to drift into bad neighborhoods, not for one moment. Always maintain positive and uplifting thought which will please God.

God is waiting for each of us to see ourselves, as He sees us. God is waiting to bless us. "He has delivered us from the power of darkness and conveyed us into the kingdom of the Son of His love (Colossians 1:13)." We were made to live in the light and have already been delivered. Align your inner vision of yourself with how God views you. God is faithful to His promises.

Make strides today to live your purpose. You were created to do wondrous and amazing things for God. Robert Schuller, the renowned pastor, stated, "Better to do something imperfectly than to do nothing flawlessly." Lean on God, He will help you succeed in your life's mission. Don't let rejection stop you. In Mathew 10:14, Jesus says to, "shake off the dust from your feet."

Life is a simple as ABC. Abundance = belief + conduct. Abundance is directly related to our ability to follow God's commands without question. Belief is focused on having steadfast faith in God, and letting God be God. Conduct is how we live our life each moment because it does matter how we live. Abundance and joy is the results of living a life which glorifies God.

"Press towards the goal for the prize (Philippians 3:14)."

Be passionate about life, and understand the big picture. God wants you to have inner joy and happiness. Albert Schweitzer said, "Success is not the key to happiness, happiness is the key to success. If you love what you do, you will be successful."

Don't ask the Lord to guide your footsteps if you are not willing to move your feet." Guidepost reader Elaine Johnson from Atlanta.

"Sometimes your only available transportation is a leap of faith." Author Margret Shepard.

Motivational Tip for Day #40

Stop what you are doing right now.

Today I want to focus on two principles: light and the heart.

The Bible speaks a lot about light, that we must stay in the light and turn away from the darkness. The first words God said in the Bible were, "Let there be light (Genesis 1:3)." These first words spoken by God are significant. "God saw the light, that it was good; and God divided the light from the darkness." This is one of the choices that every human has, to live in the light and not in the darkness. God is the light and He wants to illuminate the way before us. The Bible explains how there is no darkness in God so when we walk in the darkness of dark thoughts or dark words, we are moving away from God.

Ephesians 4:22-23 states, "You must put aside your old self which has been corrupted by following illusionary desires. Your mind must be renewed by a spiritual revolution (be renewed in the spirit of the mind)." As a follower of Christ, we are advised to put off the old self because that old self is 'of the world'. The old self was nurtured and conditioned from living in the darkness. But if we walk completely in the light, God's words will change your heart. "Keep your heart with all diligence, For out of it spring the issues of life (Proverbs 4:23)." We must closely guard what we see because what we see enters our mind and then goes to our heart.
"This is what I shall tell my heart, and so recover hope: the favors of Yahweh are not passed, his kindnesses are not exhausted. They are renewed every morning (Lamentations 3:21-22)."

God wants to come into our hearts and work wonders in our lives. Today open the door of your heart fully to God's redemptive love. God's love can redeem you, change you and fill you with more inner joy than you could have ever imagined.
"Not that I have become perfect yet: I have not yet won, but I am still running to capture the prize for which Christ Jesus captured me (Philippians 3:12)." This above verse is so profound because it tells us that there are higher levels we can strive for to become a better person. The Apostle Paul knew that with constant effort we could move closer to the mind of God.

God provides great instruction on how to have an abundant life. "My son, give attention to My words; incline your ear to my sayings. Do not let them depart from your eyes: Keep them in the midst if your heart; For they are life to those who find them, and health to all flesh (Proverbs 4:20-22)."

Ask God today to help your to live fully in the light and change your heart so that love envelopes it completely. God is faithful to His promises.

"Fear not, for I am with you; Be not dismayed, for I am your God. I will strengthen you, Yes, I will help you, I will uphold you with My righteous right hand (Isaiah 41:10)."

Be encouraged and uplifted today because it's never too late to be the person that God intended you to be!

Motivational Tip for Day #41

Stop what you are doing right now.

Today's tip builds on yesterday's as it is focused on the heart.

Jesus tells us that the greatest law is this, "You shall love the Lord your God with all your HEART, with all your soul and with all your strength. This is the first commandment, and the second, like it, is this: You shall love your neighbor as yourself (Mathew 22:37-39)." Jesus puts the heart first. Love must be in the heart first, both love of God and love of everyone else.

According to doctors, the heart is formed before the brain in the womb. Jesus did not suggest that we love God and others with all our heart - - this is commandment, not an option. It's the greatest commandment according to Jesus.

In Proverbs, we learn a lot about the heart. "Keep your heart with all diligence, for out of it spring the issues of life (4:23). And my favorite, "For as a man thinketh in his heart, so is he (23:7)." Everyone could take more time each day to focus on their heart, because it is the key to living a full, abundant life.

Jesus explains in Mathew 12:35, "A good man out of the treasure of his heart brings forth good things, and an evil man out of the evil treasure brings forth evil things." It's the heart, not the mind where the battle takes place.

In Isaiah 29:13, we see a familiar theme in today's world. "These people draw near with their mouths and honor Me with their lips, but have removed their hearts far from Me." The heart is the battlefield, and the devil knows this. The devil tries to take small portions of our hearts each day through unforgiveness, resentments, anger, grudges, envy, jealousy and other negative feelings. First Samuel 16:7 illuminates the truth, "The Lord looks at the heart."

We are commanded by God to love, because God is love. The love must emanate from the heart. Those who have been hurt or have had a broken heart, allow the Holy Spirit to heal your heart. Help yourself by loving those who aren't lovable. It starts with you!

It starts with me! I must allow love to penetrate the deep recesses of my heart too, into those places where I have carried the pain, sadness, disappoints, shame, hurts, resentments, anger and failures.

God has a plan for your life as explained in Jeremiah 29:11-14, "I, alone know the plans I have for you, plans to bring you prosperity, and not disaster...."

Now here is a scary fact, satan (devil, evil one, adversary, prince of lies, prince of darkness) has a plan for you too. His plan to take your heart, one piece at a time. Don't give in to those negative, ungodly feelings or emotions.

God's plan for us is that we should not be tossed around, to and fro, by every little problem. When we put God's Words deeply in our heart, abundance will flow out.

There are no little sins. James 2:10 states, "For whoever shall keep the whole law, and yet stumble in one point, he is guilty of all." If we love God, we will keep His commandments according to His word. The whole law must be accepted and applied completely to one's heart. Now, we all fall short of the glory of God and sin but we have a choice as whether we live in willful sin each day. We have a choice to not keep doing the same sins each day, the Holy Spirit works in us to strengthen us where we are weak. We have a choice to move beyond the pain of the past. It's a choice that God has given everyone. We can rise above the pettiness of daily life. Be part of the solution, God's solution, by sharing the love inside of us with everyone. The world does not need any more chaos entered into it; and chaos on the inside brings chaos to the outside.

"Many sorrows shall be to the wicked; But he who trusts in the Lord, mercy shall surround him. Be glad in the Lord and rejoice, you righteous; and shout for joy, all you upright in HEART! (Psalm 32:10-11)." God wants us all to have inner joy and peace in our heart but it's up to us. Read this verse: "Work out your own salvation with fear and trembling; for it is God who works in you both to will and to do for His good pleasure (Philippians 2:12-13)."

Without a thorough knowledge of God's Word and how to apply it, satan is able to trick and lead us into the darkness. Through God's grace or unmerited favor, we have been forgiven so we must forgive others. We are loved, so we need to love others. God has given us many glorious divine promises, to include the ability to receive the Holy Spirit through faith.

Know who you are through Jesus Christ today!

Tell yourself, "I am because God said I am. I can, because God said I can." Believe completely in the following promise from God, "Be of good courage, And He shall strengthen your heart, All you who hope in the Lord (Psalm 31:24)."

If you believe in your heart that you are an overcomer in Jesus Christ, you will become an overcomer!

Motivational Tip for Day #42

Stop what you are doing right now.

Gordon MacDonald says, "People who are out of shape mentally fall victim to ideas and systems that are destructive to the human spirit. They've not been taught how to think, nor have they set themselves to the life-long pursuit of the growth of the mind, so they grow dependent upon the thoughts and opinions of others." The only opinion that matter is that of God's, living a life pleasing to God. I will add to the above quote that some people are out of shape spiritually which makes them subject to the whims of daily life. They are like a roller coaster, up and down, subject to the winds of change whenever a challenge comes into their life.

God has empowered us. "The steadfast love of the Lord never ceases, his mercies (compassions) never come to an end; they are new every morning; great is your faithfulness (Lamentations 3:22-23)."

"For God has not given us a spirit of fear, but of power and love and of a sound mind (2 Timothy 1:7)" I have mentioned this verse before but it bears repeating because the devil always try to influence us to think negatively. How we think is so important. Every person has random, fearful or negative doubts that come into their minds but it's our choice whether to believe and dwell on these thoughts. God has given us the power to choose what we focus on. It's part of our battle each day to not give any ground to the devil.

"Those who wait for the Lord, who expect, look for, and hope in Him, shall renew their strength (Isaiah 40:13)." If we focus on serving God and not our lower selves (ego, pride, vanities, complaints, grumblings, murmurings and other untoward Godly actions), we will be victors.

Some people view 'set backs' as obstacles or adversity but perhaps God is 'setting you free' to go out and live your dream unencumbered. God empowers each of us to be overcomers. Many times what we view as 'set backs' is actually God 'setting us free' and 'setting us in motion' to succeed. God wants to help you succeed! While you are striving forward and waiting expectantly to be blessed, there is something that many people fail to do -- Bring others to the truth.

Today I wanted to focus on the great commission. "And Jesus said unto them, 'Go into the world and preach the gospel to every creature (Mark 16:15)."

In Mathew 28:19-20, Jesus said, "Go therefore and make disciples of all nations, baptizing them in the name of the Father, Son and of the Holy Spirit, teaching them to observe all things that I have commanded you; and lo, I am with you always, even to the end of the age. Amen." These are the last words spoken by Jesus as recorded in Mathew. Once we find peace, it's our job, our duty to show others that living in misery is not what God wants for them.

If you give back to God in tangible ways by showing others the path to salvation, you will get your mind off of whatever petty problems or challenges that may be bothering you, and you will be carrying out the wishes of Jesus. Once we have found that inner joy, it's our job to love others enough to show them the path.

"Now we have received, not the spirit of the world, but the Spirit who is from God, that we might know the things that have been freely given to us by God (1st Corinthians 2:12)."

"Therefore let us pursue the things which make for peace and the things by which one may edify another (Romans 14:19)."

By carrying out the Great Commission of Jesus Christ, we will be set in motion to achieve our own dreams!

"Sometimes when things are falling apart, they may actually be falling into place." Guidepost reader Donna Chnupa of Dublin, CA.

"Whenever you are blue or lonely or stricken by some humiliating thing you did, the cure and the hope is in caring about other people." Diane Sawyer, anchor of ABC's World News.

Motivational Tip for Day #43

Stop what you are doing right now.

True happiness is found in pursuit of knowing God. Temporal possessions, honor, fame, pleasure, and power are inadequate and disappointing goals; only the happiness that comes from loving God cannot be taken away by misfortune. This was a major theme espoused by Anicius Manlius Severinus Boethius through his great work, The Consolation of Philosophy published circa 524.

Too many people seek the wrong things in life, and are influence by the wrong things in life. It's all about God and the love that he has for us. God dwells within our soul, and our soul longs to stay in communion with God. God wants all of us, not just the little piece we wish to give him.

Do you want an abundant life? A life filled with inner joy and contentment?
We must live in love by trying to demonstrate God's love a little more each day.
Below are promises from God in Psalms. Believe completely and live in Love, and you will be blessed.

Meditate on the below promises this day:

"For you have armed me with strength for the battle...(Psalm 18:47)."
"Let the words of my mouth and meditation of my heart, be acceptable in Your sight, O lord, my strength and Redeemer (Psalm 19:14)."
"The secret of the Lord is with those who fear Him, and He will show them His covenant (Psalm 25:14)."
"The Lord will give strength to His people, the Lord will bless His people with peace (Psalm 29:11)."
"The angel of the Lord encamps all around those who fear Him, and delivers them (Psalm 34:7)."
"Delight yourself also in the Lord, and He shall give you the desires of your heart (Psalm 37:4)."
"But the salvation of the righteous is from the Lord; he is their strength in the time of trouble (Psalm 37:39)."
"For in You, O Lord; I hope... (Psalm 38:15)."
"I waited patiently for the Lord; and He inclined to me, and heard my cry....and set my feet upon a rock, and established my steps. He has put a new song in my mouth (Psalm 40:1-3)."
"For this is God, Our God forever and ever; He will be our Guide, even to death (Psalm 48:14)."
"The Lord is on my side; I will not fear. What can man do to me? (Psalm 118:6)."
"This is the day the Lord had made; We will rejoice and be glad in it (Psalm 118:24)."

The divine promises above are full of great wisdom and can help you navigate through the challenges of daily life. The devil or adversary wishes you influence you negatively so that you will forget the Lord's promises. But the devil is a liar because "The Lord is my light and my salvation; whom shall I fear? The Lord is the strength of my life...(Psalm 27:1)."

Be encouraged today, God loves you with a love so amazing that it's too great to fully understand (Ephesians 3:19)! If we do our part, God is faithful and will do His part. Live in love today!

"The spiritual and the interior are superior to the material and exterior." Meister Eckhart

Motivational Tip for Day #44

Stop what you are doing right now.

Today's tip will be focused on how God's system's work.

"I, the Lord, search the heart, I test the mind, Even to give every man according to his way, according to the fruit of his doings (Jeremiah 17:10)."

"Knowing that whatever good anyone does, he will receive the same from the Lord, whether he is a slave or free (Ephesians 6:8)."

"Do not be deceived, God is not mocked; for whatever a man sows, that he will also reap (Galatians 6:7)."

God's system works the way it is designed to work. If we focus on doing our job by showing, living and being love, God is faithful to His promises. The more we sow love, the love we will receive in kind. In Galatians 6:9, it becomes even clearer, "And let us not grow weary while dong good, for in due season we shall reap if we do not lose heart." So many people will try to make amends with someone they are upset at, but when that person does not respond immediately as we want, we give up. The devil loves when we grow weary and stop doing good.

The Bible says that we should repay evil with good. Keep sowing seeds of love today even to those that you may have given up on, there are benefits to doing our job that we can see, but God sees it and it pleases Him. It's not about what others think about us, it's all about serving God and loving the things that God loves.

"Therefore, if anyone is in Christ, he is a new creation; old things have passed away; behold, all things have become new (2nd Corinthians 5:17)." Today if you want to live for Christ, do His will and not your will. If we are to call ourselves Christians, we need to put away the old things, old beliefs, old grudges, old ideals and old attitudes. Today's question for ourselves: If we want to be Christ-like, are we still dealing with people in old ways. Today from now on, let us truly live for Christ and show love to even the unlovable because God loves them too, just as we should.

Today ask the Lord to do the following: "May the Father of our Lord Jesus Christ enlighten the eyes of our heart, that we might see how great is the hope to which we are called (Ephesians 1:17-18).

God is faithful to His promises. God loves you in a manner that we should try to imitate in our dealings with others.

Be encouraged because God has instilled in each of us unlimited potential to be better than we ever imagined. The Holy Spirit inhabits and empowers each of us so that we can achieve the dreams God put on our heart!

"Everything God does is purposeful. And Since God is in each of us, each of us has a purpose." Iyanla Vanzant, life coach and relationship expert on the OWN network.

"Happiness is not the absence of problems, it's the ability to deal with them." Steve Marbol, author of Life, the Truth and Being Free

Motivational Tip for Day #45

Stop what you are doing right now.

Today's tip is centered on hope, and reframing your definition of that concept.
God's hopes for our lives are so much greater than our own. We must align our level of hope and expectancy with that of God's. Many people hope so little, and actually hope in negative ways because they dwell on negative things more than anything else. Too few people ask God routinely, 'God let me do something astounding today for your glory.' Today, tell yourself, I will hope boldly!

Hope is a positive force in the universe. Hope is connected to faith because when faith is weak, so is the people's hope. Radical faith and radical hope produces radical results.

"I pray that God, the source of all hope, will fill you completely with joy and peace because you trust in Him. They you will overflow with confident hope through the power of the Holy Spirit (Romans 15:13)."

"When doubts filled my mind, your comfort gave me renewed hope and cheer (Psalm 94:19)."

Learn to hope expectantly, stretch your faith and hope each day. Hope produces a creative positive energy in our life which leads to abundance.
Hope is centered in God and his plans for our life. Hope is positive and love based. Hope must be 'of God' to be effective. Our hope should glorify God. Having steadfast joyful expectation each day will result in a beautiful and fulfilling life.

"Let us hold fast the confession of our hope without wavering, for He who promises is faithful (Hebrew 10:23)."

"So be strong and take courage, all you who put hope in the Lord (Psalm 31:24)." Living a hope-filled life reduces worry, stress and anxiety because it's about trusting God. Many say they trust God but they worry each day about every little thing. True hope strengthens. "The Lord is good to those who hope is in Him, to the one who seeks Him (Lamentations 3:25)." Our plan for a successful, God-conscious life is simply stated in the above verse.

We need to live a life with bold hope. Waiting, trusting and hoping in God creates a strong connection to Him. As we wait, we show faith through our hopeful thoughts. In John 14:1, Jesus said, "Do not let your heart be troubled. Trust in God, trust also in Me." We must trust God completely. If we do, worries and anxieties will melt away.

Nathaniel Hawthorn said, "No man for any considerable period can wear one face to himself, and another to the multitude without finally getting bewildered as to which may be true."

So many people fail to maintain control over their thought life and hope life. God is constantly trying to bless us and show us the true path. We must be disciplined in how we hope. Errant random negative thoughts should never be allowed to grow inside our hearts. Maintain a firm hold on the reigns of your heart. Allow yourself to love radically by loving everyone with a love pleasing to God. Allow yourself to hope radically, hoping to live a life which glorifies God in all you do.

Mike Murdock stated, "The atmosphere you create determines the energy you unlock." Ensure that your hope is using the right key to unlock the future you desire. Reframe your definition of hope. Hope loves, helps, forgives, encourages and uplifts. Hope never judges, never complains, never hurts or harms. Hope is righteous, so hope right. Hope loves, what God loves.

Be uplifted today!! Hope boldly that God is moving you towards the dreams of your heart.

"For I know the plans I have for you, declared the Lord, plans to prosper you and not to harm you, plans to give you hope and a future (Jeremiah 29:11)."

I can never mention this verse too many times because it's a promise from God that no one should ever forget! Hope is a tool that anyone can use to live an abundant life!

"The last of the human freedoms, to choose one's attitude in any given circumstance, to choose one's own way." Viktor Frankl, sole remaining member of his family who survived the Nazi death camp.

Motivational Tip for Day #46

Stop what you are doing right now.

Today we will focus on where the greatest battle take place each: the mind.
The Apostle Paul stated in 2nd Corinthians 10:4-5, "For the weapons of our warfare are not carnal but mighty in God for pulling down strongholds, casting down arguments and every high thing that exalts itself against the knowledge of God, bringing every thought into captivity to the obedience of Christ."

The above verse of scripture is so rich and full of wisdom, the greatest battle any of us will face is the battle within ourselves. There is an old quote which states, "I have met the enemy, and it is myself."

Many of us continue to be our own worst enemies. Many people walk around defeated believing every errant negative thought that enters their mind. God has placed a vision in everyone's heart but we can only reach that goal when we actually believe the promises of God and not the lies of the devil. Do not be deceived, satan is real and wants to steal your dreams. satan is constantly trying to make you believe that you are less than are, but satan is a liar.

God is God and will do what He has promised. That said, each of us also has a responsibility to do our part. God will pull down every stronghold facing us but we must bring every thought into captivity so that we only dwell on those uplifting, positive and encouraging thoughts. You can create the outer world you wish to live in by taming the inner world.

God knows each of us by name, and His vision for our lives are so much bigger and greater than most of us can imagine. God sees the person we were created to be and provides guidance each day to be that person. "Therefore we make it our aim, whether present or absent, to be well pleasing to Him (2 Corinthians 5:9)." What are you aiming for today? Our aim should be to have thoughts pleasing to God.

Jesus said in 2 Corinthians 12:9, "My grace is sufficient for you, for My strength is made perfect in weakness." Grace is the unmerited favor that God has given us freely and abundantly. Those of you, who think you are weak, understand that Jesus has given us unmerited favor and abundance. They thought Jesus was weak but He conquered death and brought us the ability to have everlasting life.

I will end this section from 2 Corinthians 13:11 where Paul writes, "Finally, brethren, farewell. Become complete. Be of good comfort, be of one mind, live in peace, and the God of love and peace will be with you."

We can become complete and be of good comfort or joy but it's on us because God has given us all we need. We are already fully equipped, we just need to believe it, and be the person God called us to be. God is for you, so who can be against you. Take charge of your life and stop giving in to and believing those negative thoughts. You are God's masterpiece and He has declared that you shall have life and have it more abundantly.

Ask God today, "Please help me to bring the thoughts within me captive, those that don't please you. I ask you to enlarge my vision today and take me to a place where I can see what you are calling me to do."

Motivational Tip for Day #47

Stop what you are doing right now.

Today we will focus on the Strength that God has put inside of us.
Psalm 138 says, "In the day I cried out, You answered me, and made me bold with Strength in my soul."

Psalm 18:39 says, "For You have armed me with Strength for the battle; You have subdued under me those who rose up against me."

In yesterday's tip, I mentioned how God has fully equipped us to have an abundant life. Today I wanted to focus on the strength inside each one of us. God has indeed made it possible for us to live a higher life. 1 Timothy 6:12 says, "Fight the good fight of faith..." Faith is a spiritual force that each one of us has abundantly inside of us. We have a choice to either believe in God and His promises or the lies of the devil. Each time you think less of yourself or decide to give in to the fear, it's the devil's voice who you are listening to. Psalm 18 above tells us that God has armed us with the strength for the battle. We know the great battle is the one we fight each day on the inside.

The Apostle Paul wrote, "Be strong in the Lord, and in the Strength of His might. Put on the full armor of God, that you may be able to stand firm against the schemes of the devil (Ephesians 6:10-11)."

The Strength is already in us, we just have to align our heart, mind and soul with that of God's. God has set us free from the bondage of the evil one, so do not fall back. Paul explained in 2 Corinthians 2:11, "We are not ignorant of his (the devil's) schemes." Satan has a plan for your life and is constantly trying to take what belongs to you. But God, has given you the strength to endure and prosper. The daily spiritual battle is only won when we keep our minds attuned to that of God and how He made us to be victors and overcomers and abundant heirs of His grace!

"Fear not; stand firm and see the salvation of the Lord, which He will work for you today (Exodus 14:13)".

Living life for God where love, abundance and joy is at the center starts with keeping our hand in the Master's hand every minute of the day.

"For you are God's own handiwork, recreated in Christ that you may do the good works that God predestined...(Ephesians 2:10)."

We only have to live a life of less than abundant, if we choose to, because that is not what God wants for us. We are fully equipped and have been given the strength for the journey. God has placed a dream on our hearts, and He wants us to live up to the potential that He has put inside of us.

Be encouraged today by believing and living by the words of God!

"To thrive is to 'realize a goal despite circumstance.' You can prosper no matter what is going on around you." Joel Osteen

"God made us to thrive, not just survive."

Motivational Tip for Day #48

Stop what you are doing right now.

Today's tip is focused on Purpose.

"And we know that all things work together for good to those who love God, to those who are called according to His Purpose (Romans 8:20)."

Having a purpose is key to life. Without purpose, life has no meaning. We are just running around trying to satisfy basic and base needs when we don't understand our purpose. Having a purpose helps to motivate us. I found my purpose by serving God and helping others. Purpose gives birth to hope from which love can flow through. We must live with intention and purpose each day understanding that fulfillment can only come when we become and do what we were born to do. Without purpose, life has no heart. And the heart is the center of being and directs our steps.

Knowing your purpose is the key to living up to your potential. To fulfill our purpose, we must live a purposeful life. What is your plan to live a life of intention and purpose? Do you have a daily life plan which you are following, or are you just being carried by the winds of existence.

Everything in life has a purpose. God is a God of purpose and has placed a dream on every human's heart. "The purposes of a man's heart are deep waters, but a man of understanding draws them out (Proverbs 20:5)."

We must have a plan in order to succeed. Plans may change but purpose is constant. We were designed for a specific purpose and God has fully equipped each of us for this purpose. God designed each of us to be unique so that we could accomplish our unique purpose in life. We were each born to accomplish a specific mission. The purpose that God has placed on our heart, is not hindered by our past. God knows your purpose, so lean on Him today. Ask God to help you identify your purpose.

God wants us to know the plans and purposes for our life, and will provide the answers to us without fail. Many times these answers come through scripture or through other people who God puts in our lives.

Life without a specific purpose is depressing because we aren't fulfilling what God has intended for us.

How to have a purpose?

First, create a vision for your life. Next, make a plan to achieve the goals to fulfill the vision. The goals that you decide on will direct your steps, your companions, your decisions, your priorities, and your level of motivation. Through this process, your purpose will emerge. The process is important. We can't discount the process.

The devil wants you to believe that you have no purpose. The devil wants you to get discouraged and to give up. But God has given each one of us clues along the way to where to go. The Bible offers guidance as to how to pursue your purpose. The process of seeking you purpose will keep you focused. "He who began a god work in you will carry it on to completion...(Philippians 1:6)." We must have faith in God to do what He says. Having a purpose lifts us during those times of despair and sorrow. Maintaining our focus and continuing the process will be its own reward many times.

Too many people settle for too little. Most people are surface dwellers, not going deep in any endeavor. But life is meant to be lived deeply. Too many people live in 'Unfinished business-land' and 'Broken promise-ville', places of their own choosing. by having a purpose we help others. What we do affect and reflect on others.

Failure is only an option, if you put it on your option menu.

Once you start on your vision quest, don't allow anyone or anything to sway you. Your purpose should be focused on following the dreams in your heart, by striving for vision fulfillment through a planned process of working on goals daily.

Motivational Tip for Day #49

Stop what you are doing right now.

There is an old spiritual song which starts like this, "Open the eyes of my heart, Lord. Open the eyes of my heart. I want to see You. I want to see You." Today we are focusing on the asking the Lord to open the eyes of our heart, by taking a walk through Proverbs.

The heart is what psychologists would call 'our subconscious mind'. Waste no more time thinking about what is done and over in the past, but focus on the present so you can realize the vision that God has put on your heart. God tell us, "Behold, I make all things new." The true Christian life is one where our hearts have been changed and transformed into a Christ-like vessel to be used by God. Our light should shine so great from our hearts, that others' path can be illuminated.

Proverbs 4:23 states, "Keep your heart with all diligence, For out of it spring the issues of life." It's the heart that we need to retrain and focus on, so that we can grow into the people that God intended us to be.

"Trust in the Lord with all your heart, and lean not on your own understanding (Proverbs 3:5)." We must trust God, to be God. We can't believe the lies of the devil over the Promises of the Creator.

"Keep My commands and live...Write them on the table of your heart (Proverbs 7:2-3)." Proverbs provides a clear understanding of why the heart is so important.

"Anxiety in the heart of man causes depression, but a good word makes it glad (Proverbs 12:25)."

"Hope deferred makes the heart sick, But when the desire comes, it is the tree of life (Proverbs 13:12)." I think the desire to live fully, is the tree of life.

Living fully, loving completely fills our heart with joy and contentment. "A merry heart makes a cheerful countenance, but by sorrow of the heart, the spirit is broken (Proverbs 15:13)."

"A man's heart plans his way, but the Lord directs his steps (Proverbs 16:9)."

Ask God to direct your steps and cleanse your heart, so the right path is clear.

"Counsel in the heart of man is like deep water, but a man of understanding will draw it out (Proverbs 20:5)." We must focus on our hearts to draw out the truth that is in there, using the Bible as a guide.

We never need to think about what others say because it's about God and serving Him. Our job is to please God, not man. "Every way of a man is right in his own eyes, But the Lord weighs the hearts (Proverbs 21:2)." At the end of time, it will only matter what God says when He looks at our hearts. We are tasked with a simple command in Proverbs 22:12, "Incline your ear and hear the words of the wise, and apply your heart to My understanding."

My favorite verse in Proverbs is 23:7, "For as a man thinks in his heart, so is he." This is the verse which guides me because it puts the responsibility on me to be better. It's my life, given by God, to use in a way to glorify Him.

"Hear my son, and be wise; and guide your heart in the way (Proverbs 23:19)."

I think this is a reference to the Way of Jesus Christ where He stated that He is the Way, the Truth and the Life. Jesus left us a comforter, the Holy Spirit, which can help us to heal our hearts and fill it with hope and love.

Do things to heal your heart each day. If your heart is heavy, give it completely to the Lord in prayer. Allow the Holy Spirit to envelope your heart. "My son, give me your heart, and let your eyes observe My ways (Proverbs 23:26)." If we give Jesus our hearts, a transformation will occur where abundance and joy will replace any sorrow, pain or hurt.

Jesus said, "Out of the abundance of the heart the mouth speaks. A good man out of the good treasure of the heart brings forth good things (Mathew 12:34-35)." We are commanded to bring forth good things through our thoughts, words and deeds. Jesus also said that "the Kingdom of God is within you (Luke 17:21)."

We have all we already need to live an abundant life; we just need to bring it out. The spirit of man is what the Bible calls, "the heart of man (Genesis 45:26-27, Romans 2:29)." Focus on your heart today by asking God to allow His words to be deeply implanted in and on your heart. Our thoughts and words that we sow flows into our heart. The heart is the soil in which our dreams flow out of, tend to the soil of your heart today.

Spiritual development is done within the heart; we must seek to live, love and hope fully and completely each day through moving our hearts closer to God.

"Let your light so shine before men, that they may see your good works and glorify your Father in Heaven (Mathew 5:16)."

Motivational Tip for Day #50

Stop what you are doing right now.

Today's tip is focused on love, a revolutionary or radical type of love within us.

If you are a reader of the Bible, you will understand how it's a powerful account of how God moved in the past and what He promises of things to come. The Bible is filled with stories of hope, but also struggle and failure. Of, promise but also of devastation. Many people chronicled in the Bible created their own problems, and they became their own worst enemy. That said, some of these same people heard God's words and put His teachings deep inside their hearts, and was rewarded, living an abundant life. We can have the same reward through Jesus Christ.

The Bible is composed of 66 books or as I call them 66 love letters from God guiding us, encouraging us, and showing us that there is a better way. We don't have to live in darkness, we can emerge from the darkness and enter into the light. One of the central themes which unfold in the Bible is redemption. We each can become the person that God intended us to be, through loving others as God loves us.

I am trying to be a revolutionary, a person who loves in a radical way. In today's society, the love which is spoken of in the Bible would be considered radical or revolutionary by today's warped standards.

Psalm 34:8 says, "Taste and see that the Lord is good." What does this mean?

1 John 4:7-13 states, "Dear friends, let us love one another, for love comes from God. Everyone who loves has been born of God and knows God. Whoever does not love, does not know God because God is love. This is how God showed His love among us; He sent His one and only Son into the world that we might live through Him. This is love: not that we loved God, but that He loved us and sent His Son as an atoning sacrifice for our sins. Dear friends, since God so loved us, we also ought to love one another. No one has ever seen God; but if we love one another, God lives in us and His love is made complete in us. This is how we know that we live in Him and He in us: He has given us of His Spirit." The above verse makes it clear as to what we need to do.

In Ephesians 4:22-24 we learn, "You were taught, with regard to your former way of life, to put off your old self, which is being corrupted by its deceitful desires, to be made new in the attitude of your minds; to put on the new self, created to be like God in true righteousness and holiness." This is the goal and what we must strive to daily. If we claim to be saved and born again, then our lives must show this fact by living a differently radical life centered in love.

1 John 4:16 states, "And so we know and rely on the love God has for us. God is love. Whoever lives in love, lives in God, and God in them."

If we live in love, we create the conditions for having an abundant life. The above verses of scripture are so beautiful and offers hope to anyone because God is love, God loves us radically, and His love is already in us.

Plato stated, "He whom love touches, not walks in darkness." Everyone can benefit from coming to a deeper understanding of a radical or revolutionary type of love. We are commanded to love others as God loves us. If our hearts are corrupted with grudges, hate, and other un-Godlike emotions/feelings, we are not following God's commandment about love, and this impedes our blessings. This is why I say that I want to be a radical, a person who loves without limits, even those who despise or hate me. I strive to love everyone, even the unlovable ones because there were times in my life when I was unlovable, and God still loved me.

There are many promises throughout the Bible including, "The angle of the Lord encamps all around those who fear Him, and delivers them (Psalm 34:7)." God protects us so that we can live a life which glorifies Him. "For everyone born of God overcomes the world. This is the victory what has overcome the world... (1 John 5:4). In Galatians 4:6, we learn another great promise, "Because you are His sons, God has sent the Spirit on His Son into our hearts..."

We have eternity in our hearts. We must put off the old self and follow God without question. Blessings come when we stop rebelling. "Grace to all who love our Lord Jesus Christ with an undying love (Ephesians 6:24)." If we say that we love God, then shouldn't we do as God commands and live in a way that is pleasing to Him.

The Apostle Paul explained the concept of love beautifully in 1st Corinthians 13. I want to highlight two short sections, "...If I have faith that can move mountains, but do not have love, I am nothing (1 Corinthians 13:2). "And now these three remain: faith, hope and love. But the greatest is LOVE (1 Corinthians 13:13)."

Wake up every morning and ask God, "Lord, give me love, radical love so that You shine through me."

Stand firm and live radically in love today--love as God loves, forgive as God forgives, and hope as God hopes.

Remember what the Apostle Paul wrote in 1 Corinthians 13:8, "Love never fails..."

Motivational Tip for Day #51

Stop what you are doing right now.

Today we will focus on the promises of God. If we meditate on the Word of God and observe God's law then we will have good success in life.

Joshua 1:8-9 states, "The book of the Law shall not depart from your mouth, but you shall meditate in it day and night, that you may observe to do according to all that is written in it. For then you will make your way prosperous, and then you will have good success. Have I not commanded you? Be strong and of good courage; do not be afraid, nor be dismayed, for the Lord your God is with you wherever you go."

I love this verse because it's a promise from God. First, we are told to meditate on God's word, day and night. Next we are told to observe or obey what has been commanded by God. This is our job, our part in the order of things. By staying focused on the Word day and night, and observing it, we are taking control of our destiny and it will lead to prosperity. Meditating on the Word means that we let it move deeply inside of us constantly, not just when we feel like it. It's so easy to slip and forget what the Lord promises us each day. This is why God reminds us that we must meditate on the Word day and night so that we stay mindful and vigilant because He knows our weaknesses.

Dr. Charles Stanley explains how God's word does several things in our life when we meditate on it each day:

1) Quiets the mind.
2) Purifies our hearts.
3) Sharpens our perceptions.
4) Clarifies our direction
5) Confirms and cautions us that we should only seek Godly council.
6) Increases our faith.
7) Guides us to success.

God's standard is so different than ours. We are actually at war against anything that sets itself up against the knowledge of God, those errant thoughts and feelings are of Satan, not God because God made us to be victors!

One of my favorite motivational and inspirational writers is Susan L. Taylor, former editor of Essence Magazine. She provides much wisdom in her book called "In the Spirit". She stated, "the search for yourself is your life's purpose." The main point is that we have to search, it will not just come to us without effort. She also explained that "living from within is an exercise in self-awareness." In this vein, she suggests that we must "move with our feet, set high goals and work towards them consistently." The last point I want to highlight from her book is that we should "challenge ourselves each moment to act only on the positive principles, the ones that we know are of God." The above suggestions are great advice for anyone who wants an abundant life.

We should understand that we can only do it with God's help, not by ourselves. Staying in the Word each day, every hour if necessary, because our journey is a personal one. What works for me, may not work for you but perhaps I can adapt what works for you, to help myself. This is what I do when I write these Tips, they are for me but perhaps they may help you or encourage you to be who God wants you to be. This is my goal each day when I awake, to strive earnestly, to be the man who God wants me to be.

God gives us such wise guidance through His word. Every time you read the Bible try these suggestions: 1) Ask God to open up your heart so that it's receptive; 2) Expect to hear God's voice; 3) Ask God to show you how to fully obey His words; 4) Ask God to change your heart and mind so that His words can change your life; 5) Ask God if He wants you to do something specific based on the Scripture you read; 6) Ask God to use you; 7) Ask God to make your heart obedient to His words; 8) Ask God to show you what to do; 9) Ask God, 'what are You trying to tell me?'; and 10) Where do I need to change, O Lord. These above ten suggestions have given me inner peace and allowed me to hear God's voice.

Once you begin to realize who you are and what you've been given by the power of God, you'll quit allowing the devil to run all over you. God commanded us to be strong and of good courage. As the people of God, you and I must shake off discouragement and rise up with courage! We must quit looking at our own limitations and failures, and start looking to God for all the answers, and rise up in the name of Jesus Christ who gives us the ability to do all things through Him!

"Let us not be satisfied with a mediocre life. Be amazed by what is true and beautiful, what is of God!" Pope Francis' Tweet for January 2014.

"It is not enough to say we are Christians. We must live the faith, not only with our words, but with our actions." Pope Francis' Tweet for January 2014.

"Love has nothing to do with what you are expecting to get; it's what you are expecting to give--which is everything." Anonymous

Motivational Tip for Day #52

Stop what you are doing right now.

"And we have such trust through Christ toward God. Not that we are sufficient ourselves, but our sufficiency us from God, who also made us sufficient as ministers of the new covenant, not of the letter but of the Spirit; for the letter kills but the Spirit gives life (2nd Corinthians 3:4)."

The above scripture touched my heart so profoundly for many reasons, and it motivates me to be a better person. First, we cannot do it by ourselves. We need to lean fully and completely trust God, who supplies all of our needs. If we need it, then God will provide it. When our lives show that we trust God completely, more blessings will come. When we worry or stress out over things, we are telling God that we don't fully trust Him.

God knows the plans and thoughts for us, "thoughts of peace and not of evil, to give us a future and a hope (Jeremiah 29:11)." When we trust God, our life shows it, it's clear because our hearts will be 'of light and love'. The second point from the above verse is that we should minister to others. When we minister to others, it helps to put the Word deeply inside of us as well. Helping others understand the word, helps us to understand the Word of God in more profound ways. We help ourselves by helping others. Third, we should follow the Spirit of Jesus' teachings and not get bogged down in small theological matter or issue. Many people will read a passage of scripture and get so focused on it that they forget the greatest law described by Jesus, "Love God with all our heart, soul and mind; and your neighbor as yourself (Mathew 22:37-40)." A Christian should focus on doing everything with love.

Love, obedience and ministering to others will heal us in ways we can't even understand or fathom. I understand that it takes training and knowledge to learn how to trust God completely, the Bible provides that knowledge. In trusting God, we open our hearts and then can start to experience God's love fully. Today, start the process of trusting God fully. It is a process that will take real effort. This trust will be evidenced when we will begin to live differently and respond in new ways to old problems. When we make a conscious effort to truly put God at the center of our lives, a new purpose and meaning will appear and the old conditioned responses start to fade away. By allowing God to fill the deep crevices of our heart, we will amaze people because we will respond in new God inspired ways. Without love and trust in God, fear and selfishness consumes our mind. Trust and fear are opposite concepts. Love casts off fear and doubt because it's rooted in a deep trust of letting God, be God.

"See then that you walk circumspect, not as fools but as wise, redeeming the time, because the days are evil. Therefore do not be unwise, but understand what the will of the Lord is (Ephesians 5:15-17)."

My goal today is to understand what the will of God is. Time is not our friend because it slows for no one, so we must make the most of each moment.

Today, please remember that redeeming the past is always possible, through making the most of the present moment!

Today, please find new ways to trust and love God. Focus on being love and a light to others, and abundance will enter your life!

"The right action is always that which will, from a purely objective point of view, have the best consequences, that is, the one that will produce the greatest good and the least evil." Bertrand Russell, one of the greatest philosophers of the 20th century.

"All human development depends of loving and being loved." Karl Rahner, one of the most important theologians of the 20th Century

Motivational Tip for Day #53

Stop what you are doing right now.

Anyone can transform their lives through the redemptive power of God's love. It's through love that we can heal ourselves from the hurts and disappointments of the past. But it starts with love, striving to understand the perfect character of love. A pure heart and the right inner spirit will help us obtain that character of love. When we trust God, He pours His love into our hearts.

"Now hope does not disappoint, because the love of God has been poured out in our hearts by the Holy Spirit who was given to us (Romans 5:5)."

Our goal should be to develop the love in our hearts by taking efforts each day to first understand what love is, the character of love. A person must understand that the perfect character of love was created within us by the indwelling of the Holy Spirit. To tap into that love, we must live in the light and stay away from those negative emotions, feelings and thoughts which is not 'of God'.

"We must develop and maintain the capacity to forgive. He who is devoid of the power to forgive is devoid of the power of love (Martin Luther King)." I love this quote because it gives good advice on how to develop that perfect character of love.

Be uplifted today because our hearts were created for love, to love and to receive love. Through the programming and conditioning of the past which comes from living in this fallen world, we have forgotten our true nature, love. We just need to understand that God already poured love into our hearts.

"You therefore, beloved, since you know this beforehand, beware lest you also fall from your own steadfastness, being led away with the error of the wicked; but grow in the grace and knowledge of our Lord and Savior Jesus Christ. To Him be the glory both now and forever. Amen (2 Peter 3:17-18)."

God knows us and the obstacles that we will face in life, including that we must grow each day to move closer to His mind. Also, we must be steadfast because the world is wicked and wanted to take us off our square. Growing spiritually is a lifelong process and our job is to let the scriptures to move us, change us.

My goal each day is to increase my understanding of God and his nature, love. Growth can occur when we grow along spiritual lines using the principles in the Bible as a guide. We must make the effort because everything in this world strives to lead us to darkness and the evil one, satan. Make sure that your spiritual journey is taking you on a positive path each day, a path composed of love.

Living in love takes an effort each day but the rewards are so amazing. Love allows us to heal, grow, transform and become the people that God wants us to be.

Be encouraged today, we are God's beloved and he has poured out His love in our hearts. "And we have known and believed the love that God has for us. God is love and he who abides in love abides in God, and God in him (1 John 4:16)."

We serve a God who is mightier than any struggles we have encountered, and who asks us to forgive, love and move in ways which allows us to know the mind of God. I end this section with three short verses from Ephesians which provides great guidance and insight:

"That Christ may dwell in your hearts through faith; that you, being rooted and grounded in love (3:17)."

"Therefore be imitators of God as dear children. And walk in love, as Christ also has loved us and given Himself for us...(5:1-2)."

"For you were once in darkness, but now you are light in the Lord. Walk as children of light (5:8)."

Are there parts of your heart which is not filled with love? Challenge your heart today to love fully and in radical new ways!

Motivational Tip for Day #54

Stop what you are doing right now.

Today's tip is focused on learning how to love in a new God-conscious ways.

God's law of love is a principle that is meant to be spread by us to others. Understanding God's design for this world allows us to be his agents in this world. When we operate in such a loving way that it shows others, God is love, we serve God as He is meant to be served.

"Walk in love... (Ephesians 5:2)." What does this mean? Have you ever thought about your daily walk, whether it's in love. it's the little details that show, we have love inside.

"Now may the Lord direct your hearts into the love of God and into the patience of Christ (2nd Thessalonians 3:5)." The definition of love in this fallen world is dysfunctional. Almost everything they we see on TV or hear today show dysfunctional types of love. We have to retrain ourselves in how to love and the perfect model of real love is described by God in the Bible. We should strive to love with our heart, completely and in whole and healthy Godly ways. Many people keep little pockets of negativity in their hearts but we must learn to open those small dark areas in the back of our hearts to God and His love. The Bible offers good and God inspired examples of how to retrain ourselves in order to love in the right ways.

What is love?

Love is steadfast. Love is not an emotion; it's a command from God. Love is not a feeling, because feelings come and go. Too often we let our feelings get in the way of our progress. Love is a perfect belief, ordered by God. Love is giving, and forgiving. Love is freely given without any expectation of return. Compassion is the emotion we feel when love moves through our hearts. Love does not do right for the wrong reasons. Love is about helping others. Love is 'of God' and of the light. Love has nothing to do with attraction because love transcends attraction. God loves us completely and commands us to love others in the same way, not just those who are lovable. Love doesn't keep a record of wrongs. Love doesn't care about the past, because love is pure. Love is an action. Love requires effort, and that effort puts us closer to God. Love is a commandment, not a choice if a person wants to be a follower of Christ. We must strive to learn how to love, using the template from God's word as the framework. Unpack and discard all those old dysfunctional notions of love today.

Colossians 2:21-23 states, "Do not touch, do not taste, do not handle...doctrines of man. These things indeed have an appearance of wisdom in self-imposed religion, false humility, and neglect of the body, but are of no value against the indulgence of the flesh."

Later we learn in Colossians 3:2 we learn, "Set your minds on things above, not on things on the earth." Our love must come from God, and then we should spread it to others.

Jesus commands us "to love God with all our heart, soul and mind. And then our neighbor as ourselves." What is left unsaid but which is vitally important is that we love ourselves first. Loving ourselves in whole and healthy ways so that we can give love to others. So many people do not love themselves through and through; they live with guilt, condemnation, shame and other negative feelings from the past. Christ died on the cross so that we could have salvation and be redeemed through His blood. Christ has forgiven us, forgive yourself and move on. When we allow those negative emotions or beliefs about ourselves to inhabit our heart, we limit the blessings in our lives.

A person without real love inside, cannot give real love to others. We can't give what we don't have. This is why it's so important to retrain ourselves to love as God has instructed us to love.

Colossians 3:12-17, describes the character of the new person. We should allow love to change us, make us new. The below section give a perfect framework of that love.

"Therefore, as the elect of God, holy and beloved, put on tender mercies, kindness, humility, meekness, longsuffering; bearing with one another, and forgiving one another, if anyone has a complaint against another; even as Christ forgave you, so you must do, but above all these things put on love, which is the bond of affection. And let the peace of God rule your hearts, which is the bond of perfection. Let the word of Christ dwell in you richly in all wisdom, teaching and admonishing one another in psalms and hymns and spiritual songs, singing with grace in your hearts to the Lord. And whatever you do in word or deed, do all in the name of the Lord Jesus, giving thanks to God the Father through Him."

Love allowed to deeply move inside our heart, allows inner peace to reign in that same place. We need to find ourselves through God and ask Him, "What is Your will for my life?' God is love and His essence of perfect love is already inside our heart, spirit and soul.

Today, see yourself as God sees you, a being of light and love!

"Love many things, for therein lies the true strength, and whosoever loves much performs much, and can accomplish much, and what is done in love is done well." Vincent Van Gogh

Motivational Tip for Day #55

Stop what you are doing right now.

Today we will focus on some ideas to help us transform our lives.

Too many people dib and dabble in change instead of having a sincere commitment to change. A person's own heart will testify against him or her when they take the wrong turn. The key is to listen to that small still voice of God along the way.

Most people abandon ship before the ship reaches the shore. To make your dreams come true and materialize, you must stay in the ship until it reaches the shores of actuality. The cycle of chaos can only change once we study ourselves by take inventory constantly. After taking an inventory, it's imperative to take those necessary course corrections to keep our ship on the right path.

I ask myself often, "Is that thought 'of God'," or "is this action 'of God'." We must do good, not just do what feels good. The indwelling of the Holy Spirit will help each of us know what is 'of God'. Reading the Bible daily will help to understand the mind of God and what is pleasing to Him. The level of your devotion will measure your strength. I want my life to honor God and I try to keep God on my mind all day long. God's laws are for our good and there is nothing there that will harm us. If we love God, then we want to please Him. God is looking for some people to bless. Ezekiel 22:30 states, "I sought for a man among them who would make a wall, and stand in the gap before Me on behalf of the land, that I should not destroy it; but found no one." I love this verse because God made us to thrive, not just survive, so when we struggle we are going against God's wishes for ourselves. The world is one of infinite possibilities and always allows a person of faith to redeem the time given to them to honor God.

Despite of the crisis, stay with your dream. Stay the course because the course is part of the process. The course will entail storms and sometimes Tsunamis but in the end, you will arrive to your destination. There is strength in the struggle but too many people panic and abandon ship before they reap the benefits of being in the ship. We must stay in the ship: fellowship (with God) and relationship (with God) and maintaining a God-ship consistently.

Ephesians 5:22-23 states, "But the fruit of the Spirit is love, joy, peace, longsuffering, kindness, goodness, faithfulness, gentleness, self-control. Against such there is no law." Verse 25 states, "If we live in the Spirit, let us also walk in the Spirit." The above traits describe how we should walk every minute of the day. We all have the seeds for our own transformation already inside of us. But we must examine ourselves deeply as described in Ephesians 6:4, "But let each one examine his own work..."

It's about staying the course, the course will lead you to having an abundant life. Ephesians 6:9 states, "And let us not grow weary while doing good, for in due season we shall reap if we do not lose heart," It's on us to save ourselves with the help of the Holy Spirit which dwells within us.

Our dreams will not realize themselves. There are times when we must be willing to suffer to achieve our dreams in order to become the person God wants us to be.

I ask myself each day, "Is God satisfied with my efforts on His behalf?" To transform myself, I had to change the very idea of myself. I had to change the conditioning of the past by doing something different, each day. I no longer leave the door open for failure. Now this doesn't mean I won't fail but because I now have a God conscious view of the world, I view failure differently. Failing in the right way with the right mindset, leads me to understand how to reach my goals in whole and healthier ways. I ask God what the failure or challenge or trial is trying to teach me. I ask God to show me where to improve and to clean my heart so I am teachable. I pray to God each day to help me, to stay teachable to His commands and to where He wants me to go.

Today, I will work on maintaining my new perspective, a view with God first, asking Him to share more of Himself with me. I read the Bible more deeply each day in order to understand what is expected of me. I trust God and believe that He is working for me good. That said, I have to do my job, and move forward in new positive ways so that I can glorify Him.

To get love, we must give love fully. With a foundation built on love, all things are possible. 1 Peter 3:4 states, "Your beauty should come from within you." We were all created by a perfect, all-powerful Creator. As His creation, we are beautiful already. God has put inside of each of us, the seeds for our transformation. Use the Bible to anchor your change, to strengthen that inner person. Strengthening that inner person will allow you to reap all the blessings that God has in store for you. We must all stay in a perpetual stage of growth, for in due time we shall reap if we do not lose heart!

Be uplifted this day because God is waiting for you to bloom so that He can send more blessing your way!

"Dear God, I pray that you open my heart and fill it with love." Iyanla Vanzant, relationship specialist on OWN network.

Motivational Tip for Day # 56

Stop what you are doing right now.

Today's tip is focused on 'right believing', believing in God centered ways in order to have an abundant life.

We have the choice each day to decide: "How we choose to believe each day; and "What we choose to believe in." By changing our 'thoughts', we can change our actual life. Too many people struggle needlessly and fight the wrong battles of the mind.

Now, you may ask what is 'right believing'. 'Right believing' is about living by the Word. Right believing puts us on a path of light. Light illuminates freedom for us and releases us from the mental prison that many have allowed themselves to be in. 'Wrong believing' puts people in a prison of their own making. A prison of wrong thoughts, demonic thoughts, dark thoughts which allow the devil to take over our hearts and minds. Even though there are no physical shackles or bars, people who don't God fully trust God by believing in the right way, are just as bound as those in a physical prison. I call 'wrong believing' those who decide to live in the bad neighborhoods of their mind. Many people chose to live in despair by having a poverty mindset. But God's Word lights our way, but it is our responsibility to trust Him fully and believe His words.

Psalm 119:105 states, "Your word is a lamp to my feet and a light to my path."

True freedom comes when we train our thoughts to conform to that of God's. One must put every thought that is not of God into captivity. By imprisoning those errant, negative thoughts, we free ourselves. When we are free, we can help lead others to the light. My job each day is to honor God with my thoughts, words and deeds so that I can lead others to Christ.

Every day, I have people ask me why I am always so happy, uplifted and encouraging of others. I explained that, "the joy of the Lord is my strength, as written in Nehemiah 8:10. I live that verse each day because it's a conscious choice to believe in the right manner. Because I know and trust the Lord, I know that it will all work out. By reading the Word of God, I know who I am and how much God loves me. I am empowered because God made me.

I often tell people that I hear God voice frequently. Some people ask why they can't hear God's voice. God's voice can be heard in many ways but the most powerful way is through His written word. This is the first way to heard God's voice. I put that word deeply in my heart each morning and throughout the day, and my day starts off with 'right believing'. "My son, attend to My words; incline your ear unto my sayings. Let them not depart from your eyes; keep them in the midst of your heart (Proverbs 4:20-21)."

The second way to hear God voice is by acting on God's words each day. Jesus said, "If you abide in My word, you My disciples indeed. And you shall know the truth and the truth shall make you free (John 8:31-32). Right believing allows us to be free. By acting on God's words and ending the process of rebellion, we open our hearts so that it can be receptive to God's voice.

The third way to hear God's voice is through the Holy Spirit which dwells in you, and which will tell you what God is saying. Jesus said, "However, when He, the Spirit of truth, had come, He will guide you into all truth; for He will not speak on His own authority; but whatever He hears He will speak; and He will tell you things to come (John 16:13)."

The fourth way to hear God's voice is to be on constant guard, and refuse to let the devil steal God's word from you. Jesus stated in Mark 4:15, "and these are the one by the wayside where the word is sown, When they hear, Satan comes immediately and takes away the word that was sown in their hearts." Many people allow circumstances or others to lead them away from God's promises.

The fifth way to hear God's voice is to choose to speak God's word. God said in Deuteronomy 30:19, "I call heaven and earth as witnesses today against you, that I have set before you life and death, blessing and cursing; therefore CHOOSE life, that both you and your descendents may live." Learn to speak in only ways that is pleasing to God, and you will hear God's voice. Many times our words show our lack of faith but today retrain your vocabulary to show your inner faith.

Right believing is truth. "If you keep My commandments, you will abide in My love...These things I have spoken to you, that My joy may remain in you, and your joy may be full. This is My commandment, that you love one another as I have love you (John 15:9-11)." If we 'right believe' and put on love, then we will have true inner joy.

All the strength that we will ever need all comes from one source, the joy of the Lord!

Motivational Tip for Day #57

Stop what you are doing right now.

Today's tip is focused on the goodness of God and praising Him always through the good times and the bad.

I have a phrase I write on all my correspondence and emails which is "God is good." This phrase for me means everything because in believing that God is good, I have hope which is manifested through my constant hopeful, loving attitude.

"For You, O Lord, I hope; You will hear, O Lord, my God. (Psalm 38:15)."

God is good, and based on his word in the Bible, I can relax and lean on Him. I praise Him because of all God has done in my life up to this point. Because God woke me up this morning to write this and for letting me see the sunshine of a brand new day, I praise Him!

"As for me, I will call upon God, and the Lord shall save me. Evening and morning and at noon, I will pray, and cry aloud, and He shall hear my voice (Psalm 55:16-17)." This is how I now live my life and I believe in His promises. I know that He is, and that I am His. "Whenever I am afraid, I will trust in You. In God (I will praise His word); In God I have put my trust; I will not fear, what can flesh do to me (Psalm 56:3-4)." I love this verse as it comforts my heart.

Anthony Robbins states in his amazing book, Awaken the Giant Within, "Too many of us leave ourselves at the mercy of outside events over which we may have no control, failing to take charge of our emotions -- over which we have all control -- instead of relying on short-term fixes." The devil loves short term fixes because he doesn't want us to Praise God or lean on God.

Today, strive to see the world as it really is, instead of through the past illusions and false internal beliefs, Decide to be different by looking at the world through a God conscious lens of love. "Turn away my eyes from looking at worthless things, and revive me in Your way (Psalm 119:37)." This is my prayer for you and me today.

My purpose today is to share the word of God with all. I have always lived with a purpose although some times the purpose was off. My purpose now is aligned with God's purpose for my life. I believe that many people are living with the wrong purpose. We are all simple creatures who tend to make everything more complicated. We can live on a higher plane even if others around us are still living in the darkness because of the strength God freely gives us. "I can do all things through Christ who strengthens me (Philippians 4:13)."

Awareness leads to self discovery which takes us on the path to find our purpose. I know God is good and like the words in Psalm, "I rejoice at Your word (Psalm 119:162)."

"For this is God, Our God forever and ever; He will be our guide, even to death (Psalm 48 14:)." Praise God all day and allow Him to be your guide today.

And remember, "Be of good courage, and He shall strengthen your heart, all who hope in the Lord, (Psalm 31:24)."

Be encouraged today because our God is an awesome God, He reigns from Heaven and Earth with wisdom, power and love.

Motivational Tip for Day #58

Stop what you are doing right now.

Are you committed to God? I ask myself each day, if am I striving towards the light or the darkness. I first committed myself to serving God and doing His will, and then he started speaking to me through His word. God is looking for people who are committed. How does one live a committed life to God? I came up with four easy steps.

The first thing that I had to understand was that God had a system and it was ordered. God's system is perfect and for our own good. "All scripture is given by inspiration of God, and is profitable for doctrine, for reproof, for correction, for instruction in righteousness; that the man of God man be complete, thoroughly equipped for every good work (2 Timothy 3:16-17)." Following God's system will allow us to be complete. John 3:27 says that "A man can receive nothing unless it has been given to him from Heaven." God's system is based on living in the light. Jesus explained in John 8:12, "I am the light of the world. He who follows Me shall not walk in darkness, but have the light of life." All good things come from the light and we must be committed to living in the light. God's kingdom is what we should seek as Jesus said in Mathew 6:33, "But first seek the kingdom of God and His righteousness, and all things shall be added to you." Following God's plan gives us meaning, direction, brings peace and gives us a future.

The second point is focused on believing that God's system is faultless. Proverbs 20:24 states, "A man's steps are of the Lord; how then can a man understand his own way." I love this verse because it's about faith. We need to have faith in God's system which will allow us to weather all the storms of life. While we go through these storms, if we believe that God is in control, then we can have a good attitude because we know it's for our benefit. Adversity is just a test so that we can become better. Proverbs 19:21 states, "There are many plans in a man's heart, nevertheless the Lord's council -- that will stand."

Third, we must follow God's system with all our heart. "The plans of the diligent lead surely to plenty, but those of everyone who is hasty, surely to poverty. Obedience is the system which opens our lives to abundance. Once we start working God's system, we must remain diligent and steadfast maintaining a good attitude while being patient. Proverbs 8:33 states, "Hear instruction and be wise, and do not disdain it." And Proverbs 3:35 states, "For whoever finds me, finds life, and obtains favor from the Lord." When we obey, we please God and find favor.

Fourth, once we obtain enlightenment and a modicum of wisdom, peace and inner joy, it's our job to bring the Gospel to others. When we learn the truth, we must share the good news with others. Ministering to others ensure that we stay mindful and steadfast. Helping others who are still in the darkness, continues to keep us on the right path.

"Life is not hard; it's only as hard as we believe it is." Be committed to living a better life with the above four points as a guide.

"The heart of the prudent acquires knowledge, and the ear of the wise seeks knowledge (Proverbs 18:15)."

Motivational Tip for Day #59

Stop what you are doing right now.

Today's tip is focused on the church.

Who is the church? The church is the body of believers. We are the church, I am the church and you are the church.

In The Revelation of Jesus Christ, John records Jesus' words where He discusses the seven churches. I look at these seven churches as how I lived my life at various times but now I strive to be the faithful church (number 6). Can you identify yourself as one of the seven churches below?

1) The loveless church: the key verses are, "Nevertheless I have this against you that you have left your first love (Rev 2:4)." "He who has an ear, let him hear what the Spirit says the churches. To him who overcomes, I will give to eat from the tree of life, which is in the midst of the Paradise of God (Rev 2:7)." Love is the basis of the Christian walk and we need to be stirred up, and return to our first love - God.

2) The persecuted church: the key verses are, "Do not fear any of those things which you are about to suffer. Indeed, the devil is about to throw some of you into prison, that you may be tested, and you will have tribulation ten days. Be faithful until death, and I will give you the crown of life. He who has an ear, let him hear what the Spirit says to the churches. He who overcomes shall not be hurt by the second death (Rev 2:10-11). Tribulations are to be expected and if we stay faithful, we will reap in due time.

3) The compromising church: the key verses are, "But I have a few things against you, because you have there those who hold the doctrine of Balaam, who taught Balak to put stumbling blocks before the children of Israel, to eat things sacrificed to idols, and to commit sexual immorality (Rev 2:14)." "He who has an ear, let him hear what the Spirit says to the churches. To him who overcomes I will give some of the hidden manna to eat. I will give him a white stone, and on the stone a new name written which no one knows except him who receives it (Rev 2:17)." Too many people compromise in life, moving further away each day from God's system in favor of the system of men. Everyone stumbles or backslides from time to time, but the Christian is about getting back up, repenting and then moving forward. "Godly sorrow brings repentance that leads to salvation and leaves no regret, bit worldly sorrow brings death (2nd Corinthians 7:10)."

4) The corrupt church: the key verses are, "Nevertheless I have a few things against you, because you allow that woman Jezebel, who calls herself a prophetess to teach ad seduce My servants to commit sexual immorality and eat things sacrificed to idols. And I gave her time to repent to her sexual immorality, and she did not repent. Indeed I will cast her into a sickbed, and those who commit adultery with her into great tribulation, unless they repent of their deeds (Rev 2:20-22)." "But hold fast what you have till I come. And he

who overcomes, and keeps My works until the end, to him I will give power over nations (Rev 2:25-26)." Many of us are our own worst enemies (like I was to myself until my eyes opened), bringing on destruction on ourselves by the decisions we make. But God will allow us to repent and return back into union with Him through Jesus Christ.

5) The dead church: the key verses are, "Be watchful and strengthen the things which remain, that are ready to die, for I have not found your works perfect before God. Remember therefore how you received and heard; hold fast and repent. Therefore if you will not watch, I will come upon you as a thief, and you will not know what hour I will come upon you (Rev 3:2-3)." "He who overcomes shall be clothed in white garments, and I will not blot out his name before My Father and before the angels (Rev 3:5)." There is such great wisdom in the above verse that it needs no explanation.

6) The faithful church: the key verses are," I know your works. See, I have set before you an open door and no one can shut it, for you have a little strength, have kept My word and have not denied my name (Rev 3:8)." "Because you have kept My command to persevere, I also will keep you from the hour of trial which shall come upon the whole world, to test those who dwell on earth. Behold, I am coming quickly Hold fast what you have, that no one may take your crown. he who overcomes, I will make him a pillar in the temple of My God, and he shall go out no more. I will write on him the name of My God, and the name of the city of My God, the New Jerusalem, which comes down out of heaven from My God. And I will write on him my new name (Rev 3:10-12)." This is the church I am trying to imitate. I have been a part of all the churches mentioned here but now I strive to be faithful. We are God's greatest masterpiece, the crown is already yours, do not let anyone take your crown. I have traveled to Jerusalem and I want to see the New Jerusalem. I also strive today to have a new name. Is this the church you are striving to be?

7) The Lukewarm church: the key verses are, "I know your works, that you are neither cold not hot. I could wish you were cold or hot. SO then, because you are lukewarm, and neither cold nor hot, I will vomit you out of my mouth (Rev 3:15-16)." "As many as I love, I rebuke and chasten. Therefore be zealous and repent. Behold, I stand at the door and knock. If anyone hears My voice and opens the door, I will come in to him and dine with him, and he with Me. To him who overcomes, I will grant to sit with Me on My throne, as I also overcame and sat down with My Father on His throne. (Rev 3:19-21)." I don't wish Jesus to vomit me out of his mouth. I used to be lukewarm but now I am on fire for God! I have seen the light and ever fiber on my being strives each day to stay in the light. I am an overcomer and you are an overcomer!

Which church are you? I never understood the above passage before but now I see that through my life I have exhibited traits from each one. I never understood that I had a choice. God is so good and merciful, Oh how I love Him because he saved a sinner like me. Try Him, he is faithful and wants all of us to prosper which is why we have his Words to help guide us to live an abundant life! Ask yourself this day, am I doing all I can for God?

Rejoice! For today you have a choice to return back to God, stir up the gifts that he has been given to you. Be passionate for God! I invite you to read Revelations chapters two and three so that you can be moved by the words of Jesus, as they moved me.

I encourage you this day to get excited about serving God! God is in your corner, and loves you unconditionally!

"Life in Christ involves constantly seeking God's purpose for our lives. As much as we may desire to fully control our own lives -- deciding where we will go, when we go, and what we will do when we go -- we know that only by seeking God's will do we arrive at the place God wants us to be." Upper Room Reader Anthony Sandusky from New York who wrote on January 18 2014 a devotional called "A life of seeking".

"The fear of the Lord is the beginning of wisdom (Proverbs 9:10)."

Motivational Tip for Day #60

Stop what you are doing right now.

Today's tip comes from 1st Peter 3:8-12 and 15-17:

"Finally, all of you be of one mind, having compassion for one another; love as brothers, be tenderhearted, be courteous, not returning evil for evil or reviling for reviling, but on the contrary blessing, knowing that you were called to this to inherit a blessing. For 'He who would love life and see good days, let him refrain his tongue from evil, and his lips from speaking lies, let him turn away from evil and do good; let him seek peace and pursue it. For the eyes of Lord are on the righteous; and His ears are open to their prayers; but the face of the Lord is against those who do evil."

Verses 15-17 states, "But sanctify the Lord God in your hearts, and always be ready to give a defense to everyone who asks you a reason for the hope that is in you, with meekness and fear; having a good conscience, that when they defame you as evildoers, those who revile your good conduct in Christ may be ashamed. For it is better, if it is the will of God, to suffer for doing good than doing evil."

The one mind is about being of the mind of Jesus Christ, and compassion for others is the act of showing love. The above passage provides clear guidance on how to live. Everyone needs to be retrained in how to live in love, true love. Having Christ on the inside allows us to walk and do right, seek peace and follow it.

Many people who are hurt, hurt others because it's what they have learned to do but the above passage discusses how we should do our job by loving and allow God to be God because he will bless us for doing good. As Christians, you and I must be different and respond differently than the world. We must reprogram ourselves along spiritual principles. As a born again Christian; we should think, speak and act differently. If we are still carrying around the baggage of the past, we can't receive all the blessings that God has in store for us.

Philippians 4:12 states that "we can do all things through Christ who strengthens me." That said, we can only have the power through Jesus Christ, when we walk in His ways. We have the power inside to respond in love instead of through pain. The Holy Spirit will empower you to be different, once you completely give God your heart.

The Christian walk required us to take action in loving ways. There is a greater reality out here than the illusionary world in which we have been living in. God looks at what we do for Him. If you move for God; God will move in your life.
Spiritual question for this day: Am I doing all I can for God? Am I passionately striving to get closer to God?

Today strive to know God in deeper ways. I have hope today because of the faith in my heart. The Lord opens doors for those who strive for Him. We must be on fire for God because He is on fire for us. With that fire stoked each day; it will burn off the bad in our hearts and allow us to get back on purpose, God's purpose for us.

Read this promise from God; write it down and carry it with you:

"No weapon formed against you shall prosper, and every tongue which rises against you in judgment, You shall condemn. This is the heritage of the servants of the Lord, and their righteousness is from Me, says the Lord (Isaiah 54:17)."

If we live in an upright manner based on the spiritual principles in the Bible, we have nothing to fear and everything to gain. Your life can be filled with abundance and joy, if you love Him as He loves you, passionately!

Be uplifted and encouraged today because the all-powerful God is working it out in your favor. Just do your part and trust God to do His part!

Motivational Tip for Day #61

Stop what you are doing right now.

Today's tip is focused on the Spirit, the Spirit of truth and error.

Too many people stumble over small points in the Bible while missing the main point, love. There is a Spirit of truth which will guide you as you open up more of your heart to the word of God.

"We are of God; he that knows God hears us; he who is not of God does not hear us. By this we know the Spirit of truth and the spirit of error (1 John 4:6)."

As we grow in Christ, we learn how to discern the Spirit of truth and it's reflected in our daily attitude and character. The Spirit of truth is relatively easy to discern to those who hear the Word and receive the Word with a ready and willing heart. Coming willingly to the light with eagerness, moves us closer to God.

It's simple to move closer to the mind of God. The problem is that many allow the spirit of error to lead them way. The source of the spirit of error, is satan. satan takes God Word out of our heart by attempting to deceived us. satan tries to manipulate and mislead us through our own human wisdom. God provides a truth that is simple for those who diligently seek it, and want it.

"Therefore, since we have this ministry, as we have received mercy, we do not lose heart. But we have renounced the hidden things of shame, not walking in craftiness nor handling the word of God deceitfully, but by manifestation of the truth commending ourselves to every man's conscience in the sight of God. But even if our gospel is veiled, it is veiled to those who are perishing, whose minds the gods of this age has blinded, who do not believe, lest the light of the gospel of the glory of Christ, who is the image of God, should shine on them. For we do not preach ourselves, but Christ Jesus the Lord, and ourselves your bondservants for Jesus' sake. For it is the God who commanded light to shine out of darkness, who has shone in our hearts to give the light of the knowledge of the glory of God in the face of Jesus Christ (2 Corinthians 4:1-6)."

This tip today is for me, to remind me to keep it simple but perhaps others will benefit from it as well. We are of God, and God is love. We are commanded by our creator to love, and with that we should do everything in love. I remind myself to make sure I put on love every minute of the day.

As I started my journey from the darkness to the light, I stopped looking for stumbling blocks and began looking for stepping stones so that I could be the man that God wants me to be. I came to believe that I never needed to be confused over some point in the Bible as long as I conducted myself in a Godly love. I long to please God now which means I live my life by loving God with all my heart, soul and mind; and my neighbor as myself (the Greatest Commandment). Loving God means that I do things that God loves and commands me to do, following the Spirit of truth. My neighbors are every human on this planet, and I am to love them as God commands me.

The Spirit of truth, the Spirit of God's Law of Love will show you the way when you allow the light to shine in every portion of your heart. It's simple; we humans make it so complicated because we don't want to truly surrender. In many ways, we are still like the stiff-necked Israelites wandering in the desert, in the spirit of error.

Too many people do not want to live as a new creature for our Creator, they prefer to hang on to their old ways trying to put a little God in their lives. God doesn't want a little of us, God wants all of our devotion and love. As I have kept it simple by focusing on the Greatest Commandment as spoken by Jesus in Mathew 22:34-40, it has allowed me to have a spiritual awakening where my life has become simple. I just have to do my job, serve and obey God, and God will do His job.

God made his system simple for we could follow it which is why Jesus gave us the Greatest Commandment, love. It's so simple, but humans love to complicate it. Don't seek to make it complicated but seek to place the Spirit of truth deep in your heart. Seek to hear God's voice by always asking God, "how can I apply this scripture to my life."

Be encouraged this day because it's simple; follow the Spirit of truth and you will have abundance in your life!

Motivational Tip for Day #62

Stop what you are doing right now.

Your walk, talk and attitude: Does it clearly tell people you are a born again Christian?

As a believer in Christ, everything about us should say that we follow something different than those in the world. Our words, thoughts and deeds should be a testimony to God, a tribute to God's great love.

As a Christian, our conduct represents our heavenly Father. We were created to glorify God through our actions. Psalms 139:14 states, "I praise You because I am fearfully and wonderfully made." Too many people allow the world to shape how they view themselves but we need to view ourselves as God sees us. God created us to glorify Him and has given us all the tools to succeed. When our efforts aligns with God's purpose for our life, meaning and joy is the result.

"Wherefore we labor, that, whether present or absent, we may be accepted of Him (2 Corinthians 5:9)." Another translation from the New King James Version states, "Therefore we make it our aim, whether present or absent, to be well pleasing to Him." Paul expresses the strong desire to be pleasing to (the concept of being 'accepted of') God. We should not seek to be accepted by man but God. We need to aim each day to seek to please God, regardless of what others say or do to us.

"Set your mind on things above, not on things on the earth (Colossians 3:2)." I love this verse because it reminds me to stay connected to God through His word. "Without faith, it is impossible to please the Lord (Hebrews 11:6)." I have hope in a brighter future and trust that God is working it all out for me. That said, the responsibility is on me to act in ways pleasing to God by showing love, compassion, kindness, forgiveness and humility to all of God's creatures.

We are called to have a steadfast, constant faith. We do this by living a life which inwardly and outwardly shows we trust and have faith in God.

"But as we have been approved by God to be put to be entrusted with the Gospel, even so we speak, not as pleasing men, but God who tests our hearts (1 Thessalonians 2:4)." We are told to be pleasing to God, not men. The world strives to move us closer to the devil, but God has given us a path to follow. The path is for our benefit and will lead to having true inner joy. Pleasing man or women will not get us into heaven, but instead we should strive to live a life which shows others the path and the light.

I started this tip off by saying our life should show others who we follow. We are God's ambassadors and as such, represent Him. "Therefore, if anyone is in Christ, he is a new creation; old things have passed away; behold, all things have become new (2 Corinthians 5:17)." It's time to truly live as a new creation by having a new walk, singing a new song, and living the new life which Christ died to give us. God has already delivered us from the darkness; it's our job to stay in the light.

With God's help, we can move mountains - - one rock at a time.

Motivational Tip for Day # 63

Stop what you are doing right now.

Today's tip is focused on service. Humans are genetically built to desire purpose and meaning in their life. Sometimes we get so focused on just trying to keep our heads above water that we forget about others.

Helping others can often be the best way to find purpose and meaning in our lives. Volunteer in your church to do something that no one wants to do, or read to an elderly person, or work in a homeless shelter, or serve as a big brother or big sister to a young person who has no one. Helping others often helps ourselves and is a way to channel the love that God has for us, to others.

When Jesus' disciples were arguing about who would obtain the place of honor in heaven, Jesus said, "Whoever desires to become great among you shall be your servant. And whoever of you desires to be first shall be slave to all. For even the Son of Man did not come to be served, but to serve, and to give His life for a ransom for many (Mark 10:43-45)."

Little things done in Christ's name; are great things. Through helping others without any expectation of benefit to ourselves, we more clearly see God's plan for our lives. Jesus always offers us to chance to understand the purpose for our lives. Serving others can give meaning to our lives in ways that one could not imagine. Helping others in new and different ways will provide so many benefits.

Your vision will become clearer through providing a service to others. It's the same with reading Bible; look at it in new ways by reflecting on what God is trying to do in your life. God is summoning all of us to be and do something unique, which adds value to the world. The next time you read scripture, ask God to show you how you can put that verse into practice in your life. God always wants to show us His vision for our lives, but we have to have a receptive heart.

"Ask God today, enlarge my vision, and take me to a place where I can see what you are calling me to do with my life."

Life is a journey and through the journey we have trials and tribulations, but God has sent us to help others along the way. Today, look for a new ways to help others, and you will be blessed!

Serving others helps us to develop God's nature in us. God is love and because we strive to be like our heavenly Father, we show our love by helping, volunteering and being God's representative on this planet.

If you want to be motivated in a God inspired way, help someone today. Show love through service, and God will pour out His blessings over your life!

Motivational Tip for Day # 64

Stop what you are doing right now.

"The Lord is near to all who call on Him, to all who call on Him in truth. He fulfills the desires of all who fear Him; He also hears their cry, and save them (Psalm 145:18-19)." This is a glorious promise from God. Many people want the promises of God but do not fully understand how to obtain it. The promise is realized through our faith. The adversary (satan) loves when we have adversity because many people are caused to stumble when the storms of life comes into their life.

To receive the promises from God, we must hold fast to our convictions in God and our confession of faith. "Let us draw near with a true heart in full assurance of faith, having our hearts sprinkled from an evil conscience and our bodies washed in pure water. Let us hold fast (be steadfast or consistent) the confession of our hope without wavering, for He who promised is faithful. And let us consider one another in order to stir up love and good works, not forsaking the assembling of ourselves together, as is the manner of some, but exhorting one another, and so much the more as you see the Day approaching (Hebrews 10:22-25)." The above verse provides guidance on how each believer should live.

Either we are going to believe God's words and be blessed; or we CHOOSE to believe the devil's lies and live a life without victory.

When we waver in our faith, we give the power to the evil one and take power away from the Holy Spirit which indwells in us. How do we waver in faith? Some people waver in faith by the thoughts that think, the words they use or the actions that take each day. These three areas testify to their wavering faith. But when we focus on honoring God with every part of life, we will start to see His promises fulfilled.

The toughest battles that we will ever fight is those in our own mind. I love this following quote, "I have met the enemy, and it is I." That quote sums up where we need to focus on - ourselves and our inner world. We need to tend to our own gardens. Some people call it doing "the hard work" or "mental housekeeping". Whatever you wish to call it, we need to do the work ourselves to reap the benefits.

Pastor Sarah Utterbach points out: "People say, 'The Lord has promised never to leave me nor forsake me', then they go back to discussing their problems. In so doing, they invalidate the power of what God said. The Holy Spirit is authorized to act on God's Word when you begin to say what God has said."

Today, do some mental housekeeping. Do the work yourself so that you can reap the great promises our Lord has promised us.

Charles Stanley in his book "How to Reach Your Full Potential For God" suggests, 'Ask yourself the following questions about everything you choose to think about:

Does this enhance my spiritual life?
Does this promote my overall well being and wholeness?
Does this uplift, edify, or inspire me to greater good?
Does this lead to holiness?
Does this increase the work of God in my life?'
Does this add to my ability to discern good from evil, right from wrong, and to determine what is God' best?'

Today, focus on holding fast to the promises of God. Be uplifted because God wants you to have an abundant life; just read His word and realize how much He loves you!

Motivational Tip for Day #65

Stop what you are doing right now.

Today's tip is focused on maturity. No wants to be immature in any part of their life. The same should be with spiritual maturity. How do we move towards spiritual maturity?

"But let each one examine his own good work, and then he will have rejoicing in himself alone, and not in another. For each one shall bear his own load (Galatians 6:4-5)."

To grow mature in the word means that we look inside and examine those areas which remains unsurrendered to God.

1 Peter 5:8-9 states, "Be controlled and alert...standing firm in the faith." Maturing in the word also will require that we have self-control and be alert to the tricks of the devil. And lastly, we must stand firm in our faith. People who are immature in Christ allow themselves to be swayed by the trials of life. We must stay steady, be sober minded and maintain calm through the storm.

We must keep on, keeping on. It's easy to claim God's promises when our life is going well but the challenge is to claim God's promises when life is falling apart. We must maintain the same strength when things look the darkest because that is how we mature. We must maintain an awareness of God's presence even when He appears to be silent in our life.

Maturing as a believer comes in the valleys, not the peaks. Rejoice in the valleys and you will see God work in your life because valleys always lead to higher places of honor.

Giving up is not who you are and neither is continuing an immature spiritual path. God wants the best for his children. Maintaining a mature spiritual walk means having the proper attitude at all times. God allows negative things to happen in our lives to teach us. Our goal should be to stay teachable while having a great attitude.

God has promised a reward for all believers. Always live with the vision of Christ before you. Maturing in the word and in spirit is evidenced by your attitude.

Paul was in a Roman prison and he rejoiced. Paul had been beaten and faced death numerous times but his attitude was always one of joy.

Read this section of 2 Corinthians 11:24-28 where Paul described what he went through, "...I received 36 lashes. Three times I was beaten with rods; once I was stoned; three times I was shipwrecked; a night and a day I have been in the deep; in journeys often, in perils of water, in perils of robbers, in perils of my own countrymen, in perils of the Gentiles, in perils in the city, in perils in the wilderness, in perils in the sea, in perils among false brethren; in weariness and toil, in sleeplessness often, in hunger and thirst, in fasting often, in cold and nakedness -- besides the other things, what comes upon me daily, my deep concern for all the churches." Even going through all of this pain, Paul thought of others. Your level of spiritual maturity is demonstrated by your attitude. We can all be like Paul.

If you are saved, God is living in you. We must strive each day to align our inner world with God's intention for our lives. Grow to be mature in God's words, looking for the lesson every day.

When people meet you, do they see the Christ in you?

I want to walk you through what Paul wrote in Philippians because he wrote this from a Roman prison.

-"Being confident of this very thing, that He who has begun a good work in you will continue it until the day of Jesus Christ (1:6)."

-"But I want you to know, brethren, that the things which happened to me have actually turned out for the furtherance of the Gospel (1:12)."

-"For it is God who works in you both to will and to do for His good pleasure. Do all things without complaining and disputing, that you may become blameless and harmless, children of God without fault in the midst of a crooked and perverse generation, among whom you shine as lights in the world, holding fast to the word of life... (2:13-16)."

-"Brethren, I do not count myself to have apprehended; but one thing I do, forgetting those things which are behind and reaching forward to those things which are ahead, I press towards the goal for the prize of the upward call of God in Christ Jesus. Therefore let us, as many as are MATURE, have this mind; and if in anything you think otherwise, God will reveal even this to you (3:12-15)."

-"Rejoice in the Lord always. Again I will say rejoice! Let your gentleness be known to all men. The Lord is at hand. Be anxious for nothing, but in everything by prayer and supplication, with thanksgiving, let your requests be made known to God; and the peace of God which surpassed all understanding, will guard your hearts and minds through Christ Jesus (4:4-7)."

-"Finally Brethren, whatever things are true, whatever things are noble, whatever things are just, whatever things are pure, whatever things are lovely, whatever things are of good report, if there is any virtue and if there is anything praiseworthy -- meditate on these things. The things which you learned and received and hear and saw in me, these do, and the God of peace will be with you (4:8-9)." These are examples of how those who want to live a mature spiritual life, should live.

-"I can do all things through Christ who strengthens me (4:13)." This is my all time favorite verse.

You can praise your way through the storm!

Today, strive to have a mature spirit in God. Ask God to help you to mature in His word so that you are a light to others!

"No one told you that the road would be easy, but if you praise as you make your way on the path of life, you will be empowered and live in abundance!" Philip Allan Turner

Motivational Tip for Day #66

Stop what you are doing right now!

"Do not be dismayed, for I am your God (Isaiah 41:10)." Too many people are dismayed so easily. We need to demonstrate our faith by not becoming discouraged when problems enter our life. God wants to show us a better way. "Lead me, O Lord...make straight you way before me (Psalm 5:8)"

God will guide you if you allow Him. The path may not always be easy but by using God's word as your compass, the journey will be more fulfilling.

The first verse in Tip mentions not being dismayed. Too many people are struggling in certain areas because of the guilt and condemnation that they heap on themselves. These people are so wrapped up in their past troubles or current obstacles that they fail to see the glory of God each day. We are called to be steadfast and to lean on the Lord. The devil wants you to believe that you are alone but God said that He would never leave you nor forsake you.

"Give your burdens to the Lord, and He will take care of you (Psalm 55:22)." Who are you going to believe this day?

Believing in God's promises require you to not be dismayed when troubles come to your door. We need to trust the Word. As James, Jesus' half brother explained in James 1:22, "Be doers of the word, and not merely hearers who deceive themselves."

Belief is a peculiar thing because it separates the real believer from those who say "play church". Jesus stated in John 11:25, "I am the resurrection and the life. Whoever believes in me will live..."

Living for Jesus requires conviction on our part because if we do our part then blessings of God will flow into our lives more abundantly!

Motivational Tip for Day #67

Stop what you are doing right now.

"God has come to help His people (Luke 7:16)."

God's got a blessing with your name on it. Many people want to the blessings from God but must understand how God's system works. First, to understand how God's system works, we must read His word and allow it to change our heart. If we want to love and honor God, then we will keep His commandments. The bible helps us to understand the mind of God. Once we understand what God wants of us and for us, we can strive to live a life pleasing to God, not man.

Each day: Dig into the Bible, searching for a revelation. Live a life of hope and Godly expectation. Expect God's blessings.

"Behold, I am the Lord, the God of all flesh. Is there anything too hard for Me? (Jeremiah 32:27)." Either we going to live a life believing God's word or not. Either we will use the Bible as our roadmap for life or not. Many people allow satan's lies to rule there life. The above verse in Jeremiah states that God can do anything. We must believe His word.

Many times we allow our blessings to fall by the wayside by believing the prince of lies, falling for his illusions. Faith can move mountains but doubt keeps us stuck and lost.

Give your heart fully to Christ. God wants all of us to be His mouthpiece for the Gospel. Stop thinking about the bad and focus your mind on God's goodness. Believe that God's word will do what it says it will. Believe that if God could change the people in the Bible thousands of years ago then God can change you. Believe!

Are you still having defeated thoughts then put more effort into reading and understanding God's infallible and perfect word each day! If we want to change, we must lean on the Holy Spirit. We cannot do it alone or by sheer human will power, we must call upon the Holy Spirit, the comforter to strengthen us.

Psalm 56:3 states, "Whenever I am afraid, I will trust in You." Trust and faith go hand in hand. Trust God to be who He is; and have faith that God is looking to bless you. Do your part and God will do His part.

Keep praising God through the good times and bad times, and you will show the devil who you follow and who you trust. There is an old song which says, "This is my story; this is my song, Praising my Savior all the day long; This is my story, this is my song, Praising my Savior all the day long."

Today, God has given us the gift of free will. We can choose to believe what the Bible says about us and prosper! God wants no one lost! God is cheering for us to be what He intended us to be. God wants us to share the Truth with others so that they may know peace and inner joy.

"But the salvation of the righteous is from the Lord; He is their strength in the time of trouble (Psalm 37:39)."

Psalm 40:3 states, "He has put a new song in my mouth..." I love God and hope this message is received in your heart because God transformed my life and I want all to find what I found. God has put a new song in my mouth and will put a new song in your to, if you will allow Him.

Be uplifted today because God has told us, "For you have armed me with the strength for the battle (Psalm 18:39)."

We have already been fully equipped by God for every good work, just believe His word today!

Motivational Tip for Day #68

Stop what you are doing right now.

God wants to get our full attention, not just occasionally or when we think of Him. God taps on our hearts and wants us to give our hearts to Him freely and completely. Trusting God to be God 24/7 is the focus of today's tip.

Romans 8:28 states, "All things work together for good to those who love God to those who are called according to His purpose." This short verse contains much truth. First, it mentions that ALL THINGS, not some but all things. Second, it states for 'good', this is not human good but Godly good which is a complete abundance and fullness that only knowing God can bring about. Third, it mentions that this promise is for all who love God: loving God means that we should work to please Him with our thoughts, words and actions. If we love someone we try to do what's pleasing to them, not what they hate. It's the same with God, we must strive to do the things that God loves. Fourth, we are being called because God is trying to get our attention. Paul was blinded on the road to Damascus by the light in Acts 9:3-6 and 9. Usually it takes a jolt of some kind to bring us around. Fifth, God has a purpose for our lives; strive to understand it through His word.

Oftentimes, it takes more than one or two sermons to get our attention, it may take years of pain and suffering. C.S. Lewis wrote in The Problem of Pain, "God whispers to us in our pleasures, speaks in our conscience, but shouts in our pains: His megaphone to rouse a deaf world." No matter what has happened in the past, tomorrow is always a new day to listen to what God is saying to you and to do His will. Once you have been aroused from the sleep of unawareness, it's time to get to work and do what God is calling you. Remember a great truth today; even though a great tragedy may have happened to you, God is working to develop our character so that we can do His will. It's about God, not us!

"I have set the Lord always before me; because He is at my right hand I shall not be moved. Therefore my heart is glad, and my glory rejoices; my flesh will rest in hope (Psalm 16:8-9)."

We have hope through our faith in God and His promises. We have love in "that God sent His only begotten Son into the world, that we might live through Him (1 John 4:9)."

Hope, Love and Faith will light your path, heal your hurts and allow abundance to enter your life if you allow it. "Love has been perfected among us in this: that we may have boldness in the day of judgment; He is, so we are in this world. There is no fear in love; but perfect love casts out fear, because fear involves torment. But he who fear has not been made perfect in love. We love Him because He first loved us (1 John 4:17-19)."

God is waiting for us to see ourselves as He sees ourselves. God is, and we are. We each need to change our aim once we become of the body of Christ, our goal should be to strive towards perfect love. Nothing is out of reach if we believe; this is a promise from Jesus Christ.

"I pray that God, the source of hope, will fill you completely with joy and peace because you trust in Him. Then you will overflow with confident hope through the power of the Holy Spirit (Romans 15:13)." This scripture is the formula for a purposeful and meaningful life full of abundance.

In Jack Taylor's book, God's New Creation, he describes statements of truth about the believer. He came to the truth in a moment of his life where he was struggling. He wrote, "One day, far away from home and alone, I seemed to be enshrouded in a cloud of anxiety, uncertainty and depression. I could not pinpoint the exact source of my problem, but the feelings had to do with my real standing with God. The more I thought, the more exasperated I became. At last I spoke of God these words, 'I would really love to know what You think of me?' The Lord began to communicate with my troubled heart, urging me to go to the Word as if saying, 'I have already made it clear what I think of you in my Word... read it!" I love this passage because so many people fail to allow God's Word to get their attention which will guide them as it was intended to do.

Too many people have lost their identity by trying to be what others want them to be instead of being who God wants them to be.

Today, trust God in new and deeper ways. God wants to get your attention today to show you the correct path which will bring peace, fulfillment and comfort!

Motivational Tip for Day #69

Stop what you are doing right now.

Today we will focus on the Great Motivator, God, and His word. Before we discuss this topic, we must understand that the devil wishes to de-motivate us by taking us off track, off God's path. satan wishes to shame you, bring up your past and get you focused on anything else except God. Let the past motivate you to be the person God intended you to be. Too many people are so self-absorbed that they forget God and focus on their own issues, problems, pains, trials and tribulations but we are commanded to focus on God, not our problems. If our eyes stays focused on God and our heart meditates on His word constantly, abundance and joy will be your reward!

Stop being self-absorbed and become spiritually-absorbed. Be spiritually ambitious each day!

"There are many plans in a man's heart, nevertheless the Lord's counsel -- that will stand (Proverbs 19:12)."

God will motivate you, if you allow Him. Our faith can be measured by our feet (our actions to move closer to God), the same with our level of motivation. I love to say that we vote with our feet because it's a tangible representation of our true internal desire to accomplish our dreams. It's the same with God. The direction of our feet demonstrates our level of faith in God. Our feet show who we follow and what we believe. God says His word is a light to our feet and God likes when we act in faith.

The devil loves to use shame to keep us bound. Our former shame can lead us to do great things for God because it ought to drive us to repentance. From repentance, we can move towards our destiny, which is greatness!

The devil uses people, friends, family members and co-workers to mislead us and misdirect us. This is why following God's word is so important to not get off track. The Bible mentions being steadfast so many times because it's in our nature to be swayed. God's word can help us to stay focused. And when you fall down, pick yourself up and know that God loves you unconditionally, then repent and honor God by moving forward. There are thoughts, words and actions which are 'of God' and those which are 'of satan'. Our goal should be to discern the difference and strive for the light.

Everyone wants God to move in their lives; God desires that we move for Him, to serve Him. Perhaps when we move our feet for Him, it will jump start the blessings in our lives.

We must want something better, to actually have a better life. Many people are ambitious but we should be ambitious spiritually. Jesus tells us, "But seek first the Kingdom of God and His righteousness, and all these things shall be added to you (Mathew 6:33)."

Take a chance today, to advance God's Kingdom. We are told to work hard to get what we want, but too few people actually strive hard to put God's word deeply in their hearts each day. These same people will cheer for worldly things, run to do worldly things but make excuses why they can't put God first in their lives. If we want God for move for us, we have to move for God. God speaks to us through his Scripture, other people and through circumstances.

"My son, give attention to my words; Incline your ear to my sayings. Do not let them depart from your eyes; Keep them in the midst of your heart (Proverbs 4:20-21)." Later in this same chapter of Proverbs we learn, "Let your eyes look straight ahead, and you eyelids look right before you. Ponder the path of your FEET, and let all your ways be established. Do not turn to the right or the left; Remove your FOOT from evil (4:25-27)." God is instructing us to look forward and move forward. The path of our feet demonstrates where we actually want to go. Today, choose to move closer to God, and watch God work in your life!

Motivational Tip for Day #70

Stop what you are doing right now.

The goal of this tip is to stress that we should pay attention to our personal growth each day, especially our spiritual growth. It's about the path we each choose to take each day by the thoughts we think, the words we speak and the actions we take. How we live our life, ever moment of each day, matters.

Damage souls attract one another just as like, attracts like. This world will damage our souls if we allow it through the media, internet and toxic people which all lead to a poisoning of the soul. Only by spiritually renewing our spirit each day, can we stay in the light. I came to understand that I had to go deeper into God's word and do additional things to grow spiritually each day. For me, going to church once a week was not enough, so I started going to church 3-4 times a week. I realized that I needed to read at least one spiritual book a week to grow. I started listening to sermons every day in the morning because it was the only way I could grow closer to God. I now have peace and inner joy because of the hard inner work I have done. My personal growth continues. If I am to maintain what I have found, I continue to do the challenging internal work with a God conscience lens to keep my hand in the Master's hand. I allowed God to speak to me and show me the way first.

"Be still and know that I am God (Psalm 46:10)." We must each not only listen but seek out that still, small voice of God. Every one of us has a personal narrative which leads to finding meaning and purpose. What does your personal narrative say? There are many tales about the hero's journey: the hero is thrust into an uncertain situation and then goes through a tragedy; it's because of the struggle that the hero learns his true destiny and after those great struggles the hero finds his love, prize or his holy grail. This is like many of us because it's never too late to be who we've might have been.

Today, I wanted to highlight some wisdom from others on parallel religious paths because it all leads to the same place if we are sincerely seeking to know God with our whole heart -- spiritual enlightenment.

"Prepare thyself, for thou wilt have to travel on alone. The teacher can but point the way. The path is one for all, the means to reach the goal must vary with the pilgrims." The Masters from the Voice of Silence. This quote is also about the hero's journey.

"The challenge before us will also be the same, to see the world with fresh eyes and to treat each moment as precious and extraordinary. May we rise to the challenge." Tim Boyd, National President of the Theosophical Society of America.

Today I ask you to consider your own pilgrimage of self exploration, has it been deep and meaningful? Today is a new day to be what God wants you to be. We often become starved for beauty and love but all we need to do is to look inside.

Joy Mills of the Theosophical Society states, "Knowing who and what we are, and with our destiny in our own hands; we are at peace within and have the courage to face the challenge before us." The path or the journey is necessary to become who God wants us to be. The Hebrews from Exodus had to leave Egypt to reach their destiny, the promised land of Canaan. The Hebrew kept looking back at Egypt but that was not the path that God had set for them. Too many of us are still stuck in an Egypt mindset but we must all leave our own personal Egypt so we can all get to our own promised land.

John Algeo stated that, "the path exist within."

In Luke 17:20-21, Jesus said, "For the Kingdom of God is within you."

"Here is the road; the light comes and goes then returns again. Be gentle with your fellow travelers. As they move through the world of stone and stars whirling with you yet every one alone. The road waits. Do not ask questions but when it invited you to dance at daybreak, say yes. Each step is the journey; a single note in the song." Arlene Gay Levine from Bless the Day: Prayers and Poems to Nurture Your Soul. Edited by June Cotner Kodansha int'l.

Fredrick the Great stated, "Every man must get to heaven in his own way." This is an important point because it's on each of us. Isaiah 42:16 says, "I will lead the blind by ways they have not known, along unfamiliar paths I will guide them; I will turn the darkness into light before them and make the rough places smooth. These are the things I will do; I will not forsake them."

God has promised that He would never leave nor forsake us. We must just believe and act on that belief each day. "Trust in the Lord with all you heart, and lean not on your own understanding; in all your ways acknowledge Him, and he shall direct your paths (Proverbs 3:5-6)."

Praise God! We have an all-powerful, all-knowing and all-present God who is waiting for each of us to surrender to Him and trust Him. He will direct our paths. Meditate throughout the day on God's word. Allow your first thought to be on the Lord. In all ways, acknowledge Him by seeking His guidance for everything. Seek Him and He will be found. God wants to bless us with favor and abundance; we just need to do our part.

Ma Jaya Sati Bhagavati stated, "When you plant a seed of love, it is you that blossoms."

"Look for a little bit of God in everyone," Guideposts reader Leonard Klappauf of Mount Pleasant, Wisconsin

Inspirational Tip for Day #71

Stop what you are doing right now.

I decided to use the term "Inspirational" instead of "Motivational" for the next thirty days because when we are inspired, we will also be motivated. I have a deep abiding passion to bring others to the light, the truth and to the knowledge of Jesus Christ. I felt inspired when I wrote these tips, and in that I was helping myself move closer to God. Many times I never knew what I would write about until I started typing. I would ask God to help me and would be led to write about the Lord and how to discern His voice.

I can't speak about what God has done in your life, but He has saved my life and set me on a better path. I want others to know the inner peace which I have gained once I gave my life to God. I aspire to inspire!

Let God reign in your life. God tells us to bring Him our first fruits. We can only bring our best to God through love. Today's tip is focused on gaining inspiration and motivation through love. God has made provision for every believer to live in victory and abundance. Our victory is through faith and love is the path to that victory!

"For whoever is born of God (that is you and me) overcomes the world. And this victory that has overcome the world – our faith. Who is he who overcomes the world, but he whoever believes that Jesus is the Son of God (1 John 5:4-5)." We are overcomers!

"The Lord appeared to him from far away. 'I have loved you with an everlasting love; therefore I have continued my faithfulness to you (Jeremiah 31:3)'." God loves us so deeply, completely and perfectly that the human mind can't comprehend it because we don't love like this unless we allow the Holy Spirit to move deeply and change our heart. I will mention several more verses on love which will help show you the way, as it was shown me. Meditate on these verses, asking God to speak to your heart.

"Love each other deeply, because love covers a multitude of sins (1 Peter 4:8)."

"Eye has not seen, nor ear heard, nor have entered into the heart of man the things which God has prepared for those who love Him (1 Corinthians 2:9)." If we say we love God then we should act in ways which will please our heavenly Father.

"For I am persuaded that neither death nor life, nor angels nor principalities nor powers, nor things present not things to come, nor height nor depth, nor any other created thing, shall be able to separate us from the love of God which is in Christ Jesus our Lord (Romans 8:38-39)." So many people allow others to move them away from God. We allow people to entice us to please satan instead of pleasing God. Someone says something unkind to us and many will respond in anger (which is not 'of God') or in unkindness in return. We must be like how the Apostle Paul described above in that nothing can persuade us to become separated from God. We all have been guilty of allowing others to steal our God inspired dreams and take us in directions away from the mind of God. Be steadfast and allow God to inspire you through love.

"The love of God has been poured in our hearts by the Holy Spirit who was given to us (Romans 5:5)." It's already inside of us because we are 'of God', and God is love. We must stay true to who God is, and what God has put inside of us. Today, love with your whole heart, and in more inspired ways, and you will see abundance and joy enter your life!

Be inspired to be who God called you to be!!

Inspirational Tip for Day #72

Stop what you are doing right now.

Inspiration comes from God and for this I thank Him. Ecclesiastes 2:26 states, "God gives wisdom, knowledge and joy to those who please Him."

When we please God, our path is so much easier. Too many people focus on pleasing people instead of God and then they are surprised when they are disappointed. People can disappoint while God will never disappoint. satan has many tricks and traps for humans. satan wants you to put your trust in humans instead of God.

Be aware of God's presence always and you will never be discouraged. God stated in Malachi 3:6, "For I am the Lord, I do not change." Wow, this is an amazing characteristic of God. People change but God never will. The same God that Abraham, Jacob, Joshua, Joseph and David served, we serve. This fact makes me what to jump for joy! God is faithful.

We have to get to know God personally. We should strive to have an intimate personal relationship with Him. God is always faithful. 2 Timothy 2:13 says, "If we are faithless, He remains faithful; He cannot deny Himself." God is who He says He is. Either we are going to believe in God or not.

Many people feel lonely but this is because they have not allowed God to come fully into their lives. satan wants you to feel lonely and abandoned but God is real and can be felt if we strive to know Him deeply through His word. His word says that God is Omnipresent, Omnipotent and Omniscient. God is also patient towards us, waiting for us to fully give our lives to Him. No matter what your yesterday looked like, God can turn your tomorrow into greatness

2 Peter 9 states, "The Lord is not slack concerning His promise, as some count slackness but it longsuffering toward us, not willing that any should perish but all should come to repentance." Many people attribute human attributes with God but His words says He will never leave us not forsake us.

"Oh, the depth of the riches both of the wisdom and knowledge of God! How unsearchable are His judgments and His ways past finding out! 'For who has known the mind of the Lord? Or who has become His counselor? Or who has first given to Him and it shall be repaid to him?' For of Him and through Him and to Him are all things, to whom be glory forever. Amen. (Romans 11:33-36)."

God ways may be mysterious but they are always wise and for our good. God wants to work it out for you but you must be faithful and patient in striving to understand Him. We can grow in the knowledge of the Lord by going deeply in His word. Too many people are just surface dwellers in life. Life is meant to be lived deeply, fully and completely. God has moved me so many times that I cannot count it anymore. Seek to go deeply into His word and into the Spirit of His words. To find deep joy, purpose and fulfillment, one must dive deeper.

"Grace and peace be multiplied to you in the knowledge of God and Jesus our Lord, as His divine power has given to us all things that pertain to life and godliness, through the knowledge of Him who called us by glory and virtue, by which have been given to us exceedingly great and precious promises, that through these you may be partakers of the divine nature... (2 Peter 1:2-4)." God is so amazingly great and his mercies endures forever. I encourage you this day to understand who He is so that you can know who you are.

"You have made known to me the path of life; you will fill me with joy in your presence, with eternal pleasures at your right hand (Psalm 16:11)." I know who God is and I know who I am. I am stronger and wiser today because of what God has done in my life. If God can move in the lives of Abraham, Jacob, Joseph, David and Daniel the God can move in your life. God is leaning towards you and want you to understand that he is the same yesterday, today and tomorrow.

Instead of focusing on yourself and your feelings today, focus on God! Instead of being self-absorbed, be self-aware of who you are in Christ Jesus. "You are a chosen generation, a royal priesthood, a holy nation, His own special people, that you may proclaim the praises of Him who called you out of darkness into His marvelous light (1 Peter 2:9)." God wants us to see ourselves as He sees us. There is no guilt or condemnation because if we fall, all we have to do is to get up and turn to God. Too many people believe the lies of satan.

Today, look at life through the eyes of God. Be aware of God's presence as you work, walk, speak and live. Believe that God already has the best worked out for you. Put your thought life under control because God has not written anyone off. God has chosen each one of us and wants to use us. We are not what people say about us, instead we are everything that God says about us!

Inspirational Tip for Day #73

Stop what you are doing right now.

Today's tip is focused on having "the strength for the journey."

"Those who hope in the Lord will renew their Strength. They will soar on wings like eagles; they will run and not grow weary, they will walk and not be faint (Isaiah 40:31)." Once we decide to live for God, we must develop a plan to retrain ourselves so we do not continue to fall for the same thinking errors. The Bible offers the solution but one must go to the Word of God first and then believe it, instead of the lies of the devil. If we do not know the tricks of the adversary or the evil one, then we will continue to fall for them.

"God is my strength and power, He makes my way perfect. He makes my feet like feet of deer, and sets me on my high places (2 Samuel 22:33-34)." God wants us to live a higher life. He has set us up to succeed and has provided the strength for the journey. "For you equipped me with strength for the battle; you made those who rise against me sink under me (2 Samuel 22:40)." God has fully equipped us to live an abundant life, a life of fulfillment and meaning is His goal for us. It starts with knowing who God is and who you are through God. "I can do all things through Christ who strengthens me (Philippians 4:13)." Believe it, repeat it, memorize it and live it!

We have all been conditioned in certain negative ways. If we want a better, more meaningful life than it starts with our thinking. We must believe that God is for us, just as His words say He is. "Be strong and do not let your hands be weak, for your work shall be rewarded (2 Chronicles 15:7)." We must believe ourselves to be strong because God commands us to be strong. We must also understand how God's system's work. We work hard and we will be rewarded. Sloth or laziness is one of the deadly sins for a specific reason. "Do not be slothful in zeal, be fervent in spirit, serve the Lord (Romans 12:11)."

We need to remember another part of how God's system works, "You need to persevere so that when you have done the will of God, you will receive what He has promised (Hebrews 10:36)." This is God's word detailing how His system works. All we need to do is to believe and put our belief into action by being intentional.

Each of us has been chosen by God for a specific purpose. There are things, emotions, feelings, people and habits which hinder us. We must know what those negative things are. "Let us throw off everything that hinders and the sin that so easily entangles, and let us run with perseverance the race marked out for us (Hebrews 12:1)." Again, God spells it out clearly and concisely so that we will not stumble.

Psalm 27:14 states, "Wait on the LORD; be of good courage, and he shall strengthen your heart; wait, I say on the Lord." God has freely given us everything we need, all we have to do is to accept these gifts, understand His system and believe His words.

I leave you with Philippians 4:8-9, "Finally, brethren, whatever things are true, whatever things are noble, whatever things are just, whatever things are lovely, whatever things are of good report, if there is any virtue and if there is anything praiseworthy --- mediate on these things. The things which you learned and received and heard and saw in Me, these do, and the God of peace will be with you." We all have a job to do and one can never read or hear the above verse too many times. As James said in 1:22, "Be doers of the word, and not hearers only, deceiving yourselves." Today I strive to move closer to God. I fall down like many but now I get back up understanding who I am in Christ.

We have all been equipped with the tools and strength to live a purposeful life. All we have to do is to see ourselves as God sees us and move forward in a Godly way. Choose to move uprightly, choose to think Godly and choose to love completely!

Saint Augustine said, "Faith and understanding go hand in hand: Understand that you may believe; believe that you may understand," and "True happiness consists in knowledge of God."

Inspirational Tip for Day #74

Stop what you are doing right now.

Today's tip is centered on opening our eyes and striving to keep them open.

"To open their eyes, in order to turn them from darkness to light, and from the power of satan to God, that they may receive forgiveness of sins and an inheritance among those who are sanctified (set apart for those in the world) by faith in Me (Acts 26:18)." Jesus spoke these words and they provide clarity to the believer. Opening our eyes and awakening to our purpose should be everyone's goal.

The Apostle Paul wrote in Ephesians 5:14, "Awake, you who sleep, Arise from the dead, and Christ will give you light." Too many people sleep walk through life or walk around blinded by the illusions of this world.

John Randolph Price writes in 'A Spiritual Philosophy for the World', "Until you transcend the ego, you can do nothing but add to the insanity of the world."

Galatians 3:29 states, "If you are in Christ's, then you are Abraham's seed, and heirs to the Promise." We all have an inheritance from God but too few people understand this fact. I used to live in the darkness and never understood that God had promised us certain things. "Whatever you do, do it heartily, as the Lord and not to men, knowing that from the Lord you will receive the reward of the inheritance; for you serve the Lord Christ (Colossians 3:23-24)." Too many people try to please man but that only leads to pain while striving for God leads to an abundant life. So many people out here have the mentality of "barely making it" based on their thoughts and words. The verse above states that we should do everything heartily or with passion. Open eyes means that we understand who we are in Christ and how much power each of us actually has inside.

Sri Nisargadatta Maharaj, one of the greatest sages in India provided much wisdom in his modern spiritual classic, "I Am That". "The false self must be abandoned before the real self can be found." He goes on to say that, "If you are truly earnest and honest, the attainment of reality will be yours." His thesis is that we can all achieve self-realization by being a true seeker of truth. "Humanity's problem lies in the misuse of the mind only. All the treasures of nature and spirit are open to man who will use his mind rightly....Clarify you mind, purify your heart, sanctify your life -- this is the quickest way to change your world." He further stated, "Pain and suffering are only the body and the mind screaming for attention." We must attend to our inner world to move forward. "Heal your mind and it will cease to projects distorted, ugly pictures... But if you disregard all teachings, all books, anything put into words and dive deeply within yourself and find yourself, this alone will solve your problems and leave you in full mastery of every situation, because you will not be dominated by your ideas about the situation." I think the main point here is that we look within and remove the internal limits and labels we put on things.

Life is an experiment with infinite possible outcomes. We must be mindful of the experiment in that there are certain paths or actions which provide for better results. Since its' an experiment, we should learn from its failures. Are you unfulfilled or unhappy? If you want more, you will have to put more in what you are doing. An open mind yields more possible positive outcomes while having a closed mind to doing new things leads to the same results.

God is faithful and just. "I, the Lord, search the heart, I test the mind, even to give every man according to his ways, according to the fruit of his doings (Jeremiah 17:10)." If we believe God is willing to do His part, then we must do our part and become self-aware!

"Who I've been is not as important as who I'm becoming" from Hope for Alcoholics, Addicts, Inmates (And those who love them), submitted by Gary L.

Inspirational Tip for Day #75

Stop what you are doing right now.

I believe that inspiration is everywhere, because God is everywhere. I believe that God is always trying to inspire us to pray more, talk and listen more to Him, turn away from sin and be faithful to the Gospel, as well as doing away with all things which get in the way of our relationship with Him. We are on this planet for such a short time and this season calls us to recognize our dependence on God. Today, be inspired to be more for God! I propose that we can all be inspired by Praying Big, Hoping Big and Loving Big because these three principles are "of God."

"There are three things that will endure - faith, hope and love (Corinthians 13:13)." I find great inspiration in these three concepts.

Pray Big: Prayer moves us closer to God, because it's He who provides all of our inspiration. "The Lord is near to all who call on Him, to all who call on Him in truth, He fulfills the desires of those who fear Him; he hears their cry and saves them (Psalm 145:18-19)." "I say to you, whatever things you ask when you pray, believe that you receive them and you will have them (Mark 11:24)."

Hope Big: Hope is a positive force inside of all of us that we will grow once we decide to believe and fully trust in God. "The Lord is good to those who hope is in Him, to the one who seeks Him (Lamentations 3:25)." Too few people actually utilize the positive energy of hope to realize their dreams. Hope is a powerful tool because it's centered on joyful expectation of receiving God's promises.

Love Big: Loving God and loving others with our whole heart will ignite blessings and move forward your inspired dreams. "I love those who love Me, those who look for Me, find Me (Proverbs 8:17)." This is a promise from God. "A new command I give you, love one another. As I have loved you, so you must love one another. By this all men will know that you are my disciples, if you love one another (John 13:34)." "Love each other deeply, because love covers over a multitude of sins (1 Peter 4:8)." There are different facets to love and we must strive to learn how to love deeply in every way and in healthier Godly ways as well. The love of Jesus Christ creates a deep attachment to the Word of God, and the force of love creates love. He who feels Christ's love, acts as Christ acted. Love enlarges the heart and frees us from the negativity which comes from living in a dysfunctional world. Love is from God and flows through God.

The young man from my class realized that motivation or inspiration was everywhere, even inside. Be encouraged today because there are many people out here who are in a worst situation than you are, and are still encouraged. I have great hope that we will all eventually grow into the people, God wants us to become. J. Keith Miller stated in his book, A Hunger for Healing, "A changed life speaks with a clarity no words can match and that what draws people ... to the church and to God." In 2 Corinthians 5:20, it states that, "We are ambassadors for Christ, as though God was pleading through us; we implore you on Christ's behalf, be reconciled to God."

One of the greatest promises from God is, "If you are willing and obedient, You shall eat the good of the land; But if you refuse and rebel (sin is rebellion), you shall be devoured by the sword; For the mouth of the Lord has spoken (Isaiah 1:19-20)."

Today, I challenge you to Pray Big, Hope Big and Love Big, and you will see blessings rain down on you.

"God dwells within the soul." Saint Teresa of Avila.

"God can be experienced by every person through the presence of the indwelling Christ or Spirit." George Fox.

"Every Human being must be respected because there is "that of God" in everyone." George Fox, founder of the Friends or Quakers movement in 17th century.

"Faith itself has no beauty unless it works by love." Thomas Watson (1620-1686).

Inspirational Tip for Day #76

Stop what you are doing right now.

Today's tip is focused on the benefits of deepening our daily/weekly spiritual practice. I was recently asked why I was so uplifted and happy each day by someone from my church. I explained what my father, a minister, told me, "A person has to make his or her spiritual practice real in order to be changed." "Real" means keeping God at the forefront of my mind each day. For example, if someone yells "Jesus Christ" out loud in jest, I would then say, "is my Lord and Savior." I found that when I placed God first in thought, word and deed, my life became easier. I explained to my friend that when I changed my perspective of how I viewed the world, my heart burst open to God's love and a new way to live came open to me. I decided to keep it simple and go on faith by believing in the following points:

1) I decided to believe that God's words were true and perfect.
2) God loves me unconditionally. God is love, so we must change how we view love because our conditioning of the past has moved us away from the Godly definition of love.
3) The ways of God are mysterious and sometimes incomprehensible but this must not change how I perceive Him or the things I must do for Him.
4) God is who He says He is and can do what He says He can do.
5) We are here for God's pleasure and to serve Him.
6) God has a plan for my life and it is for my ultimate good, even if it doesn't seem that way to me. See point three again. Also, when I make the wrong decision, He still loves me and desires that I learn from my mistakes.
7) I am who God says I am, and I can do what God says I can do.
8) I cannot do it alone. I must put God first in everything I do.
9) There are two forces in this world trying to influence me: the darkness and the light.
10) The current world will attempt to lead me to the darkness while God wants me to choose the light.
11) I can choose which path I want to take. God wishes that I choose Him knowing that when I strive to do His will, my way will be made easier. Choosing the path of darkness, in any way, will lead to a more difficult path for me.
12) How I think matters; how I speak matters; and how I act matters even more.
13) Through a painstaking self assessment, I can begin to turn away from the darkness in order to move closer to my God inspired purpose.
14) I must strive each day to move closer to God and deepen my spiritual practice
15) The enlightenment I have found, can be easily lost.
16) Repeat the steps in order to maintain spiritual, mental and physical balance.

I use the following quote to describe how inner joy can enter our hearts. "Until we have a direct encounter with God's love, it will more challenging to change." Only by deepening our daily spiritual practices each day and week, can we maintain our focus on God and the life He desires us to live.

We can never engineer our own transformation; if we try it will generally be self-centered. "Now we have received, not the spirit of the world, but the Spirit who is from God, that we might know the things that have been freely given to us by God. These things we also speak, not in words which man's wisdom teaches but which the Holy Spirit teaches, comparing spiritual things with spiritual. But the natural man does not receive the things of the Spirit of God, for they are foolishness to him; nor can he know them, because they are spiritually discerned. But he who is spiritual judges all things, yet he himself is rightly judged by no one. For 'who has known the mind of the Lord that he may instruct Him?' But we have the mind of Christ (1 Corinthians 2:12-16)." Spiritual wisdom will save us and allow us to lead a life of purpose and meaning.

"If indeed you continue in the faith, grounded and steadfast, and are not moved away from the hope of the Gospel which you have heard, which was preached to every creature under heaven, of which I, Paul, became a minister (Colossians 1:23)." This is my aim today, to continue in the faith and stay grounded in truth. It's all about striving each day to "have the right relationship with life and God."

"Watch your thoughts; they become word.
Watch your words; they become actions.
Watch your actions; they become habits.
Watch your habits; they become character.
Watch your character; they become your destiny." Anonymous

Inspirational Tip for Day #77

Stop what you are doing right now.

Today we will focus on 'letting go'. When I mention letting go, I mean to let go of the old ideas about ourselves so we can see ourselves as God sees us. Too many people are only partially 'there' for God but God wants us to be 'all in' for him. We are called to be new creations in Christ once we become born again but too many people continue to hold on to old ideas and old values while sprinkling a little Christ here and there. Letting go also means to let go of the old notions of God and serving Him. As a born again believer, we need to cast off and completely let go of 'the old' in order to make way for a new Christ-like life.

First and foremost, we can only move to be who God wants us to be by allowing our faith to increase. The Apostles said to Jesus Christ in Luke 4, "Increase our faith." We often hear that we should, "let go and let God," Although this is a platitude, it's something that everyone should do because without letting go of the old self, we can't reap the great blessings that God wants us to have. Only a surrendered life can obtain total abundance.

Charlotte Sophia Kasl stated in her book, 'If the Buddha God Stuck', "Change requires deep questioning, internal shifts, giving up the known, and often the images of who we think we are." This advice is so amazingly helpful for those who want a better, higher quality of life. Letting go of the old self is a challenge and it can only happen when we understand our infinite and limitless potential through the Holy Spirit. I often tell people that Jesus is the center of my joy, but some people don't understand what that means in practical terms. My joy is connected to what God allowed His Son, Jesus of Nazareth, to do on the Cross at Calvary because of his unconditional love for us. I now have hope because of my faith.

The Apostle Paul wrote the following in Romans 8:25-28, "But if we hope for what we do not see, we eagerly wait for it with perseverance. Likewise the Spirit also helps in our weaknesses. For we do not know what we should pray for as we ought, but the Spirit Himself makes intercession for us with groanings which cannot be uttered. Now, He who searches the heart knows what the mind of the Spirit is, because He makes intercession for the saints according to His purpose." God desires that we share our heart with Him, not a little piece of it, but all of it. He even provides us with the Greater interpreter to help us as we pray. We have all been perfectly positioned to succeed.

Irenaeus stated, "The glory of God is man fully awake, and the life of man is the vision of God."

So many people are sleepwalking through life not understanding their full potential. Letting go of any of the negative perceptions so that love can flow, is an important step in becoming who we were intended to be. I never understood until I sought God with all my heart that the Lord's plans for me were so much greater than I ever imagined previously for myself. Even if we fall down or go through a painful tragedy, God can still use us because He has a plan for our lives. We can become fully awake by letting go of the old beliefs about God, others, and our life purpose. If we are holding any negative beliefs or feelings for anyone, you are holding yourself back.

Love in action is our goal. Love must be sincere and all-encompassing. If you say that you are a Christian and have hatred or unforgiveness inside of you, you are not honoring Jesus Christ. I can declare that this day, I have love for everyone who has crossed my path or ever done me any wrong because I want to become more than I was. I want to honor God by wishing everyone love, light, and inner joy. I came to understand that certain emotions and feelings interfere with how God moves in our lives. The Bible says that there is no darkness in God. God is perfect and our goal should be to get closer to God by rooting out those things from our old life. It's a fact; you cannot claim to be different in Christ, by doing the same old things of the past.

Unconditional surrender to the will of God is the goal for today. Surrender those old thoughts, feelings, emotions, and attitudes of the past so you can receive what God wants to give you. In surrendering, we show that we are fully trusting God completely. Surrendering to Christ is the most important part of living a Christ-like life. Too many people conditionally surrender to God. Our diet each day should include a steady feeding on God's word. God wants us to completely surrender and give Him our total devotion and love.

If your life is not what you want it to be, try something different. When we align our lives with how God sees us and with what God wants for our lives, the Holy Spirit is able to help us navigate the unsteady waters of life. Don't waver when adversity comes on; show God that you are trusting in Him despite of what you may see in the natural. True faith is demonstrated in the valleys as opposed on the mountain tops.

"If you are not reading your Bible every day, then you are not living a Godly life," Charles Stanley.

Once you give God your first fruits, a series of infinite possibilities will start to emerge in your life. Jesus surrendered His life for you and me, we should at least surrender our will to Him. In Isaiah 50:11, we see that walking by our own fires only results in torment of the heart and mind. We cannot do it alone and we were not meant to do it alone. Life is like a one person's race guided by an all-powerful, all-knowing, and all-present God. Without that guide, it becomes infinitely more difficult to run the race.

Be encouraged today, Jesus left us a Comforter to help us, the Holy Spirit. The price has been paid, and the gifts are just waiting for you to pick them up!

On 17 October 2011, Victoria Osteen posted, "God wants us to be constantly growing and rising to new levels in this life...If we are going to experience all that God has for us, we can't just stay where we are; we have to be bold, we have to stretch, and we have to step out of our comfort zones." At the end of her post she said, "Each time you stretch, you are tapping into gifts and abilities He has deposited on this inside of you. Just like treasure hunting, each experience causes you to dig deep into the riches within."

Inspirational Tip for Day #78

Stop what you are doing right now.

Today we will focus on how God is the "God of new beginnings." You can always change what you are doing now in order to create a new future for yourself. If we challenge ourselves to always embrace new healthier ideas, we can move is more positive directions. We hold the creative power of the universe inside of us because we were created in the image of God. "...God breathed into his nostrils the breath of life; and man became a living being (Genesis 2:7). Our nature is divine by definition but too many people remain unaware of the power inside of them. Many people are driven by their demons, often forgetting that greatness is their destiny. Worry, fear, doubt and other negative emotions have taken over their central processing unit.

"Do not fret or have anxiety about anything, but in every circumstance and in everything by prayer and petition with thanksgiving, continue to make your request known to God (Philippians 4:6). 1 Peter 5:6-10 states, "Casting the whole or your care (all your concerns) on Him, for He cares for you affectionately and cares about you watchfully. Be sober, be vigilant; because your adversary the devil walks about like a roaring lion, seeking whom he may devour. Resist him, steadfast in the faith, knowing that the same sufferings are experienced by your brotherhood in the world. But may the God of all grace, who called us to His eternal glory by Christ Jesus, after you have suffered a while; perfect, establish, strengthen, and settle you."

Worry and inner peace do not mix. Fear is the tool of the devil. Many people go through life waiting for the next shoe to drop. It's like they are expecting bad things to enter into their life. When one believes in Christ Jesus fully, a peace settles over them because they understand that even if we suffer a while, God will strengthen and settle us. Too few people actually expect daily blessings in their lives. Now, if you ask them this question, they may say "Praise the Lord, I expect blessings" but their thoughts, speech and actions throughout the day paint a completely different picture. Their thoughts and words invalidate their blessings because it displays a mentality of defeat.

We were meant for so much more but because of the effects of the defeats, sorrows, grudges, unforgiveness, hurts, disappointments and anger -- we become less than who we were meant to be. Life is a journey of infinite possibilities. Does your life say this or are you still putting yourself in a box? Are you still limiting your blessings? Life was meant to be a journey of growth and evolution but many are resistant to their destiny. I have learned that it's my journey; I can choose to use this opportunity for spiritual development and emotional healing. We can always start again because God is faithful in His desire that no one remains lost. As the Bible says, Don't lose heart for in due time, we shall reap.

Aristotle stated that "We cannot learn without pain. Tony Dungy, the former Super Bowl winning coach and player, stated in his book Uncommon, "...and without the negative feedback of pain that God allows in our lives, we would miss many of life's most important lessons (Page 97)." Pain is one of life's greatest teachers, if we learn the lesson and move on.

The key is to put God first; we must each seek the Lord first. Many people turn to God after thinking of all other worldly cures but God wants us to cast our cares on Him first. God, according to His word, wants us to rely on Him fully. The devil wants us to turn away from God and put our faith in every other idol or possibility. God's will is that we lean on Him.

Don't invalidate your blessings by putting your faith in a small box. Eliminate all self imposed limits. Dream big and sing a new song today for there is greatness in your DNA. No more self-imposed limits is the power phrase today. God sees us as limitless. It's time to see yourself the same way, a creation from an all-powerful, all-loving God who wants the very best for you. God is for you and wants you to soar.

As Jesus stated in Mathew 9:29, "...according to your faith, let it be done."

Today, move out in faith and in the direction of your dreams!

Inspirational Tip for Day #79

Stop what you are doing right now.

Today's tip is focused on encouragement. I wanted to provide words of encouragement to everyone out there.

First, everyone should know that God is the Great Encourager! God have provided us 66 love letters (the 66 books in the Bible) to encourage us!

Psalm 32:8, "I (God) will instruct you and teach you in the way you should go; I will guide you with my eye." God wants to show us the way, the right way.

"But those who seek the Lord shall not lack any good thing (Psalm 34:10)." God created us to serve Him and to be His light in the world. We are to be encouragers. By encouraging others, we also encourage ourselves. Jesus was an encourager!

Today, help to build others up, to embolden them to have courage for the journey ahead.

Many people struggle with the weight of the world on their backs, but God made us to be overcomers and more than conquerors. Focus on your God and not your issues. Talk about the greatness of your God and not your problems. The weight of the walk can get heavy at time but God wants us to be His hands by helping others move forward. We can often be inspired through encouraging others.

We were meant for so much more. So today, I am encouraging you to focus on what God is trying to do in your life. There are times when we are so busy going through life that we forget that God creates purpose in the heart of every moment. God guides us and provides opportunities for us to move to higher levels. The dream only dies when the dreamer's fire dies out. We must constantly keep those internal fires stoked.

"But sanctify the Lord God in your hearts: and be ready always to give an answer to every man that asks you a reason for hope that is in you with meekness and fear (1 Peter 3:15)" Many times, once we take our eyes off of our problems and strive to inspire others, our great purpose will become known to us.

"He (God) heals the brokenhearted (Psalm 147:3)." Be encouraged today, knowing how much God wants for you. We were meant to soar, not to be mediocre. Psalm 27:1 states, "The Lord is my light and my salvation, who shall I fear. The Lord is the strength of my life; Of whom shall I be afraid." King David knew what we should all know, we are not in this alone. There are times when God is not going to change our circumstances but instead wants to change us so that our circumstances do not bother us anymore.
God told Joshua, "Be strong and of good courage; do not be afraid, not be dismayed, for the Lord your God is with you wherever you go (Joshua 1:9)." Just as God was with Joshua, God is with us. The same DNA in Joshua, is in us. God wants the best for us. We are the children of God and as such, already have greatness inside of us.

Today, I want to motivate you to give your very best for God, for yourself and to others!

We must remember that the most powerful force in the universe resides in us. In Luke 17:21, Jesus said, "For indeed, the kingdom of God is within you."

Inspirational Tip for Day #80

Stop what you are doing right now.

Today we will focus on "the plank".

Jesus said in Mathew 7:1-5, "Judge not that you be not judged. For with what judgment you judge, you will be judged; and with the measure you use, it will be measured back to you. And why do you look at the speck in your brother's eye, but do not consider that plank in your own eye? Or how can you say to your brother, 'Let me remove the speck from your eye'; and look, a plank is in your own eye? Hypocrite! First remove the PLANK from your own eye, and then you will see clearly you remove the speck from your brother's eye."

Today I wanted to focus on removing the plank in my eye so I can move closer to God. I have lots of planks in my eye. A plank is a stronghold in your life or a weakness, foible, fault or other deficiency. I wanted to focus on burning off those ungodly things in my heart which displeases God. I am striving, making an effort and working hard to change my thinking, speech and actions so that I can be a living testimony to the redemptive power of God's love. I am not judging others but instead am tending to my own garden. I am working on my side of the street so I can be whole and healthy. My focus is my inner world so that I can be a light in this world.

The plank will always cause us problems especially since the devil knows our weaknesses. The devil wants us to not focus on our own issues, but instead on our neighbors, co-workers, spouses, or relatives' problems. Today I wanted to focus on a single issue because it's so important to develop the inner person so that we can allow more blessings to flow into our lives. God wants to help us to truly be His children in every sense.

God promised to deliver us, if we call on His name. Today, I want to focus on my planks so I can be a healthier human being. As I continue to walk in a Godly direction each day, I continue to self-assess and work out my own issues, so my problems don't become your problems. Dealing with our own deficiencies is one of the best ways to honor God.

The devil is known by many names; the thief, satan, the evil one, the adversary and the prince of lies. Jesus describes the devil's job in first part of John 10:10, "The thief does not come except to steal, and to kill and to destroy." The devil wishes to steal your dreams and God's blessings; and kill your ability to move closer to God. The devil knows that when we judge others, we are attempting to usurp the place of God. Also, by judging we are going against the direct wishes of Jesus in Mathew 7:1-5 as detailed above but also in Luke 6:37-42. This was so important that it was recorded in two separate Gospels. When we judge, we take our eyes off of God. The devil is tricky because he knows that if I judge you, I will have the illusion of temporarily feeling better about myself. This will feed my ego which will start to ease God out. When I focus on how wrong you are, it interferes with my ability to look inside of myself. Our goal is to please God, and by His own words, God is the one who will judge us.

Thus, today I am looking for planks in my own eye so I can cleanse my heart to move closer to the mind and heart of God. I am focusing on my 'planks'.

Life question for today: Are there any planks obscuring your vision?

The second part of John 10:10 are Jesus' words, "I have come that they may have life, and that they may have it more abundantly." We are meant to have an abundant life! Be uplifted today because God wants to direct your footsteps into your own personal 'Promise land'.

Jesus explained in John 8:32, "And you shall know the truth and the truth shall set you free." Today, I am looking at my planks so I can become free.

The purpose of this tip is to stress the need to continue self-assess ourselves using Godly principles, so we can continue to transform ourselves into the people God intended us to be.

Inspirational Tip for Day #81

Stop what you are doing right now.

Today's tip is focused on the notion of "life, liberty and the pursuit of happiness" through a God-conscious lens.

This phrase was the notion that Thomas Jefferson made famous as he stated that we have certain inalienable rights. I wanted to use this phrase in a Godly manner. As a Christian, we also have certain rights as the children of God.

Life: Jesus stated in John 14:6, "I am the way, the truth and the life. No one comes to the Father except through Me." I believe that these words highlight the need to understand the words of Jesus deeply and fully through our heart. In Deuteronomy 30:15-19, God stated, "See I have set before you today life and good, death and evil. In that I command your today to love the Lord you God, to walk in His ways, and to keep His commandments, His statutes, and His judgments, that you may live and multiply; and the Lord your God will bless you in the land which you go to possess. But if your heart turns away so that you are drawn away, and worship other gods ad serve them, I announce to you today that you shall perish; you shall not prolong your days in the land which you cross over the Jordan to go in and possess. I call heaven and earth as witnesses today against you, that I have set before you life and death, blessing and cursing, therefore choose LIFE, that both you and your descendents may live." God wants us to have life! Jesus stated in John 10:10, "I have come that they may have life and have it more abundantly."

Liberty: In Luke 4:17-19, Jesus was handed the book of the prophet Isaiah (Isaiah 61:1), and when He had opened the book, He found the place where it was written: "The Spirit of the Lord is upon Me, Because He has anointed Me to preach the Gospel to the poor; He has sent Me to heal the brokenhearted, to proclaim LIBERTY to the captives and recovery of sight to the blind, to set at LIBERTY those who are oppressed; to proclaim the acceptable year of the Lord." Many people are captive to their thoughts and their actions but through Christ, they can be free. Many are spiritually blind and actually are the cause of their own oppression. Anyone can be set free through choosing a better path through Jesus Christ.

The pursuit of happiness: We have to keep on, keeping on while we pursue Godly happiness. The Apostle Paul states in Philippians 2:12-13, "...Work out your own salvation with fear and trembling. For it is God who works in you both to will and to do of His good pleasure." We must strive or pursue what we desire because anything worth having, must be pursued diligently. Psalm 30:5 states, "For His anger is but for a moment, His favor is for life; weeping may endure for a night, but JOY comes in the morning." As it says in Psalms, "This is the day the Lord has made, we shall rejoice and be glad in it." Joy and happiness is a choice for the believer. Jesus stated in John 15:11, "These things I have spoken to you that My joy may remain in you and that you joy may be full." We can have hope in Jesus. "These things I have spoken to you, that in Me you may have peace. In the world, you will have tribulation; but be of good cheer, I have overcome the world." We have many promises in the Bible but these are the a few of the greatest.

Today, I want everyone reading this to live, be free and pursue Godly happiness knowing it's that same thing God wants for you.

"...the Spirit of God dwells in you (1 Corinthians 3:16)." Be uplifted today, know that God is for you and wants the best for you!

Today pray try this short prayer: "Speak Lord, Your servant is listening."

Inspirational Tip for Day #82

Stop what you are doing right now.

Today's tip is focused on 'today'. Living today fully with our eyes on God.

"Do not remember the former things, Nor consider the things of old. Behold, I will do a new things, Now it shall spring forth; Shall you not know it? I will even make a road in the wilderness and rivers in the desert (Isaiah 43:18-19)." God tells us to move forward and not to remember the past. Too many people get distracted by the past and taken off a Godly path. Today is called the 'present', because it's a gift from God. Strive to do a new thing.

The Apostle Paul stated in Philippians 3:12-14, "Not that I have already perfected; but I press on, that I may lay hold of that for which Christ Jesus has also laid hold of me. Brethren, I do not count myself to have apprehended; but one thing I do, forgetting those things which are behind and reaching forward to those things which are ahead, I press towards the goal the prize of the upward call of God in Christ Jesus."

Once we are saved and born again, we are a new creation in Christ. Our thoughts, speech and actions should be different as those still in the world. We must forget the past so we can become the people that God want us to become.

We must move forward with a new perspective, a God-conscious view of the world. "For I rejoiced greatly when brethren came and testified of the truth that is in you, just as you walk in truth (3 John 1:2)." It's important to move forward in truth. The path forward is narrow and can be tricky because there are many diversions. We must stay focused and engaged in the present. Jesus said in Mathew 7:13-14 "Enter by the narrow gate; for wide is the gate and broad is the way that leads to destruction, and there are many who go in by it. 'Because' narrow is the gate and difficult is the way which leads to life, and there are few who find it." The Bible tells us that eye haven't seen not ear has heard that great things God has in store for those who love Him. Anyone can enter but all must strive. I know that I desire to find it. Are you striving this day to find it?

Today, tell yourself that you will strive to keep your eyes on this day, maximizing every possibility, in order to be fully engaged and productive for God.
Be uplifted this day because God is trying to lead you into new areas of abundance; perceive it!

Inspirational Tip for Day #83

Stop what you are doing right now.

Today's tip is focused on complete 'commitment'.

Too few people are actually fully committed to God. We need to fully commit to God by staying in close proximity to His word each day. I love, love, love the mighty Word of God! It gives me such great peace and joy because it speaks to my heart. I never knew what great wisdom, guidance and comfort the Bible had in it. Too many deny the authority of the Bible or deny parts of the scripture. I believe what God says in His word without questions and my life is so much better, easier. I had to stop questioning and start believing without reservations. Reservation will destroy you. The writers of the Bible went through the same things that we are going through today. The Biblical stories could be on the Jerry Springer show or the Maury show today.

"O GOD, You are my God; Early will I seek You; My soul thirsts for You; My flesh longs for You in a dry and thirsty land where there is no water (Psalm 63:1)." Are you thirsting for God each day? Thirst to know more of Him through His word. I like this analogy of thirst because while the body can live without food for weeks, we can only live without water for a few days.

Jesus explained in John 7:37-38, "If anyone thirsts, let him come to me and drink. He who believes in Me, as the Scripture has said, out of his heart flow the rivers of living water." Living water will allow you to traverse those dark times so that you can be led back into the light. When we fully commit to God, an interesting thing happens, blessings and abundance enters our life in the most remarkable ways. Luke 18:27 states that, "What is impossible for men, is possible for God." We all have an inheritance to accept, which comes from fully committing to the way of God, not the ways of man.

"my soul follows close behind You (God); Your right hand upholds me (Psalm 63:8)." If our soul follows close behind God, we will stay in a fully committed mode. When we seek after and pursue God, the quality of our life will change. I am free now on the inside because I am fully committed to God. I am excited to write about God, talk about what God has done in my life. I am excited to spread the Gospel of Jesus Christ. I tend to His garden each day, and trust God to tend to my garden.

"Look to yourselves, that we do not lose those things we worked for, but that we may receive a full reward. Whoever transgresses and does not abide in the doctrine of Christ does not have God. He who abides in the doctrine of Christ has both the Father and the Son (2 John 1:8-9)."

Life questions for us all: Is our daily walk one where we are striving to abide in the doctrine of Christ or are we unsteady in our walk? Do your thoughts, words and actions demonstrate that you have God in you?

Today have a fully committed type of faith. Our faith gives God something to work with. Tell God that you trust His timing and show Him that you are fully committed by learning more about Him through His word each day!

We must be fully committed to God, always seeking to stay true to Him and His 'work' so that we may receive the promised blessings and abundance in our lives. Look back at the stories in the Bible with reassurance and then look forward with hope knowing that God is the same, yesterday, today and tomorrow.

Inspirational Tip for Day #84

Stop what you are doing right now.

Today's tip is focused on "strengthening the inner person" through deepening our spiritual practices through love.

The Apostle Paul stated the following, "that He would grant you, according to the riches of His glory, to be strengthened with might through His Spirit in the inner man, that Christ may dwell in your hearts through faith; that you being rooted and grounded in love, may be able to comprehend with all the saints what is the width, length and height -- to know the love of Christ which passes knowledge; that you may be filled with all the fullness of God. Now to Him who is able to do exceedingly abundantly above all that we ask or think, according to the power that works in us (Ephesians 3:16-20)."

Today, our goal is to focus on strengthening the inner person. The great news is that God will help us to achieve this goal. When we put Christ deeply in our hearts, the reward is peace and inner joy. A deep abiding love of Christ, demonstrated by a changed heart, will give us the knowledge we need for the journey. God wants us to be filled with His fullness. I read this passage and was touched by its richness. It touched the deep recesses of my heart and I felt God's presence inside. The last line of the verse is a great promise. God can do great and abundant things in our life when we seek to Him. Lastly, we already have the power inside of us. We are "of God" and He wants us to have an abundantly full life.

Always keep God at the forefront of your thoughts and heart each day, call on Him and speak with him all throughout the day. He wants us to lean on Him. All that we ask or think is an expression of our love for God. Love will free you and ignite blessings in your life!

Strengthening the inner person requires a commitment to engaging in healthy, spiritual thoughts and habits. There is a path which leads to a rich and fruitful life, that path is love. "How can a young man cleanse his way? By talking heed according to Your word. With my whole heart I have sought You; Oh, let me not wander from Your commandments! Your word I have hidden in my heart, that I might not sin against you (Psalm 119:9-11)." This verse provides guidance on how to stay on the path. In life, people pursue many desires with much passion but God wants us to pursue Him more that those earthly endeavors. In order to move to closer to Him, we must seek to know God with our whole heart. It's easy to wander or drift away from God's word but through diligently seeking God each day by reading His word and hiding it in our heart; we will be in a position to reap all the benefits of being the sons and daughters of the Most High God!

Every morning I start my day with a grateful heart. "O give thanks unto the Lord, for He is good; for His mercy endures forever (Psalm 136:1)." I want to jump for joy each morning at God's mercy because He gave me another chance to praise and serve Him. I have real inner joy today because I understand what God wants for me. I just have to continue to mature in His word, working on cleaning my heart to that I can understand what He wants of me. I cannot enunciate how much I love reading God's word!!

Strengthening that inner person is easy once we allow God's love to touch our hearts each day, and then we can use His love to be love!

Be encouraged today knowing that the love that God has for you is unconditional, and He wants you to have a full and abundant life!

Inspirational Tip for Day #85

Stop what you are doing right now.

Today I wanted to discuss "giving God our best".

I started by asking myself, am I doing all I can each day for God? I realized that I could read more of my bible each day. I discovered that I could do more for God each day. I started allowing God to move even more inside of me. I starting asking myself this question each day, "Am I giving God my best today?" These questions started to lead me in new spiritual directions.

The amazing gospel singer Kirk Franklin has a song called "Give me" where he says, "Get the actors off of stage and let church begin". Ask yourself, "are you one of these actors?

If you move for God each day, you will start to see God moving more in your life. How to give more of ourselves each day when time is finite. I provide the following suggesting using Biblical scripture on how to give God more.

"Be thankful always". Having a mindset of gratitude jump starts an opening of blessings in our life. I thank God for the smallest wonders each day. "In everything give thanks; for this is the will of God in Christ Jesus for you (1 Thessalonians 5:18."

This is the will of God for us to give thanks. If we complain or grumble, we tell God that we are satisfied with what's in our life. When we cease to give thanks, we are going against God's will. "Delight yourself also in the Lord, and He shall give you the desires of your heart (Psalm 37:4)."

"Praise God throughout the day." Having a mindset of faith and belief in God. Many people forgot who God is or how all powerful God is because they start to worry about their little problems or dwell on the issues of this world instead of God. In my church, there is a saying, "When the praises go up, blessings come down. I praise Him while I walk, eat, sit, watch TV and throughout the day. This is also about communicating with God throughout the day because God wants to hear from His people. "Rejoice always, pray without ceasing (1 Thessalonians 5:16-17)."

"Love with your whole heart." Master the Divine art of love. Jesus is calling us to do two things: to consider our own sinfulness and to forgive others. I strive each day to 'be love'. In being love, I strive to love the unlovable because it's easy to love those who love us. Loving with our whole heart is about getting ourselves right with God because God is love. Let's master loving everyone so that God will have compassion on us. Many people want blessings in their life but are unwilling to get right with God.

"That Christ may dwell in your hearts through faith; that you being rooted and grounded in love (Ephesians 3:17). Our faith must be grounded and rooted in love. Our every action should say we serve a loving God. Jesus said in John 13:35, "By this shall all will know that you are my disciples, if you have love for one another (John 13:35)." John recorded more about love in 1 John 4:16, "And we have known and believed the love that God has for us. God is love, and he who abides in love abides in God, and God in him."

"Share the gift of salvation with others." Through our changed heart, we seek to look for opportunities to bless others. Tell others what Jesus has done in your life. Today, I declare that Jesus Christ has saved me and given me a new opportunity to serve Him. Jesus Christ saved my life when I wanted to end my life. I am uplifted and full of inner joy because of what Jesus has done in my life.

Take the opportunity today to help others find the path to salvation. 2 Timothy 4:2 states, "Preach the word! Be ready in season and out of season. Convince, rebuke, exhort, with all longsuffering and teaching." Jesus said in Mathew 28:19-20, "Go therefore and make disciples of all nations, baptizing them in the name of the Father and of the Son and of the Holy Spirit, teaching them to observe all things that I have commanded you, and lo, I am with you always, even to the end of age." This is called the great commission, and it's commanded by Jesus to bring others to the Truth of the Gospel.

"You therefore, beloved, since you know this beforehand, beware lest you also fall away from your own steadfastness, being led away with the error of the wicked; but grow in the grace and the knowledge of our Lord and Savior Jesus Christ. To Him be the Glory both now and forever. Amen (2 Peter 3:17-18)."

2 Timothy 3:16 states, "All scripture is given by inspiration of God, and is profitable for doctrine, for reproof, for correction, for instruction in righteousness, that the man of God may be complete, thoroughly equipped for every good work." We can only be fully equipped by learning and obeying God's word.

If you want to see God move powerfully in your life, move powerfully for God!!
Give God your best today!

Inspirational Tip for Day #86

Stop what you are doing right now.

Today's tip is focused on "Godly positivity"

"But you, beloved, building yourselves up on your most holy faith, praying in the Holy Spirit, keep yourselves in the love of God, looking for the mercy of our Lord Jesus Christ unto eternal life (Jude 20-21)."

There are times when we must build our own selves up in this world. Don't let every negative thing inside of your inner person. Use the Word of God as an anchor to center you on who you were created to be. Don't listen to every negative report or every criticism. Negativity can poison your spirit if you allow it to enter. Stay in peace and trust God to work it out. Don't waste emotional energy on the negative. When others start down that negative path, redirect it to the positive. Don't feed into unGodly thoughts, words or actions.

Stop getting offended at those around you because that takes your mind off God, but instead become focused on God's word and His plan for your life. Offense is another trick of the devil because the evil one wants you to get sidetracked and distracted so that they will take your eyes off of God and way from your destiny. You can't achieve your destiny by focusing on others or the negative. The devil's job is to get you wandering from your path or race. Run your own race, a Godly race!

If we stay focused on the love of God then it will show in our speech, dialogue with others, thoughts and actions. You can't be a positive Godly person, focusing on the negative. Don't let every negative thought grow into worry, when that unGodly thought comes, refocus your attention and energy onto the positive nature of God.

Focusing on your illness, sickness, pains, weaknesses and other negative issues, can limit your blessings because it interferes with what God is trying to do in your life. You can't have a positive life, dwelling on negative people or negative things in your life. Focus on your growth or the lesson God is trying to show you.
Leaning on God is so important because it allows us to move from a spirit of defeat to one of victory. "Now to Him who is able to keep you from stumbling... (Jude 24)."

God will help us to keep from drifting off but we have to seek Him first. I use the example of a home burglar alarm, it only works if you arm it and then lock your door. Just because you have the alarm does not mean it will work unless you do your part, set the alarm and lock the door. Serving and honoring God is the same way, many know of God and attend church regularly but have not allowed God to deeply affect their lives on the inside. For example, when something bad happens in their life, they look to natural solutions before giving it to God. Or, when some little setback comes into their life, they speak negativity or defeat into their lives or just think general negative thoughts.

Proverbs tells us to guard our hearts. It's important to guard what you think about or dwell on. Doing our part means to allow God to continually inhabit our hearts by keeping his Words on our lips. God works! I testify this day that He has changed my life and allowed me to sing songs of joy even under the worse circumstances. Every day and throughout the day, I praise Him! We can praise our way through problems.

In Hosea 4:6, God says, "My people are destroyed for lack of knowledge. Because you have rejected knowledge, I will also reject you from being priest for Me..." Many lack knowledge of who God is, lack knowledge of whose they are, lack knowledge of the power inside of themselves, lack knowledge of the great things God has for those who love Him, and lack knowledge of how God system works.

There are many Christians who can recite verse after verse of scripture but their lives don't demonstrate they have God in their heart. Our God is a positive God and He wants us to have an abundant life! This is why God sent His Son, so that we have life and have it more abundantly!

Today, show God you love Him by trusting Him fully and staying positive. Understand that God gave us His word to encourage us. Sometimes, we have to not look to others to encourage us or inspire us, but we must encourage ourselves. King David wrote the Psalms to encourage himself and future generations. God inspired David so that we would be inspired. Don't let the negativity to enter or poison your spirit.

Charles Stanley states that when discouragement comes on, we need to encourage ourselves like David did in 1 Samuel 30. When David was defeated and his family was taken captive, the people rose up and wanted to stone David. Instead of being dismayed, David encouraged himself. Charles Stanley recommended five ways to encourage ourselves:

1-Pause and be quiet before God. Don't get stressed.
2-Ask God for guidance first.
3-Open the word of God and ask Him where you should read.
4-Recall God's help in previous times.
5. Obey God even if we are fearful.
I think it comes down to staying positive in Godly ways, by living our spiritual practice each day.

Wayne Dyer states in his great book, The Power of Intention, on page 61, "To realize your desires, match them with your inner speech. Keep all inner talk focused on good reports and good results. You inner speech mirrors your imagination, and your imagination is your connecting link to Spirit. If your inner voice is in conflict with your desires, your inner voice will win. So, if you match desires with inner speech, those desires will ultimately be realized."

Joyce Meyer says in the introduction of her great inspirational work, Power Thoughts Devotional, "Many years ago, I was extremely negative. My thoughts were all negative, so the words of my mouth were negative, and therefore my life was negative. When I really began to study the Word and to trust God to restore me, one of the first things I realized was that the negativity had to go.... It wasn't easy, but God taught me that I can choose my thoughts and control the way I think and speak. I don't just have to think every old thing that falls into my head. I can think things on purpose that will positively affect my life. I can think in line with God's Word and speak it as my daily confession. I can overcome negative thinking by setting my mind and keeping it set on things above. And you can too."

All three of the above inspired teachers provide guidance on how to live an abundant life. As Jesus said in John 7:38, "He who believes in Me, as the Scripture has said, out of his heart will flow rivers of living water."

We must guard our hearts. Some translations say 'guard' and the NKJV says, "Keep your heart with all diligence, for out of it springs the issues of life (Proverbs 4:23)." We must maintain a positive countenance no matter what happens; confidently knowing that God is at work behind the scenes.

The Bible says, "If God is for us, who can be against us (Romans 8:31)."

That said, we must be for God. Be love, be positive, be a Godly example to others, be faithful, be a light, be knowledgeable of who God is, be knowledgeable of who you are and how much power God has given you today!

"Everyone is born a genius, but the process of living de-geniuses them." Buckminster Fuller

Inspirational Tip for Day #87

Stop what you are doing right now.

Today, impress God! God is perfect but people are defective and fallible. Too many people try to impress other humans instead of striving to impress God. Let God reign in your life this day. When I speak of impressing God, I mean seeking to please Him. We can please God by striving to walk in love each day, and by having good and honest intentions in everything we do.

1 Corinthians 15:57-58 states, "But thanks be to God, who gives us the victory through our Lord Jesus Christ. Therefore, my beloved brethren, be steadfast, immovable, always abounding in the work of the Lord, knowing that your labor is not in vain in the Lord."

If we aim to please God, we will be rewarded in more ways that just material. Are you tired of the same type of life? Do you want a more abundant life? So many people are still lost or wandering aimlessly through their day with no real purpose or passion. Purpose allows us to live an abundant life. When we seek to impress God by bringing Him our very best, all other things fall into place. Proverbs 20:5 states, "The purpose of a man's heart are deep waters, but a man if understanding draws them out." God is purposeful God and each of us has a God-inspired purpose but misdirected action and negative energy take us away from our purpose.

Miles Munroe states in *The Pursuit of Purpose* that, "Plans change but purpose is constant…Purpose transforms mistakes into miracles and disappointments into testimonies…God's purpose is not hindered by your past…God never requires anything of His creations that He didn't already build into them…You have what you need to be who you are…Purpose permits a view of life that looks beyond the apparent surroundings and the obvious pitfalls…Purpose keeps you focused." God wants us to live purposeful and that happens by striving to impress God!

Choose today, whom you will serve. We should all move to get right with God. Today, why not say something radical like, "Here I am Lord, use me." I decided to a few years ago to help myself by helping others. I was depressed from losing my job and house but once I started focusing on my God instead of my problems the quality of my life improved. Once we get right with God, the stressors or anxieties of the past will be more manageable. I now want to glorify God with my actions. Glorify God this day with your actions and watch God work in your life.

Proverbs 14:12 states, "There is a way that seems right to a man, but in the end the way is death." We need t seek to please God, and impress Him because man's ways will only lead to a dark and painful life.

The life we live is our testimony, it shows whom we love. People, who love God, talk about God. We must stay steadfast by constantly praising and worshipping our Lord instead of focusing on our problems. God loves when we guard out thoughts and words so that they honor Him. When the Hebrews were freed from bondage in Egypt, they left Pharaoh and headed towards the Promised Land but their hearts were still in Egypt. The Hebrews spoke about returning to Pharaoh and their old life in Egypt. We must all leave our own personal Egypt. We must leave Pharaoh too! When we are born again, we must be different in every way. We must walk, talk and speak differently. The Hebrew left their physical captivity but their minds and hearts were still held captive. Let captivity go! Do a new thing today! Can those around you tell that you are a follower of Christ? If not, today is the perfect day to impress God.

David said, "my heart is fixed on God." If you love God, testify for Him! If we profess Christianity, our life should demonstrate a change which directs others to the light.

Jeremiah 15:16 says, "Your words were found and I ate them, and Your word was to me the joy and rejoicing of my heart; For I am called by Your name, O Lord God of hosts." Allow your heart to sing with songs of joy because of who the Lord is and whose you are. Impress God by staying steadfast and walking in love as you go through your day. When our vision is refocused on God, our life changes and becomes fuller and more meaningful.

Have passion for God and learning His word each day. God is impressed when we seek Him with all our heart, soul, mind and strength. Go rewards the faithful!!

Be uplifted today knowing that God wants the best for us, and such, shouldn't we give our very best to Him!!

Inspirational Tip for Day #88

Stop what you are doing right now.

"Pain is inevitable, suffering is optional." Hanuki Murakami author of *What I talk about when I talk about Running*

Too many people choose to suffer by the decisions that they make each day. I found peace through God's word and you can too. Derek Prince discussed in his great book, *Foundational Truths for Christian Living*, the three effects of God's word:

1. *God's word produces faith, and faith, in turn, is directly related to God's word because faith is believing and acting upon what God has said in His word.*
2. *God's word, received as incorruptible seed into a believers hearts, produces the new birth – a new spiritual nature created with the believer and called in the Scriptures 'the new man'.*
3. *God's word is the divinely appointed spiritual nourishment with which the believer must regularly feed the new nature within him if he is to grow into a healthy, strong and mature Christian."*

Life is as simple or as hard as each one of us make it. It's simple but we humans make it so complicated. If we read God's word continually and believe that His word will do what it says it will do, our lives will easier.

We suffer when we forget why God created us; to serve Him. We suffer when we don't understand how much God loves us. We suffer when we lose sight of what God believes about us. We suffer when we are unaware of how we are supposed to live. We must regularly feed our new nature because the world seeks to return us back to our old nature. Once we have clarity of mind and a clean heart, its incumbent on us to maintain healthy habits to continue to walk in truth and love.

God's word is settled in heaven and only through reading the word of God do we know How to live and How to love. Many Christians still do not understand what sin is or how to live by God's word.

Dr. Gene Hooker wrote a book called, *Born a Slave to Sin*, "It is the sin of unbelief that separates mankind from God. It is the sin of unbelief that condemns man. It is the sin of unbelief that sends souls to hell. 'But without faith it is impossible to please Him: for he that comes to God must believe that He is, and that He is a rewarder of them that diligently seek Him (Hebrews 11:6)." It is a sin to disbelieve or doubt God. The request that God answers is the request that is made in faith. But doubt and disbelief cancels our prayer request. Every act we perform is either Godly or it is ungodly, there is no neutral ground in God's service. We are either for Him or we are against Him…There is no need to be confused over whether it is right or wrong, God's word is very clear on rights, wrongs, do's and don'ts for the Christian."

Jeremiah 10:14 states, "Everyone is dull-hearted without knowledge…" The knowledge of God's word will enlarge our heart and allow wisdom to enter it. God has given us the most amazing gift, His word, to help guide us. When Jesus was in the wilderness for 40 days, He fasted and the devil tempted Him by saying, "If you are the Son of God command this stone to become bread. But Jesus answered him saying, "It is written, 'man shall not live by bread alone, but by every word of God (Luke 4:3-4)." The word of God is precious and a light to our feet.

I love the words from God in Deuteronomy 30:20, "that you may love the Lord your God, that you may obey His voice, and that you may cling to Him, for HE is your life and the length of your days; and that you may dwell in the land which the Lord swore to your fathers, to Abraham, Isaac, and Jacob to give." God has promised that He would never leave nor forsake us, and that He wants to lead us to our own personal Promised Land but we must cling or hold fast to His word.

Today, focus on God's word, looking for new insight and new ways to please God because one small step of obedience is a giant step to blessings.

"What lies behind us and what lies before us are tiny matters compared to what lies in us." Oliver Wendell Holmes.

"Sin is the lack of understanding of our purpose." Ravi Zacharias

Inspirational Tip for Day #89

Stop what you are doing right now.

Today, our focus is on having big, Godly dreams! Have a bigger dream for yourself each day. God wants us to constantly be rising in our lives. Nothing stagnant can prosper; we must grow and mature in all areas of our lives. God wants us to increase our knowledge of His will for our lives. God wants every facet of our lives to be prosperous but we need to get rid of small minded or limited thinking. ["And we know that all things work together for good to those who love God, to those are the called according to His purpose (Romans 8:28)."]

Anticipate supernatural increase! ["Eye has not seen, nor ear heard, Nor have entered the heart of man the things which God has prepared for those who love Him (1 Corinthians 2:9)."]

Expect God to do great things in your life. Imagine your future the way you want it. [Jesus said in Luke 12:32, "Do not fear, little flock, for it is your Father's pleasure to give you the Kingdom."]

Conceive it!

God will make it happen but we must have the vision to see out dreams come to pass. [Jesus said in Mathew 19:26, "...With men this is impossible but with God all things are possible."]

Believe it!

Look through eyes of faith and not through what we see in this natural world. Believe that God will pour out His immeasurable favor on you. Expect God's blessings and favor! [Jesus said in Mark 9:23, "If you can believe, all things are possible to him who believe."]

God is constantly planting seeds in our lives so that we can grow into the people He wishes us to become, but it starts with maintaining steadfast faith. Don't let the enemy steal your seeds, your dreams or your joy. God wants you to be filled with hope and love each day. [Jesus said in John 10:10, "The thief (devil) does not come except to steal, and to kill and to destroy. I have come that they may have life, and that they may have it more abundantly."]

Each day, God is trying to promote us and give us greater anointing but we must perceive it. Once we perceive God's presence in our lives, then we must do our part. ["But do you want to know, O foolish man, that faith without works is dead (James 2:20)?"] God is trying to use us, to be His hands in this world. We must remain faithful and encouraged even when things may not appear in the natural to be going well. Where do you dream you will be in one year, five years or twenty years from now? Dreams must be nurtured and the seeds that God puts in our lives must be watered through effort on our part. [Jesus explained in Mathew 21:21-22, "...Assuredly, I say to you have faith and do not doubt, you will not only do what was done to the fig tree, but also if you say to this mountain, 'Be removed and be cast into the sea', it will be done. And whatever things you ask in prayer, believing you will receive."]

Make God first in your life, and watch God work. [Jesus stated in Mathew 6:33, "But first seek the kingdom of God and His righteousness, and all these things shall be added to you."]

Let God's seed grow each day by putting forth the effort to fulfill your God inspired mission. God wants big things to happen in your life because He is a God of abundance. He desires that we increase and mature in every aspect of our lives. God is Divinely abundant and wants us to have a full life. God's dreams for us are so much bigger than our dreams for ourselves. [Jesus said in Mathew 13:18-23, "Therefore hear the parable of the sower: when anyone hears the word of the kingdom, and does not understand it, then the wicked one comes and snatches away what was sown in his heart. This is he who received seed by the wayside. But he who received the seed on stony places, this is he who hears the word and immediately received it with joy; yet he has no root in himself, but endures only for a while. For when tribulation or persecution arises because of the word, immediately he stumbles. Now he who received seed among the thorns is he who hears the word, and the cares of this world and the deceitfulness of riches choke the word, and he becomes unfruitful. But he who hears the word and understands it, who indeed bears fruit and produces: some a hundredfold, some sixty, some thirty."]

Let the seeds of God's favor take root in your life by keeping the Lord first in your life. He is well able to move in a supernatural manner in our lives because He is an awesome God! [Jesus said in John 15:7, "If you abide in Me, and My words abide in you, you will ask what you desire, and it shall be done for you."]

Be full of joy each day! [Jesus said in Mark 6:50, "...Be of good cheer! It is I; do not be afraid."]

Live with enthusiasm because if you don't waiver or grow tired, your miracle is right around the next corner. Change your thinking and expect good things to happen each day to you. ["May the God of hope fill you with all joy and peace in believing so that you may abound in hope by the power of the Holy Spirit (Romans 15:13)."]

Don't take for granted the little miracles each day so that you can be ready for when the great miracle comes. God has plans to prosper you, and He wants you to have zest for the life He has given you. When you get excited about your God, favor and blessings will more easily enter your life. Your destiny can start today when you strive to do what you love. ["But those who wait on the Lord shall renew their strength; they shall mount up on wings like eagles, they shall run and not be weary, they shall walk and not faint (Isaiah 40:31)."]

You purpose is jumpstarted by being passionate about God and serving Him. He is looking for people to bless. The Lord wants to open doors for you and we should expectantly look for His blessings each day. Don't let anyone take your zeal or your joy. Get excited about your life; show God that you want to Glorify Him through your actions. [Jesus explained in John 17:13, "But now I come to You, and these things I speak in the world, that they may have My joy fulfilled in themselves."] Approach life with excitement and enthusiasm, and watch God work. ["This is the day that the Lord has made; we will rejoice and be glad in it (Psalm 118:24)."]

The above promises are encouraging and uplifting for all those who put their trust in God! ["...If God is for us, who can be against us (Romans 8:31)?"] Either we are going to believe His word and live a life which clearly demonstrates God's truth; or we choose to live below our birthright and accept the devil's lies. Choose Life, choose light, choose the Lord and His righteousness this day, and watch God work in your life!

"Blessed is everyone who fears the Lord, who walks in His ways. When you eat the labor of your hands, you shall be happy and it shall be well with you (Psalm 128:1-2)."

Inspirational Tip for Day #90

Stop what you are doing right now!

Today's tip is called "giving up is not an option." Too many people allow "giving up" to be an option on their menu of life but God did not send His son for us to live a defeated life. He has specifically stated that, "But you are a chosen generation, a royal priesthood, a holy nation, His own special people, that you may proclaim the praises of Him who called you out of the darkness into His marvelous light (1 Peter 2:9)." Fear comes from the darkness but the Lord offers light and love to everyone unconditionally!

The absence of faith creates the internal conditions for fear. Too many people live and operate in a constant state of fear. Fear grips, trips and strips away our blessings from God. Fear tells God that we don't believe, and unbelief is a great sin in God's eyes. Fear leads to doubt, despondence, depression, sadness and other negative emotions. The devil loves when we are afraid and don't fully trust God. Fear is not how God designed us to live. There are people out there afraid of everything, even success.

Stop being afraid of the change that God is trying to put in your life. Too many people are scared of the solution that God is share with them. Sometimes, God puts the solution right in front of us but we refuse to accept it. Stop focusing on the fear because it takes away from your divine nature. God is always trying to give us a solution but we are a stubborn people like the Hebrews of the Old Testament who thought they could do it their way. Faith and fear are opposites. You can't be afraid and say that you are trusting in God. Faith will allow you to move through the storms with a great attitude while fear keeps you dwelling on the past.

Opportunity awaits but you must plan for your destiny. If you can overcome your fear then you can reach towards your blessings and ultimately your destiny. Too many people are paralyzed by fear and never reach their Godly potential. We can't believe in people but we can always believe in God. Put your complete trust in God today. Too many people allow the storm to reach deep into their soul. They talk about the past more than they talk about their God. They let the trauma seep in and change the course of their destiny. Everyone has gone through trauma, but we weren't created to stay broken. You must tell yourself that you will not let the spirit of fear into your soul. When fear overcomes our faith, then God's favor is hindered in our lives.

You can make it but you must keep fighting. Fear constrains while faith frees and empowers us. The below scriptures provide clear guidance and truth.

--"Let us hold fast the confession of our hope without wavering for He who promised is faithful (Hebrews 10:23)."
--"But without faith it is impossible to please Him, for he who comes to God must believe that He is, and that He is a rewarder of those who diligently seek Him (Hebrew 11:6)."
--"For God has not given us a spirit of fear, but of power and of love and of a sound mind (2 Timothy 1:7)."

--"There is no fear in love; but perfect love casts out fear, because fear involves torment. But he who fears has not been made perfect in love (1 John 4:18)."
--"Be anxious for nothing, but in everything by prayer and supplication, with thanksgiving, let your request be made known to God (Philippians 4:6)."

Fear is not 'of God'. Fear will always strip, grip and trip you. The good news is that God says that we must operate in faith. Tell yourself that you have hope and help in the Lord! Fear leads to anxiety and to poor health. Many times our poor health can be attributed to inner fears and worries.

Wally Amos the founder of famous Amos Cookie Company and the author of Man With No Name wrote, "When we have faith, we reinforce our subconscious to make our lives move forward and flourish. We create our own circumstances, and our subconscious merely reproduces in our environment what we conjure up in our minds..."

See and seek the future you want. Do not doubt ever. Focus on the daily blessings that God has put in your life. Be thankful for all that has come into your life thus far. Be grateful and stay in faith!

Norman Vincent Peale stated in "In God we Trust, "You can't get much faith through a person who is filled with sin, wrong, and guilt. To have a flow of this power through a personality, to release it, you must have a transformed personality. You have to get rid of hate, ill will, grudges, and sins, for they block power. Only a little power trickles through, not enough to give great strength.

So form in your mind a picture of yourself believing, achieving, what God wants you to do and to be. Cleanse yourself so that His power may get through you. No matter what obstacles are before you, if you will cleanse yourself and believe, you will obtain absolutely astonishing feats."

Throw back your shoulders, let your heart sing, let your eyes flash, let your mind be lifted up. Live with verve and victory and enthusiasm, such as you never lived before. Leave those old negative defeats at the alter of God. And like Joan of Arc, let Him touch your bright and shining sword and storm the walls of defeat to conquer them."

Robert Schuller stated, "I'd rather attempt something great and fail than attempt nothing and succeed." What great work are you attempting this day?"

As God stated in Isaiah 41:10, "Fear not, for I am with you; do not be dismayed for I am your God. I will strengthen you, Yes, I will help you. I will uphold you with My righteous right hand." What a glorious promise. Accept His promise today!

In the Bible, God tells us so many times in His own words that we should not fear but instead have steadfast faith. Today, tell yourself that you will serve the Lord in truth and deed by not living with fear or doubt.

Be encouraged today, for the Lord, your God, loves you unconditionally and wants you to have an amazingly abundant life!

Cicero stated, "Gratitude is not only the greatest of virtues, but the parent of all others.

"I must be willing to give up what I am, in order to become what I will be." Albert Einstein

"Fully functioning, mature persons are continually growing, for they realize that maturity is not a goal, but rather a process..." Leo Buscaglia

Inspirational Tip for Day #91

Stop what you are doing right now.

"For if by one man's offense (Adam and Eve's sin and rebellion) death reigned through the one, much more those who receive abundance of grace and the gift of righteousness will reign in life through the One, Jesus Christ (Romans 5:17)."

Joyce Meyer, one of my most favorite anointed ministers stated, "God wants us to think, speak, and behave rightly, so He gives us what we need in order to do those things. God will never require us to do something without giving us what we need to do it. God gives us the gift of righteousness so we can become righteous in what we think, say and do! (Power Thoughts Devotional March 21)."

It matters how we live every minute of the day. There is a verse in Psalm 19:14 which say, "Let the words of my mouth and the meditation of my heart be acceptable in Your sight, O Lord, my Strength and my Redeemer."

I studied this verse in Psalm and God put it on my heart that everything we do should have the goal of being acceptable in His sight. I started thinking about my thoughts, words and actions to see where I needed work. After an honest assessment, I realized that I had work to do so I could get closer to God. The Bible states that there is no darkness in God, only light. I thought about those times when my thoughts, words or actions were dark or ungodly in nature, clearly unacceptable to God. I analyzed those times where I was unable to hear God's voice and I understood why I felt disconnected from God. It's difficult for us to understand what God was trying to tell us when we walk in darkness, God is love and light.

Today, I challenge all of us to ask this question: Do we know what is acceptable in God's eyes? The Bible provides that knowledge clearly in passages like in Galatians 5:22-25, "But the fruit of the Spirit is love, peace, longsuffering, kindness, goodness, faithfulness, gentleness, self-control. Against such there is no law. And those who are Christ's have crucified the flesh with its passions and desires. If we live in the Spirit, let us also walk in the Spirit." Our goal is to first analyze our own actions and then to repent (turn away) from those which are not acceptable or pleasing to God, in order to begin living and walking in the Spirit. Challenge yourself today to allow the Word of God to dwell deeply inside of you so that the inner change is clearly seen on the outside by others. Be a light to someone else who is still in the darkness.

Many times it's our desire to get angry, hold grudges, be envious or jealous, judge or do other things which are not acceptable to God. Many people are waiting for God to move in their lives, but God requires us to do what is pleasing to Him and then we will be blessed.

God's system is perfect and is designed for us to prosper. We are to live a new life through Jesus Christ but that is not possible doing the same of things that we did in the past. This very moment is a new opportunity to change in a Godly way for Jesus whereby your life can become a testament which glorifies God and bring others to Him! What better legacy could one leave on this planet than for others to see a Christ-like behavior which shows others the way!

Be encouraged this day because God is cheering for you to be who He created you to be!

Inspirational Tip for Day #92

Stop what you are doing right now.

Today's tip is focused on serving the Lord.

"I (God) have given you a land for which you did not labor, and cities which you did not build, and you dwell in them; you eat of the vineyards and olive groves which you did not plant (Joshua 24:13)."

Joshua told the people, "Now therefore, fear the Lord, serve Him in truth, and put away the gods which your fathers served on the other side of the River and in Egypt. Serve the Lord! And if it seems evil to you to serve the Lord, choose for yourselves this day whom you serve, whether the gods which your fathers serves that were on the other side of the River, or the gods of the Amorites, in whose land you dwell. But as for me and my house, we shall serve the Lord (Joshua 24:14-15)."

Our primary job on Earth is to serve and honor God. Many people have either forgotten this or never knew this fact because their lives are so self-absorbed that they have very little time for God. Some of us, me included, have wandered through life having no idea of why we are here on this planet. While others know they should serve God but they still aim for worldly things first and their actions say they serve a different god or idol than the Lord. This latter description was also me at times because my actions said that I didn't have a sincere belief in God, but through the magnificent grace or unmerited favor of God everyone has a choice this day whom they will serve.

Jesus said in Mark 7:6-7, "Well did Isaiah prophesy of you hypocrites, as it is written: 'This people honors Me with their lips, but their hearts is far from Me, and in vain they worship Me, teachings as doctrines the commandments of men." I was guilty of this before I gave my heart to God and allowed Him to work in me. Many people today attend church and say nice godly words but their heart is far from the Lord. I have made a pact with God that I will now serve Him with sincerity and truth. This day would be an excellent day for all people to make the same pact with God, to serve Him in truth.

Jesus stated in John 12:26, "If anyone serves Me, let him follow Me; and where I am, there My servant will be also. If anyone serves Me, him My father with honor." If we serve Him in truth, then God will honor us. God wants us to freely choose Him and serve Him with an open and willing heart. We are to love God with all our heart, soul, mind and strength. I have written about this in previous tips but wanted to say that if we did love God with all our heart, soul, mind and strength then we would serve Him gladly and in truth.

Today, I still fall down and miss the mark because we all sin but I now know my purpose, to serve God with my talents and with my whole being. I want God to one day say to me the same words that Jesus said in the parable of the Talents in Mathew 25:14-21, "Well done, good and faithful servant." All of us have God-given talents and abilities; we must use them to glorify God. Ask God today, "Please show me what I can do to serve You, to honor You with the abilities You have given me. May my life be a living sacrifice of love and effort for Your honor."

So if you have fallen down and have missed the mark as well, shake off the dust from your sandals, get up and start anew knowing that God loves you unconditionally. Leave any shame or guilt in the past because that is 'of satan', not 'of God'. We all have the ability to the people that God wants us to be but it starts with serving Him.

Today is a new day to serve God. The Lord is waiting for His good and faithful servants to return to His service. As Jesus stated in Mathew 6:33, "But seek first the Kingdom of God and His righteousness, and all these things shall be added to you."

Be inspired today knowing that Mathew 6:33 is a grand promise for all of God's people!

Inspirational Tip for Day #93

Stop what you are doing right now.

"The book of the law shall not depart from your mouth, but you shall meditate in it day and night, that you may observe to do according to all that is written in it. For then you will make your way prosperous, and then you will have good success (Joshua 1:8)."

Today's tip is focused on 'good success.' Do you want good success? I think most people would say yes, but are you willing to do what is necessary for good success?

The above Scripture is an amazing promise for us. Living a Godly life will lead to success. God has given us so many wonderful promises in the Bible but the above is one of the greatest of the Old Testament along with the rest of Joshua 1:1-9. Earlier in Joshua 1:5, God says, I will be with you. I will not leave nor forsake you." Many people will read these verses but real faith in the spirit in which it was written will elude them. We have the same promises in our life that Joshua had, if we follow Jesus.

Let's focus on the word 'meditate' in the above verse. God says that we shall meditate on it day and night. Too few people actually mediate on a scripture. Instead, they quickly read a verse of scripture before running to work or before they go to bed. A few minutes of moments of reading God's word will not help us when things go badly or we get down. We must infuse His words into our hearts. To meditate on God's word means that we read a verse with thoughtfulness, believing and absorbing it. Some of you may ask, "How can I meditate on a particular verse when I am so busy?"

Here is one suggestion: We can meditate on it by first writing it down after we read it. Then carry that verse with you during the day, referring back to it often. Ask God to show you how you can apply it to your life. Ask God to help you absorb it into your heart. Look at the verse and pray over it every hour looking from revelation from God.

God doesn't want us to fail. Every Christian must agree with God so as not to live a defeated or 'less than' life. God wants to show us the way to good success as He stated to Joshua. We should not let God's word depart from our hearts or mouths as we go through each day. Our Godliness should always shine through in everything we do.

We are to keep God first in everything but many people's very words set them up for a 'less than' life. God challenges us to be better so that we can glorify Him. God wants us to have good courage and to not be swayed by the storms of life. God told Joshua in chapter 1:1-9 three times to "be strong and of good courage." God knew that it would be possible for Joshua to be afraid when he used natural vision instead of through faith filled lens. Joshua was given the mighty promise of entering the Promised Land but God had to remind him three times how to get there. Why? Because it's easy to get discouraged when we forget the promises of God but the Lord gave us the key by explaining we need to mediate on His word.

Susan Taylor, the former editor of Essence Magazine, stated in her amazing book, *In the Spirit,* "Renew your attitude about yourself…Take charge of the thoughts and feelings you have about your life…Renew your faith in yourself and your oneness with God." I believe that this can only come about by following Gods guidance in Joshua 1:8.

When we put God's word deeply into our hearts; we become calm, fearless and firm walking in confidence because we trust God. There are many people out here who just have not been able to understand the type of life that God wants for them or how to connect with God because they are not allowing God's word to go deeply inside their hearts. If you want to have good success, make an effort each day to meditate on God's word.

Too many people just exists, don't be one of those people. Stay focused and 'in the Spirit' each day by mediating on God's word.

Be encouraged today because God thinks you're special and knows your name (Psalm 139:1-2).

Sufi mystics explain there are two paths of transcendence: one is to look out at the universe and see yourself; and the other path is to look within and see the universe.

"Remember that God will meet your level of expectancy. Reprogram your mind for Godly success and raise your level of expectation by seeing world through a God-conscious lens. Belief starts on the inside, and is demonstrated through our thoughts, words and actions." Philip Allan Turner

Inspirational Tip for Day #94

Stop what you are doing right now.

There is an old quote which says, "A wise man will befriend the sorrows that move into his life." I believe that this statement is about changing our perception. Many people know that right thing to do, but then decide to do the unhealthy or unGodly things which do not lead to an abundant life.

Today's tip is about changing our perspective which allows us to perceive the totality of the blessings entering our lives each day. Everyone who wakes up, is given a gift. Count your blessings each morning when you wake up by thanking God for being who He is, and then your health, next the loving people in your life and then the other wonders which are currently in your life. The gift of life, the gift of another day, is special but many do not perceive this fact. Each day we get a "do over" whereby we can change our path and pivot into the right direction.

Too many people sabotage themselves each day. No one is usually involved in this process except the people themselves. Stop sabotaging yourself today by realizing that it is not God's plan for your life. Each day is a gift where we can vote with our feet. The word sabotage comes from the French word, sabot, which were the wooden shoes they wore to work in the factories of that day. When the workers decided to strike because of poor working conditions, they took their wooden shoes (sabot) and threw them into the machinery which caused a work stoppage. The sabots destroyed the internal mechanisms of the machines. Many people are voting with their feet when they sabotage themselves, as they throw their shoes into their own way.

Too many people fail to pivot but instead keep doing the same things excepting a different result. The physical act of pivoting requires a person to plant their foot and then turn in a different direction but too few people actually turn in a different direction. We can't expect to live a different life by doing the same things from the past.

Past performance is predicative of future results.

"Ponder the path of your feet, and let all your ways be established (Proverbs 4:26)."

Faith in Christ does not make us immune to problems or storms (even the self-inflicted storms) of life. Belief in Christ allows us to understand that there is a great force working to help move us out of the storms with inner peace. Sometimes our inability to love God or ourselves as we should causes us to stumble back into the same traps of the past.

Blake William said, "Life is a series of decisions and living with the consequences." When we pivot into a different direction, we need to change our perspective so that we do things differently. Pivoting is about moving from fear to faith, worry to hope, from loss to gain, and regret to expectancy. Change is natural and scientific because when we get better in dealing with ourselves, our life gets better.

Break the unhealthy patterns of the past. Allow yourself to be free and be loved. Miracles happen each day but many fail to see them for what they truly are.

Jesus stated in John 8:31-32, "If you abide in My word, you are my disciples indeed. And you shall know the truth, and the truth shall make you free."

Too few people are actually on "Team Jesus." What team do your actions say you are on? If we continue in His word, then we are real disciples. Our dedication to Christ is measured by our obedience to His word. If we question His word, resent His word, or avoid obeying His word by interpreting some preferred meaning of our own, we can't live an abundant life. Everyone needs to examine the genuineness of our belief in Jesus by choosing to vote in Godly ways with our feet.

Each of us was created in God's image according to the word in Genesis. In that vein, we were created to be like God in the way we think, act and respond to the events of life. The Apostle Paul urged Christians to stop living like people of the world. Each day, we have to choice to be renewed in the image of God.

Reading the Bible deeply each day helps us to understand several important facts:

--The specialness of maintaining a close relationship with God, and how this relationship will improve the quality of our lives.
--How special we are in God's sight, because He loves us with an unconditional love.
--The type of life that God wants us to live.
--God wants us to see ourselves as He sees us, His greatest creation.
--How seriously God views sin, and how much God wants us to turn from sin.

Our perceptions of life, affect the quality of our lives. Today, focus on having a Godly perspective in everything you do.
Be inspired this day because God wants all of us to live an abundant life!

Inspirational Tip for Day #95

Stop what you are doing right now.

Today's tip is focused on 'happiness'. What is happiness?

Happiness is a state of being attained through Godly living, which is available to all of us. Happiness is not the goal; it's a way of life occurring when we change our thinking, attitudes and the condition of our heart. When a person becomes born again and allows Jesus to completely enter their heart without reservations, the chains of our inner prison will dissolve and happiness because our new state of mind and heart. Reservations will always keep us from living an abundant life, the life that God promised us in His Word. Fully commit today to a better life!

The Apostle Paul wrote from a Roman jail in Philippians 4:11, "For I have learned in whatever state I am, to be content."

Imagine a life where people were content in whatever state they found themselves in. Everyone has a belief system in their minds whether they realize it or now. Many of our belief systems are based on untruths or outright lies. Jesus said the truth will set us free; truth will also lead us to happiness.

Pope Francis tweeted in October 2013, "The secret of Christian living is love. Only love fulfills the empty spaces caused by evil....To follow Jesus means to share His merciful love for every human being."

The Pope's quote is very profound because love is the way to inner joy. Our job is to love others and it's impossible to separate the Christian life without love. We can't have an abundant life, full of inner fulfillment and joy without love, a deep radical type of love which we learn through God's word.

I believe the process of spiritual growth allows us to be content and have inner joy. God is not satisfied with people staying the same, stagnant. The New Testament discusses being a new creation in Christ, moving forward and not returning to things of the past. I believe happiness can be found through the Word of God. When we read the Word of God each day and apply it to our hearts, we start to change because our spirit is being fed in healthier ways.

"Blessed is everyone who fears the Lord, who walks in His ways. When you eat the labor of your hands, you shall be happy, and it shall be well with you (Psalm 128:1-2)." This is a clear formula for all of us when we obey the Lord and work hard, we will be happy.

1 Samuel 3:1 stated, "The Word of the Lord was precious (rare) in those days; there was no widespread revelation." It's the same today where the Word of God is even more precious in this chaotic world we live in. The Word helps us to stay on the right path, a

Godly path. The Word provides encouragement, strength, guidance, faith, hope, love and happiness. I always become so content when I read about how much God loves me and want me to succeed. Happiness can only be found through a specific path founded on the Word of God.

On March 25, Joyce Meyer stated in her great book, 'Power Thoughts Devotional', "The Bible teaches us that our words have power and we get exactly what we speak. Along with that, our thoughts affect our moods and attitudes. In other words, your attitude in life affects your altitude in life, meaning your attitude determines how far you can go in life -- how far you can go in pursuing your dreams, relationships, business, etc."

When we keep our mind focused on God's Words throughout the day, inner joy is attainable. When we think Godly thoughts and speak Godly words throughout the day, happiness becomes our default.

Be encouraged this day knowing that God wants you to be happy!!

Inspirational Tip for Day #96

Stop what you are doing right now.

Today's tip is focused on 'forgiveness' in order to live a more abundant life. Being able to forgive is a skill which needs to be nurtured each day. Forgiveness is so important that several evangelists and ministers have written whole books on it including Joyce Meyer and T.D. Jakes.

Jesus explained in Mathew 6:14-15, "If you forgive men their trespasses, your heavenly Father will also forgive you. But it you do not forgive men their trespasses, neither will your Father forgive your trespasses." Forgiveness is not a request but a command from God for the Christian, just as love is a commandment. I posit that one can't love completely as God commands with unforgiveness in our hearts.

This scripture should be enough regarding forgiveness for those wanting to live a Christ-like life but I wanted to provide some additional details regarding forgiveness. Forgiveness frees us and releases positive energy into the Universe. Letting go not only sends positive energy into the world but also frees our attention to focus on more positive matters. Mother Teresa stated, "To be able to see God in the silence of our hearts, we need a pure heart. A pure heart only can see God; can understand what He speaks to us." Our hearts cannot be pure when we still hold on to old grudges, hurts and pains from the past. A heart filled with unforgiveness is not pure. Unforgiveness takes up emotional space which should be used for love. When I decided to forgive everyone in my life who I perceived had done wrong to me, a peace came over me and I was able to love God more deeply, and the love others more deeply.

I believe that most beautiful example of forgiveness was when Jesus was on the cross in Luke 23:32-32. The passage in Luke explains it simply, "There were also two others, criminals, led with Him to be put to death. And when they had come to the place called Calvary, there they crucified Him and the criminals, one of the right hand and the other on the left. Then Jesus said, 'Father forgive them, for they do not know what they do'..." We, as Christians, are supposed to be Christ-like, meaning that we should follow His example.

God provides us much guidance regarding forgiveness throughout the scripture because He knew we would have a problem with that Godly concept. Colossians 3:13 states "Bear with one another, forgiving one another, if anyone has a complaint against another; even as Christ forgave you, so you also must do."

According to King Solomon in Proverbs, conduct is the best indicator of character. If someone says that he or she is a Godly person, their words can only be proven through consistent actions (Proverbs 20:11). While words and pretty speech can be deceiving, behavior never lies. As followers of Jesus, we demonstrate our love for Him by what we do each day, not just what we say. As love is 'of God', forgiveness is also a Godly trait.

I have released all my past negative and unGodly feelings towards others. I only have love for those who have wronged me in the past. I pray the same for them, as for myself; that we all grow closer to God. And to anyone I have wronged, I am sorry and ask you to forgive me because unforgiveness is not good for you. I wish everyone an abundant life. Loving our enemies is part of our core beliefs as Christians. Jesus explains in Mathew 5:44-45 that if someone is an enemy, we should love them. If they curse us, we should bless them. If they hate us, we should do good to them. If our enemy goes out of the way to hurt us, we should respond by praying for them. God always wants us to respond in love. Everyone who has entered my life in any capacity, I pray blessings over their lives and offer them love.

T.D. Jakes stated in his book, 'Let it Go', "The other insidious danger of not practicing forgiveness is that we become contagious carriers of the very offenses that we ourselves have suffered." Forgiveness is a Christ like attribute while unforgiveness is 'of satan'. Who are you trying more to be like this day? God is asking you to forgive.

Unforgiveness is like a cancer inside of us because it causes other ills within us. Just as untreated cancer spreads throughout the body and starts to kill other systems, so does unforgiveness. Unforgiveness starts to spread to the mind, body and spirit. Unforgiveness is a darkness which can cause all types of physical illnesses because of the resentment and bitterness which can spring from it. Negativity can make you physically sick according to doctors. More importantly, negative feelings like unforgiveness in our hearts interferes with our communication with God, who has no darkness in Him. Unforgiveness is a seed of negativity which grows into feelings of resentment and unkindness spreading through our hearts. Unforgiveness creates negative conditions inside of us which prevents us from hearing God's voice and loving in whole and healthy ways. Unforgiveness leads to pride, moodiness and bitterness. The devil wants you to hold grudges and resentments against others. God wants you to forgive. Who will you follow today?

Many times, the person we are mad at doesn't even remember the offense. We are just carrying that baggage for no Godly reason allowing it to make us bitter, and it consequently interferes with our Godly blessings. Romans 12:17 states, "Never pay back evil for evil to anyone..." Because Christ forgave us for our sins, we are called to do the same.

One of the greatest stories in the Old Testament of forgiveness is Joseph in Genesis 50:15-21. After Jacob dies, the father of Joseph and his brothers, the brothers feared revenge from Joseph. Could Joseph really forgive his brothers for selling them into slavery? But to their surprise, Joseph not only forgave them but reassured them that he would take care of them and their families. Joseph forgiveness was complete and sincere as he explained in the 21st verse, "So therefore, do not be afraid; I will provide for you and your little ones." Because God forgives us even when we do not deserve it, we should also graciously forgive others even when they do not deserve it.

In Luke 11, Jesus taught His disciples to pray. In that prayer, Jesus made forgiveness the foundation of the relationship with God. God has forgiven our sins, so now we must forgive others who have wronged us. To remain unforgiving shows our lack of love for God and His laws. Sin is rebellion to God's laws, so when we do not forgive, we sin.

Forgiveness brings true inner joy. God is perfect and forgives our transgressions and doesn't count our sins against us. Shouldn't we strive to do the same so that we can demonstrate our love for God? Jesus told us to love God with all of our heart, soul and mind. If we truly love God, we should do what pleases Him.

Forgiveness frees you. Do yourself a favor today, let it go. Eject any ill will you may have for anyone. Save yourself by wishing only love and well-being for anyone who has wronged or hurt you. The Bible says that we should pray for our enemies. If you are not where you want to be in life, perhaps there is unforgiveness in your heart holding you back. Perhaps that unforgiveness is preventing you from being who Christ intended you to be. Help yourself this day by forgiving.

"Indeed, man wishes to be happy even when he so lives as to make happiness impossible." Saint Augustine.

"Success is not the key to happiness. Happiness is the key to success." Albert Schweitzer.

"To be without some of the things you want is an indispensable part of happiness." Bertrand Russell.

Inspirational Tip for Day #97

Stop what you are doing right now.

Today's tip is focused on connecting to God in a deep and genuine way.

Are you content? Do you feel powerful or powerless? Are you living an abundant life or just getting by? Too many people just exist from day to day but God wants us to be happy and fulfilled.

Jesus said in John 10:10b, "I have come that they many have life, and that they may have it more abundantly." Later in John 15:11 Jesus stated, "These things I have spoken to you, that My joy may remain in you, and that your joy may be full." Jesus spoke about joy again in John 16:24, "Until now you have asked nothing in My name. Ask, and you will receive, that your joy may be full." John 17:13 provides additional facts about joy from Jesus, "But now I come to You, and these things I speak in the world, that they may have My joy fulfilled in themselves." Jesus spoke about joy so much because it's a destination that is attainable for all, and desired for all by God.

I was recently thinking about why some people 'get it' vis-a-vis their spiritual enlightenment and others do not. Why do some find inner peace through a deep spiritual practice while others continue to go through the motions each week? Religion is supposed to change us by making us better people and moving us closer to God. Once we are aligning our mind to that of God's mind, our perspective changes from a worldly one to a Godly one. We perceive things differently, understanding what's important which provides new clarity and peace.

Why are we here on this planet? Is to collect toys, cars, jewelry, houses, clothes and other natural prizes or is there some other reason why God put us here.

The Bible states that we are here to serve Him and are here for His pleasure. If we are here to serve God then we should seek to enter into a genuine relationship with Him so we can move from having an attitude of this world in exchange for a God-consciousness.

How do we get there?

A person must sincerely want it, a deep and abiding relationship with Jesus Christ. Some people are addicted to their particular negative way of life. Some people are addicted to a type of inner sadness. Too many times in life, people will strive passionately for worldly things, but not for God. What does that say about their commitment to God? What does that type of life say about what we actually love? Too many people are self-absorbed and still wonder why they are living a "less than" life. Only a God-absorbed life can achieve abundance and inner joy.

As Christians until we allow Christ to touch our hearts, change can't occur. Proverbs 23:7 states, "For as a man thinks in his heart, so is he." Thus we have to live by a set of principles which will help transform our heart.

I used to view things through a worldly lens but now I perceive things through a Godly lens. I decided that I could use the paradigm from the world of espionage to help me after I read the Bible and saw that spies were a common theme in there. For example, Moses sent spies to Canaan to reconnoiter the Promised Land, and Joshua sent out spies to Jericho forty years later. Collecting intelligence for the acquirement of political information or military order of battle plans has been going on since the book of Genesis. According to books by former intelligence officers on how to recruit a source, the intelligence officer spots, assesses, develops and then recruits the source. This same method can be used to get closer to God.

Spot - the conditions in which we live; how the enemy works; how God's system operates; and who you are. The below verses of scripture in each section can provide some enlightenment.

--Romans 3:23 states, "For all have sinned and fall short of the glory of God."
--Romans: 6:23, "For the wages of sin is death, but the gift of God is eternal life in Christ Jesus our Lord."
--2 Timothy 4:5, "But be watchful in all things, endure affliction, do the work of an evangelist, fulfill your ministry."
--1 Peter 5:8, "Be sober, be vigilant; because your adversary the devil walks about like a roaring lion, seeking who he may devour."
--Galatians 6:7, "Do not be deceived, God is not to be mocked; for whatever a man sow, that he will also reap."
--Romans 8:6, "For to be carnally minded is death, but to be spiritually minded is life and peace."
--Romans 8:28, "And we know that all things work together for good to those who love God, to those who are called according to His purpose."

Assess - yourself to include strengths and weaknesses, as well as your inner environment.

--1 Corinthians 11:28, "But let a man examine himself..."
--Galatians 6:4, "But let each one examine his own work..."
--2 Peter 3:11, "Therefore, since all these things will be dissolved, what manner of persons ought you to be in holy conduct and Godliness?"
--2 Timothy 3:16-17, "All Scripture is given by inspiration of God, and is profitable for doctrine, for reproof, for correction, for instruction in righteousness that the man of God may be complete, thoroughly equipped for every good work."
--1 Corinthians 16:14, "Let all that you do be done with love."
--Jesus said in John 8:32, "And you shall know the truth and the truth shall make you free."

Develop - your higher, Godly traits.

--Romans 12:2, "And do not be conformed to this world, but be transformed by the renewing of the mind, that you may prove what is good and acceptable and perfect will of God."
--2 Corinthians 10:5, "...Bringing every thought into captivity to the obedience of Christ."
--Jesus stated in Mathew 6:33, "But seek first the kingdom of God and His righteousness, and all things shall be added to you.
--Philippians 2:12, "...work out your own salvation with fear and trembling."
--Ephesians 6:10-11, "Finally, my brethren, be strong in the Lord and in the power of His might. Put on the whole armor of God, that you may be able to stand against the wiles of the devil."
--James 1:22, "But be doers of the word, and not hearers only, deceiving yourselves."
--Colossians 3:2, "Set your mind on things above, not on things on the earth."

Recruit or acquire - your desired results: inner peace, joy, abundance and a deep abiding relationship with God. Once Godly enlightenment is gained, we must maintain healthy spiritual habits to keep us on the path of light and love.

--Galatians 5:22-25, "But the fruit of the Spirit is love, joy, peace, longsuffering, kindness, goodness, faithfulness, gentleness, self-control. Against such there is no law... If we live in the Spirit, let us also walk in the Spirit."
--Colossians 3:14, "But above all these things put on love, which is the bond of perfection."
--1 Corinthians 13:13, "Now abide faith, hope, love, these three; but the greatest of these is love."
--2 John 1:8, "Look to yourselves, that we do not lose those things we worked for, but that we may receive a full reward."
--Ephesians 5:8, "For you were only in darkness, but now you are in the light in the Lord. Walk as children of light."
--1 Peter 2:9, "But you are a chosen generation, a royal priesthood, a holy nation, His own special people, that you may proclaim the praises of Him who called you out of darkness into His marvelous light."

I believe the process listed above, connected to the above anchoring Biblical verses, can assist anyone in getting closer to God and His son Jesus Christ which will lead to an abundant life.

Inspirational Tip for Day #98

Stop what you are doing right now.

Today's tip is focused on sin.

What is sin? It is rebellion from God's law but more specifically it is missing the mark. God has given us a purpose and when we aim sincerely for His target, we enter the zone of blessings. God's favor or blessing zone is where we operate consistently in His system. Of course we fall down but our aim and goals, as a born again believer, has changed because we now know what is pleasing to God.

The wages of sin is death (Romans 6:23) and just one sin is enough to condemn us (Romans 3:23). There are no small sins. There is a key difference is between committing a sin, and continuing to live in willful sin. When we fall down, our job is to repent and then strive to sin no more. Sin keeps us from God's best and hinders our ability to hear God's voice. Everyone sins but our job as the faithful is to not remain in sin by repeating the same mistakes.

In Romans 1:24-25, the Apostle Paul writes, "Therefore God also gave them up to their uncleanness, in their lusts of their hearts, to dishonor their bodies among themselves, who exchanged the truth of God for the lie, and worshipped and served the creature rather than the Creator who is blessed forever. Amen."

The above verse is powerful, insightful and revealing. God has given us the choice of who we want to serve, Him or the devil, the prince of lies. God gave us free will which allows us to grow into the people God wants us to be but for some it's almost a curse as they consistently choose the wrong things.

Many people do not even know what is pleasing or displeasing to God. Now, most Christians know the Ten Commandments but there is much more we need to know as Christians. We need to know what God considers sin to be in order to avoid it.

Living outside of God's laws will lead to captivity; first of the mind, spirit and soul but for some it can then lead to captivity of the body as will. Today's tip is to motivate people to search out what God considers sin in order to please God and live a better life. There is a better, higher way but sin will keep you from that life.

Here are some examples of what displeases God and is considered sin:

"Now the works of the flesh are evident, which are: adultery, fornication, uncleanness, lewdness, idolatry, sorcery, hatred, contentions, jealousies, outburst of wrath, selfish ambitions, dissensions, heresies, envy, murders, drunkenness, revelries, and the like; of which I tell you beforehand, just as I also told you in time past, that those who practice such things will not inherit the kingdom of God (Galatians 5:19-21)." This is clear as the verses describe and it will keep us from heaven.

"But now you yourselves are to put off all these: anger, wrath, malice, blasphemy, filthy language out of your mouth. Do not lie to one another, since you have put off the old man with his deeds (Colossians 3:8-9)."

"But without faith it is impossible to please the Lord, for he who comes to God must believe that He is, and that He is a rewarder of those who diligently seek Him (Hebrews 11:6)." Doubt is a sin and too many people live a life of unsteady doubt instead of a life of steadfast faith.

If a person has a job, they will find out what pleases their employer and seek not to do those things displeasing to their boss. Well, our job is to serve God first and foremost, so we need find out what pleases and displeases God.

"Do not love the world or the things of the world, if anyone loves the world, the love of the Father is not in him. For all that is in the world -- the lust of the flesh, the lust of the eyes, and the pride of life -- is not of the father but is of the world (1 John 2:15-16)."

Unforgiveness, anger, envy, greed, lust, revenge, laziness, judging others and the like are sins and displeases God. The Christian must know the specific details of how to be a servant of Christ. I hope this tip motivates others to read more of the God's word to understand how to live so that they can live an abundant Godly life.

We can choose our own master, the Lord or satan. We must commit ourselves to a Godly life because in Christ we have a new life, new nature and new freedom. Because we love the Lord with all of our heart, soul and mind, we want to please Him.

Christ gives us power but sin keeps us from that power. Remember this verse: "I can do all things through Christ who strengthens us (Philippians 4:13)."

Inspirational Tip for Day #99

Stop what you are doing right now.

Today's tip is focused on the help available to those believers who love God in spirit and truth; His Holy angels.

"The angel of the Lord encamps all around those who fear Him, and delivers them (Psalm 34:7)."

There are mysteries in history which defy explanations. We cannot completely understand the mysteries of the universe but we get a glimpse and a better understanding through God's word. The Bible gives us strength and guidance for daily living. We learn how others dealt with adversity and the tools available to us when we obey God. When a person has a passion for Godly living and an excitement about learning more about their heavenly father, supernatural doors open. No one is perfect but we can become so much better than we currently are. We can also attain a quality of life previously undreamed of when we completely surrender to the will of God. We have great power in us because we are 'of God', and because of the Holy Spirit which indwells in us. Today, I want to discuss another benefit of being a true servant of the Lord; access to His Holy angels.

Holy angels are special, supernatural beings who serve God and help carry out His work on Earth. They bring God's message to people (Luke 1:26), give guidance (Exodus 14:19), carry out punishment (2 Samuel 24:16), patrol the Earth (Zechariah 1:9-14) and fight the forces of evil (2 kings 6:16-18 and Revelation 20:1-2). The Bible discusses angels throughout the Old and New Testaments because they are an extension of the will of God.

Even though angels are usually invisible to us, angels are real because the Word of God says they are. The important part of this concept is that angels are more involved in our daily lives that we realize. One of the primary purposes of angels is to be servants or ministers to those who are to inherit salvation. "Are they not all ministering spirits, sent forth to minister for them who shall be heir of salvation (Hebrew 1:14)."

In Psalm 103:20 we learn, "Bless the Lord, you His angels, who excel in strength, who do His word, heeding the voice of His word." When we obey God and live within His system, we have access to His supernatural ministers. It's all about God and His plans for our lives. When we are in line with God's word, the angels heed His word and assist us. God is able to dispatch any number of angels necessary to do His will.

"For He shall give His angels change over you, to keep you in all your ways. In their hands they shall bear you up, lest you dash you foot against a stone (Psalm 91:11-12)." When we please God through our praise, worship, thoughts, words and actions, we gain supernatural assistance.

Angels have great wisdom because they are, "to know all things that are in the earth (2 Samuel 14:20)." Because the angels follow God's will and have great wisdom, they are interested in God's plans for us, and have roles in those plans.

1 Peter 1:12 states, "To them it was revealed that, not to themselves, but to us they were ministering the things which now have been reported to you through those who have preached the gospel to you by the Holy Spirit sent from heaven -- things which angels desire to look in into." Angels are like God's secret agents who are interested in the well-being of God's other creatures, humans. They are our guardian angels and provide assistance in times of need. By serving God faithfully, we can gain God's favor whereby His angels help us to have an abundant life.

God is the same yesterday, today and tomorrow. What God did for His servant Daniel, He will do for us. "Then Daniel said to the king, 'O king, live forever! My God has sent His angel and shut the lions' mouth, so that they have not hurt me, because I was innocent before Him'... (Daniel 6:21-22)."

Today, be uplifted and encouraged knowing that when you do the will of God, an angel will be encamped around you to assist you in order to have an abundant life!

Inspirational Tip for Day #100

Stop what you are doing right now.

Today's tip is focused on staying teachable, focused and steadfast in faith. Being teachable is an important Godly principle to live by each day.

"These were more fair-minded than those in Thessalonica, in that they received the word with all readiness, and searched the Scriptures daily to find out whether these things were so (Acts 17:11)."

Staying teachable and focused on the word of God is key to having an abundant life. The word of God provides so many amazing benefits. There are 66 books in the Bible and 774,746 words (depending on the translation). In the word is life but we must allow the word to fall on fertile ground in our hearts by reading the words slowly, daily and prayerfully. God speaks to us through His word. When you have a problem, go to the word asking God to show you the answer. If you are a believer, God will speak to you. Reading it slowly allows it to get into your heart; reading it daily allows us to stay steadfast in faith so the seeds are not taken out of our heart; and reading it prayerfully will allow God to clearly speak to us. If you live in the world, you will need to counter balance all the unGodliness that we hear, see and think each day. The Bible's purpose is to teach us but it will not do us any good if we don't want to be taught. Moses, Davis and Paul were all taught by God. When we allow ourselves to be taught God's word whereby we live by it, then we are blessed.

In the Old Testament, the freed Hebrew slaves continued to rebel and stay stiff-necked which caused God to punish them. When we refuse to heed God's word then we are asking to be separated from God's goodness. Ecclesiastes 2:36 states, "God gives wisdom, knowledge and joy to those who please Him." We please God when we listen to Him and obey Him. God never gives us a command without giving us the grace and strength to obey it. That said, we have free will whereby God allows us to decide how we wish to live. Staying teachable gives us to have a Godly perspective, allowing us to move beyond ourselves and our ego and pride.

If you stay teachable, God will restore, your body, mind and spirit. Living in sin has a ripple effect in our lives which cannot be seen sometimes. God's love has the same ripple effects as well. When we stay teachable and aligned with His word, God's favor is allowed to bloom. Some people go to church every week and are still lost. Many of these church goers are not teachable because they hear the word of God but don't allow it to enter their heart and change them. If we are a believer in truth then we will look for ways to live a Godly life. God inhabits the praise of His people but many people speak more about their problems or the world than about the greatness of their God. God is pleased when we speak about Him and revel in His glory.

Nothing is more important than being spiritually fit. Are you spiritual fit? Do you work out daily with God's word through prayer and prayerful reading? God's favor rests on those who walk in His way. Read, heed and seek truth through the word of God. Fully commit today to God by beginning a training program to be more Godly. Are you responding in the same ways to things of the world this year than you did before you became a believer in Christ?

God stated in Isaiah 42:16, "I will lead the blind by ways they have not known, along unfamiliar paths I will guide them; I will turn the darkness into light before them and make the rough places smooth. These are the things I will do; I will not forsake them."

Are you praying for your enemies as the Bible commands or are you still holding grudges? Do you love God with all your heart so that you willingly obey Him? Are you loving all of the Lord's people in the Godly way? Are you learning to love more deeply and fully each day? God is love. Is love the foundation of your operating directive or mere words to you? God does not want you to have a chaotic life but chaos on the inside will only create chaos on the outside.

Are you focused each day on learning more about God? God challenges us in His word to live for Him. Are you meeting God's challenge each day?

Accept the challenge of life, to live your life for God. When you allow God in your life completely, you will feel energized and empowered. "Therefore, He says, 'Awake you who sleep, arise from the dead, and Christ will give you light.' See then that you walk circumspectly, not as fools but as wise, redeeming the time, because the days are evil. Therefore do not be unwise, but understand what the will of the Lord is (Ephesians 5:14-17)." I love this verse because it shows how God is trying to guide us in the right manner. Each day is a gift from God and we must treat it as such.

Be a rock and steadfast in your daily walk. Persevere to the end by continuing on faith and walking in love. We each have the choice of which path we want to walk each day. Are you choosing the healthy path each day or are you too busy to do things which show you actually love yourself.

I believe in the transformative and redemptive power of God's word and His love. We must each have a hunger for the Godly things in life as we have for worldly things. Allowing God to instruct, correct and guide us is part of this process to live a life of abundance. We all have been fully equipped by God for our assignment. Many people still are not using their God-given talents each day. They have allowed the devil to steal their seed. In John 10:10, Jesus stated that, "the thief does not come except to steal, and to kill, and to destroy. I have come that they may have life, and that they may have it more abundantly." The adversary wants to steal your dreams, kill your hope and destroy your destiny. But Jesus has told us in His own words that He came so that we may have a full and a joy-filled life.

God has given each of us a gift for a particular assignment, what are you doing this day to complete your Godly assignment? We each have an assignment. Are you reading God's word each day looking for God to speak to your heart? Jesus says that satan loves bitterness, offense, resentment, unforgiveness and anger. If there are still negative energies or emotions in your heart then you are being held from being your very best, and not allowing Jesus to teach you.

Being teachable for some is the exact opposite of how they live their life; they will resist even the healthiest things. We have a choice each day, to live a "less than" or a "more than" life.

Look inside for strength and happiness first. If you can't find it then you most definitely need more of God's word on the inside. Ask God to teach you and then listen to what His word has to tell you. When you are still bound with unGodly emotions, you are not free to be who God created you to be.

Faith grows when we open up our hearts to Godly principles. Break the chains of mental slavery. Jesus tells us in Mathew 5:6, "Blessed are those who hunger and thirst for righteousness." Later in Mathew 5:48, "Therefore be perfect, just as your Father in heaven is perfect." We can only get there by staying teaching to the word of God. Too many people strive for too little and too few people stay teachable daily.

"The Lord says, 'I will guide you along the best pathway for your life. I will advise you and watch over you (Psalm 32:8)." Why continue to do things your way instead of a Godly way. If you want a better quality of life, where you eat the best fruits God has to offer, and then allow God's word to envelop your heart. Ask God for assistance like David did in Psalm 51:10-12, "Create in me a clean heart, O God, and renew a steadfast spirit within me. do not ask me away from Your presence, and do not take Your Spirit from me. Restore to me the joy of Your salvation, and uphold me by your generous Spirit."

I want to leave you with what I consider 12 important life truths to tell yourself:

1) God loves me unconditionally and needs me to unconditionally surrender.
2) God wants me to have a whole, healthy and abundant life.
3) This life will require me to go through some adversity, pain and disappointments.
4) From adversity, I will learn some valuable lessons.
5) its through these lessons that I learn the real meaning of my purpose.
6) God gave me a guide book (the Bible) which will provide me with encouragement, guidance and wisdom.
7) In the Bible, God advises me to love, forgive and hope without limit.
8) If I follow the wisdom in the Bible, then my path will be easier and more abundant.
9) Believe that God is guiding me to a greater end.
10) Search diligently for the lesson in each moment which God is trying to show me with an open, obedient and willing heart.
11) Have faith that God is in charge and that He has a plan for my life.
12) Stay in constant daily, even hourly communication with God through His word, prayer and meditation, and doors will come supernaturally open.

Today is another chance to be who God wants us to be. Tell yourself that you will make every effort to be steadfast in faith and teachable. Live a radically different today and watch God work!!

"Someday is not a day of the week." From Church Signs: Little Sayings to Help You on Your Way

"I will give you a new heart and put a new spirit within you; I will take the heart of stone out of your flesh and give you a heart of flesh (Ezekiel 36:26)."

The last 80 tips are called Spiritual Refreshers and I begin each with the phrase, "Take this time to spiritually reflect on the following point."

Spiritual Refresher for Day #101

Take this time to spiritually reflect on the following point: Godly perseverance.

"Blessed is the man who perseveres under trial, because when he has stood the test, he will receive the crown of life which the Lord has promised to those who love Him (James 1:12)."

Life gives us tests from time to time and sometimes during these tests there are pop quizzes in life. Each test is a super opportunity to demonstrate our great love for God. satan tests us in the world constantly to see how we will react, to see if we will deny Jesus through our reactions. The adversary (satan) will constantly seek to put adversity in our path. Each time we are tested, it's a glorious opportunity to serve God by reacting in a Christ-like manner. Trials and tests come into our lives in order to test our faith and to strengthen us.

In the book of Job, he lost everything when he was tested by satan. "And Job said, 'Naked I came from my mother's womb, and naked shall I return there. The Lord gave, and the Lord has taken away; Blessed be the name of the Lord.' In all this, Job did not sin nor charge God with wrong (Job 1:21-22)."

Adversity, tests and trials help to strengthen our faith and are part of the journey. We should rejoice when we have an opportunity to show the world that we are new creations in Christ. We should be happy to show unbelievers that we are believers by our attitude. We have a choice each day to serve God by living in light and love. Anyone can say that they are Christian but when the test comes, do others see Jesus living in you?

satan has a job to do each day; he strives to move us away from God and will use anyone for his demonic purposes. Too many people want the blessings but are unwilling to do what is necessary to gain God's favor. There are many 'lite Christians' or part-time Christians out here. The Christian life is built on doing the hard internal work while leaning on the Holy Spirit to help us be Christ-like. Many Christians want to be entertained in church, and then go on living the same type of life during the week. The 'great work' occurs on the inside and is demonstrated through our daily walk. Your job as a Christian is to preserve, reconcile and give hope to those around you.

As Christians, the Bible says that we should be the light of the world. That's what Jesus said in His sermon of the Mount, "Let your light so shine before men, that they may see your good works and glorify your Father in heaven (Mathew 5:16)." When the test comes, show the world a different path by demonstrating love and your new Christ-like behavior.

Today is the day where you could bring someone to Christ through your actions.

Spiritual Refresher for Day #102

Take this time to reflect on this point: Renewing our minds.

Three Biblical verses will anchor this Godly principle:

--Ephesians 4:21-24 says, "If indeed you have heard Him and have been taught by Him, as the truth is in Jesus Christ: that you put off, concerning your former conduct, the old man which grows corrupt according to deceitful lusts, and be renewed in the spirit of your mind."

--Romans 12:2 states, "And do not be conformed to this world, but be transformed by the renewing of your mind, that you may prove what is that good and acceptable and perfect will of God."

--3 John 1:11 says, "Beloved, do not imitate what is evil, but what is good. He who does good is of God, but he who does evil has not seen God."

See God for yourself. Anyone can read the Bible and renew their minds through the power of the Holy Spirit. The Lord only wants our obedience. If we give God our best, then we will be blessed. As a born again believer, we must live differently than unbelievers.

How do we renew our minds?

Jesus' own words provide the solution in John 14:15-18, "If you love Me, keep my commandments. And I will pray the Father, and He will give you another Helper, that He may abide with you forever -- "the Spirit of truth", whom the world cannot receive, because if neither sees Him nor knows Him; but you know Him, for He dwells with you and will be in you. 'I will not leave you orphans; I will come to you.'" Later in John 14:26-27 Jesus states, "But the helper, the Holy Spirit, whom the Father will send in My name, He will teach you all things, and bring to your remembrance all things that I said to you. Peace I leave with you. My peace I give to you; not as the world gives do I give to you. Let not your heart be troubled, neither let you be afraid." The process is clearly discussed above and the Lord will give us the answers we want freely through His word and through prayer.

The Holy Spirit is available to all Christians. All we need to do is to lean on the Holy Spirit for that internal change to take place. We can change our behavior by living intentionally for Christ. Psychologists say that "Behavior is what we do, not what we think, feel or believe." We can change our behavior because as born again believers, we have a Helper.

Ralph Marsden stated, "Excellence is not a skill, it's an attitude." If we step out boldly in faith, we can do anything. Get excited about the life that God has given you each day. Read your Bible daily listening expectantly for God's small still voice. Also, listen to sermons expecting to hear God's voice. Faith is about Godly expectancy. When we read God's word, we need to listen for God's voice asking for the Lord to show us the way.

Renewing one's mind is about seeing things in a Godly manner instead of in the natural. Believe as you read that you are being changed on the inside. Make God's desires, your desires and watch blessings enter your life. Our love of God must be evident in our daily walk and this can only come about when we renew our minds.

Be fearless today, don't wait move towards God in more bold ways. We are all stronger that we know, have faith that God has given you a purpose to fulfill. Diligently strive to fulfill your divine ministry and God will give you the answers you seek.

Spiritual Refresher for Day #103

Take this time to spiritually reflect about this point: Having a God Consciousness.

It's critical to stay engaged with our feelings and attitudes throughout the day. The devil can gain an opening into our lives when we walk around in a spiritual daze. Many Christians still fail to keep God first in their lives on a practical level. Practically, we need to be intentional in maintaining a conscious state where God is constantly at the forefront of our minds.

1 Timothy 1:6 states, "But certain individuals have missed the mark on the very matter (and) have wandered away into vain arguments and discussions and purposeless talk."

We must train ourselves to not allow the devil to gain a foothold. Too many people's internal GPS is fixed closer to the devil's frequency because they respond in ways that are more pleasing to satan then God.

Don't give the devil an opening in your life. The best way to keep the devil at bay is to stay aware of how you feel, what you are thinking, what you are saying and what you do each day. The devil hates when we maintain internal Godly awareness.

"Behold, I give unto you power to tread on serpents and scorpions, and over all the power of the enemy: nothing shall by any means hurt you (Luke 10:19)."

God has given us the power to control our thoughts. When something negative happens to you or a person is unfair or rude or mean to you, your initial reaction may be negative but by being aware, you have the power to immediately view it through a God conscious lens. You can immediately remember an appropriate scripture which will comfort you or you can use that opportunity to forgive as Jesus commands us to do or you can express the Christian value of compassion and pray for them. We have the power and the ability to move beyond our old responses. We can learn to show love in everything we do. Too few people actually use the divine power they have within themselves or the power of the Holy Spirit which dwells in them to respond in more Godly ways.

What you think and what you say matters to God. We reap what we sow. The energy we put out in the world affects the quality of our lives each day.

Today focus on Godly triage: Stay engaged with your thoughts, words, actions and feelings throughout each day. Next, start practicing to respond in more Godly ways by utilizing the tools that the Lord has given us. God has told us in His word that, 'He will never leave nor forsake us'. Believe that you, as a child of God, can like more Christ-like each day. While we can always ask God for help in defeating the enemy, much of it is on us because God has given us all we need to walk in a Christ-like manner, His word. Get in God's word so you can be better equipped for the daily battle.

Today is a new day to walk for Christ in a radically different manner from now on.

Remember the key to living a Godly abundant life is to keep God first, every minute of the day. God wants our total devotion each day!

Spiritual Refresher for Day #104

Take this time to spiritually reflect about this point: A Christ-like attitude.

"This is the day the Lord has made; we will rejoice and be glad in it (Psalm 118:24)."

"You shall be happy, all it shall be well with you (Psalm 128:2)."

"The Lord has done great things for us, and we are glad (Psalm 126:3)."

Jesus said in Mark 6:50, "Be of good cheer!..."

Biblical scriptures speak of having a Christ-like attitude because it's a Godly principle that allows us to have an abundant life.

Viktor Frankl, a Jewish psychiatrist, spent WWII in a concentration camp where he lost his wife and child and a manuscript that was his life's work. In the death camp, Frankl became interested with the question of why some people in the difficult circumstances of the camp quickly gave up and died, while others not only survived but grew stronger. He concluded that the difference was attitude and how various people perceived their experience. He stated, "Everything can be taken from a man but one thing: the last of human freedoms, the ability to choose one's attitude in any given set of circumstances, to choose one's own way."

When we focus on having a Christ-like attitude, we perceive life differently. The greatest way to have a Christ-ness is to put on love and walk in love.

Hermann Hesse stated, "We insist that life must have a meaning -- but it can have no more meaning that we ourselves are able to give it. Because individuals can do this only imperfectly, the religions and philosophers have tried to supply a comforting answer to the questions. The answers all amount to the same thing: love alone can give life meaning. In other words: the more capable we are of loving, and giving ourselves, the more meaning there will be in our lives."

Too many Christians are still angry, unforgiving, impatient and unloving; and they wonder why their lives aren't better. Life gets better when we get better. The best way to put on a Christ-like manner is to love unconditionally as God loves us.

Anais Nun stated, "We don't see things are they are, we see them as we are." Rick Warren expands on this in his amazingly inspiring book, The Purpose Driven Life, when we says, "the way you see your life, shapes your life."

This is why is vitally important to have a Christ-like attitude. Ask yourself this day, in which areas can I have a more Christ-like attitude. Ask God to show you today where you can improve. The Christian walk is one of growth and maturing in His word, if you are not growing then stagnancy will not lead you to an abundant life.

Each day, refocus on developing a Christ-ness in your attitude and maintaining an inner Godly perception, and watch God work!

Spiritual Refresher for Day #105

Take this time to spiritually reflect on these points: Our hearts and walking in the light.

"For God who commanded the light to shine out of darkness, hath shined in our hearts, to give the light of knowledge of the glory of God in the face of Jesus Christ. But we have this treasure in earthen vessels, that the excellency of the power may be of God and not of us (2 Corinthians 4:6-7)."

The Bible is a book which provides God's guidance to believers. The Bible is a simple book for those who read God's word with a willing heart but can be difficult for those who are still living in rebellion. The Holy Book starts out with God giving Adam and Eve a blessed life in Paradise until they rebelled and the fall of mankind takes place. But because God is merciful, man's rebellion did not derail God's plan to fill this natural world with His glory. We have the potential for new life through God's son, Jesus Christ. The Bible provides guidance and wisdom from God of how we can regain a right standing relationship with the Lord so that we can gain everlasting life. In the Bible, God provides examples of how His prophets obeyed and lived an abundant life, while others who didn't obey were punished. We are provided histories of Godly men and women who learned how to live for God. Two themes that ring clearly in the Bible are that we must cleanse our hearts and stay in the light instead of the darkness.

The above scripture records that God wishes His light to shine in our hearts. God is trying to help His people live an abundant life. It's important that we all work on our hearts daily by longing for His light. God sets our hearts aflame that we, like a full moon on a clear night, might cast His brilliant light across the expanse of a darkened world. We must long for the light and declare the goodness of God each day.

1 Peter 2:9 states, "that you may proclaim the praises of Him who called you out of darkness into His marvelous light." Once we understand our mission (to serve God), it's our job to help others find what we have found. One doesn't have to be perfected to help others. When you allow God to work through you, you can bring others to the Truth which also helps you to stay in the light.

Jesus is the light of the world and our job is to connect our inner light with His light each day. Jesus declared in John 8:12, "I am the light of the world. Whoever follows me will never walk in darkness but will have the light of life."

There are many Christians who know about Jesus, but don't actually know Jesus on a personal and intimate level. These "Burger King" Christians want it their way instead of following God in truth and love. "A man's heart plans his way, but the Lord directs his steps (Proverbs 16:9)."

Are you striving to know Jesus more each day by reading His words? What additional time have you given God this day to know Him and His son?

Today focus on walking in the light in more deep and Godly ways whereby you can be a light to others.

Spiritual Refresher for Day #106

Take this time to spiritually reflect on this point: Being strong and of good courage!

The below two verses discusses the Godly principle of being strong and of good courage:

"And David said to Solomon his son, Be strong and of good courage, and do it: fear not, nor be dismayed: for the Lord God, even my God, will be with you; He will not fail you, nor forsake you, until you have finished all the work for the service of the house of the Lord (1 Chronicles 28:20)."

"Be strong and of good courage, fear not nor be afraid of them: for the Lord your God, He is the One who goes with you. he will not leave nor forsake you (Deuteronomy 31:6)."

God understands that in life, we will falter and experience fear from time to time which is why He reminds us 11 times in the Bible 'to be strong and of good courage'. The people we encounter in life can cause us to doubt or be fearful at times but God doesn't desire that His people experience anything but the best out of life. Eleven times in the Bible God reminds some of His greatest prophets to "Be strong and of good courage because even the most Godly people need to be encouraged from time to time. We read this Godly principle three times from the lips of Moses, five times in Joshua, two times from David, and once from Hezekiah.

I believe that there is so much more to the above simple phrase. We should be strong in faith, in sprit, in love and in following the Lord's path. When we follow the Lord's commandment of being strong and of good courage, we are comforted and urged onward even when we don't feel like it because God's words empowers us. Having courage in the face of adversity is how God wants us to live. We should have courage in all that we do even if someone tells us we can't do it then we must keep on pushing forward to achieve our dreams. I don't know about you, but sometimes I forget who I am in Christ because I allow the world to get to me or sway me. I allow ungodly people to influence me and it takes me off my path but I have learned that God's word will take me back to the right path.

Psalm 119:105 states, "Your word is a lamp to my feet and a light to my path." Sometimes when I am daunted or discouraged, I just have to read how God offered encouragement to some of His mighty men and women of valor, and this encourages me.

We should never allow anyone to negatively influence us because God has the final say so in our lives. In Psalm 119:89, we read "Forever, O Lord, You word is settled in heaven." We can all do great things for God but we must stay strong and follow our Godly dreams without being distracted. The devil loves when we are distracted or led in unproductive directions. We should just focus on glorifying God in all that we do. While we may not be Moses, Joshua, Picasso, Shakespeare, Lincoln or Churchill, God has given us many talents which when utilized to glorify Him, will please the Lord.

Remember this day that God wants us to be strong and of good courage. Do everything with Godly strength and courage!!

Spiritual Refresher for Day #107

Take this time to spiritually reflect on this point: living a Godly life.

I wanted to focus on how we can live a Godly life in a fallen world. I first should define what living a Godly life means: It's seeking to know God's divine nature in deeper ways, and then obeying Him. This doesn't mean that we never sin but when we do sin we immediately confess it, repent and then move on. To follow God's path means to come to understand our divine nature and live according to it. Paul stated in Colossians 1:27, "which is Christ in you, the hope of glory." With Christ inside us as born-again believers, we are assured of glory. We may not be sinless but we can live righteously.

2 Peter 1:2 states, "Grace and peace be multiplied to you in the knowledge of God and of Jesus our Lord (1), as His divine power has given to us all things that pertain to life and godliness (2), through the knowledge of Him who called us to glory and virtue (3), by which have been given to us exceedingly great and precious promises (4), that through these you may be partakers of the divine nature, having escaped the corruption of the world through lust (5).

I wanted to break down the above piece of scripture into the five points:

1) When we have Jesus on the inside, He is our focus as we live each day, and it allowed us to know peace because we trust Him and His plan for us.
2) Jesus offers to give us part of His power which will help us to navigate the challenges of life. We will know how to live an upright life in alignment with God because His word provides the necessary guidance.
3) Jesus is calling us to know Him intimately so that we can have a virtuous life.
4) There are so many promises that Jesus has given us but we can only receive it through the indwelling of the Holy Spirit.
5) A divine nature is a holy nature. We can get there by knowing Jesus and allowing the holiness of God to flow through us.

"Now Godliness with contentment is great gain (1 Timothy 6:6)." When we agree to live a Godly life, we invite the Holy Spirit to come in to enable and strengthen us. Jesus says in Revelation 3:19-21, "As many as I love, I rebuke and chasten. Therefore be zealous and repent. Behold, I stand at the door and knock. If anyone hears My voice an opens the door, I will come in to him and dine with him, and he with Me. To him who overcomes I will grant to sit with Me on my throne, as I also overcame and sat down with my Father on His throne." Jesus is ready, willing and able to save us. To ignore Jesus' love is spiritually dangerous because Jesus voice is the voice of love. Jesus says we should be zealous or impassioned for the Godly life in order to achieve salvation. We should be should seek to fellowship with Jesus each day so that He can transform our life. Jesus' voice is the voice of love.

In Rick Warren's The Purpose Driven Life, he states, "There are three barriers that block our total surrender: fear, pride and confusion. We don't realize how much God loves us, we want to control our own lives, and we misunderstand the meaning of surrender." There too many confused Christians out here today. Godly people want to obey God's word. "Therefore be imitators of God as dear children. And walk in love... (Ephesians 5:1-2)." Later in the same book, we learn, "For you were once in darkness, but now you are light in the Lord. Walk as children of light (for the fruit of the Spirit is all goodness, righteousness and truth (5:8-9)."

"Finally, brethren, whatever things are true, whatever things are noble, whatever things are just, whatever things are pure, whatever things are lovely, whatever things are lovely, whatever things are of good report, if there is any virtue and if there is anything praiseworthy -- mediate on these things (Philippians 4:8)." This is the Lord's template on how to live a Godly life.

Each day, we must check our spiritual vital signs, and live intentionally and purposely for God. We should know how God wants us to live, and this happens by diligently reading His word daily. Each day, seek to have a deeper relationship with God. Have a new goal each day, to live a more Godly life. God is light and love, and we receive His promises by seeking after the things which God loves.

Spiritual Refresher for Day #108

Take this time to spiritually reflect on this point: Rejoicing in the Lord!

I wanted to use the two below verses to anchor this spiritual principle:

"Rejoice in the Lord always. Again I will say, rejoice! (Philippians 4:4)."

"Rejoice always, pray without ceasing, in everything give thanks; for this is the will of God in Jesus Christ for you (1 Thessalonians 5:16-18)."

When we rejoice in our heavenly Father, we take our minds off our problems. Too many people are too self-absorbed to enjoy their lives fully. We please God when we focus on rejoicing in Him.

Moving for self-absorbed to being God-focused is the goal of this tip. Too many people talk about their problems, infirmities, injuries, illnesses instead of focusing on the greatness of their God. We are urged to grow in knowledge of God in the scriptures. Becoming mature in God's word should be the goal of all born-again Christians. This above spiritual point is more important than many people realize because when you, "delight yourself also in the Lord, and He shall give you the desires of your heart (Psalm 37:4)."

When one rejoices in the Lord, we seek opportunities to please Him. "My little children, let us not love in word or in tongue, but in deed and in truth (1 John 3:18)." When a person rejoices and delights in the Lord, we want to follow our God in truth and spirit. 1 John 4:19 states, "We love Him because He first loved us." God delights in His people so we should delight in Him.

******
I wanted to note some of my favorite Joel Osteen quotes because he always rejoices in the Lord:

"Quit questioning God and start trusting Him."

"it's vital that you accept yourself and learn to be happy with who God made you to be. If you want to truly enjoy your life, you must be at peace with yourself."

"We may get knocked down on the outside, but the key to living in victory is to learn how to get up on the inside."

"God wants you to have a good life, a life filled with love, joy, peace and fulfillment. That doesn't mean it will be always easy, but it does means that it will always be good."

"Keep doing the right thing. God is building character in you, and you are passing the test. Remember, the greater the struggle, the greater the reward."

"You will never change what you tolerate."

"It's our faith that activates the power of God."

"God will not pour fresh, creative ideas into old attitudes."

"If you can see the invisible, God will do the impossible."

"You may be sitting around waiting for God to change your circumstances. They you're going to be happy, then you're going to have a good attitude, then you're going to give God praise. But God is waiting on you to get up on the inside. When you do your part, God will begin to change things and work supernaturally in your life."

"You must make a decision that you are going to move on. It won't happen automatically. You'll have to rise up and say, 'I don't care how hard this is, I don't care how disappointed I am, I'm not going to let this get the best of me. I'm moving on with my life."

"No matter how many times you get knocked down, keep getting back up. God sees your resolve. He sees your determination. And when you do everything you can do, that's when God will step in and do what you can't do."

I love Joel and Victoria Osteen's ministry because they are great examples of how to always rejoice in the Lord. The above quotes motivated and inspired me, and I hope they do the same for you.

******

When we rejoice in God, we are encouraging ourselves to be who the Lord created us to be. Spend your thought life, rejoicing in the Lord. Each day, be diligent in letting others know what God has done for you. Take an active role in spreading the good news of Jesus Christ to others. Let your speech show the world that you are Christ-like in word and deed! Many people don't realize how much power they have in which direction their lives will go. We can all have an abundant life when we start to have a Christ-ness in everything we do.

Rejoice in the Lord always, and watch God work in your life!!

Spiritual Refresher for Day #109

Take this time to spiritually reflect on this point: Characteristics of the Christ-like believer.

"And when John had heard in prison about the works of the Christ, he sent two of his disciples and said to Him, 'Are You the Coming One, or do we look for another?' Jesus answered and said to them, 'Go and tell John the things which you hear and see: The blind see and the lame walk, the lepers are cleansed and the deaf hear; the dead are raised up and the poor have the Gospel preached to them (Mathew 11:1-5)."

I wanted to break down each of the points explained by the Christ in the above scripture:

Spiritual blindness: When we allow Jesus in our hearts, our natural vision changed. We are no longer blinded by the illusions of the world. We see for the first time in our lives because we now have a God-consciousness when we look at the world. We see through the lens of 'love'. Spiritual blindness keeps us from living up to our full potential. God wants us all to live fully and abundantly whereby we no longer are ignorant to the tricks of the devil; because we see the world through God's scriptures and are not negatively affected by those still walking in darkness instead we are moved to compassion to help show others the way. "The eyes of your understanding being enlightened; that you may know what is the hope of His calling, what are the riches of the glory of His inheritance in the saints, and what is the exceeding greatness of His power towards us who believe according to the working of His mighty power which He worked in Christ when He raised Him from the dead and seated Him at His right hand in the heavenly places (Ephesians 1:18-20)."

Walking in the Spirit: We can now walk in the Spirit when we make our spiritual practices real. We are no longer spiritually blind so we now seek out how to walk daily in the Spirit. In Galatians 5:16-26, the believer learns what it means to have Christ-like characteristics: love, joy, peace, longsuffering, kindness, goodness, faithfulness, gentleness and self-control. Take a few moments and completely read and meditate on this section of Galatians so that you cannot walk lamely or crippled in the world.

Spiritual lepers: Being cleansed through the blood of Christ, we no longer are unclean like lepers of old. Once we begin to end our spiritual blindness by seeing the world through a Godly lens, we begin to walk in the Spirit. This is possible because of the work Jesus Christ did on the cross. We are clean because of the great love God had for us that He sent His son to die for us (John 3:16). Once we encounter Jesus in truth and spirit, we are cleansed of our sins and walk to passionately serve Christ. We have a new aim in life and strive to fully honor the sacrifice of Jesus. Our hearts are cleansed and we passionately seek the things of God, and not man.

Deaf: After we allow Christ to live in us, we now hear the word in ways we could not have imagined. We not only hear God's words through our ears but His words are placed on our hearts as a born-again believer. We can hear God's word in the manner it was intended, to change us so that we become like Christ. We see and hear in a Christ-like manner. We no longer question the Gospel but instead seek for ways to apply it to our lives. We are looking for ways to hear God's voice through the Word. Psalm 46:10 states, "Be still and know that I am God." When we are now living a Christ-like life, we regularly hear God's voice and our life are enriched beyond words. God speaks to us and we can hear it because we have put off the old person and are truly a new creation in Christ.

Alive: We are now alive in Christ and can bring the Truth to others. We understand who we are in Christ and have a passion for life that we never had before. We are spiritually alive and have fully accepted Christ in our hearts. We have fully surrendered and see the beauty of God's system. We are changed and alive for the first time in our lives! We live fully because Christ lives in us. Living according to God's system makes us alive. Ephesians 2:1-10 states, "And you He made alive, who were dead in trespasses and sins..." Take the time to read this short passage because it explains it beautifully. As Paul stated in Galatians 2:20, "I have been crucified with Christ; it is no longer I who live, but Christ lives in me; and the life which I now live in the flesh I live by faith in the Son of God, who loved me and gave Himself for me." This verse is so beautiful because it says how we should live.

Poor in Spirit: Our goal once we start this journey for Christ is to help others gain wisdom and Godly insight as well. This process of helping the poor in Spirit, helps us. So no matter where you are in your walk, help others grow in the knowledge of Jesus Christ. When we accept Jesus completely and willingly in our hearts, we want to obey because we love God with our whole heart. Jesus tells us in Mathew 28:19-20, "Go therefore and make disciples of all nations, baptizing tem in the name of the Father, and of the Son and of the Holy Spirit, teaching them to observe all things that I have commanded you; and lo, I am with you always, even to the end of the age." By telling others our testimony of how God has worked powerfully in our lives, we glorify God and help to bring others to Christ.

The above verses in Mathew were actual miracles done by Jesus but it's also an analogy of how many people live today: blind, lame, deaf, unclean and dead. John the Baptist is not mentioned too many times substantively in the Gospel but Mathew felt that it was important to mention the story of John in prison. John didn't ask for any material objects to make him physically comfortable but wanted to be spiritually comforted by knowing if Jesus was indeed the Anointed One the world was waiting for. John was dedicated to truth in ways that's hard for us to imagine today. We should all desire to have the same characteristics of those touched physically by Jesus because God has given us an opportunity to allow Christ in our hearts!

I wanted to highlight the above scriptures so that you would perhaps see the words of Jesus in a different light. With Jesus in our lives, we are different in every facet. If you are not acting, thinking and speaking in new Christ-like ways each day, then perhaps this spiritual refresher may inspire you to live more fully for Christ each day.

Spiritual Refresher for Day #110

Take this time to spiritually reflect on this point: Faith.

According to the Apostle Paul, "And now abide faith, hope, love, these three: but the greatest of these is love (1 Corinthians 13:13)."

Although no believer can doubt that without love in their hearts, they cannot experience the nature of God. I wanted to speak on faith today. I cannot discuss everything about faith in this short format but instead wanted to focus on a few points to meditate on this day regarding faith.

What is faith?

"Now faith is the substance of things hoped for, the evidence of things not seen (Hebrews 11:1)." Faith is a concept that each believer must understand fully and deeply. Many people say they have faith but the very words don't show that they really do. Is this you?

The book of Hebrew discusses faith so clearly. "But without faith it it impossible to please Him, for he who comes to God must believe that He is a rewarder of those who diligently seek Him (11:6)." True faith acts on and believes in God's Word. God has made ample provision for every need in our life. The Lord just wants us to believe His word and then accept the promises that He has laid out before us.

Our feet (i.e. our thought, words and actions) show our faith each day. Do people see you and think to themselves, there goes a person of deep faith? My goal today is to provide a spiritual refresher to both the reader and myself.

Faith is always spoken of in the present tense because it's what we need to have it daily as a believer. Hope is focused on the future but faith is rooted in the present. True faith should be experienced in the now and practiced in all that we think, say or do daily. Faith is a practice, a daily process of moving closer to God. God wants us to have a steadfast faith and this can only be done by getting deeply into the Word of God each day. The Word of God steadies us, and reminds us of how to live daily in a world full of sin and unbelievers.

There are days that my thought life wavers and I allow certain negative thoughts to come into my mind which doesn't show faith. I have learned that I have full control over what I decide to dwell on in my mind and what I decide to say. I don't have to focus on every random thought that pops into my mind shows doubt. I must always remember that God is my creator and I am His created. I have the choice to believe and when I have any doubts, I go to the Bible for spiritual refreshing.

"So then faith comes by hearing, and hearing by the word of God (Romans 10:17). The Word of God is the key to building faith. The more time the believer spends reading the

Bible, the better equipped they will be to navigate in a world where the devil walks around like a roaring lion.

Anyone can have deep faith. "God has dealt to each one a measure of faith (Romans 12:3)." We are already fully equipped and prepared to live a life of constant faith. We can choose to dwell on uplifting thoughts, believing that God has a plan for us as detailed in Jeremiah 29:11. Take time now to read this verse in Jeremiah.

The Apostle Paul discussed faith throughout many of his epistles. "That He grant you, according to the riches of His glory, to be strengthened with might through His Spirit in the inner man, that Christ may dwell in your hearts though faith; that you, being rooted and grounded in love (Ephesians 3:16-17)." Faith is the 'sine quo non' or essential ingredient for us as believers. In Romans 4:20, Paul wrote that "Abraham did not waver at the promise of God through unbelief, but was strengthened in faith, giving glory to God."

Doubt doesn't please God. Faith pleases God and empowers us because it's the cornerstone of the Christian walk. After Jesus restored the sight of the blind man in Mark 10, He said, "Go your way; your faith has made you well." Faith in Jesus can do amazing things to include moving mountains as Jesus explained in Mathew 17:20. Our faith brings glory to Him.

Faith is discussed so much in the Gospel and in the scriptures because everyone has the potential to doubt and waver but staying in God's word allows us to shake off that doubt. Genuine faith is not based on emotions or feelings but instead upon what God has revealed in His word. I love this short verse in Habakkuk 2:4 which says, "But the just shall live by his faith."

Today, take an honest assessment through a Godly lens of your thought life, speech and actions in order to see where you can increase your faith. The Hebrew word for 'belief' (aman) in the Old Testament also means 'to stand firm, to not waver, to trust, to be certain or sure, or to have faith in something. Faith pleases God and we can all practice our faith in deeper ways each day. Strive (make additional efforts) to demonstrate to God (through your actions) your renewed faith this day, and watch God work in your life!!

Spiritual Refresher for Day #110

Take time to spiritually reflect on this point: God's perfect timing.

In the 11th chapter of the Gospel of John, we learn of the death of Lazarus. When Jesus arrived at Bethany, Lazarus' sister, Martha, tells Jesus that, "Lord, if You had been here, my brother would not have died. But even now I know that whatever You ask of God, God will give to You (11:21-22)." It had been four days since Lazarus had died and Martha had thought that it was too late but Jesus said, "Your brother will rise again." Martha said to Jesus, "I know that he will rise again in the resurrection at the last day." Jesus said to her, "I am the resurrection and the life. He who believes in Me, though he may die, he shall live. And whoever lives and believes in Me shall never die. Do you believe this?" She said to Him, "yes, Lord, I believe that You are the Christ, the Son of God, who is to come into the world (11:23-27)." Jesus told those there to remove the stone in front of the tomb and said, "Lazarus, come forth!" Lazarus arose from the dead.

I retell this story of Jesus as an analogy to show that it's never too late for God because He operates in His own time. We must stay in faith and believe that God's timing is perfect. Even when it seems as if it's too late, God can move in miraculous ways. Martha did her job and believed, and we must continue to do our job and believe as well. When we have faith, we trust Jesus to take care of us in His time, not our time. Many times when we are seeking something to happen now, it would actually be bad for us to get when we want it. God sees all and knows all. God's timing is perfect and when we live in faith and by faith, we can have a stress-free abundant life knowing that God is in charge.

Patience is an important quality when waiting for God to bless us. "But you, O man of God, flee these things and pursue righteousness, godliness, faith, love, patience, gentleness. Fight the good fight of faith...that you keep this commandment without spot, blameless until our lord Jesus Christ's appearing, which He will manifest in his own time... (1 Timothy 6:11-16)."

Part of fighting the good fight of faith is to be patient, fully trusting God, to be God in His magnificence. We should trust God to know what's best for us because the Lord is absolutely sovereign, omnipotently rules everything everywhere. We must understand that God knows the plans He has for us, plans to prosper us and not harm us. Patience is a spiritual virtue that takes practice daily.

Each day, all believers have a job to do and part of that is to walk in faith, living a Godly life. We can have inner peace and joy when we completely surrender to God's will for our lives. We must do our part to strive each day to glorify God in everything we do. Be encouraged this day knowing that God is in charge and His timing is perfect.

Spiritual Refresher for Day #112

Take this time to spiritually reflect on this point: our spirit and the Holy Spirit.

Your inner spirit was made to connect with the Spirit of God. We are directed by God to live a life whereby we walk by the fruits of the spirit. We can't do that alone or on our own, but through the Holy Spirit we can do great things which will glorify God. Although sheer willpower will not get us to where we want to be; the Holy Spirit is ready, willing and able to help us live more fully, in whole and healthy ways.

Ephesians 5:18 simply says, "...be filled with the Spirit." Kenneth and Gloria Copeland write in their book, *He Did It All For You,* that "The Spirit of God living within your spirit can reveal to you the inside of God, the heart of the Father. The Holy Spirit, who knows all the deep things of God, desires to come and live in you to teach you the profound and unsearchable wisdom of God...The deep things of God can enter into the heart of man only by the Spirit of God." 1 Corinthians 2:9-10 discusses the above points.

God's Spirit feeds our inner spirit and empowers us to do more than we can do on our own. People often attempt things by sheer willpower but without actually leaning on the Spirit to help them, it's difficult. It can be a challenge to stop the same old bad habits but the Holy Spirit can help us to actually live a different, higher life. There can't be any real change without taking it out of our hands and putting it into the hands of the Master. The key to tapping into the Holy Spirit is to get deeply into God's word each day, speaking honestly and truthfully with God throughout the day and asking Him to empower us to develop new Godly habits.

Proverbs 18:14 states, "The spirit of a man will sustain him in sickness, but who can bear a broken spirit?" By developing our inner spirit, we will begin to live an abundant live in spirit. There are many Christians out here with a broken spirit and they do not know it. Many of these 'believers' are stuck in their old habits; their old life with a little church window dressed, and are disconnected to the Holy Spirit.

But today is a new day and it's never too late. God is an Awesome Being of new beginnings. Joyce Meyer explains that it's never too late to be the person God called you to be but it requires effort on our part. Anything worth having take effort and developing a relationship with the Holy Spirit is no different. When our spirit connects with the Holy Spirit, a great change begins within us. We start to see things differently and discern things in new Christ-like ways. We must be intentional in striving to connect with the Holy Spirit. Every believer should have a spiritual plan to allow God's spirit to work in them.

The following verses of scripture provide some insight into what is available to you:

"The very Spirit of Jesus Christ is in the believer's spirit (Galatians 4:6)."

"Only your spirit, deep inside you, really knows all that God has given you (1 Corinthians 2:12, 6:19)

"The Spirit of God himself dwells in you (1 Corinthians 3:16)."

"Jesus Christ gives His Spirit to you, and His Spirit gives you life (1 Corinthians 15:47)."

"His Spirit is in your heart (2 Corinthians 1:22)."

"The Spirit of God writes on your heart (2 Corinthians 3:3)."

"The Spirit gives you God's own life (2 Corinthians 3:6)."

"The Power of Christ Himself dwells in the believer (2 Corinthians 12:9)."

"God's Spirit dwells in you (Romans 8:9)."

"Christ Himself is in you (Romans 8:10)."

"The Father dwells in you (Romans 8:11)."

"Go inside where the Lord dwells, in your spirit, to pray (Ephesians 6:18)."

The above verses are promises but they will not be realized until we connect in truth and in spirit with the Holy Spirit. When we live by the spirit of the Bible and passionately search to know more of the Spirit of God, we will be rewarded with wisdom and insight. Our Godly mission is to develop strong spiritual muscles by studying the Bible deeply, and speaking openly and honestly with God throughout the day so that He can show us the things He desires us to know. God wants to be our best friend. As we continue to learn to speak more openly with God daily, He will show us through His scriptures of how we can attain abundance in spirit.

Be uplifted today knowing that there is great power awaiting you. Today choose to live differently, in and through the Holy Spirit, so that you may live the life God envisioned for you, a life of abundance!

Spiritual Refresher #113

Take this time to spiritually reflect on this point: Walls between us and God.

Many Christians still have walls between them and God. Some are mad at God or resentful for things that have come into their life. There are some people who have dwelled for years on these walls which have kept them from knowing God intimately. We are all tasked to draw closer to God but it can only happen when we tear down those walls. Everyone has walls in their hearts but the key is to recognize where these walls are and seek God's help to remove them.

What are walls?

We have walls of unforgiveness, bitterness, anger, hate, envy, greed, resentment, jealousy, complaining, grumbling, disappointment, sadness, doubt, fear, unthankfulness and the other ungodly emotions. satan loves walls because it allows him to get into our hearts, pushing God away.

The anchor verse for this spiritual point comes from James, the half-brother of Jesus Christ. "Draw near to God and He will draw near to you. Cleanse your hands, you sinners; purify your hearts, you double minded (James 4:8)."

God has no darkness in Him, He is pure light and love. Our walls interrupt our communion with God. We are called to draw closer to God but we can't get closer to God with these walls still in our hearts.

James said that we should cleanse our hands and purify our hearts. Many people often use the excuse that they are working on their walls but with Christ in our hearts, we can change in a moment, not years. Too many people limit God and think of God as the unbeliever. God is well able and willing to change us instantaneously. In order to draw closer to God we need to forget our old identities.

Isaiah 43:18-19 provides more guidance for the believer, "Do not remember the former things, nor consider the things of old. Behold I will do a new thing, now it shall spring forth; Shall you not perceive it?"

Too many Christians still view the world through their old self instead of through Christ. Once we understand where we should go, we should look inside to find those ungodly walls. God is well able to tear down the walls so we can glorify Him. I say today with joy in my heart that I am happier and full of a joy because of what Christ has done to my heart.

The change begins on the inside by allowing the Holy Spirit to work on our hearts. Do not leave any mental space for unbelief. Do not leave any room for satan to enter your heart. To activate the power of the Holy Spirit in your life, we all must tear down the walls in our hearts. We all must remove those last remaining walls or any other impediment between us and God. It starts with reading the word, doing more spiritual activities with fellow believers, helping others and most importantly loving others.

God is love and we are called to love Him with all our heart, soul, mind and strength. We are also told to love our neighbor as ourselves. Many people are still struggling with this point and need to allow Jesus fully and completely in their heart so that they can fully accept the glorious promises of Christ.

There is a great song which says, "I'm trading my sorrows...", but we cannot trade our sorrows until we tear down those ungodly old beliefs or attitudes which keep us from God's very best. The lifestyle of the believer should be evident to all those around them, so they be a light in the world to others.

Today, be inspired to act for the Lord! Be in-spirited with the Holy Spirit! Have a passion and enthusiasm for God. If we listen, learn, absorb and embrace God's ways; we will be blessed.

Practice 'wall destroying' spiritual principles today: love, smiling, joy, gratitude to everyone especially those who you have withheld this to in your old life.

Instead of dwelling on your walls, dwell on God's goodness. Allow your heart to sing this day without the walls of yesterday.

Spiritual Refresher for Day #114

Take this time to spiritually reflect on this point: Building Godly character.

Ephesians 4:22-24, "Take on an entirely new way of life - a God fashioned life, a life renewed from the inside and working itself into your conduct as God accurately reproduces His character in you (The Message)."

The New King James version of Ephesians 4:22-24 says, "that you put off, concerning your former conduct, the old man which grows corrupt according to the deceitful lusts, and be renewed in the spirit of your mind, that you put on the new man which was created according to God, in true righteousness and holiness."

I wanted to provide the two translations as a way to provide more clarity on this point. Rick Warren states in The Purpose Driven Life that, "God's ultimate goal for your life on earth is not comfort, but character development.... Christ likeness is all about transforming your character, not your personality."

Later in Pastor Rick Warren's great work, he states, "God wants you to develop the kind of character described in the beatitudes of Jesus (Mathew 5:1-12), the fruit of the Spirit (Galatians 5:22-23), Paul's great chapter on love (1 Corinthians 13), and Peter's list of the characteristics of an effective and productive life (2 Peter 1:5-8). Every time you forget that character is one of God's purposes for your life, you will become frustrated by your circumstances."

Our Godly character can be developed by examining ourselves through a spiritual lens with the focus on our hearts, and then pivoting in a new Godly direction. "The spirit of man devises his ways. Keep your heart with all diligence for out of it are the forces of life (Proverbs 4:23)." Our hearts are the rudders of our ships.

I love Proverbs because it provides such amazing Godly wisdom on how to live and build those spiritual muscles. Proverbs 22:17b states, "And apply your heart to knowledge..." Proverbs 23:12 states, "Apply your heart to instruction..." Knowledge and instruction helps us to build Godly character. In Hosea 4:6, we learn, "My (God) people are destroyed for lack of knowledge..." Godly character is composed of a willingness to learn more about the character of God so that we can become like our Lord.

The heart is the place where Godly character is developed. We each can choose which seeds or ideas we plant in our hearts each day. The heart governs our thoughts, words and deeds. Proverbs 23:7 is my favorite verse because it says, "For as he thinks in his heart, so is he." Godly self assessment and development will lead the believer to paths which are pleasing to the Lord.

How do we build Godly character: By flooding our hearts with the word of God.

There is another verse that is critical, "Therefore be imitators of God as dear children. And walk in love, as Christ also has loved us and given Himself for us... (Ephesians 5:1-2)." The world seeks to separate us from God. Every believer needs to understand how satan works in order to overcome his tricks. "But those things which proceed out of the mouth come forth from the heart; and they defile a man (Mathew 15:18)."

Many people worship in church for an hour or two but the real battle occurs outside of church during the week. Our hearts shows God who we are trying to imitate. "A man's heart deviseth his way (Proverbs 16:9)." Search your heart this day in order to make the necessary adjustments in your life to live in a more Godly way. This is my wish for you and for me.

I wanted to provide six simple verses of scripture to keep in mind when you study the Word of God:

Believe it (John 6:69)
Honor it (Job 23:12)
Study it (Ezra 7:10)
Love it (Psalm 119:97)
Obey it (1 John 2:5)
Preach it (2 Timothy 4:2).

Jesus tells us, "The Kingdom of God is within you (Luke 17:21)." We are given all the tools we need to build Godly character, and the heavy lifting is on us each day. Be encouraged knowing that by building Godly character it's part of the process that God has set before us in order to have an abundant life here and to have everlasting life in the future. Remember that this planet is not our home but a temporary place of residence until we can go home to Heaven.

Spiritual Refresher for Day #115

Take this time to spiritually reflect on this point: Living a spiritually radical life!

For anyone who reads the Bible, it becomes immediately clear that Jesus was a radical, a revolutionary. Jesus taught the truth of God and turned the beliefs of His day upside down. Jesus taught radical love! If you just look at His major concepts such as loving your enemies and how sin starts in the heart, it's easy to see how His radical views was difficult for the people to understand and accept then, and even more so now.

I wanted to focus on the first six phrases recorded in the Gospel of Mathew as spoken by Jesus Christ:

1) "Permit it to be so now, for thus it is fitting for us to fulfill all righteousness (3:15)."
[Our aim is to be righteous or in right-standing with God. Righteousness means that we live a life pleasing to God. Seek to know more of God this day by learning what is pleasing and displeasing to Him through His word.]

2) "It is written, 'Man shall not live by bread alone, but by every word that proceeds from the mouth of God (4:4)."
[How should we live? By God's word. The word of God provides all the direction and guidance a person needs to live an abundant life. The Word of the Lord will keep us uplifted and edified so that we can live the type of life that God intended us to live.]

3) "It is written again, 'You shall not tempt the Lord your God' (4:7)."
[We tempt God by speaking words displeasing to Him and then by expecting God to still bless us. Many people call on God when they need Him while still refusing to by Hi laws. We are told, "Do not be deceived, God is not to be mocked for whatever a man sows, that he will also reap (Galatians 6:7)." When we live a life which is not aligned with God's plans for us, and still expect God's blessings, we are tempting God. Many 'Burger King' Christians -those who want it their way, when they want it- live a life of rebellion and still look to obtain God's best.]

4) "Away with you satan! For it is written, 'You shall worship the Lord your God, and Him only you shall serve (4:10)."
[We are commanded to love God with all of our heart, mind, soul and strength (Deuteronomy 6:5)." Many people still worship idols in their life. The first commandment in Exodus 20:3, "You shall have no other Gods before me." There are people who spend more time with their hobbies then serving their God. Also, there are people worshipping objects, jewelry, cars, houses, alcohol or drugs, and even their own feelings. An idol is anything that interferes with worshipping and serving the Lord. Are there idols still in your life?]

5) "Repent, for the Kingdom of heaven is at hand (4:17)."
[It matters how we live. it matters what we think, say or do because our faith is demonstrated through our actions. Isaiah 29:13 states, "Therefore the Lord said,

'Inasmuch as these people draw near me with their mouths and honor Me with their lips, but have removed their hearts far from Me." God wants our whole heart. If we are still holding grudges or not loving with our whole heart, then we are not honoring God. Jesus came so that we would turn away from our old life in order to embrace a new radical life of living for Him.]

6) "Follow me, and I shall make you fishers of men (4:18)."
[There is two parts to this verse. First, Jesus commands us to follow Him. We should follow Him in truth and in spirit in all that we think, say or do. By following Jesus' teachings by the letter and in the spirit, we will be able to stay on a path pleasing to God. The radical teachings of Jesus leads to having life and life more abundantly (John 10:10). Second, Even in this earliest part of the Gospel of Mathew, we are being commanded to win souls for Christ. Jesus tells Peter that he will become a fisher of men. The Great Commission is that all Christian are commanded by Jesus in Mathew 28:19 to make disciples of all nations. This commission helps all believers to stay on a Godly path.]

I wanted to take these first six simple phrases by Jesus to explain how a believer can live a Godly life from it. Jesus was a radical and wants us to be radical in our faith. We must step out in faith attempting to imitate Jesus. Today, live a radical life of faith by moving forward in Godly new ways. This day, look for opportunities to live according to Jesus' words by living a spiritually radical life!

Spiritual Refresher for Day #116

Take this time to spiritually reflect on this point: God's Grace.

"And after you have suffered for a little while, the God of all grace, who called you to His eternal glory in Christ, will Himself perfect, confirm, strengthen and establish you (1 Peter 5:10)." Joyce Meyer said that the above is one of her favorite verses in the Bible. I was listening to her sermon on grace and I was motivated to further study God's grace.

One study Bible I consulted defined Grace as "God's gift of good things which are not deserved especially salvation." Further, another commentary Bible explained that, "Grace is God's voluntary and loving favor given to those He saves. We can't earn salvation, nor do we deserve it. No religious, intellectual, or moral effort can gain it because it comes only from God's mercy and love. Without God's grace, no person can be saved. To receive it, we must acknowledge that we cannot save ourselves, that only God can save us, and that our only way to receive this loving favor is through faith in Christ."

I realized that grace came back to faith because 'without faith, it's impossible to please the Lord'. The Apostle Paul stressed that nobody is good enough to save himself or herself. If we want to avoid punishment and live eternally with Christ, all of us, must depend totally on God's grace. God offers His grace freely to the believer. I have provided a few verses on grace below:

--"The Law came in so that the transgression would increase; but where sin increased, grace abounded all the more (Romans 5:20)."

--"And He (Jesus) has said to me, 'My grace is sufficient for you, for power is perfected in weakness.' Most gladly, therefore, I will rather boast about my weaknesses, so that the power of Christ may dwell in me (1 Corinthians 12:9)."

--"For by grace you have been saved through faith; and that not of yourselves, it is the gift of God (Ephesians 2:8)."

God's grace is free and available to all believers. As Christians we have access to God's unmerited favor or grace, not as a result of any effort, ability, choice, or act of service on our part. However out of gratitude for this free gift, we seek to help and serve others through love in order to glorify God. Our love of God inspires us to respond to others with a deep love because we want to please God, and not because we want anything from God. We were created to serve God, and the Lord wants us to respond to life's challenges with praise, joy and gratitude.

What else does God's grace provides us?

God's grace gives us power to do things that we never could on our own. Most believers do not understand the power they have inside of them. They limp through life at times not feeling the great power flowing through them because of God's grace. I came to understand that I may not ever fully understand this divine concept as long as I strive to live a Godly life each day. My daily goal is to honor God with my thoughts, words and actions each day, and I realize that if I do things which glorify God, His grace will be with me.

"But He gives a greater grace. Therefore it says, 'God is opposed to the proud, but gives grace to the humble' (James 4:6)."

There are many concepts in the Bible that we may not understand completely but as believers we walk by faith we walk, and that opens up infinite possibilities. I asked God to explain His grace to me and Ephesians 3:16-20 was placed on my heart, "...that He would grant you, according to the riches of His glory, to be strengthened with might through His Spirit in the inner man, that Christ may dwell in your hearts through faith; that you, being rooted and grounded in love, may be able to comprehend with all the saints what is the width and length and depth and height -- to know the love of Christ which passes knowledge; that you may be filled with all the fullness of God. Now to Him who is able to do exceedingly abundantly above all that we may ask or think, according to the power that works in us."

I may not understand God's grace but I felt the Lord place the above verses on my heart to show me that if I am grounded in love, then I will be better able to comprehend how to live a Christ-like life. Grace is free and is offered to those who walk in truth and in spirit because of God's unconditional love for us.

Be encouraged today knowing that your Godly efforts are not in vain!

Spiritual Refresher for Day #117

Take time to spiritually reflect on this point: Pleasing God.

"Most of all, let love guide your life (Colossians 3:14 Living Bible)."

Walking in love pleases God and only by pleasing God can we enter Heaven. There is an amazing song that I love to sing called, "They will know we are Christians by our love." Unless we show unconditional love as Jesus commands us each day, we are not doing our job. Love pleases God and we are told to love God, and then to love others with the same intensity.

The Ten Commandments are an amazing set of laws because six of the commandments deal with our relationship with others, while four deals with our relationship with God. The key to it is about being in a right relationship with God and with others. The only way to do that is through love. I put together a few simple points to keep me focused on my job on pleasing God:

1) Focus on the things that you have in common with others, not the differences. Look for the bit of God in everyone.

2) Realize that everyone is entitled to have a bad day. I have bad days so I know other humans must have bad days too.

3) Showing compassion and kindness to everyone at all times may be the only opportunity a person gets to see our Christ-like character each day. We can actually win souls to Christ by walking in love at all times (emphasis added).

4) Love the unlovable. Pray for those who you have grudges or anger against when you pray for yourself.

5) Make the first move. God expects us to make the first move in love because we will be evaluated by our love.

6) Allow every thought or word you speak be a prayer to God. Honor God in how you think and speak each day. "Every thought should be a prayer. The attitude of prayer should become a habit (Thomas 'Stonewall' Jackson)."

The development of Christ-like character takes time, and it's on us to take the time each day to learn what pleases God and then strive to please Him. Learning to please God in all we do is about building new habits and unlearning old habits. Many believers are still easily swayed by a few harsh words from others. They seek to please their egos and lower self instead of God. If we seek to please God in all that we do, we will start to see God work more powerfully in our lives. Rock Warren states in "The Purpose Driven Life that, "God develops the fruit of the Spirit by allowing you to experience circumstances in which you're tempted to express the exact opposite quality."

"...And we also glory in tribulations, knowing that tribulation produces perseverance: and perseverance builds character; and character builds hope. Now hope does not disappoint, because the love of God has been poured out in our hearts by the Holy Spirit who was given to us (Romans 5:3-5)." It's all about changing our perspective in order to know our true purpose in life.

Once I realized that my job was to serve and honor God, I saw the things which happened to me in a different light, in a spiritual light. My attitude changed and the quality of my life improved significantly. I became free when I started pleasing God and stopped seeking to please man.

"Whatever you do, work at it with all your heart, as working for the Lord, not for men, since you know that you will receive an inheritance from the Lord as a reward (Colossians 3:23-24a NIV).

Too many people are people-pleasers and not pleasers of their God. The people-pleasers will say they put God first but internally, they are still conformed to this natural world instead God's Kingdom. The Bible states that we should first seek the Kingdom of God and then all things will be added to us (Mathew 6:33). Too few people actually live in this Christ-life manner as they are still motivated by the world's material things as well as reacting to people instead of being moved by God. Too many believers are still swayed by shiny objects and the opinions of others instead of spiritual truth. People have a passion for things of the world vice a passion for Christ. When our aim stays fixed on Christ, the quality of our life will increase.

I can testify this day that God-pleasers will eat from the best of the Lord. My life became blessed when I surrendered to the Lord and acquired a new life goal, to be a pleaser of God.

Be uplifted today knowing that there is a better way, a Godly way which is grounded in love and leads to abundance!

Spiritual Refresher for Day #118

Take this time to spiritually reflect on this point: Serving the Lord.

The four anchor verses for this principle are provided below:

1) "And it shall be that if your earnestly obey My commandments which I command you today, to love the Lord your God and serve Him with all your heart and with your soul (Deuteronomy 11:13)."

2) "Then Samuel said to the people, 'Do not fear. You have done all this wickedness; yet do not turn aside from following the Lord, but serve the Lord with all your heart (1 Samuel 12:20)."

3) The Apostle Paul wrote, "For God is my witness, whom I serve with my spirit in the gospel of His son, that without ceasing I make mentions of you always in my prayers (Romans 1:9)."

4) The Apostle Paul also wrote, "Not with eye service, as men pleasers, but as bondservants of Christ, doing the will of God from the heart (Ephesians 6:6)."

We are called to serve God with all our heart and soul in the first verse. When a person is earnest in serving God, they do it in order to honor and bring glory to God. "Whatever you do, do it all for the glory of God (1 Corinthians 10:31)." Loving God goes hand and hand with serving Him. We were created to serve God and our true purpose in life can only be found through the Lord. Many people want meaning and purpose in their lives but they can't get it chasing things of this world. Meaning and purpose comes from serving God.

Samuel explained to the people that they needed to serve God with their whole hearts, and Paul's apostleship was a testament to fully serving God. Many people are looking for God to bless their lives but the best way to get a blessing, is to be a blessing to others. When we help others, we are also ministering to them as Jesus explained that He came to serve, not to be served. "Just as the Son of Man did not come to be served, but to serve, and to give His life as a ransom for many (Mathew 20:28)."

In John 13, Jesus washed the feet of His disciples. God gave His Son to the cross so that we may have everlasting life. Jesus came to serve as a ransom for our sins so that we could have salvation; and it's in that spirit we should willingly help others and serve God diligently.

Today, I have a passion and enthusiasm for God, and all things Christ related. I wasn't always this way but when I suffered tragedy in my life, I turned to God and a new way of life emerged. I started reading the Bible and got deeply into the 'Word' where I found true inner peace. My 'life-quake' was the best thing that ever happened to me because it opened the eyes of my heart and God's great love poured in. I learned to love God with all my heart, soul and mind - in truth and in spirit. In turn, I learned to love myself and then started loving others as well. It's still a challenge to love others as myself but I am getting better each day because it's a part of serving God.

Another aspect of serving God as a Christian is to bring others to Him. As believers, we strive to win souls for Christ because we love Him and want others to find what we have found through Christ. Every believer has a unique ministry which can be used to glorify the Lord. Rick Warren's states in his great book, 'A Purpose Driven Life', "In the Bible, the word 'minister' and 'servant' are synonyms, just as ministry and service. If you are a Christian, you are a minister, and when you're serving, you're ministering."

The passion that I have for God is expressed in my attitude daily because one way I serve the Lord is with a Godly attitude and by showing love for others. I serve God by trusting him to be who He says He is, and believing that He has a plan for my life. I serve God by sponsoring a daily prayer group and teaching free classes to others. I give of myself so that others can see the Christ in me, which glorifies God. I strive to be an ambassador for Christ by sharing my gifts to those who don't know Christ. When asked why I do what I do, I say, "I do this to glorify God because as Christians we are known by our love." My testimony is demonstrated through my actions. I serve God when I tutor men in reading skills and when I teach public speaking. I give lectures on what God has done in my life and in my heart. When I pray, I ask God to send me to help others. Today, seek to serve God by finding a way to help others for no personal gain.

One of my favorite verses in the Bible about serving God is from Joshua. "And if it seems evil to you to serve the Lord, choose for yourselves this day whom you will serve, whether the gods which your fathers served that were on the other side of the River, or the gods of the Amorites, in whose land you dwell. But as for me and my house, we will serve the Lord. (Joshua 24:15)." Today, I choose, with a willing heart, to serve the Lord.

Take your passion and enthusiasm this day, and channel it in serving the Lord! You will find that through providing help and assistance to others that you yourself will be the one blessed. It's though service and volunteering that others can see the Christ in us.

Spiritual Refresher for Day #119

Take time to spiritual reflecting on this point: Going deeper into God's Word.

Humans were made to grow up. We start out in our mother's womb and after we are born, our bodies and mind starts to mature and grow. We grow in knowledge and mature in numerous ways as we reach adolescence. Once we are adults, we start to delve deeper into worldly matters. We get more serious jobs and then we will start mastering skills which will allow us to be productive employees for companies. As adults, people generally want to increase their responsibilities at work and get deeper into their worldly job. Today's tip is focused on seeking a deeper relationship with God so that we can be in right-standing with our Lord. Our Job is to serve the Lord with our whole heart and that can only be done by growing in spiritual knowledge.

"That we should no longer be children, tossed to and fro and carried about with every wind of doctrine, by the trickery of men, in the cunning craftiness of deceitful plotting, but....may grow up in all things into Him who is the head - Christ (Ephesians 4:14-15)."

We were not created to remain spiritual infants. Rick Warren explains in 'A Purpose Driven Life', "that millions of Christians grow older but never grow up. They are stuck in perpetual spiritual infancy, remaining in diapers and booties."

Too few Christians go deep into God's word; yet, they still expect to obtain all the benefits of being a Christians without doing any of the hard work. Kind David asked the Lord, "Examine me, O Lord, and prove me; try my mind and heart (Psalm 26:2)." Many Christians would fail miserably if God examined their heart. I failed in the past but I have a new mission now, to have a deep intimate relationship with God. Now, I want to go deeper into this point because it's not about being perfect but instead striving for perfection. Too few believers strive each day to be Christ-like. Many Christians don't even understand the basic tenets of how to live a Christ-like life. They are like babies asking to be spoon fed God's word by the minister or by others instead of seeking the Gospel for themselves. We must seek God for ourselves by throwing off the old inner man, so that we can nourish our new Christ-like self.

King David stated in Psalm 27:4, "One thing that I have desired of the Lord, that will I seek: That I may dwell in the house of the Lord all the days of my life, to behold the beauty of the Lord, and to inquire in His temple." The Bible said that David was a man after the Lord's own heart. David sought the Lord diligently with his whole heart. I want God to eventually say that I sought Him diligently. I never used to go deep until I truly allowed Christ to reign in my heart. I was one of those Christians who went to church on Sunday but during the week I did my own thing for the most part. I never went deep into the Word of God and I never passionately sought the Lord out. But God (I love the 'But God' parts in the bible) showed me a different, higher way and I took responsibility for my own spiritual growth. I got serious with God and God got serious with showing me His way.

Many believers want signs from God but the Lord has already given us so many powerful signs. I have heard some Christians speak about how God feels far way but He is the same yesterday, today and tomorrow. It's only our simple human perception that changes from day to day. To maintain the correct type of spiritual perception, we must fill our hearts with God's word each day.

Pastor Rick Warren of Saddleback Church stated that, "God's Word generates life, creates faith, produces change, frightens the Devil, causes miracles, heals hurts, builds character, transforms circumstances, imparts joy, overcomes adversity, defeats temptation, infuses hope, releases power, cleanses our minds, brings things into being, and guarantees our future forever!" This is probably the best definition of what happens when we deeply study the word and allow it to fill our hearts.

My father, a minister, told me that if I over-filled my spiritual cup each day then there would be no room for anything unspiritual to get in. I have learned that this is so true because the devil constantly seeks to take us off our path. Many Christians still don't understand that the choice of how they want to live is up to them. By going deeper into the Bible, we start to clear hear God's voice. God often speaks to me through His word. Before I start to read the Bible each day, I ask God to speak to me, and to show me in what areas I need to grow up.

By studying the Word, we gain insight into the mind of God, and what pleases Him. "As newborn babes, desire the pure milk of the word, that you may grow thereby (1 Peter 2:2)." Delving deeper into the Word of God is the only way to live a Christ-like life. It will not happen by placing the Bible under our pillows, hoping that through osmosis we will gain a deeper understanding of our purpose and how we should be living. Today, I wanted to encourage all believers to have a new daily goal, diving deeper into God's word.

How to go deeper into the Word of God?

One way to do this is to study other translations of the Bible in order to see the Lord's Words in a fresh light. Many times because we have studied the same translation over years, we have become so familiar with the words that we fail to gain any new insight. I encourage my readers today to use different translations (comparing ones that perhaps you have never read before) so that you can read God's truth in new ways. Ask God to show you new truth and insight before you read it and you will be rewarded. Ask God to allow your heart to be more open to what He wishes to teach you as you read these new translations. When you start to go deeper into God's word, your relationship with God will become richer, more intimate and you will start to live a more abundant life!

Spiritual Refresher for Day #120

Take this time to spiritually reflect on this point: Understanding your enemy.

The enemy is satan, the same enemy of God and Christ. 1 John 4:6 says, "We are of God...", and because of this fact the devil hates us and wants us to fail. Too many Christians do not understand who the real enemy is or how the enemy works to lead them down the wrong path. Too many believers are actually their own worst enemy, fighting the wrong battles in their minds and hearts each day but the true enemy is the devil. The devil has many names: the adversary, the evil one, Beelzebub, the deceiver and the prince of lies among other names. The devil is real and he has a host of earthly assistants who help to carry out his chief goal, to keep God's children out of heaven. Some of the devil's helpers are witting of who they are actually working for, but most of his helpers have no idea that they are actually assisting the devil in keeping believers out of heaven. I had to look inside myself to make sure I wasn't one of the devil's unwitting helpers. I realized that I was one of satan's unwitting helpers so I decided to change teams; I am now on Team God! I ask myself each day, who am I serving? That question keeps me focused on God and serving Him. Ask yourself today, are you furthering the kingdom of God or satan's mission.

The devil has many tools at his disposal to include disappointment, discouragement, shame, guilt or just generally influencing us to think that we are not worthy of God's love. We are worthy of God's love and we were created by a perfect God who only makes masterpieces. We are of God, as recorded by John. One person can make a difference in this fight and we are commanded to be soldiers in the army of God. The fallen angels who supported Lucifer are now called demons and they help him. There are many people today with demons in them, like in the days of old. Look at the TV shows and the reality shows of today, and you will see many willing helpers of satan. The themes in the Bible are being played out today. Solomon said that there is nothing new under the sun.

The anchor verses for today are listed below:

"Fight the good fight of faith, lay hold on eternal life, to which you were also called... (1 Timothy 6:12)." This is part of our job description each day. Fight the right battle, the good fight of faith and not the wrong battles in your mind.

"Resist the devil and he will flee from you (James 4:7)." We have hope because God tells us that if we resist the devil, then we will run.

"He who sins is of the devil, for the devil has sinned from the beginning. For this purpose the Son of God was manifested that He might destroy the works of the devil (1 John 3:8)." When we sin, we are furthering the mission of satan on earth. Every one sins but to stay in willful sin, without true repentance, we are not seeking first the kingdom of God. We must understand what pleases satan and what pleases God. After that, we must decide who we want to put first in our lives each day. Love and forgiveness pleases God;

while hate and unforgiveness pleases satan. Know yourself first and then seek to learn the tricks of the enemy so that you can resist him. 1 Corinthians 2:11 states, "lest satan should take advantage of us; for we are not ignorant of his devices." The believer must know who the real enemy is and how to fight against his tricks.

"So the great dragon was cast out, the serpent of old, called the devil and satan, who deceives the whole world; he was cast to the earth, and his angels were cast out with him (Revelations 12:9)." The devil's realm is earth. satan can never return to the glorious light of heaven and thus he doesn't want us to see God's Glory either. 1st Peter provides details of how we should live and who our enemy is. "Be sober, be vigilant; because your adversary the devil walks about like a roaring lion, seeking whom he may devour. Resist him, steadfast in faith... (1 Peter 5:8-9)."

The word of God provides all the information we need to live an abundant life. God repeatedly tells us how we should live and who our real enemy is. John 10:10 states, "The thief comes not, but to steal, kill and to destroy..." This is his job to steal our destiny, kill our dreams and to destroy our lives. When I was living in the darkness, the devil didn't have to worry about me because I didn't know who he was or what his mission was. But God, saved me and explained what I must do and now its part of my life mission to show others what God has put on my heart.

The rest of John 10:10 provides Jesus' words the hope that we may be assured of, "...I have come that they may have life, and that they may have it more abundantly."

Be encouraged today knowing that this refresher may have assisted you in knowing a little more about the enemy of God, so that you can live the life that God intended you to live!

Spiritual Refresher for Day #121

Take this time to spiritually reflect on this point: Repentance.

Today is Resurrection day and I wanted to discuss one of the most vital points of the Christian faith, repentance. We all need to have a right understanding of the nature of repentance. I started studying this point in order to better understand it myself. I found through deep reflection and study of God's word that there was more that I needed to do in this spiritual area. I decided to put this concept higher on my priority list after I examined my own brokenness from living in this fallen world. I wanted to mature in understanding how to walk in Christ.

The word repent is often translated from the Greek verb 'to perceive or to understand'. Therefore repentance involves a radical change in a person's perception of things, his or her view of reality. The illusions of the past are cast off (or the scales have fallen from their eyes) in order to perceive matters as a true child of the living God. When we are born again, the Spirit of God regenerates a person's heart and mind. I realized that I had to be genuinely sorrowful for the sin I committed by striving to turn away from it. I had to turn my back of all things from the past which was not of God so that I could receive the promises of God. In sum, repentance is focused on building the inner person in new radical Christ-like ways so much so that one hates the sins of the past.

The prophet Ezekiel stated in 14:6, "Thus says the Lord God: 'Repent, turn away from your idols, and turn your faces from all your abominations." Later in 18:31 it says, "Repent, and turn from all your transgressions, so that iniquity will not be your ruin. Cats away from you all the transgressions which you have committed."

John the Baptist spoke directly about repentance in the wilderness of Judea. "Repent, for the kingdom of heaven is at hand (Mathew 3:2)." John spoke of repentance as a radical turning from sin which became manifest in the fruits of righteousness. John stated, "Therefore bear fruits worthy of repentance...Therefore every tree which does not bear good fruit is cut down and thrown into the fire (Mathew 3:8 and 10)."

The start of Jesus' public ministry echoed what John the Baptist preached. The first words recorded in Mathew 4:17 by Jesus were, "Repent, for the kingdom of heaven is at hand." These words set the tone for Jesus' entirely earthly ministry. Repentance was a constant theme taught by Jesus which is why I wanted to focus on this spiritual concept today. Jesus also commanded His disciples to preach repentance as well. We are called to be Christ-like and should live a repentant life and preach this Godly point as well.

Jesus said, "Remember therefore from where you have fallen; repent and do the first works, or else I will come to you quickly and remove your lamp stand from its place --- unless you repent (Revelation 2:5)."

"And saying, 'Men, why are you doing these things? We also are men with the same nature as you, and preach to you that you should turn from these useless things to the living God, who made the heaven, the earth, the sea, and all things that are in them, who in bygone generations allowed all nations to walk in their own ways (Acts 14:15-16)."

"Truly, these times of ignorance God overlooked, but now commands all men everywhere to repent (Acts 17:30)."

"I kept back nothing that was helpful, but proclaimed it to you, and taught you publically and from house to house, testifying to Jews, and also to Greeks, repentance toward God and faith toward our Lord Jesus Christ (Acts 20:20-21)."

"Therefore, if anyone is in Christ, he is a new creation; old things have passed away; behold, all things have become new (1 Corinthians 5:17)."

"Now then, we are ambassadors for Christ, as though God were pleading through us: we implore you on Christ's behalf, be reconciled with God. For He made Him who knew no sin to be sin for us, that we might become the righteousness of God in Him (1 Corinthians 5:20)."

What is repentance?

A calling to change our ways from worldliness to Godliness. Repentance is focused on living a new life through Christ in order to glorify God. We are called to be like Christ, not like the world around us. We are urged to strive after a higher life, not a lower life. Repentance is an imperative for us as believers in Christ. In this vein, I wanted to list a few characteristics of true repentance:

-Change of mind
-Change of heart
-Walking in love
-Sorrow for sin
-personal acknowledgment and confession of sin
-Turning away from sin
-Turning to God for reliance in all matters
-Practical obedience
-Continuance of following after things of God in order to maintain a state of deep repentance.

Be encouraged today, knowing that God sent His son for our salvation because He loved us first. Now, it's our turn to move to repentance because we love Him!

Spiritual Refresher for Day #122

Take this time to spiritually reflect on the following point: Abandoning the prison of our own making.

Many people live their lives inside a prison of their own making. These unfortunate souls are constantly reliving the sorrows of the past and the tragedies of yesterday. Too many people are caught in a loop of depression and sadness which makes up the walls of their prison. One Victorian Poet stated, "Stone walls does not a prison make."

In Luke, 4:18-20, Jesus read from book of the prophet Isaiah (61:1), "The Spirit of the Lord God is upon Me, because the Lord has anointed Me to preach good tidings to the poor; He has sent Me to heal the broken hearted, to proclaim liberty to the captives, and recovery of sight to the blind, to set at liberty those who are oppressed (the opening of the prison to those who are bound)..." Jesus closed the book after reading the verses and then said, "Today this scripture is fulfilled in your hearing (Luke 4:21."

Jesus came to free us from the prison of our own making. Growing up in this fallen world, we start to build the walls of our prison, and thereby put limits on ourselves and God through the journey. God is infinite and all-powerful but we start to put God in a box over time. After we start limiting God, we then start to limit ourselves and what we can do. When we start speaking limitations over our own lives, it cripples us and takes away the power given to us by God. But Jesus came to free us from sin and from mental bondage. Paul stated in Ephesians 5:16-17, "See then that you walk circumspect, not as fools but as wise redeeming the time, because the days are evil. Therefore do not be unwise, but understand what the will of the Lord is." God want none of His children to be imprisoned, God's will is that we be free.

"I, the Lord, have called You in righteousness, and will hold your hand; I will keep you and give you as a covenant to the people, As a light to the Gentiles, to open blind eyes, to bring prisons from the prison, those who sit in darkness from the prison house (Isaiah 42:6-7)."

Many Christians still live in darkness instead of the Glorious light of God, because they are still blinded by the illusions of the world. God sent His Son to help us find the light and to tear down the self-imposed walls of our prison.

John Spilsbury of Bromsgrove, who was confined in Worcester Jail for the testimony of Christ, bore this witness: "I shall not henceforward fear a prison as formerly, because I had so much of my Heavenly Father's company has made it a palace for me." Another, in similar case, testified: "I thought of Jesus until every stone in my cell shone like a ruby."

Everyone has a choice in how they choose to perceive the world. We can see the world through a God-conscious lens or through mental slavery to unhealthy habits. I once heard a story of two prisoners in a cell looking out at the night sky; one of them looked out and only noticed the bars while the other man only focused on the stars.

Psalm 142:7 states, "Bring my soul out of prison, that I may praise You name; The righteous shall surround me, for You shall deal bountifully with me." When John the Baptist was in prison, he sent two of his followers to find out if Jesus was indeed the Christ. John didn't want any help in the natural but sought to know if Jesus was the one (Luke 7:18-23). It's our job to seek after Jesus with all our heart, soul, mind and strength so that we can be free on the inside.

Many people's souls are bound, yet they still have no clue. The devil loves when this is the case with believers. The spirit of humans was created for eternity, God made us for eternal life. We must all search our hearts, minds and spirits so we can ensure that we stay aligned with the will of God.

The Apostle Paul was in a Roman prison and stated in Philippians 4:11, "Not that I speak in regard to need, for I learned in whatever state I am, to be content." Paul was in a prison and understood that happiness comes from within. His words were seasoned by the words of Jesus Christ and he thrived because of the Christ inside of him. Paul stated he had learned to be content, and it's a template for us in that we need to learn to be content as well. Spiritual growth through learning allowed Paul to be free on the inside. later in Philemon while still in prison, Paul stated in the first lines, "Paul, a prisoner of Christ Jesus....Grace to you and peace from God our Father and the Lord Jesus Christ." Paul focused on His God and not his problems. We all need to focus on the greatness of our God and not the bars of our internal prison.

I wrote this step because I searched my heart, soul and mind to see the areas where I was still bound. I saw that satan still had me bound in some areas so I created a plan to fix the areas where I needed work. Today, I work my salvation plan diligently because it's my priority. When I completely surrendered to the Lord and opened my heart to the great redemptive power of God's love, the walls of my mental bondage ended. Praise God!

I encourage my readers to do what is suggested in 1 Corinthians 11:28, "let a man examine himself..." and then use the Bible to free yourselves in order to live a Godly, more abundant life.

Spiritual Refresher for Day #123

Take this time to spiritually reflect on this point: Eradicating limiting thoughts.

This refresher is focused on training our mind to put an end to the limits we put on ourselves and on God. Our identity should be in Christ Jesus whereby we view the world through the word of Jesus and His Father. As we get older, we tend to create limits inside of us and then transfer these same limits to God. Many people drift through life thinking that they are powerless But God wants our thoughts to be focused on Him, and deeply engaged in an intimate relationship with Him. We must stay close to God everyday so that we can live the abundant limitless life that God has in store for us.

When Jesus said, "It is finished," on the cross, it was at the time that we became fully equipped for any job or mission. We can do great things for God. Jesus said in Mark 9:23, "If you believe, all things are possible to him who believe." Too few Christians actually live a life which shows they truly believe. Later in Mark 16:17-18, Jesus said, "And these signs will follow those who believe: In My name they will cast out demons, they will speak with new tongues; they will take up serpents; and if they drink anything deadly, it will by no means hurt them; they will lay hands on the sick, and they will recover."

Our belief must be unwavering. When errant thoughts come into our minds, we must immediately go to God's word to renew our thinking, to get back on God's track. We must train ourselves to maintain a steadfast faithfulness to live the type of life God wants us to live. Now, this verse in Mark 16 is not to say that we have permission to live a reckless life. We are not to just grab a snake or drank poison on purpose to test God but if we we have accidents, through the indwelling of the Holy Spirit we have the power. God's will for us is not to live a life with self-imposed limits. 'God willing' is a saying I heard in the Middle East regularly; this is an interesting saying because many people put limits on what God's will is. By reading the Bible, we get an idea of what God wants for us, and it is not to live a life with human imposed limits. God is vast and limitless and He wants His greatest creations, us, to have an abundant life.

God gave us the power. Jesus stated in Acts 1:7-8, "It is not for you to know times or seasons which the Father has put in His own authority. But you shall receive power when the Holy Spirit has come upon you..." We will never know all the mysteries of life but I choose to believe that with faith, I can do anything. Jesus tells us in Luke 18:27, "The things that are impossible with men are possible with God." Many believers talk a lot about faith while living with doubt and fear. If we can retrain ourselves to always go to God's words when those doubts come into our minds, we will be able to live a more Godly life.

In John 8:32, Jesus said, "And you shall know the truth and the truth shall set you free." The truth will free us from limited, small minded (natural) thinking. The truth is centered on knowing ourselves and our limitations so that we can overcome them. Many people live in fear of confronting their limits and thus continue to limit themselves. In

Philippians 2:5, Paul tells us to have the same attitude as Christ Jesus." When our identity is fully connected with Jesus, we come to understand that our greatest weaknesses can be used to glorify God. The Bible is full of imperfect, weak and ordinary people who went on to do mighty things for God. God can use anyone who is in Christ because the Lord is never limited by our limitations.

The Apostle Paul stated in 2 Corinthians 12:9-10a, "I am glad to boast about my weaknesses, so that the power of Christ may work through me. Since I know it is all for Christ's good, I am quite content with my weaknesses (New Living Translation)."

I want to explain this verse because there are many misunderstandings about it. We are not to boast about our weaknesses just to do so because that is complaining but do it to bring glory to God because it shows with Christ we are overcomers and can conquering our self-imposed limits. Some people may read the above verse and believe its okay to talk or dwell on their hurts, disappointments or weaknesses from the past but Paul is showing that it's alright to admit our weakness so that WHEN we overcome them, God gets even more of the glory. There is a best-selling book about a man born with no legs or arms but who had went on to achieve an amazing abundant life, Nick Vujicic. On the cover of the book was a picture of him without arms and legs with a huge smile on his face because he is content with his 'apparent' weakness. To this man, his weakness was his strength and his attitude glorifies God and encourages others by allowing them to see that if this man could do amazing feats and live a full life, then others can as well. Nick is an Australian evangelist and successful motivational speaker.

The mature Christian understands that limitations should motivate and encourage them to lean more on God while staying focused on serving God in truth and Spirit, and with a Godly positive attitude. Too many people wallow in self-pity and sorrow but we are told that we are more than conquerors. The greatest narratives from humans often come from those who experienced great loss or pain. Our limitations increase our ability to be compassionate to others who are still living in the darkness but should never hinder us from glorifying God in everything we do. The Lord gives the believer strength to overcome anything.

I came to understand that I have to believe with my whole heart that I serve a God of breakthroughs. Doubt doesn't please God. God sees us as we are and not who we think we are. God put on my heart to know that there are no limits to what I could do for Him, so I strive to glorify Him through my writing.

Some of the greatest heroes of the Bible had limitations, and God still used them. Moses killed a man and was slow of speech but he became arguably the greatest prophet in the Old Testament. David committed adultery and had Bathsheba's husband sent to a war zone so that he would be killed but God said David was, "a man after My own heart (Acts 13:22)." Many of those recorded in the bible realized that their limits did not keep them from serving and honoring God while moving on to do great things.

We must identify and embrace our weaknesses so we can move beyond them. Ephesians 4:13 says, "I can do all things through Christ, who strengthens me." God understands our limitations but gave us the power to overcome through Christ and the Holy Spirit which indwells us. Too many Christians know the words from the scriptures but fail to live it. Many believers have memorized the words with their tongues but their hearts are far away from God's truth. The words and thoughts of these 'Sunday Christians' don't demonstrate a real reliance or belief in God. They speak defeat over their lives and focus on their limits instead of their God. God is limitless and made us to be the same. We can overcome anything through belief. Roman 1:17 says, "The just (righteous) shall live by faith." I never knew how much power I had through Christ and how my destiny was tired to my faith. Faith is about believing in the unseen.

Reading the Bible deeply allows the believer to know how to live, what to think and in which ways they can serve the Lord. Our God is a limitless, all-powerful Divine being. In Colossians 3:17, we read, "And whatever you do in word or deed, do in the name of the Lord Jesus..." If we keep this in mind and remove the limits from our minds and spirits, we will be overcomers in everything we do.

Too many people are walking three steps behind where God actually wants them. We need to step up to be the people God intended us to be. Step up and believe in new radical ways today!

Break out of the old ways of thinking and speaking. The enemy (devil) is supposed to be under our foot, not on our backs. We all need to step up to win souls for Christ. Step into your blessings by stepping up for Jesus!

Spiritual Refresher for Day #125

Take this time to spiritually reflect on this point: spiritual diligence.

Today I will be working out of the book of Ecclesiastes. King Solomon, the son of David, was the wisest man in the world. He stated that, "there is nothing new under the sun (Ecclesiastes 1:9)." This is why the Bible is so amazing because it speaks to us today. After I read the Bible, I realized the same things which had occurred in the past were also occurring today. One only needs to see any of the reality shows of this generation and it brings to mind the things of Sodom and Gomorrah. I heard one minister say that if God waited too much longer for the end of time, that He would have to apologize to the inhabitants of Sodom and Gomorrah. This is a joke but our salvation is no joke. Our society may have become more technologically advanced but society has also become more morally bankrupt and corrupt. I used to follow the world and sought out worldly pleasures but today I diligently seek after God. I understand now that that God gave us His words to help us live an abundant life, and it's through our steadfast diligence that we can be spiritually prosperous.

"In the morning sow your seed, and in the evening do not withhold your hand; for you do not know which will prosper (Ecclesiastes 11:6)."

Many believers don't understand the value of sowing spiritual seeds for God each day. The above verse is focused on being spiritual diligent. Too few believers maintain a diligent spiritual practice for the Lord. When I speak of diligence, I am referring to what we think, speak or do so that it is aligned with what pleases the Lord. Our thought life matters, our words matters and how we live matters.

"Do not let your mouth cause your flesh to sin, nor say before the messenger of God that it was an error (Ecclesiastes 5:6)." Our words can cause us to live a defeated life because when we speak curses or any negative word about ourselves, we allow that energy to enter our lives. Our words should always be used to craft the type of life we want, not complain or grumble. God wants us to praise Him continually and to be thankful. God wants believers to be examples to non-believers. As new creations in Christ, we are commanded to speak in new Godly ways. We should not use the same speech as we did as non-believers. We should not respond to people in the same unGodly ways but be a light by responding in love in all that we do.

There are times when people say they have made a mistake and sinned but it was not an error but a choice. I came to realize that the unGodly decisions I made in the past were my choices, it was not a mistake but a choice which pleased satan. Today, I strive to make decisions which please God.

Our God is an awesome Divine Being of second chances. Jesus came not for the righteous but for sinners. We have the possibility to have our second act be even greater that the first act. "The end of a thing is better than its beginning (Ecclesiastes 7:8)." We always have the choice of how we want to live each day.

"Let us hear the conclusion of the whole matter: Fear God and keep His commandments, for this is man's all. For God will bring every work into judgment including every secret thing whether good of evil (Ecclesiastes 12:13-14)." God is the ultimate judge so I don't need to be judgmental, I just need to spread the truth of the Gospel with love.

One of my favorite heroes of the Bible is Joshua Bin Nun, the faithful servant of the Lord and the steadfast companion of Moses. God gave Joshua a plan for success. "This book of the law shall not depart your mouth, but you shall meditate in it day and night, that you may observe to do according to all that is written in it. For then you will make you way prosperous, and then you will have good success (Joshua 1:8)."

The above verses from God tell us how to be spiritually diligent?

1) Keep the Word (the Bible) in our mouth and hearts.
2) Meditate day and night on the Lord's Words.
3) Do what the Word says.

Being spiritual diligent brings great rewards here and in the afterlife. "For God gives wisdom and knowledge and joy to a man who is good in His sight (Ecclesiastes 2:26)." Being spiritually diligent is about growing strong in the Lord because it pleases Him and allows abundance to enter our lives.

I also wanted to leave you with four simple points which helped me to spiritually mature and helps me to be diligent in my spiritual practice:
-Pray and read the Bible each day looking for new insights from the Lord.
-Attend church regularly, looking to become of part of the church family.
-Fellowship weekly with other Christians through Bible studies and worship groups.
-Tell others what Jesus has done for you.

Remember the devil is content to let us profess Christianity as long as we do not practice it. Be encouraged this day knowing how much God loves us and wants us to succeed!

Spiritual Refresher for Day #126

Take this time to spiritually reflect on this point: The narrow way.

"Enter through the narrow gate; for the gate is wide and the way is broad that leads to destruction, and there are many who enter through it. For the gate is small and the way is narrow that leads to life, and there are few who find it (Mathew 7:13-14)." The words from Jesus provide great insight into the Christian walk. I will be working from this verse today.

The gate which leads to eternal life is called narrow because it's a path which is different from how unbelievers live. The narrow way is a path defined by the will of God. God's will is clearly defined through His commandments, precepts, commands and the Good News as spoken by Jesus Christ. There is no excuse to not know the will of God for the believer.

The redeemed of God's do not walk aimlessly but purposely and intentionally in order to live within His will. The Bible lays out the way for the believer; and Jesus' words lights the straight path for us. Jesus is the way, the truth and the life (John 14:6). It's only through imitating Christ that we can inherit the kingdom of God.

The narrow way requires discipline and focus because the narrow way is often marked with difficulty and struggle. It's not an easy road but nothing worth having in life is easy. Many Christians want to keep one foot in the natural world and another in God's world but we are called to be new creations in Christ. We are called to give up our old ways and establish new Christ-like ways. 2 Corinthians 5:17 state, "if anyone is in Christ, he is a new creation; old things have passed away; behold all things have become new." If we are to call ourselves Christian, then we must live differently. We must think, speak, and act differently than from before we came to the truth, otherwise we are hypocrites. Hypocrites will not see the kingdom of God according to Jesus.

Too few people actually live a new life, but instead want to sprinkle a little Christ on themselves in order to continue doing things their way. As Christians, we are commanded to be separate from the world in how we act and live. There will be times when not conforming to the world will cause problems but suffering for Christ is a reward unto itself.

Our way only leads to destruction and perdition. The way of Christ leads to life, and life more abundantly! Many people may wonder what's the different between suffering in the world and suffering for Christ. The difference is the reward. When a person allows Christ in their heart and starts to genuinely serve God, the sufferings of this world is no longer an issue because our perspective has changed, and nothing is as difficult as it was before. Being in Christ is the only way to salvation and that means that everything will not be roses but because of what Christ did on the cross, we have hope in a brighter tomorrow.

2 Timothy 3:12 states, "...And all who desire to live Godly in Christ Jesus will suffer persecution but as Christ we praise when we suffer affliction because for Christ sake. Paul stated in 2 Corinthians 4:8-9, "We are hard-pressed on every side, yet not crushed; we are perplexed, but not in despair; persecuted but not forsaken; struck down, but not destroyed -- always carrying about in the body the dying of the Lord Jesus, that the life of Jesus also may be manifested in our body." Living in Christ brings hope because of the awesome unconditional love that God has for us.

God will go to great lengths to help us, even allowing us to suffer so that we gain a new perspective. I love what God has done in my life because I may have lost all material things, I have gained the greatest gift ever. I now know who I am through Christ.

The broad way is the way of the world. The broad way is the way of the flesh, it's a childish way. We have too many childish adults attending church every week. We as Christians must long to mature in God's ways, being responsible for our own salvation. The broad way is one of self-gratification. The scripture tells us that men by nature are lovers of self (2 Timothy 3:2), lovers of money (2 Timothy 3:2), lovers of this world (1 John 2:15-17), and lovers of pleasure instead of lovers of God (2 Timothy 3:4). The broad way is the natural way because it filled with superficial distractions. The broad way is led by the devil and not the Spirit. "We know that we are if God, and the whole world lies under the sway of the wicked one (1 John 5:19)." This is the evil one's world and he has recruited many to help him lead the rest to hell. Some of satan's best assistants are unwitting of their participation in his great plan. Many believers actually put more chaos in the world then non-believers. These 'Sunday Christians' are unforgiving, unloving (or only loving to those who love them), selfish, undisciplined, unfocused and easily swayed by the devil. The broad way is darkness in every sense.

The narrow way is the way of light. To maintain our walk in the narrow way, Christ's way, we must remember to walk in the light with Christ at our core every moment of the day because in due season we will reap the goodness of the land. The Bible tells us that, "...you may know what is the hope of His calling, what are the riches of the glory of His inheritance in the saints (Ephesians 1:18)." The reward is so great when we strive to walk on the narrow path; just as the punishment is too great for those who walk the broad path, destruction.

Minister Paul David Washer puts it this manner, "Since God's purpose is also His people's good, we seek to walk the narrow way and stay within the safety and blessedness of His will revealed in His commandments and wisdom. Furthermore, we also seek to work out our salvation in fear and trembling, knowing that it is God who is at work in us both to will and to work for His good pleasure (Philippians 2:12-13). Having such promises as these, we discipline ourselves for the purpose of Godliness (1 Timothy 4:7)." The narrow way is defined by living by the fruits of the Spirit. The narrow way leads to the upward call of God in Christ Jesus (Philippians 3:13-14)." The narrow way is the only way!

I found new meaning in these verses and I plan to strive even harder to know God's will for my life by going deeper into His word. I encourage everyone to do the same, and God willing we will be together in Heaven for eternity!

Spiritual Refresher for Day #127

Take this time to spiritually reflect on this point: Right relationships.

Life is about relationships, and the most important relationship in our lives in our relationship with God. The Bible lays out from Genesis to Revelations how to get back into right relationship with God after the fall of man. We also need to focus on getting in right relationship with ourselves and with others. According to the Robb Report Health and Wellness issue, 26 percent of Americans reported having a mental health disorder over a 12 month period. It has also been reported that 50 million Americans are on anti-depressants. Some of these people have legitimate mental issues and those issues should be addressed by medical professionals. The people in the survey self-reported that they had mental illness. Too many people bring more serious issues into their lives by believing they are broken but God creates only masterpieces and has made a way for all people to be whole and compete. It's all about perception, how we view God, ourselves and the world. Whatever illness we may think we have, it can be lessened by being in right relationship with God, ourselves and others. A right relationship is a whole and healthy relationship.

Many of the people who reported that they have mental illness often fail to understand the amazing power of God because when we get in right relationship with God, restoration of our mental health is possible, and we can be better than we previous imagined. Being in right relationship with God can heal even the greatest ills. There are many people in this world who don't know that our goal is to be in right relationship with God because the Lord is the God is restoration.

"This I recall to my mind, therefore I have hope. Through the Lord's mercies are not consumed, because His compassions fail not, they are new every morning; great is Your faithfulness. 'The Lord is my portion,' says my soul, 'therefore I have hope in Him!' The Lord is good to those who wait on Him, to the soul who seeks Him. It is good that one should hope and wait quietly for the salvation of the Lord (Lamentations 3:21-26)." Understanding who God is helps us to navigate in this fallen world.

How does one get in right relationship with God, ourselves and others? Through Love. The epistle of Colossians provides vital information on how to be in right relationship.

"Since you have been raised to new life with Christ, set your sights on the realities of heaven, where Christ sits in the place of honor at God's right hand. Think about the things of heaven, not the things of earth. For you died to this life, and your real life is hidden with Christ in God...Have nothing to do with sexual immorality, impurity, lust and evil desires. Don't be greedy, for a greedy person is an idolater, worshipping the things of this world...But now it the time to get rid of anger, rage, malicious behavior, slander, and dirty language. Don't lie to each other, for you have stripped off your old sinful nature and all its wicked deeds. Put on your new nature, and be renewed as you learn to know your Creator and become like Him...Since God chose you t be holy people He loves, you must clothe yourselves with tenderhearted mercy, kindness, humility, gentleness, and patience. Make allowance for each other's faults, and forgive anyone who offends you. Remember the Lord forgave you, so you must forgive others. Above all, clothe yourselves in love, which binds us all together in perfect harmony. And let the peace that comes from Christ rule in your hearts...Let the message about Christ, in all its richness, fill your lives (Colossians 3:1-16)."

The above verses are a template on how to live in right relationship with God and others. There is also a hidden point in the above verses in that the qualities listed about is how we should treat ourselves. For example, we need to not get angry with ourselves or lie to ourselves or be unkind to ourselves. So many people live with shame, condemnation, guilt and other negative emotions with themselves each day. These negative emotions prevent us from being who God made us to be. We must be in right relationship with ourselves so that we can love God and others. Too many otherwise healthy people are spiritually and mentally unhealthy because they allow old negative thought to take root inside their hearts and minds. The devil doesn't want us to be might people of valor but instead fearful and doubtful each day. satan wants us to think we are less and unworthy but that is not what the Word of God says. God says that we have been made for every good work. Colossians 3:17 explains it clearly, "And whatever you do or say, do it as a representative of the Lord Jesus, giving thanks through Him to God the Father."

The goal is to do more of the above, not just be content to think we do enough. The devil tells us that we are doing enough but God tells us to "reach forward to those things which are ahead, press towards the goal for the prize of the upward call of God in Christ Jesus (Philippians 3:13-14)." We must continually strive each day to better our relationship with God, ourselves and others. Do you have an action plan to get into right relationship with God, yourself and others? If you don't have a plan then you are probably just drifting and that is one of the devil's greatest tools. Drift is not 'of God' because God is purposeful and intentional. There is nothing in the Bible where people are told to drift but instead we are told to act as representatives or Ambassadors of Christ. Christ was in right relationship with the Father, and our Goal is to do the same. The Ten Commandments are about being in right relationship with God and others. Four of the Ten Commandments deal with our relationship with God and six commandments are about our relationship with others.

God's story is one of love for us and His attempts to bring us into right relationship with Him. As sincere believers, we have new hearts and minds whereby Jesus lives in us every minute of the day. It's time to assess our relationships with God, ourselves and others. Many people are still living with deep hurts within them which are not what God wants for us. We are to put away the old feelings, believes and attitudes so that Christ can reside in us. Until we completely move away from the past, and look to God in truth in Spirit, we will continue to be shallow immature believers. These us great profit in obeying God because He focuses on restoring relationships. We must truly love God, ourselves and others with all of our heart, soul, mind and strength so that we can receive the inheritance as proper children of the living God.

Spiritual Refresher for Day #128

Take this time to spiritually reflect on this point: Your spiritual priorities.

I wanted to ask a question for this tip; do you have any spiritual priorities? Have you articulated your spiritual priorities to yourself, or to God?

Once you have your spiritual priorities, then the next step is about applying these principles to our lives. The greatest priority for any believer is to be ready when Jesus returns. We should all live in such a way that we are anticipating the return of Jesus. No one knows when Jesus will return so we must focus on being ready at any time. In Mathew 24:42-44, Jesus stated, "Watch therefore, for you do not know what hour your Lord is coming...Therefore you also be ready, for the Son of Man is coming at an hour you do not expect."

Our greatest spiritual priority is to be ready for the Lord's return. It's our responsibility to be ready and internally motivated to live a Godly life. There so many verses in the Gospel which states that we must be ready. In Acts 1:7, Jesus says, "it is not for you to know times or seasons which the Father has put in His own authority." In Revelation 22:7, the next to last verse in the Bible, Jesus says, "Surely I am coming quickly." The key to this verse is not focusing on 'when' but believing that He is coming and that we must be ready all times. Living right must be a priority for all Christ-like believers. We must be focused on Jesus Christ so that we live in a Godly manner each day. If we all eagerly anticipate the Lord's return, we will be motivated to live a higher life, a Godly life. How often do you think about the return of Jesus?

I never considered my spiritual priorities before I surrendered my will completely to Christ and allowed Him to enter my heart. I still have struggles but I have a goal and focus each day. I now think about these issues because no one knows when the end will come. Perhaps my life will end before the end of days, so I must be ready. Part of my spiritual priorities is to understand my responsibilities for my own spiritual salvation. There are four responsibilities the believer should keep in mind:

1) We must watch faithfully, always maintaining a Godly mindset. Living engaged for God.
2) We should wait peacefully, not living with worry or anxiety because our joy is in the Lord.
3) While we're waiting, we must work diligently for the Lord. Working for Christ must be a priority for the Christian.
4) Lastly, we should worship joyfully, seeking opportunities to serve, praise and worship the Lord.

If every believer lived in a manner whereby they eagerly awaited the return of our Lord, imagine how much more amazing our daily lives could be. If all believers spent and invested their time wisely in Godly ways, the church would not be in the state it is in today. There is more of God to have for every believer, and when we get better the quality of lives will improve.

Spiritual question for today: Does God have our complete attention?

I realized that God wanted me to live intentionally and purposefully for Him each day, not drifting through the days unfocused. God doesn't want our leftovers but He wants our first fruits, thus I decided to write down my spiritual priorities, and they are listed below:

-Wanting to know more about the mind of God. Each day, I will do this by reading the Bible in deeper way, and seeking to live inside of God's will.
-Longing to be closer to Jesus. I will spend more time with Jesus through studying the Gospels, attending Bible studies and reading spiritual books.
-Desire to know what pleases and displeases God. Listening more closely for God's voice through prayer and staying tuned to God's frequency. Living in the Christ zone where blessings flow more abundantly.
-Gaining more knowledge on how to live a righteous life. I will study different translations of the Bible in order to find new spiritual truths and to get deeper into God's word.
-Building a deeper, more sincere relationship with God. I will work harder to get closer to God by speaking to Him throughout the day, living by His spiritual principles and by living with God at the forefront of my mind.
-Winning souls for Christ. I will take more opportunities to testify for God.
-Living in a way which allows me to be ready to receive Christ when He returns. I will live in love by serving God through a dedicated ministry to help others. Living Godly each day!

These are my spiritual priorities today, what are your spiritual priorities today? Have you taken the time for God to outline your spiritual principles today? The more we focus on God, the more truth becomes available to us.

Many Christians don't understand that the real test occurs every day outside of church. It easy to praise the Lord in church each Sunday but the challenge is to praise the Lord throughout the week when the barbs and spears are coming at us. I thank the Lord when I have the opportunity to be tested because I know this builds faith.

God has my complete attention this day! I still fall down and make many mistakes but I am fully engaged with God now. I praise God that I have learned that I should have spiritual priorities today. I learned the greatest lesson of my life when I went through my greatest tragedy and was forced to my knees, I learned how to look up, to my heavenly Father, and the scales on my eyes fell from off and I was freed. Rejoice this day knowing that the King is sitting on the throne and that Jesus has died for us so that we may have life and have it more abundantly!

Spiritual Refresher for Day #129

Take this time to spiritually reflect on this point: Genuine belief in Christ.

Today's refresher comes from the Gospel of John 20:19-29. The words in the parenthesis are my comments.

"That Sunday evening the disciples were meeting behind locked doors because they were afraid of the Jewish leaders (Jesus had been crucified and his disciples were fearful that the same fate would await them). Suddenly, Jesus was standing there among them! 'Peace be with you,' He said. As He spoke, He showed them the wounds in his hands and his side. They were filled with joy when they saw the Lord! (the disciples fear turned into immediate joy when they saw Jesus). Again, He said, 'Peace be with you. As the Father has sent me, so I am sending you (Jesus was commission them).' Then He breathed on them and said, 'Receive the Holy Spirit. If you forgive anyone's sins, they are forgiven. If you do not forgive them, they are not forgiven.'" One of the disciples, Thomas, nicknamed the twin, was not with others when Jesus came. They told him, 'we have seen the Lord.' But he replied, I won't believe it unless I see the nail wounds in His hands, put my fingers into them, and place my hand into the wound in his side (after all Thomas has seen and heard, he still doubted).' Eight days later the disciples were together again, and this time Thomas was with them. The doors were locked; but suddenly, as before, Jesus was standing before them (Jesus didn't need to use a door because He is the door). 'Peace be with you', He said. Then He said to Thomas, 'Put your fingers here, and look at my hands. Put your hand into the wound in my side. Don't be faithless any longer. Believe!' 'My Lord and my God!' Thomas exclaimed. Then Jesus told him. 'You believe because you have seen me. Blessed are those who have not seen and yet have believed.'"

Christianity is a rescue religion and I can testify to this fact because Jesus Christ saved me in more ways than one. Christ came to save us from our sin. I praise God for what He did for us, because of His great love for us. The above text is so rich because it was right after the crucifixion of the Christ and the disciples were fearful. Christ conquered death and then completed what He has started by ensuring His disciples were saved from their own fear. The disciples were on the run not understanding the next steps in their journey. The disciples didn't completely understand what Jesus had been telling them about His resurrection from the dead although they were with Him for three years. The disciples were sad and disappointed because they still were holding on to a different idea of a Savior, not a savior who died a sinner's death on the cross. They had lost faith but Jesus knew exactly what was needed when He appeared and breathed on them whereby giving them Holy Spirit. I think it interesting that Jesus had to show up and show some of them his wounds so that they would believe. The first words that Jesus said were 'Peace Be with you'. He says it several times because it was His intent they those commissioned to spread His gospel would be at peace. After Christ had died, His closest companions were still not carrying Jesus inside of them. I love these verses because once Jesus was on the scene, they were at peace and then they had joy.

When we allow Jesus to enter our hearts, we too can receive the gift of the Holy Spirit. Paul writes that the power which resurrected Christ is in us. Many times in life people run from one thing to another thing just like the disciples were running and locked themselves in place to hide from the Jews. What I see in this verse is that today there are many people who have locked their hearts away from Jesus today. They have put their hearts behind a lock door of past hurts and sorrows but Jesus can enter in an instant. Many people are never satisfied nor are they at peace in this fallen world. Many people can understands what it feels like to be on the run from some real or imagined threat or even from the past in general. I remember when I was running from God Himself. God had been knocking on my heart for years but I kept pushing the Lord away. God had to get my attention and I praise Him for it. Although I wanted inner peace, I wasn't willing to come to the Lord on my own but God never gives up on anyone. I believe it's innate in every human to strive for peace, to be content or secure. No one longs to constantly live in a state of fear. Our goal is to become whole and healthy in every manner. Many people believe that they are too broken to have peace but Jesus can break through the hardest of hearts so that peace can enter.

Many people are still running each day, to a destination they don't know. These runners are not satisfied nor are they whole. These 'believers' are fearful and waiting for the next shoe to fall. Instead of living with hopeful expectancy in Christ, they are living an unfulfilled life of disappointment and sorrow. Jesus is waiting for you so He can say, "peace be unto you." Jesus told Thomas, 'Don't be faithless anymore, believe! If we truly believe that Jesus conquered death then we should believe that through Christ we can do all things. So many 'Christians' still limit themselves, and by extension, they limit God. These 'Christians' make their feelings into their idols which they believe over their God. I only have compassion for those who need to see in order to believe because I used to be one of these people. In reality, people don't need to see Jesus to believe because even if they saw Christ after a short time they will still not believe just like the disciplines. The disciples saw every miracle even how Jesus raised the dead. John wrote that Jesus performed many more miracles than he recorded in his Gospel but they still didn't believe in the impossible (John 20:30-31).

We have even more help from God and Jesus Christ which provide all the explanation we need. The disciples didn't have all the revelations that we have in the 66 books of the Bible. Either we are going to believe and trust God fully or not. Thomas the disciple is like many people who after seeing so much Divine evidence, they still need more convincing but Jesus said that 'blessed are those who have not seen and yet believed'. I don't know about you but I don't need to see anything else because of what God has done throughout my life. Jesus wants everyone to have peace.

There are at least eight reasons why people have no peace in their lives:

1) People are too suspicious and too full of resentment. Trust is hard to come by these days. Faith is the foundation of the believer. Romans 10:9 states that "that if you confess with your mouth the Lord Jesus and believe in your heart that God has raised Him from the dead, you will be saved," There are many people who claim to be Christians but they

really don't believe in their heart. For example, people immediately call the doctor for the smallest ailment instead of taking it boldly to the throne of grace first. There are too many Christians who are faith-deficient.

2) People who are still living in the past rather than focus on the promises of Christ. They dwell on the past by carrying over grudges and hurt which should have been long gone. The past must be left there so we can enjoy this day. Paul stated in Philippians 3:13-14 states, "forgetting those things which are behind and reaching forward to those things which are ahead."

3) Too busy trying to fight, battle and argue on things they cannot change. Fighting the wrong battles in their minds. We can't handle everything but we serve a God who can. Focus on what we can change and stop worrying about the things we can't change. The serenity prayer says "God grant me the serenity to accept the things that I can't change, the courage to change the things I can, and the wisdom to know the difference." We all need to learn how to be at peace with the things we have no power over. As a follower of Christ, once we give it to the Lord in prayer, we are to walk confidently believing that it is being handled even if we don't understand or see it in the natural. It's about faith!

4) People are disconnected from the present. Too few people actually enjoy the moment. Too many people are still living in the past or too focused on the future to see the beauty and enjoy the moment. God wants us to be engaged in every moment so that we can serve Him and honor Him. It's difficult to glorify God reliving the hurts of the past or holding grudges from yesterday or worrying about tomorrow.

5) People are too filled with self-pity and other self-absorbed behavior. Too many adult wine and cry much too often. They glorify their problems and minimize their God. There is little genuine thankfulness for the life they already have, they allow their self-pity to dishonor God. We must honor and glorify our Lord and Savior all throughout the day.

6) People have moved away from old fashioned values such as love, forgiveness, peace, kindness, self-discipline, and the other fruits of the spirit. These people do not build on a foundation which produces peace. Peace can only occur on a Godly foundation.

7) Too many people expect too much from themselves. Unrealistic expectations lead to unfulfilled lives. There is no honest self-assessment of their own abilities. People put too much pressure on themselves instead of having realistic plans and goals. We are 'to examine ourselves' according to the Bible (Galatians 6:4).

8) People have no peace because they are not connected to something bigger than themselves. These people are not anchored in Godly principles because there is no sincere connection to God and His son, Jesus Christ. They have yet to allow Christ to enter their hearts completely. They don't truly know Jesus. When we allow Jesus Christ and His teachings to permeate our hearts, minds and souls; a fruitful and abundant life will result. I feel sad for those Christians who know no peace or joy because this is not

what God has intended for followers of Christ. If you are reading this message, take this time to make a spiritual action plan in order to allow Christ to completely enter your heart. Do something radical to honor Christ each day! Commit to living a true Christ-like life from now on so you can be a follower of Christ in truth and in Spirit.

Jesus has appeared to us and it's our responsibility to allow Him to enter every facet of our life. Christ is not only to be worshipped in church but in our hearts every moment of the day. If we as believers keep Christ in our hearts every minute of the day, there would be no room for any negative thoughts or beliefs. Christ on the inside allows us to be at peace. Christ empowers while fear constricts and limits. Christ didn't die on the cross so that we would live a defeated life. Christ came so that we may have life and have it more abundantly (John 10:10). Too many Christians live a life far from what God has imagined for us. If we want the abundant life that Christ spoke about, we must continue to live a life which honors Christ in all things we think, say or do!

Be uplifted today, understanding how much Jesus Christ loves us, He came to rescue us and to set us on the right path. Jesus is the Way, the Truth and the Life! Our lives can only become full when we allow Christ to reign in it!

Spiritual Refresher for Day #130

Take this time to spiritual reflect on this point: Allowing Christ to find you.

Jesus stated in Mathew 18:11, "For the Son of Man has come to save that which was lost."

There are many Christians today who are still lost and living in the darkness. Although they have heard the Word, those good spiritual seeds still continue to pass through their hearts without taking hold. The Apostle Paul was not one of these people because when he heard the word, and accepted the calling. I really relate to the Apostle Paul because of his dramatic conversion. Paul said in Philippians from a Roman prison, "Not that I have already attained, or am already perfected; but I press on, that I may lay hold of that for which Christ Jesus has also laid hold of me (3:12)." As a born-again Christian, I make mistakes and fall as a follower of Christ but I now have purpose through Christ because I understand what is expected of me. I read Paul's words and they touch my heart, motivating me to be better each day.

Paul was on the road to Damascus when he saw a light from heaven which knocked him to the ground. Jesus asked Paul (then named Saul) why was he persecuting Him (Acts 9:3-4). I had a similar moment at the lowest point in my life when I wanted to end my life and I also heard the voice of the Lord tell me that it was not my time and that I had work to do for Him. I was lost, living in the darkness but through God's amazing grace, I was saved. This message is for those who are still living a partial darkness, thus they are still lost.

Jesus told Paul that, "...I now send you to open their eyes, in order to turn them from darkness to light, and from the power of satan to God, that they may receive forgiveness of sins and an inheritance among those who are sanctified by faith in Me (Acts 26:17-18)." The 13 Epistles of Paul provides much clarity on how to turn from the darkness and embrace the light. Today, I strive for the prize of the upward call of God in Christ Jesus.

The Bible discusses light and darkness throughout the scriptures. In Genesis 1:3, God said, "Let there be light, and there was light. And God saw the light, that it was good; and God divided the light from the darkness." The idea of light and darkness is a concept anyone can understand. Light allows us to see, to live and to thrive. Light is essential to life while that which is in darkness doesn't grow or prosper. We are lost in the darkness, living without hope. Jesus explained in the Gospels that He didn't come for the righteous but for those who are lost. Jesus provides direction to those who are still confused and blown about by their perceived difficulties of the world. The Bible tells us that we will have difficulties and that it is to be expected. So if I know this fact, all I need to do is to work harder to strengthen my inner man each day so when the storms come, I'm ready. Today, I want to connect the ideas of living in the darkness and being lost.

"Then Jesus spoke to them again saying, 'I am the light of the world. He who follows Me shall not walk in darkness but have the light of life (John 8:12).''

In my past when I wasn't a believer in Christ in truth and spirit (I called myself a Christian but my life didn't testify to this fact and I understand that I was playing church), I was so lost and I didn't know it. I thought I know it all but I knew nothing. Jesus says that He is the truth, the way and the life. We have to understand where we are, if we are to move out of the darkness. In Mathew 5:16, Jesus says, "Let your light shine before men, that they may see your good works and glorify your Father in heaven." Our job is to glorify God, and living in the darkness does not glorify God.

I was lost and didn't even know it, just as there are Christians today who attend church each week who are still lost and living in the darkness. Ask yourself, am I still living in partial darkness? Those lost sheep are easily identified by their thoughts, speech and actions because it testifies to who they are and in what condition their hearts are in. Jesus explained that we will known by the fruits of our labors.

Jesus challenges us to be perfect, not to be stay broken. "Therefore you shall be perfect, just as your Father in heaven is perfect (Mathew 5:48)." Now no one can be perfect but we can strive for a Christ-like existence. Too many people don't strive nor do they actually challenge themselves to be better for Christ. Jesus said in Mathew 7:21, "Not everyone who says to Me, 'Lord, Lord, shall enter the kingdom of heaven, but he who does the will of My Father in heaven." I don't want to be one of those unfortunate souls.

Jesus explained in Mathew 22:13, "Then the king said to the servants, 'Bind him hand and foot, take him away, and cast him into outer darkness; there will be weeping and gnashing of teeth." And again in Mathew 25:30 Jesus says, "And cast the unprofitable servant into the outer darkness. There will be weeping and gnashing of teeth." Separation from God's will result in eternal darkness. For those who are in darkness now, there reward will be even more darkness, forever.

I was once lost and now I am found, and it's my responsibility to make sure that I stay in the light, and spread the truth of the Gospel to all. There are those out here who operate in confusion without understanding what the will of God is. The Lord wants none of us to be lost nor living in darkness without hope. But God loves us so completely and fully, that He understands our confusion and wants to help. The Lord sent His son in order to be the way for our salvation.

Today, commit to the way of the Lord and seek to know more of Him each day!

Spiritual Refresher for Day #131

Take this time to spiritually reflect on this point: Developing a thirst for God.

Jesus said in John 7:38, "He who believes in Me, as the Scripture has said, out of his heart will flow rivers of living water."

Blaise Pascal described the thirst for God in terms of a God-shaped vacuum in the human soul. I believe there is a basic human need for a relationship with God, but sin keeps many from recognizing this basic need. Too many people try to fill this void for God with worldly things. Nothing can fill that unique God-shaped space in our soul, except for God. In this vein, we need to develop a thirst for God.

Faith connects us to God while sin separates us from God. The biggest sin of humans is seeking independence from God. We think we can do it ourselves and only go to God after we try other remedies or cures. Seeking things of the world first will always cause us to fall short.

"Bring my sons from afar and my daughters from the ends of the earth,... whom I created for my glory (Isaiah 43:6-7)." God made us to magnify His glory and greatness. Every human should live to glorify God. "So whether you eat or drink or whatever you do, do it all for the glory of God (1 Corinthians 10:31)."

Many Christians don't quite understand that success has nothing to do with material things or accolades from others but success should be focused on our identity in Christ. It matters not what others think, only what God thinks. I ask myself throughout the day: Do my actions, thoughts and speech glorify God in all that I do? Do I thirst to honor God; do I put God first in my heart? Is it God's words that I strive to glorify?

"Therefore, since a promise of entering His rest, let us fear lest any of you seem to have come short of it. For indeed the Gospel was preached to us as well as to them; but the word which they heard did not profit them, not being mixed with faith in those who heard it (Hebrews 4:1-2)." It's our duty as believers to make sure that we profit and benefit from hearing the words of God. It does no good to just hear the word, say a halleluiah, and then just keep on living a broken and defeated life. The author of Hebrews explains throughout that we shouldn't come short of the eternal rest offered by God. The great news is that it's never too late!

I remember how I used to live before I came to the truth of Jesus and allowed Him to live in my heart. I used to get excited after hearing a great sermon but then I would leave the church and the message would eventually fade away. I never understood that it was my responsibility to make sure that the truth stayed in my heart. I came to understand that I had to keep putting the word deeply in my heart so that I stayed focused on the upward prize which allowed me to also live an abundant life here. God put it on my heart that I had to develop a thirst every day to receive His promises. Thus, each day when I wake up, I start my day with the word of God and continue to lean on it throughout the day so that I never run low of spiritual fuel.

The Lord's word is the spiritual fuel we need to navigate through life's difficult waters. Many believers fail to understand that we all need a daily influx of spiritual fuel each day to live. The amount of spiritual fuel that each believer needs is different. For me, I need to read the bible morning, noon and night so that I stay balanced and on pace to maintain spiritual wellness inside of myself but perhaps you are going through something and need more of God's word. I learned that it was my responsibility to determine what I needed to satisfy my soul daily. It all started with developing a thirst each day so that I overflow my internal spiritual cup each day so that nothing negative can get in. If I overfill that reservoir, then I am better equipped for the battle of life.

"Let the word of Christ dwell in you richly in all wisdom, teaching and admonishing one another in psalms and hymns and spiritual songs, singing with grace in your hearts to the Lord. And whatever you do in word or deed, do all in the name of the Lord Jesus, giving thanks to God the Father through Him (Colossians 3:16-17)."

The devil wants us always to believe that we are doing enough for God. We can never do enough so we must push ourselves each day to put God first and develop a spiritual thirst for His word like we have a thirst for water. Paul writes that nothing "shall be able to separate us from the love of God which is in Christ Jesus our Lord (Romans 8:38-39)." It our responsibility to make this verse a reality each day for us by not letting our circumstances get to us where we forget that God has a master plan for our lives.

God has the answer!

As James stated in 1:22, "Be doers of the word, and not hearers only, deceiving yourselves." I used to deceive myself but that is what the devil wants so I choose today to be a doer of God's word. I do this by developing my thirst for God's word each day. When we thirst for God, He thirsts for us. "Now may the Lord direct your hearts into the Love of God and into the patience of Christ (2nd Thessalonians 3:5)."

Jesus told the woman at the well in John 4:14, "Whoever drinks of the water that I shall give them will never thirst. But the water that I shall give him will become in him a fountain of water springing up into everlasting life." Develop a thirst today for Jesus because He is the living water we need to satisfy all our needs.

Today, live your life every moment believing that "If God is for us, who can be against us (Romans 8:31)."

Spiritual Refresher for Day #132

Take this time to spiritually reflect on this point: Strengthening our inner being.

The Apostle Paul stated, "I pray that out of His glorious riches He may strengthen you with power through His Spirit in your inner being, so that Christ may dwell in your hearts through faith. And I pray that you, being rooted and established in love, may have power, together with all the saints, to grasp how wide and long and high and deep is the love of Christ, and to know this love that surpasses knowledge -- that you may be filled to the measure of all the fullness of God (Ephesians 3:16-19)."

The above verses are so rich, and are one of my favorites. It lays out a framework and a promise for us. I long for Christ to dwell deeply in my heart, and I focus on being rooted and established in love because love gives us power. Christ loves us so deeply that words can't express it. Our identity must be in Christ and not through anything else. If the followers of Christ, truly saw themselves as Christ sees them, then they would be able to tap into an ample supply of power to do anything.

The devil wants to separate us from the love of God. Not that the devil can separate God's great love for us but the evil one clouds our perception so that we perceive God less then who He is. The devil's goal is to continue to get the humans to mess up and veer off God's path. The adversary looks for people to work through just as God looks for people to work through. The devil uses the spirit and attitude of the weak, those without a solid foundation in Christ, to do his bidding. This is why we must strengthen our inner person each day. There are so many churchgoers who are unwittingly serving the prince of darkness each day. The devil wants to destroy us and we must get our attitudes and spirits right to keep the devil at bay. The devil wants to get in our ear and direct us to his path.

Establishing spiritual barriers is the key to living an abundant life. We can establish spiritual barriers to keep the devil out by staying in the Lord's Word. The devil rebelled and loves the rebellious. The devil constantly attempts to speak to us. Be careful to what voice you listen to. Check in with God's word each day to confirm what you are listening to.

God tells us to love and the devil tells us to hold grudges and to hate. Don't blindly fall into the devil's trap. God wants us to love, as He loves. Although it's difficult at times, God wants us to be like His son and love. It's important that we love, to even love those who spite us or hate us because that is what pleases the Lord. Our hard work leads us to heaven. Jesus said, "I know your deeds, your hard work and your perseverance (Revelations 2:2)." Without effort, change is impossible but our Lord tells us that our work is not in vain.

2 Timothy 2:19 states, "Nevertheless, God's solid foundation stands firm, sealed with this inscription: 'The Lord knows those who are His,' and Everyone who confesses the name of the Lord must turn away from wickedness."

Doubt and lack of Godly faith is wickedness and does not please God. Many believers feel they are good enough, but good enough will not get us into heaven. We must keep striving each day to know more of God, and to build an intimate relationship with Him. The Bible says that we are prepared for every good work but preparation is not enough. We must work hard within God's boundaries. We must lay aside our own agenda, get out of our way and serve God in truth and spirit.

Do you know what serving God in truth and spirit means? If not, don't you think it's important to learn what this means? It's time to get deeper into the Bible so that you know the truth. Be refreshed through God's word this day. We are each responsible for our own salvation.

We must internalize change. If we don't deal with our negative issues and traits, then we force others to deal with them. We each need to tend to our own gardens. Living a Godly life does not mean we live in the absence of fear, stress, anger, anxiety and other negative emotions but we know how to manage them so that they no longer rule our lives.

Our character is a result of our search for wisdom, the people whom we associate with, how we choose to spend our time, and the discipline that we impose on ourselves and our attitude. Character is the total sum of our habits and nothing shows a person's inner character more than his/her habits. Developing good spiritual habits strengthens us on the inside. He or she who endures to the end, shall be saved says the Bible. Helen Keller said, "Character cannot be developed in ease and quiet. Only through the experience of trial and suffering can the soul be strengthened, vision cleared, ambition inspired and success achieved."

I love this quote by Jim Rohn, "If you really want to do something, you will find a way; if you don't, you will find an excuse."

The choice is always ours as to how we want to live. This is why God tell us in Deuteronomy 30:15-20, "See I have set before you today life and good, death and evil.....therefore choose life..." The ancient Hindu text from the 5th century B.C., the Bhagavad Gita, says "The mind acts like an enemy for those who don't control it."

Once we strengthen our inner person, everything else starts to fall into the right place. Today understand that we have the power because we are 'of God' and each moment has the promise in it for enlightenment. And we can't be enlightened without living and walking in the light. The goal of our spiritual practices is to bring about liberation, inner freedom, happiness and joy; if this is not the case with you today, then it's time to look deep inside and make a radical change.

Be encouraged today knowing that with Christ on the inside, brings peace into our lives!

Spiritual Refresher for Day #133

Take this time to spiritually reflect on this point: Defining what Jesus means to you.

Jesus asked His disciple, "Who do people say the Son of Man is?"

I decided to ask myself, who do I say Jesus is? There are so many answers I could give to include what is said in Romans 3:25, "God put (Christ) forward as a propitiation by His blood, to be received by faith. This was to show God's righteousness, because in his divine forbearance he had passed over former sins." Or I could choose the verse, "In this love, not that we have loved God but that He loved us and sent His son to be he propitiation for our sins (1 John 4:10)."

I could also say that Jesus was the unblemished lamb who took our place because the wages of sin is death. Jesus made a way for us by His ultimate sacrifice. Galatians 3:13-14 states, "Christ redeemed us from the curse of the law by becoming a curse for us...He redeemed us in order that the blessing given to Abraham might come to the Gentiles through Christ Jesus, so that by faith we might receive the promise of the Spirit."

These verses discuss what Jesus did but I still ask myself, 'Who do I say He is?' Some say that Jesus was a great moral teacher while others don't truly believe He was even that.

I say that Jesus was the Son of God! I say Jesus is also the Guide by which we learn how to get to His Father. "Whoever believes in the Son has eternal life; whoever does not obey the Son shall not see life, but the wrath of God remains in him (John 3:36)."

I say that Jesus is life! "Whoever has the Son has life; whoever does not have the Son God does not have life (1 John 5:12)." Having Jesus is about having Him in our hearts. By allowing Jesus to guide us, we have life, an abundant life. There are so many 'Christians' who don't really know Jesus is. I say this because these Sunday Christians continue to live a life below what Jesus has promised them.

Jesus is my Guide! Jesus stated, "For I did not come to call the righteous, but sinners, to repentance (Mathew 9:13)." Praise God, this is me! He came for me, to guide me to the right path.

One of the most beautiful verses in the Bible is written by King Solomon, one of the wisest men ever to walk the earth. "God has put eternity into man's heart (Ecclesiastes 3:11)." How do we tap into that force? We tap into our divine nature through Christ.

Who do I say Christ is? Christ is my Bridge!

Bridges allow people to cross over an obstacle in order to continue on their journey safely. Jesus is that bridge which allows us to traverse the tribulations and trials of life so that we can have a full life today. Jesus is the bridge between God and the world. "I am the way and the truth and the life. No one comes to the Father except through me (John

14:16)." These are His words describing how it's only through Him that we can see the Father.

Jesus stated in Revelation 2:2-5, "I know your deeds and your toil and perseverance...But I have this against you, that you have left your first love. Therefore remember from where you have fallen, and repent and do the deeds you did at first; or else I am coming to you and will remove your lamp stand out of its place -- unless you repent." There are two points I want to discuss here. First, Jesus is the Judge. Many people don't completely that they will be judges by God's standard, not human standards. Second, I wanted to stress that we rekindle our love for Christ by being love, showing love, forgiving and being a light to others. We honor God and His son through our faith expressed through our thoughts, words and actions.

Most believers had a deep love for Christ when they first heard of Him but overtime they conform to the world by starting to hold grudges, judge others, holding anger in their hearts and other things Jesus explicitly spoke against. Their love for Christ waned because they stopped being a disciple of Christ. We show our love for Christ by following Him. Are you striving to be more Christ-like each day or are you still responding in the same worldly ways to your circumstances?

Jesus is my rock and my foundation! Jesus stated, "Therefore whoever hears these saying of Mine, and does them, I will liken him to a wise man who built his house on the rock: and the rain descended, the floods came, and the winds blew and beat on the that house; and it did not fall, for was founded on the rock (Mathew 7:24-25)." Jesus allows me to go through life with a happy countenance each day. Jesus in my heart allows me to weather any storm with a song on my lips.

Jesus is my brother! Jesus states in Mark 3:35, "For whoever does the will of God is My brother and My sister and mother." He is my brother because I seek to do His will in everything I do. I still make mistakes but I know the way now and strive each day to fight my nature to honor Jesus. I know Jesus is love because God is love. I know Jesus is rooting for me to be like Him. I strive now to be a follower of Jesus in truth and spirit.

Jesus is the Answer, my answer in how to live! Jesus provides me all I need each day to be happy, to live a higher more fulfilling life. Jesus wants the same for you too!

Jesus is my Rescuer! Jesus explains in John 3:17 and 20-21, "For God did not send His son into the world to condemn the world, but that the world through Him might be saved....For everyone practicing evil hates the light and does not to the light, less his deeds should be exposed. But he who does the truth comes to the light, that his deeds may be clearly seen, that they have been done in God."

The knowledge of Christ should change us. Today, I write these words as a refresher for others and myself. Christ gave all believers a great commission in Mathew 28 and in Mark 16. Jesus said, "God therefore ... teaching them to observe all things that I have commanded you...(Mathew 28:19-20)."

Psalm 100:2 says, "Serve the Lord with gladness." Today I serve Christ because I love Him with all my heart, soul, mind and strength. Who do I say the Son of Man is? Today I happily say that Jesus is my everything!

Today, Make Jesus your everything, in thought, word and action!

Spiritual Refresher for Day #134

Take this time to spiritually reflect on this point: God's mercy and His portion.

This morning I asked God to put something on my heart to write about and two scriptures came to my mind: His mercy endures forever, and the Lord is my portion. I couldn't remember where there verses were but I opened my Bible for my daily morning Bible study and it opened to Psalm 107:1 which says, "Oh, give thanks to the Lord, for He is good! For His mercy endures forever. Let the redeemed of the Lord says so, Whom He has redeemed from the hand of the enemy." Wow, thanks oh Father for showing me where this was.

I believe God wanted me to make sure that I always remember how great the Lord is regardless of the situation I am in. I felt God comforting me by saying, "I am good and My mercy will endure forever, stay on My path." No matter how many times I may fall down, as long as I stay focused on God by serving Him and telling others what He has done for me, all will be well with my soul. This verse says that those who are redeemed should say so. This is a direct reference to our responsibility to reach out to the unsaved or to the lost Christian to share the Gospel. Have you ever taken the opportunity to share the Gospel message of salvation with someone who didn't know the Lord?

Jesus said in Mark 16:15, "Go into the world and preach the Gospel to all creation." The Lord Jesus is calling us to tell others about Him. Do you love Him enough to start obeying Christ today?

The next page my Bible turned to was in Lamentations 3:21-26: "This I recall to my mind, therefore I have hope. Through the Lord's mercies we are not consumed, because His compassions fail not. They are new every morning: Great is your faithfulness. 'The Lord is my portion,' says my soul, 'Therefore I have hope in Him!' The Lord is good to those who wait for Him, to the soul who seeks Him. It is good that one should hope and wait quietly for the salvation of the Lord." I gained so much from these verses. I felt the Holy Spirit showing me the points to focus on and have listed them below:

--Hope comes from knowing God.
--The Lord's mercies come up again. Remember that He is merciful for those who fall or stray.
--God's compassions is renewed each morning, He is faithful in a Divine way.
--The Lord is my portion. My soul tells me this means that the Lord's promises will come to fruition.
--Hope comes up again because it's a Godly principle. Our requirement is to get our soul right and to keep it in a right state.
--Hope allows me to stay uplifted with inner contentment because I know that those who wait on the Lord will have salvation. Believers who have hope will never be disappointed because Godly hope does not disappoint. If you are living without hope or in a state of sadness or disappointment, then it's time to seek Him in deeper ways.

I praise the Lord this day because He shows me the way! I was also shown the following verses from Hebrews 10:22-25, "Let us go right into the presence of God with SINCERE hearts fully trusting Him. For our guilty consciences have sprinkled with Christ's blood to make us clean, and our bodies have been washed with pure water. Let us hold tightly without wavering t the HOPE we affirm, for God can be TRUSTED to keep His promise. Let us think of ways to motivate one another to acts of LOVE and GOOD WORKS. And let us not neglect meeting together, as some people do, but ENCOURAGE one another, especially now that the day of His return is drawing near." I highlighted the words which spoke to me and I hope they encourage you as much as they did me. My soul praises the Lord this and every day! Thank you oh heavenly Father!

Today, I love God in truth and in spirit. I love the Lord with all my heart, soul, mind and strength. Today, I am happy because I can hear the Lord's voice as a seeker of light and love! Today I hope that this message speaks to your heart as you read it so we can all strive to be the people God intended us to be.

Spiritual Refresher for Day #135

Take this time to spiritually reflect on this point: Godly encouragement!

God is always encouraging us to be the people who He intended us to be. Too many Christians don't perceive it and are still stuck in the same old way of believing and living their lives.

The Apostle Paul stated, "Let your conduct be worthy of the Gospel of Christ (Philippians 1:27)." Is your conduct worthy of the Gospel of Jesus Christ? This is a life question I had to ask myself.

God has given us the Gospel to save us, to rescue us, to redeem us and to give us hope. Don't block God's blessings in your life by refusing to renew your minds through His word. God has entrusted us with this life so that we may glorify Him. "For it is God who works in you both to will and to do for His good pleasure (Philippians 2:13)."

God didn't create us to be 'less than' He imagined us to be but for greatness. We were created for greatness! I wanted to write this twice because so many Christians don't understand this simple point in practice. They live defeated, speak defeat; and they live a limited life with limiting thoughts. Galatians 5:1 states, "Stand fast therefore in the liberty by which Christ has made us free, and do not be entangled again with a yoke of bondage." It makes me so sad that so many Christians don't realize that Jesus came to free us. Many continue to live by the old, unGodly ways instead of embracing what Jesus did for them on the cross. I never understood this before I fully surrendered to Christ. I used to sprinkle a little Christ in my parts of my life where I would say Hallelujah but then live a life outside the will of God. I never understood that Jesus came to bring truth, to be truth and lead us to truth. Jesus specifically stated that John 8:32, "And you shall know the truth, and the truth shall make you free." In John 14:6, Jesus stated, "I am the Way, the Truth, and the Life."

"For he who serves Christ in these things is acceptable to God and approved by Men (Romans 14:18)." When we serve Christ, we are automatically approved by Him. There is no need to seek approval from humans because only Jesus is perfect. Does your life testify that you are serving Christ, that you know Christ? This is another serious question I asked myself when I surrendered to Christ. It's actually a question I have to ask myself daily because the world seeks to always drag us down to sin and an unGodly lifestyle.

God is the Great Encourager! Do you know that? Are you still leaning on things of man to help you when God said He will take care of all our needs? In Romans 15:13, we read, "Now may the God of hope fill you with all joy and peace in believing that you may abound in hope by the power of the Holy Spirit." Praise the Lord! God on the inside provides comfort, hope, joy and peace. The Holy Spirit comes to believers, that is to those who believe in truth and spirit. We all have the same potential to be Godly, living up to our potential. God sent Jesus to heal those with broken hearts. If we believe this truth, once we allow Christ in our hearts, we have to live a life which testifies to that changed life.

In Joyce Meyer's Power Thoughts Devotional on May 4, she discussed how Jesus doesn't want us to forget Lot's wife who was turned into a pillar of salt by looking back. Lot's wife disobeyed God's command and looked back. Jesus mentions in Luke 17:32, "Remember Lot's wife!" Joyce states, "In other words, stop looking back. The past is finished. Look to the future ahead! Begin to see, think on, and talk about the future God has planned for you, and you will soon make progress in the right direction. If there is anything you need to let go of, there is no better time that now!" Amen sister Joyce! Too many believers disobey God each day by focusing on the past instead of the hope we have in Christ Jesus.

God wants us to be encouraged so that we can encourage others! Even when I don't feel like encouraging others, I do it because of the hope and faith I have in God. The Bible tells me that I am to be Christ's ambassador. I can't do this by living the same type of broken life I lived as an unbeliever. I can't call myself a Christian and still live as I did in the past.

One of the greatest encouraging verses in the Bible outside of John 3:16, which is the greatest, is Romans 8:28, "And we know that all things work together for good to those who love God, to those who are called according to His purpose." What an amazing promise! We must be 'intentional and on-purpose' believers. Jesus told the little girl who was dead in Mark 5, 'Talitha Cumi' which means 'lamb, arise'. Today Jesus is telling us to arise. Don't continue doing the same things as we did in the past believing that it's the will of Christ. God's will is not for us to live below our inheritance which we gained through the death of Jesus on the cross. Christ wants us to live a new life which says "Behold, I am doing a new thing, can't you perceive it." Isaiah 43:18-19 says, "Do not remember the things of old. Behold, I will do a new thing, Now it shall spring forth; shall you not know it."

God is the Great Encourager! From the beginning, His word was created to help us return into right relationship with Him. "The Lord your God has chosen you out of all the peoples on the face of the earth (Deuteronomy 7:6)." What God promised in the Old Testament is even truer in the New Testament through His son Jesus Christ. God chose us by sending His Son to save us.

"You have made them a little lower than the angels and crowned them with glory and honor (Psalm 8:5)." That is us, we were crowned with glory and honor, don't you see it? Christ's kingdom has not fully come, but it has started its advance in the lives of those who follow Christ. Paul wrote such beautiful encouraging words in Romans that it's one of the chapters I return to often. "So now there is no condemnation for those who belong to Christ Jesus. And because you belong to Him, the power of life-giving Spirit has freed you from the power of sin that leads to death....those who are controlled by the Holy Spirit think about things that please the Spirit. So letting your sinful nature control your mind leads to death but letting the Spirit control your mind leads to life and peace... You are controlled by the Spirit if you have the Spirit of God living in you...And Christ lives with you...The Spirit of God, who raised Jesus from the dead, lives in you (Romans 8:1-2, verses 5-6 and 9-11)." These verses lift me up and give me the strength each day because I understand whose I am. I am an overcomer and so are you! Stop living a 'less than' life, and start living the life of abundance God promised.

"You make known to me the path of life; in your presence there is fullness of joy; at your right hand are pleasures evermore (Psalm 16:11)." These are beautiful encouraging words from our Heavenly Father. When I think of other encouraging verses from God, I am reminded of 1 Corinthians 2:9, "What no eye has seen, no ear heard, nor heart of man imagined ...God has prepared for those who love Him." Wow! Today, I am excited and encouraged by God's word!

Remember what is said in 2 Chronicles 15:7, "Be strong and do not let your hands be weak, for your work shall be rewarded!" Hebrews also provides a similar promise, "If we are faithful to the end, trusting God just as firmly as when we first believed, we will share in all that belongs to Christ." We have all we need to be successful and spiritually prosperous each day through the word of God, what's holding you back. I often tell people that I have met the enemy, and it is I. But today, I know that my internal enemy has been bound because of what Jesus did for me. I also read the end of the Book, and know who wins in the end! Praise the Lord! This day, I will strive to keep my hand in My Redeemer's hand and honor God through my actions so I can bring glory to Him!

Be encouraged today knowing that God is for us, and trying to lead us to greatness for His glory!

Spiritual Refresher for Day #136

Take this time to spiritually reflect on this point: Understanding our Divine nature.

"You are of God, little children, and have overcome them, because He who is in you is greater than he who is in the world (1 John 4:4)."

Jesus says in Luke 17:21, "the kingdom of God is within you."

Ralph Waldo Emerson stated, "What lies behind us and what lies before us are tiny matters compared to what lies within us."

Every born-again believer has the ability to overcome the demons of this world. We are victors through Christ because once we allow Christ into our hearts; we become inheritors of the promise. We are overcomers through Christ. Jesus lives in us when we follow Him in truth and spirit. When we act on God's words each day, we acquire a level of peace and protection that the unbeliever or those still in the darkness don't have. When I allowed Christ to enter my heart, soul and mind; I was able to walk through the darkest of paths without a care in the world. The things which bothered me before, no longer were an issue for me. Now, I must admit I still face the same issues but because of my faith in Jesus, I no longer have the same anxiety about those things I can't control. I understand that God has given me the power to decide what I want to focus on and where I put my internal energies. God has given me the power to discern. This ability to discern truth is one of the great gifts we receive from the Holy Spirit.

So many people are still looking for the internal switch but the switch is wherever we think it is. My switch is centered on my faith in Jesus and what He did for me on the cross. Each morning I decide that I will have a great attitude and that nothing will distract me, and it comes to pass. Each day I fully engage my heart, soul and mind on Christ. Too few Christians are fully engaged with who they are through Christ. I have control over the switch because God gave me this power.

"We are of God. He who knows God hears us; he who is not of God, does not hear us. By this we know the spirit of truth and spirit of error (1 John 4:6)." I now understand which is which, truth and error, because those former thinking errors have been fixed and healed through Christ. In 1 John 4:8, we learn, "He who does not love does not know God, for God is love." The spirit of God is based on love. Loves heals the brokenhearted but we must allow the love of God to enter our heart. I have forgiven all those who harmed me in my life and this has given me the power to have access to God's love. I found out that the grudges I held inside my heart, took space away from my heart, where God commanded me to love.

Og Mandino stated, "The prizes of life are at the end of the journey, not near the beginning; and it is not given to me to know how many steps are necessary in order to reach my goal. Failure I may still encounter at the thousandth step, yet success hides behind the next bend in the road. Never will I know how close it lies unless I turn the corner. Always will I take another step. If that is of no avail, I will take another, and yet another. In truth, one step at a time is not too difficult. I will persist until I succeed." I love this quote because it's how I feel each day. I persevere each day because of Christ.

My aim for this day: I persevere knowing that I have the power, and my work is not in vain because I am seeking a higher prize, the Kingdom of God. I strive each day to pursue a passionate life, fully engaged, so that I can please God. I will work to glorify God in all that I do because it's about God and not me. I will love everyone even those who are unlovable; I will forgive even those who are not repentant; and I will not judge those who are still in the darkness because I was once there. I will work to bring others to the light, so that they will be able to know the Gospel of Jesus Christ. I will strive to serve God in all that I do, understanding that my nature was created by God and that the Lord has given me everything I need for an abundant life!

Spiritual Refresher for Day #137

Take this time to spiritually reflect on this point: Focusing on the Godly guidance.

The Bible offers so much wisdom to the believer including encouragement, guidance, peace, joy, rest, healing and truth. I wanted to focus on a few verses written by the Apostle Paul in his epistles. As you read them, ask God to show you new meaning and insight into these verses.

"Christ is inside the believer (Galatians 1:16)"

"A man who has become truly righteous has become righteous by faith. It is this man who has life (Galatians 3:11)."

"The very Spirit of Jesus Christ is in the believer's spirit (Galatians 4:6)."

"Christ lives in you and is being formed in you (Galatians 4:19)."

"The Lord alone causes you to love (1 Thessalonians 3:12)."

"God teaches you how to love others in the local ecclesia (1 Thessalonians 4:9)."

"Only your spirit, deep inside you, really knows all that God has given you (1 Corinthians 2:12, 6:19)"

"His spirit is in your heart (2 Corinthians 1:22)."

"The Spirit of God writes on your heart (2 Corinthians 3:3)."

"The Spirit gives you God's own life (2 Corinthians 3:6)."

"The believer can see the unseen (2 Corinthians 4:18)."

"The power of Christ himself dwells in the believer (2 Corinthians 12:9)."

"God's spirit swells in you (Romans 8:9)."

"The Father dwells in you (Romans 8:10)."

"His strength is your strength (Ephesians 6:10)."

"You are filled with all spiritual wisdom (Colossians 1:9)."

"It is a speaking Lord who dwells in you (Colossians 3:16)."

"Getting to know Christ Jesus personally and internally is the most unsurpassable of all values (Philippians 3:8)."

"All your supply for all your needs is in an indwelling Lord (Philippians 4:19)."

When we are children, we learn how to walk, read, ride a bike and to do other things. As believers, we need to learn the truth of the Gospel, and how to apply it to our lives in a faith-filled walk. So many Christians say that God is first place in their hearts, but this is clearly not demonstrated each day as they constantly put others things before spending time with the Lord through His word. We have power in us, but it can only be tapped into by getting to know Jesus intimately. Many Christians know of Jesus but don't really know Him. They superficially read the word and think that is enough but the world we live in is constantly trying to negatively influence us towards the darkness.

What is the secret of the Christian life?

Is it obedience, worship, praise, forgiveness, serving others, prayer or something else? I believe its love, a deep abiding Godly love which inspires us to do the above happily and eagerly. When we love how God commands us to love, we will live be living by the Spirit. I have been a failure in my Christian walk, but God, has inspired me to not be content each day. I strive, fight, and exert effort to not live as a failure but as a victor in Christ. I strive with my heart and soul to radiate the Christian life through me. So many Christians are content with being failures. I say this because they are striving with much passion to live a Christ-like life. I want my thoughts, words, actions and walk to totally tell everyone, I am a follower of Christ. I want to radiate a light so bright that others are drawn to it, and I can testify that the light they see is because of Christ.

The best testimony for any Christian life is a fully lived, fully realized life of abundance where others say, "I want what he or she has." Today is a new day, and I will do new things for Christ because I love Him with all my heart, soul, mind and strength. Jesus said that, "Loving God is the greatest commandment, and loving others is the second." This is why I say the secret of the Christian walk in love. As Christians, we must lay hold of that higher life that resides inside of us, for that life alone can live the Christian life in truth and spirit.

John Donne stated, "I neglect God for the noise of a fly, the rattling of a coach, the creaking of a door." Is this you? This used to be me and I still have challenges but I know what I am supposed to do each day. I know the truth now and I know I have meaning through the Jesus Christ. I am spiritually aware now, thanks to the Holy Spirit. I am fully engaged with Christ Jesus each day! My daily goal is living higher life and the above verses allow us to know that we are already equipped for every good work.

Jeremiah 15:16 says, "Your words were found, and I ate them, and Your word was to me the joy and rejoicing of my heart; I am called by Your name, O Lord God of hosts." Today, I am hungry for God's word! Are you hungry for God's words each day? Today, I am changed! My desires and goals are different because I have renounced the negative things of my past and embraced the light of Christ. Have you allowed Christ to change your heart? 2 Corinthians 4:16 tells us, "Therefore we do not lose heart, even though our outward man is perishing, yet the inward man is being renewed day by day." Praise the Lord, this is how I feel! These words are for all of us. We all have the same opportunity for spiritual enlightenment. Are you utilizing the tools that God gave you to achieve a higher state of spiritual awareness? I ask myself these questions each day so I can live as a new creation in Christ.

Be encouraged this day knowing, "For you are the temple of the living God (2 Corinthians 6:16)." Today, I am different because I live by these words, "Thanks be to God for His indescribable gift! (2 Corinthians 9:15)."

You are more that you believe you are! You can do more than you believe you can! God's dreams for us are greater than ours, so let Him guide you today. Believe the Lord's words today in truth and spirit!

Spiritual Refresher for Day #138

Take this time to spiritually reflect on these two points: Spiritual awareness and inner well-being.

The opposite of spiritual awareness is spiritual ignorance; and the opposite of inner well-being is inner dysfunction. You probably ask why should I mention the opposite of my two points. I raise these two negative points so that we can avoid them. We must not stay unaware of the devil's tricks. I think spiritual ignorance and inner dysfunction are two of the greatest impediments or stumbling blocks to being the people God intended us to be.

Webster's Dictionary defines ignorance as, "lacking knowledge; showing a lack of knowledge of intelligence; the state of being unaware." This last part is where I want to focus because so many of my Christian brothers and sisters are spiritually unaware, and this unawareness is their undoing. God knows that we will make mistakes and fall down but too many believers claim they made a mistake when in actuality they made a bad choice. I believe ignorance can be also defined by the repeated bad choices we continue to make in life. We make bad choices because we don't know a specific choice is outside the will of God. Living outside the will of God is a part of living in spiritual ignorance. We must seek to be spiritually aware of what is pleasing to God. The key to life is to be spiritually mature and grow so that we make better, more Godly decisions each day. The Bible is framework to show us how to live a Godly life, a life within the will of God.

Webster's dictionary defines dysfunction as, "failing to perform its proper function normally; an irregularity in functioning of any given thing." If our job is to serve and love God with all of our heart, soul and mind each day then many Christians are failing to perform their proper function normally. These Christians are living in a state of dysfunction because they are living outside of God's will. Being spiritually ignorant is not what God wants for us, and living outside of God's will is responsible for many of the issues, problems and tribulations which we bring on ourselves.

Also, when people are ignorant of their true purpose, they live a dysfunctional type of life, which is displeasing to God. When we live outside the will of God, we suffer and pain enters into our lives. We drag chaos into everything we do when we are unaware and dysfunctional. But God, who mercies renew each morning, gives us hope and an opportunity each day to be more Christ-like. As new creations in Christ; we are reborn, changed and dedicated to living differently through and because of Christ. The Holy Spirit empowers us and guides us through our spiritual awakening. We are transformed.

Romans 12:2 states, "And do not be conformed to this world, but be transformed by the renewing of your mind, that you may prove what is that good and acceptable and perfect will of God."

2 Corinthians 3:18 states, "But we all, with unveiled face, beholding as in a mirror the glory of the Lord, are being transformed into the same image from glory to glory, just as by the Spirit of the Lord."

The Bible tells us to awake from the sleep of the past. Ephesians 5:8-10 states, "For you were once in darkness, but now you are light in the Lord. Walk as children of light for the fruit of the Spirit is in all goodness, righteousness and truth. Finding out what is acceptable to the Lord." This verse speaks directly to spiritual ignorance and being responsible for knowing what is acceptable to God. We are commanded to be transformed which means that we become spiritually aware. And a few verses later, we are told, "Awake you who sleep, arise from the dead, and Christ will give you light (Ephesians 5:14)." There are too many Christian zombies walking around here saying 'empty words of praise' while in reality they are still ignorant of 'what is acceptable to the Lord.'

Jesus told us in John 8:12, "I am the light of the world. He who follows Me shall not walk in darkness, but have the light of life." To not live a dysfunctional life, we must follow Jesus completely without reservations. Too many Christians have reservations. You can tell who they are by their words, such as, "Well, I will follow Christ, if I have time" or "I'll give God more time once I get more time" or "I'm too busy to read more of the Bible" or something like these excuses. These Christians speak more about their problems and excuses than the greatness of their God. God's own words tell us that He wants us to have an abundant and full life, not a defeated broken life of 'barely making it'. There are too many people in churches who still have a victim mentality instead of a victor mentality. They say they have victory in Jesus but its just empty words. In John 14:17, Jesus tells us, "The Spirit of truth, whom the world cannot receive, because it neither sees Him nor knows Him; but you know Him, for He dwells with you and will be in you." When the Holy Spirit spoke to me, I was shown the Spirit of truth. The main different now is that I am on the purposeful and intentional path, and I know Jesus personality and intimately.

If when we seek to follow Christ, then we are Christians. If we choose to not follow Christ in Spirit and truth then we are hypocrites or worse, unbelievers in the eyes of God. I no longer want to live in ignorance nor live a dysfunctional life so I choose to follow Christ. I am tired of my mess and my goal is to take every step with my hand in the Master's hand.

Ignorance and dysfunction doesn't have to be our only options. We were created to live an abundant life for God's pleasure, a life where we pursue the things of God with passion, and where the things of the world are secondary. Too few Christian live a life testifying to this fact. Once we accept Christ, it's our job to know the duties, rights and responsibilities of a believer. We can't get the promises without the putting in the work. We can't stay ignorant nor dysfunctional all our lives because that dishonors God.

Jeremiah 17:10 states, "Even to give every man according to his ways, according to the fruit of his doings." We will reap exactly what we sow each day in our thought life.

There are Christians who still don't know that their thought life can keep them from the kingdom of God. We must put all unGodly thoughts into captivity so that we can serve the Lord and allow Him to work in our lives. Too many Christians are allowing their old life and old attitudes comingle with their new life in Christ. Don't let you past continue to be a stumbling block but instead let it motivate you to testify to what Christ has done in your life so that you can help others find their way.

Today seek the Lord and His word with all your heart so you can be spiritually aware and have inner well-being! Be encouraged knowing that it's what God desires for us: spiritual awareness and inner well-being!

Spiritual Refresher for Day #139

Take this time to spiritually reflect on this point: Inner rebirth!

"Therefore if any man be in Christ, he is a new creature: old things are passed away; behold, all things are become new."

Through the blood of Christ, we are reborn. With that rebirth, there are things which we need to place on the table and things which we need take off the table. The things of the past need to be taken off the table while new Godly habits should be added. One translation of the above verse says, "that any man who is in Christ Jesus is a new species of being that never existed before." This is so beautiful!

God put this on my heart one day when I was reading the Bible, "Don't be victim to my circumstances; but instead allow the Holy Spirit to help me master my circumstances so that they no longer bother me. I was told to use my circumstances to motivate me, and to not defeat me." We are changed because of the Holy Spirit which dwells in us. Being in Christ means that we are 'saved, healed and delivered. The Bible says that when we made Jesus our Lord, we become one spirit with Him. This said, God gives us free will to live how we want to live. If we want to profess Christianity while still maintaining the same type of lifestyle or unGodly habits then God will allow us to live that way. God will not force anything on us. We must come sincerely and honesty to Christ because the Lord knows our hearts if we are genuine. We will not inherit the promises with one foot in the past and the other foot in the kingdom of God.

Acts 20:32 says, "And now, brethren, I comment you to God, and to the word of His grace, which is able to build you up, and to give you an inheritance among all them which are sanctified." The word can only build us up if we allow it and if we get deeply into it. The inheritance doesn't just come without effort on our part; we have to choose our path every minute of the day.

The key to inner rebirth is through love. Too few people actually know what love it. Once we are reborn through Christ, the love of God has been born within us. But unless we take action, then the love will remain hidden in us. If you are holding any grudges against anyone or holding on to past hurts or harboring hatred or dislike for people in your past, you will not be able to fully activate the love inside to help you be reborn. God is love and unless we start loving as God loves, then we are just putting a little window dressing on our old lives. Love is the most powerful force in the universe and by acting on the knowledge of God's word we are like Paul says a banging cymbal in 1 Corinthians 13, lots noise and nothing else.

Ask God today to show you how to love as He loves. Without the love of God working inside of us, we are still lost. God has sent His Spirit of love to live in us and to teach us how to truly love. The decision is on each believer as to whether they will work to perfect the love of God in their life. If you still have issues with people in your life, then God still has issues with you. I had to cast off the old resentments and bitterness towards those who I felt had wronged. When I did this, I started to live and God allowed my broken spirit to be healed.

Kenneth and Gloria Copeland stated in their book, *He did it all for You*, "Learn to believe in love. It's the most powerful force in the universe. Walk in love by faith in the Word. Walking in love is walking in the spirit, it's walking as Jesus walked. Love never fails. Nothing works without love, and there can be no failure with it. When you live by love, you cannot fail. It takes faith to believe that love's way will not fail. The natural mind cannot understand that because the natural man and his world are ruled by selfishness... His selfishness shuts the door to the love of God, and he wins up on his own." The Copelands say that we should love in a revolutionary fashion based on God's word. We can't be reborn with allowing love to rule our hearts. Too many Christians focus on protecting themselves instead of loving completely and allowing Jesus to protect them. Believers should believe in truth and spirit!

To be reborn we must bury the past and renew our thinking through the word of God. If you keep reading God's word, it will get through the thickest skulls. I know because I used to hard-headed and intransigent when it came to wanting to change but I choose to allow Jesus into my hearts and with Him, I also obtained the Comforter (Holy Spirit) who taught me a radically different path to follow. Today I strive to radically love, radically forgive, and radically hope in a better tomorrow as a follower of Christ!

How do we support the rebirth process?

1) Read the Bible.
2) Study God's word by cross referencing the scripture and using other translations. This step is about getting deeper into the word in order to understand how a born-again believer should think, speak and act.
3) Ask God to show you more of Himself. Seek revelation every time you study the Bible. Ask God to reveal His will for your life. Ask God to show you in which areas you need more work in order to imitate Christ.
4) Apply what you have learned from the three above steps. Obey God's word because you love Him and have been reborn, not because of obligation. Look for the internal areas you have neglected over the years. Pursue change because you are now a new creation in Christ and have a new goal in life.

I have been given an amazing gift and I wish to share it with the world. The gift of inner peace and the inspiration to spread the Gospel. I used to be led by the world at every given turn but now my joy and strength is in the Lord and not in the world. The world didn't give me this peace, and the world can't take it away. It was through the words of God and His Son, Jesus of Nazareth, that I dried my tears and cast off the darkness so that I could allow the light to enter my heart. I smile, I dance and I sing every day, even on the bad days, because my worse day with Christ is better than my best day without Him! Today, I celebrate because I have Christ!

Spiritual Refresher for Day # 140

Take this time to spiritually reflect on this point: Standing out for Christ.

When people ask me how I am, I say I'm outstanding but what I mean is that I'm 'standing out for Christ'. Sanctification is about being set apart from the world. As Christians, we should stand out so much so that people say, "He's or she's a Christian, look at their light. Look at the peace they have. Look at their walk!" The Bible says that our light should shine so brightly, it shows others the way.

Paul tells Timothy, "Pursue righteousness, Godliness, faith, love, endurance and gentleness. Fight the good fight of faith. Take hold of the eternal life to which you were called when you made your good confession in the presence of many witness (1 Timothy 1:6)." We should walk in such a way that others clearly see what we are about.

Can others see the Christ in you?

We stand out for Christ by fighting the right battles. Paul later tells Timothy, "For God did not give a spirit of fear (or timidity), but a spirit of power, of love and of self-discipline (2 Timothy 1:7)."

The right battles are the ones of faith, not rehashing the same old battles in our minds. Both the Old and New Testaments say we should be set apart from the unbeliever. Psalm 4:3 states, "But know that the Lord has set apart for Himself him who is Godly; the Lord will hear when I call to Him."

2 Corinthians 5:20 provides clear guidance on how we should live, "Now then, we are ambassadors for Christ, as though God were pleading through us: we implore you on Christ's behalf, be reconciled to God." This verse is so rich because is explains that it's the role of every believer to walk as examples of Christ. We must cast off, discard, eliminate and eradicate our old value systems, priorities, beliefs and plans. We must embrace a newness in to order to develop a new spiritual perception on how to live.

Paul drew from Isaiah 52:11 when he wrote in 2 Corinthians 6:17 about the command to be spiritually separated, "Therefore 'Come out from among them and be separate, says the Lord. Do not touch what is unclean, and I will receive you.'" As new creations in Christ, we are to make a clean break from all sinful habits and patterns. This can be a challenge on our own but through Christ we can do all things which strengthen us (Philippians 4:13). God gives us power when we stand out for Him. The more wisdom we gain, the more peace that enters our hearts.

Here are some suggestions on how to stand out for Christ:

Think the way God thinks, and not like the world.
Develop a daily spiritual plan for victory.
Feed your faith daily.

Stand strong in faith during adversity.
Release the past.
Be joyful always!
Be thankful always!
Forgive quickly and completely.
Always stay focused on God.
Spread the Gospel to others.
Focus on your job: Loving, serving, honoring God in all we do.
Walk boldly in faith.
Hope boldly!
Love boldly!

We can't honor and worship God when we are still living in the past. This is why there are so many verses in the Bible about moving forward, and not looking back. The crown of life is ahead of us, not behind us. Christianity is a religion focused on internal change through faith in Jesus Christ. We live in the present while believing and striving in such a way each day that we honor the Lord, so that through God's grace we will be allowed to have everlasting life. Too many Christians are still living in the past; holding on to old hurts, grudges and resentments. These people are not standing out for Christ but instead they are allowing the devil to ride on their backs. The Christ-like follower lives a new life in the here and now, knowing that it matters how he or she lives. Staying focused on the present moment with Jesus Christ at the center, we grow in appreciation of the things we have and seek out opportunities to stand out for Christ.

There are a few verses in Romans which summarizes sanctification. "And do this, knowing the time, that now it is high time to awake out of sleep for now our salvation is nearer than we first believed. Then night is far spent, the day is at hand. Therefore let us cast off the works of darkness, and let us put on the armor of light. Let us walk properly, as in the day, not in revelry and drunkenness, not in lewdness and lust, not in strife and envy. But put on the Lord Jesus Christ, and make no provision for the flesh, to fulfill its lust (Romans 13:11-14)." These are beautiful verses. Our goal each day must be centered on being transformed into the very image of Jesus. We must make no provision for the world, but instead make all provision and planning for success by imitating Jesus Christ.

Dynamic evangelist Jesse Duplantis explains in 'The Battle for Life', "Some people can't accept what the Word say because they still cling to guilt and shame. You may be one of those types of people. You may think that what you did in the past was so bad that you don't deserve to he helped through the battles of life. That's a lie. Jesus' blood washes you clean, and there is no reason for you to feel any guilt over the past. God lives you with an unconditional love....Disappointment is on the greatest tools satan uses against the Body of Christ. He will always try to get you disappointed in yourself, your family, and in your social life. He wants you to replay every mistake and become preoccupied with past losses." I used to dwell on past mistakes a lot which didn't honor God. I had no control over my through life and the devil had control over what I thought. I gave the devil the power and he took it. Christ didn't die for us to feel powerless.

We are supposed to act likes victors not victims. There's victory in Jesus, not defeat. When you allow the devil to rule your thoughts, you invalidate what Christ did on the cross. I broke out of the old habits of the past by reading the Word. When I started studying the Word and came to understand that I had all the power. I had the power to decide what I wanted to think about. I could think about all my past mistakes or failures, or I could dwell on the greatness of God. When the devil comes into my mind, I can immediately choose to place my thoughts on Jesus. I can change the channel from the devil's channel, to God's channel. The key to standing out for Christ is to help yourself. Participate in your own rescue!

The next time the devil starts speaking in your ear, don't allow his words to gain a foot hold. As Jesus said, "Get behind me satan"; we can say the same thing. We must be focused, disciplined and steadfast in our thought life by not allowing the devil to play his movie in our mind's eye. You are the director and Jesus is the producer. We can stand out for Jesus by staying focused on the future prize. The devil has many tricks he can place in your thoughts, if you allow him. The devil loves to get you to put off your spiritual well-being for worldly matters. Standing out for Christ is centered on prioritizing what's important to you. Is the world more important than the kingdom of God? Instead of laying down when satan tells you to lie down, stand up for Christ!

We need to put the devil under our foot and keep him there. The longer we allow unGodly thoughts to be played in our head, the further we move from Godliness. God is looking for believers to bless. To receive those great promises and blessings, followers of Christ must take a stand and stand out for His son, Christ Jesus.

Spiritual Refresher for Day #141

Take time to spiritually reflect on this point: Love, love and love! Living a life filled with love.

The purpose of this refresher is to see where you are not loving and show more love in those areas. Love is like a river flowing through our hearts, we can't damn off part of the flow expecting there not to be an impact on the total amount of water flowing down stream. When we stop love from flowing through our heart, we start down a dark path that moves us towards the goals of the evil one. When we don't practice love each day, we are guaranteed to stumble. Only love can heal us and empower us!

"May you experience the love of Christ, though it is too great to understand fully. Then you will be made complete with all the fullness of life and power that comes from God (Ephesians 3:19)."

We can't be who God intended us to be if we are still holding old grudges, bitterness, resentments and other unloving feeling towards others. This is why I started this refresher by saying this tip is focused on learning how to love everyone especially those who you have issues with. This tip is centered on loving the unlovable so that you may experience the full blessings of the Lord. Loving others is what God has commanded us to do.

The Apostle Paul tells us to, "live a life filled with love, following the example of Christ. He loved us and offered Himself as a sacrifice for us, a pleasing aroma to God (Ephesians 5:2)."

Susan Taylor, the former editor in chief of Essence Magazine says in her book 'In the Spirit', "We are created in the image and likeness of the Loving Spirit that created us. Each of us is perfect and powerful child of God, a holy light...When you are loving, you are living righteously. So despite the possibility of hurtful experiences, you can never lose...The highest power is love and it protects us and all of creation. Love is the very nature of the energy we call God."

When we limit love in our hearts, we limit ourselves. We have been created so that we glorify God but many Christians live a life which dishonors God and then they seek to justify their behavior. We call God a liar because we belittle Him. I used to do this by saying, "I can't love like that...or...You don't know what they did to me... or...I just can't do it." Either we believe God or not. "Now all glory to God, who is able, through His mighty power at work within us, to accomplish more than we might ask or think (Ephesians 3:20)." We can do all things through Christ who strengthens us. If only our limited thinking which limits the potential miracles which are possible in our lives. The Bible says that we can't say that we love God, whom we haven't seen, and then say that we don't love our neighbor who we have seen. This is not the Godly way! I want to live a Godly existence because I'm tired of living a 'less than' life.

When we love, we are empowered and we are connected to God in truth and spirit. It's no trick that loving people gets more breaks and blessings in life. Those who love in truth and in spirit, always seeking to honor the Father, are the ones who benefit the most from God's mercy.

Jude explained that "we must build each other up in your most holy faith, pray in the power of the Holy Spirit, and await the mercy of our Lord Jesus Christ, who will bring you eternal life. In this way, you will keep yourselves safe in God's love (20-21). We can only gain the benefits within God's perimeters.

Susan Taylor explains that "Bitterness limits you, your energy and your happiness...Love is a magnet; it attracts the best of everything...When you love, you are doing God's work." These are such beautiful words. I can see the love in which it was written by Ms. Taylor. People who help us to understand God's love are doing God's work as well. I love to write things which glorify God and there is nothing which glorifies God more than writing about His great love for us.

Living in love is not a natural response for us which is why we must learn what it is and push ourselves to follow this path each day. There are Christians out here who wonder why they are still living such a difficult life, why they struggle each day. This is not the type of life God intended for us but God has given us the greatest wisdom, guidance and direction, the rest is on us. Here is the key, we are fully equipped for every good work but we must stay focused on God, Godly thoughts and Godly actions to inherit all the great Godly promises.

When we fail to live a life filled with love, the results can only be one of struggle. I decided that my desire for a better life was more important than my pride which wanted to keep me living the same type of broken life. I got tired of my brokenness and my internal perception of my internal brokenness. Many people's main issue is their perceived brokenness, their lack of self-love. My first breakthrough came through when I started seeing myself as Jesus sees me. I started to focus on studying who I was through Christ. I never knew that love was the center of my faith. Because of God's great love for me, He gave His son. I never knew that as a Christian we are to be known by our love for others.

I never knew the two greatest commandments were to love God with all my heart, soul and mind; and loving others being the next greatest commandment. Now that I know, I have a loving and willing obligation to love all regardless of who they are or what they have done to me. I read Jesus' words about the Pharisees and Sadducees and their hypocrisy and asked myself: Do I want to be one of those hypocrites? Do I just want to be a 'window dressing' Christian where I look good on the outside but the inside is still in the darkness of disarray and chaotic. No is my answer. I want people to look at me and say, "there goes a follower of Jesus Christ!"

There is a great song which states, "They'll know we are Christians by our love, by our love." I changed the song and now sing, "They'll know I'm a Christian by my love" because I need to keep Christ real and personally meaningful to me each day. I need to remind myself at all times that I need to stand out as a Christian.

Don Miguel Ruiz says in *The Mastery of Love*, "Humans live in continuous fear of being hurt, and this creates big drama wherever we go...Love is always kind...Love is unconditional...Love is not about concepts; love is about action. Love in action can only produce happiness. Fear in action can only produce suffering. The only way to master love is to practice love...We have so many self judgments that we can't possibly have any self-love. And if there's no love for ourselves, how can we even pretend that we share love with someone else? The way you react has been repeated thousands of times, and it becomes a routine for you. You are conditioned to be a certain way. And that is the challenge: to change your normal reactions, to change your routine, to take a risk and make different choices. If the consequences are not what you want, change it again and again until you finally get the results you want...You will know you have forgiven someone when you see him/her and you don't feel anything anymore. You will hear the name of the person and have no emotional reaction. When you can touch a wound and it doesn't hurt then you know you have truly forgiven...Forgiveness is the only way to clean the emotional wounds. Forgiveness is the only way to heal them...Love is the medicine that accelerates the process of healing...There are millions of ways to express your happiness, but there is only one way to really be happy, and this is to love. There is no other way. You cannot be happy if you don't love yourself...When you become wise, you respect your body, you respect your mind, and you respect your soul. When you become wise, your life is controlled by your heart, not your head. You no longer sabotage yourself, your own happiness, or your own love. You no longer carry all that guilt and blame; you no longer have those judgments against yourself, and you no longer judge anyone else. From that moment on, all the beliefs that make you unhappy, that push you to struggle in life that make your life difficult, just vanish...When you love with no conditions, you the human and you the God, alight with the Spirit of Life moving through you. Your life becomes the expression of the beauty of the Spirit. Life is nothing but a dream, and if you create your life with Love, your dream becomes a masterpiece of art."

Don Miguel Ruiz provides such great advice on how to view and express love. He explains the concept and characteristics of love so that we can live a life filled with love. We all must learn how to love in healthier ways because if we can't love our God with everything, or ourselves completely, then how can we expect to truly love anyone else. We must cleanse our hearts of all unrighteousness so that we can begin to love with our whole heart. I had to throw away everything I knew about love and start over by studying Godly or Divine love first and then I studied what others said about Godly love with an open and willing heart.

Dr. Wayne Dyer explained about living in love in his book, 'The Power of Intention', "Love is the force behind the will of God...Pour your love into your immediate environment and hold to this practice on a hourly basis if possible. Remove all unloving thoughts from your mind, and practice kindness in all of your thoughts, words and actions. Cultivate this love in your immediate circle of acquaintances and family, and ultimately it will expand to your community and globally as well. Extend this love deliberately to those you feel have harmed you in any way or caused you to experience suffering. The more you can extend this extend this love, the closer you come to being love." The closer we are to 'being love', the closer we are to God, because God is love!

Our goal must be a divine form of love, not the dysfunction type of love we have grown accustomed to giving and receiving. Divine love is defined by its characteristic of loving the unlovely. Divine love is selfless and inspires obedience. Jesus stated in John 14:21a, "Whoever accepts my commandments and obeys them in the one who loves me." When we love God, we willingly want to obey the Lord command to love. Divine love is love that is given to someone who is absolutely helpless, clueless and unworthy because they are unable to offer it in return and does not deserve it - just like we don't deserve it from Jesus. We are to give to others what God and His son, Jesus Christ, gives us - unconditional love!

I wanted to end this refresher with four verses from the Bible. Our job is to continually think of them, study them and apply them and we will see God work mightily in our lives!

"The love of God has been poured out in our hearts by the Holy Spirit who was given to us (Romans 5:5)."

"I love those who love me; those who look for me find me (Proverbs 8:17)."

"Love each other deeply, because love covers a multitude of sins (1 Peter 4:8)."

"A new command I give you: love one another. As I have loved you, so you must love one another. By this all men will know that you are my disciples, if you love one another (John 13:34)."

Spiritual Refresher for Day #142

Take this time to spiritually reflect on this point: Being fully engaged with Christ.

Too many Christians fail each day to fully engage their faith because they allow their inner critic and other negative energies take over. When we are fully engaged in taking control of our spiritual life, we understand that nothing is too hard for God. Faith is allowed to flow through us without doubt. A person with a fully engaged spirit understands that no matter what happens, God is still on the throne and all will be well. I hope this message refreshes your desire to follow Jesus in truth and spirit, and rekindle a deep reverence to study God's word.

In 2 Timothy 1:6-7, Paul tells Timothy, "Therefore I remind you to stir up the gift of God which is in you through the laying on of my hands. For God has not given us a spirit of fear, but of power and of love and of a sound mind." This is one of my life verses because there are times when fears and doubts enter my mind but by being fully engaged I understand how God made me to live and this allows me to stay anchored to stay the course. When we are fully engaged, we restrain the inner critic and don't allow their thoughts to run wild without putting every thought into captivity. When we fully commit to God, we receive power to take control of our thoughts.

Today, fully engage in life and serve God because this is how we move into abundancy and the blessing zone.

Own it! Own your faith each day! Don't allow anyone or anything to take you own a Godly path. This is perhaps the greatest truth God has put on my heart. I used to allow people or circumstances to affect my mood and attitude but when I decided to own it, joy became my default.

Today, own your own salvation, and stop running away from what God is trying to teach you. There are many Christians out here who are partially engaged with life and partially engaged with God each day. The individuals only give God their seconds and wonder why they are not living a victorious life, they life they desire.

Today, ask God to speak to you. Ask God to show you what He wants you to do. Ask God to use you to be His hands. Listen with your hearts when you read the word of God, without guilt, but with a loving sincerity to do His will.

Jesus said, "If you love Me, keep My commandments. And I will pray the Father, and He will give you another Helper, that He may abide with you forever --- the Spirit of truth, whom the world cannot receive, because it neither sees Him nor knows Him; but you know Him, for He dwells with you and will be in you. I will not leave you orphans; I will come to you (John 14:15-18)." Jesus has promised us that we will never be alone. The power is always in us, ready to be activated so we can bless others.

Too many people want around in shame, guilt and condemnation but this is not God's will for us to walk around with a heavy burden. God loves us to completely and unconditionally, it's never too late to be a child of God in truth and spirit. "All who are led by the Spirit of God are children of God (Romans 8:14)." Being fully engaged allow us to stay focused on our true Godly nature and how God sees us. Isaiah 61:7 states, "Instead of your shame you shall have double honor, and instead of confusion they shall rejoice in their portion. Therefore in the land they shall possess double; everlasting joy shall be theirs." This is the inheritance for those believers who fully engage their faith. We have been redeemed by the blood of Christ Jesus, and I encourage you to live fully, by owning your faith each day.

Victory comes from God when we give the Lord our all. When we put God in the first position in our hearts, we will know the truth. Being fully engaged allows us to not forget the truth because the devil is always on the prowl to take the seeds of our faith away from us. When we own it, we focus on nurturing our seeds of faith each day. From those seeds, joy and contentment will spring!

Many Christians create so many excuses why they can't live the Christ way of life. They belittle their God by how they live, because their words may say they are Christian but their lives show they have not changed on the inside. We must take responsibility as believers in Christ, if we want to become the person God intended us to be. There are so many broken-spirited Christians in church each Sunday who fail to understand why God created them. Jesus came to heal our broken-spirits but we must own it and fully engage with Him through prayer, study of His word and application of the faith on a daily basis. It matters how we live, what we believe, what we think and what we say each day.

Everyone has moments of sorrow or sadness and that is normal but we have the power through Christ to decide whether we dwell on those moments or not. "Therefore since God in His mercy has given us this new way, we never give up (2 Corinthians 4:1). Jesus has given us a new way to live and satan wishes us to remain in the darkness and lost. "satan, who is the god of this world, has blinded the minds of those who don't believe. They are unable to see the glorious light of the Good News. They don't understand this message about the glory of Christ, who is the exact likeness of God (2 Corinthians 4:4)." Don't keep continuing falling for the tricks and illusions of the evil one. God is giving us the truth in what the enemy is trying to do to us. We must not give up or give in to the darkness which is 'of the devil'.

"That is why we never give up. Through our bodies are dying, our spirits (our inner being) are being renewed every day. For our present troubles are small and won't last very long. Yet, they produce for us a glory that vastly outweighs them and will last forever! So we don't look at the troubles we can see now; rather, we fix our gaze on things that cannot be seen. For the things we see now will soon be gone, but the things we cannot see will last forever (2 Corinthians 4:16-18)."

God is so loving and merciful that He wants no one to be lost but instead all to know Him intimately. Intimate knowledge of Christ provides a level of comfort and peace which transcends any feelings of brokenness. For many believers, their brokenness comes from their own perceptions of a dysfunction instead of a real medical condition. My goal in this refresher is to inspire Christians to fully engage and own their faith. "My sheep hear My voice, and I know them, and they follow me (John 10:27)." Once we fully engage and work to stay engaged, we will start to hear God's voice speak to our hearts.

"He gives power to the weak, and to those who have no might He increases strength (Isaiah 40:29)." Once we put God first and fully engage, we are then empowered to do the other things we need to do in our lives. Many Christians often say they don't have enough time but when we give the Lord our best efforts first, our way is made easier so what took hours before to complete, will now take less time. God gives us what we need and the move effort we give Him, the more He gives us.

"And Jesus answered and said to him, 'Get behind Me, Satan! For it is written, 'You shall worship the Lord your God, and Him only shall you serve (Luke 4:8)." As the Lord's greatest creations, we must understand that it's on us to understand our purpose: to serve the Lord. When we serve God completely and fully, the Lord directs our steps into areas where our skills and talents will flourish.

When we own our faith, miracles happen. "The steps of a good man are ordered by the Lord, and He delights in his way. Though he fall, he shall not be utterly cast down; for the Lord upholds him with His hand (Psalm 37:23-24)." So many Christians have fallen away from how they originally worshiped the Lord, but God is merciful and compassionate. We should shake the dust off our sandals and then keep moving forward. We each have a Godly destiny and no one can play our parts but us. "Therefore we also, since we are surrounded by so great a cloud of witness, let us lay aside every weight, and the sin which so easily ensnares us, and let us run with endurance the race that is set before us (Hebrews 12:1)." Our destiny cannot be realized outside of God's will. When we fully engaged, God will show us our destiny and leads us to new areas of abundance.

Be encouraged today knowing that God is ready, willing and able to be fully engaged with us! Thus, choose to fully engage God this day, and watch the blessings come!

Spiritual Refresher for Day #143

Take this time to spiritually reflect on this point: Taking care of your Spirit.

"All things are lawful for me, but all things are not helpful....Do you not know that your bodies are member of Christ (1 Corinthians 6:12 and verse 15)." Later in the same chapter we learn, "Or do you not know your body is the temple of the Holy Spirit who is in you, whom you have from God, and you are not your own? For you were bought at a price; therefore glorify God in your body and in your spirit, which are God's (1 Corinthians 6:19-20)."

There is so much wisdom in these verses I wanted to break them down. First, the world offers each of us many choices but not all of them are 'of God' nor are they good for us. As Christians, we are given choices each day but we must be mindful that we belong to Christ and the Holy Spirit dwells in us. This means that we have the responsibility to live Godly. Our spiritual health matters even more than physical health. The Bible tell us that our physical bodies may be dying each day but our spirit can live on forever when we are in Christ. The opportunity for everlasting life is based on the price Jesus Christ paid on the cross.

Humans are spiritual people and there is nothing better for us than spiritual health. In 1 Timothy 4:8, Paul explains, "For bodily exercise profits a little, but godliness is profitable for all things, having promise of the life that now is and of that which is to come." Our bodies are only important in this realm but when we take care of our spirit, it's like putting money in the bank of life for our future.

Our inner spirit is that secret inner source. The spirit is important and must be fed daily through reading and obeying the bible, devotionals, inspirational writings, bible studies, volunteering, prayer and listening God's voice. The spirit should be nurtured and fed so that it matures as well. When we spiritually mature, we start to put away the pride of life and the ego. Pride and ego keeps people's spirits bound by unclean spirits of the devil.

Faith, hope and love help us to take care of our spirit. Building our faith, requires us to stay steeped in hope and walk in love will allow our spirits to mature. Faith is the backbone for hope and love because they go hand in hand. We are told in Hebrews 11:1, that faith is about believing in the unseen, and having a confidence in the invisible. We should be people of great faith. My hope is based on believing that I can do all things through Christ and that I can overcome every temptation. I strive to be hopeful every day. Hope has allowed me, to be like the Apostle Paul when he wrote in Philippians from a Roman prison, to be content in whatever state I'm in. Love is an action, not a feeling, but a command from God which allows our spirits to sing and prosper. We are called to become people of love.

Stephen Arterburn stated in his book, Regret-Free Living, "Trust that God is full of love -- is love -- and that no matter of wilderness we find ourselves traveling in, he's there, ready to guide us to goodness." Faith, hope and love can heal the most broken spirits.

The Gnostic Gospel of Phillip says, "Faith is our earth, in which we take root; hope is the water through which we are nourished; love is the air through which we grow; gnosis (knowledge) is the light through which we become fully grown."

"All of us who have had the veil (of unbelief) removed can see and reflect the glory of the Lord. And the Lord -- who is the Spirit -- makes us more and more like Him as we are changed into His glorious image (2 Corinthians 3:18). One of our jobs is to work to conform our spirit into a thing of beauty thing, something pleasing to God. We, humans, are amazing beings, created in God's image with eternity created in our hearts.

Until we have a direct encounter with God's love, we will not change. We each must be willing to let God change us, to refine us, to direct our every step. The best way to take care of our spirit is to stay teachable.

"God knew His people in advance, and He chose them to become like His Son, so that His Son would be the firstborn among many brothers and sisters (Romans 8:29)." We, as believers, are a part of the body of Christ and a member of His family. Our Lord empowers us and we can connect to the spirit through prayer, hope and love.

Our potential is limitless. We have the Holy Spirit inside of us and God routing for us on the outside. We are set up for success, spiritual success. Our spirit was created to prosper beyond this world of tears and pain. We were born to represent our heavenly Father on this plane of existence. We were created for greatness in order to glorify God! The Lord wants us to strive to be more and more like Him each day. Being Christ-like is our goal and we do this by feeding the Spirit at every opportunity.

Spiritual Refresher for Day #144

Take this time to spiritually reflect on this point: Spiritual absolutes (or truth).

I have always gotten a lot of spiritual knowledge from my parents, even though I didn't always listen. I now strive to listen to all they say especially in spiritual matters. My parents are Godly people who always strived to help me by providing me a foundation in God. I never quite understood until I personally encountered God's great love and now I hope to help others who may be lost. My parents understood that those who put their trust in God would be blessed. Blessed means that we enter into the happy condition of those who revere the Lord and do His will. I came to understand that they wanted me to understand spiritual truth. In this vein, my mother recently sent me a letter and said I should meditate on Psalm 1. I decided to focus this refresher on the 1st Psalm because it's about life's two roads where the life of a faithful person is contrasted with the life of a faithless person. God reveals His directive for life in this short Psalm. Psalm 1 is like a blueprint or framework for the overarching way we should live.

Psalm 1 says, "Blessed is the man who walks not in the counsel of the ungodly (or wicked), nor stands in the path of sinners, nor sits in the seat of the scornful; but his delight is in the law of the Lord, and in His law he meditates day and night. He shall be like a tree planted by the rivers of water, that brings forth its fruit in its season, whose leaf also shall not wither; and whatever he does shall prosper. The ungodly are not so, But are like the chaff which the wind drives away, therefore the ungodly shall not stand in the judgment, nor sinners in the congregation of the righteous, For the Lord knows the way of the righteous, But the way of the ungodly shall perish."

The first thing I wanted to mention is that God's Words are always confirmed by His word. God's Words will keep us from wrong thoughts, words, and actions. I have broken down the verses and used other verses as a way to absorbing and meditating on this Psalm as my mother suggested.

--Godly people will be blessed. Proverbs 4:4 states that, "He also taught me, and said to me: 'Let your heart retain my words; Keep my commands and live.'" This reiterates how obedience leads to an abundance life because joy is found in obeying God. There are only two paths in life: that of Godly obedience which leads to joy; and that of rebellion which leads to destruction.

--Sitting with sinners corrupts our soul. As Christians we are called to love all but those in our inner circle should be help our walk, not hinder it. Jeremiah 15:17 says, "I did not sit in the assembly of mockers, nor did I rejoice; I sat alone because of Your hand, for You have filled me with indignation." At times our Godly walk, can be a lonely earthly walk but that's okay since God is always with us. God has told us that He would never leave us nor forsake us in Hebrew 13:5. There are always Godly believers who are out here looking to help us and we can always seek them out to help them. If our goal is to spend eternity with God then it's critical that we make sure we are spending time with the right people. This said, we are to witness to unbelievers but we must not join in or imitate their sinful behavior.

--Delighting in, taking joy in, cherishing, and valuing God's law must be our daily aim. Psalm 119:14 states, "I have rejoiced in the way of Your testimonies, and much as in all riches." And the 16th verse of Psalm 119 says, "I will delight myself in Your statues; I will not forget Your word." Joshua stated in 1:8, "This Book of the Law shall not depart from your mouth, but you shall meditate in it day and night, that you may observe to do according to all that is written in it. For then you will make your way prosperous, and then you will have good success." God provides spiritual truth from the beginning and throughout His word so that we will be prosperous and live a successful life. Meditating on God's words means that we spend time reading and thinking about it. It also means that we ask God to show us where we should change so that we are living a life pleasing to God. By asking the right spiritual questions, we learn the right spiritual truths. The more we study the Word, the closer we get to God.

--Trees grow when they have a water source, just like we will grow when our source is the law of the Lord. Trees which have been watered have deep roots which prevent storms from blowing it to and fro. The God's word always us to remain firm in life when the storms of life try to uproot us. In Jeremiah 17:7-8, we read a similar truth, "Blessed in the man who trusts in the Lord, and whose hope is the Lord, For he shall be like a tree planted by the waters, which spreads out its roots by the river, and will not fear when heat comes; but its leaf will be green, and will not be anxious in the year of drought, nor will cease from yielding fruit." Now this will not mean that we will never have adversity or difficulty. While we may never be guaranteed health, wealth or earthly success; we can gain wisdom when we have God's Word in our hearts. God becomes our source, just as water is the tree's source of life.

--We are told what happens with those who decide to live in the darkness, an ungodly life; we will be separated from God and His glorious light. Those who decide to live outside of God's will and His law will not escape God's judgment. Those who seek guidance for life in God's law rather than from the world will be blessed. When our goal is to honor God in all we do, we gain His favor and we are grounded and steady, not easily swayed to the world. "They are like straw before the wind, and like chaff that a storm carries away (Job 21:18)." Chaff is very light and is blown away by the wind while the good grain falls back to earth. Chaff is a symbol of a faithless life that drifts along without direction. The chaff is like many people who have no true foundation in Christ. Good grain is a symbol of a faithful life that can be used by God. Unlike grain, we can choose our direction in life.

In Deuteronomy 30:15, God tells us, "See I have set before you today life and prosperity, death and adversity; in that I command you today to love the Lord your God, to walk in His ways and to keep His commandments and His statutes and His judgments, that you may live and multiply, and that the Lord your God may bless you in the land where you are entering to possess it." In verses 19-20, God states, "...So choose life in order that you may live, you and your descendants, by loving the Lord your God, by obeying His voice, and by holding fast to Him, for this is your life and the length of your days, that you may live in the land which the Lord swore to your fathers..." Moses told Israel that God wanted His people to choose life so that they could continue to enjoy His blessings. God's telling us this same thing in this first Psalm.

--Our reward is clear. "The Lord knows the days of the upright, and their inheritance shall be forever (Psalm 37:18)." I connect this to what Jesus said in John 3:16, "For God so loved the world that He gave His only begotten Son, that whosoever believes in Him shall not perish but have eternal life." Our reward for living a Godly, upright life is eternal life. Our faith is based on believing and trusting that God will do what He says He will do. There are times when the devil tries to influence me and It's hard for me to stay focused but I have learned that by staying deeply in God's word, fellowshipping with other believers each day, reading Godly and spiritual books, staying in prayer, my challenges are reduced and my joy is increased. Hebrews 10:35 states, "So do not throw away your confidence; it will be richly rewarded. You need to persevere so that when you have done the will of God, you will receive what He has promised." Psalm 1 is a promise and a warning, its law and wisdom.

Be encouraged today knowing that God's Word is given to help us, instruct us, guide us into the right path, a less painful path. God loves us so much that He constantly trying to reach us to us, to comfort us and to deliver us. God loves us unconditionally and with a love so great and incomprehensible that He gave us a body of teachings and law so that we can know what He expects from us and how we should live.

"His Word is a lamp unto my feet, and a light unto my path (Psalm 119:105)."

Spiritual Refresher for Day #145

Take this time to spiritually reflect on this point: Being reconciled with Christ.

No one likes separation, such as being separated from love ones or from friends. Imagine what it would be like to be separated from God's love and light for eternity. If we are cast down in hell, we will be cast down for eternity. In Luke 16:20-31, we learn about a rich man who is sent down to hell where he was in torment. The rich man asked Abraham to send Lazarus, who is in heaven, to go to his father's house to warn his five brothers about the hellfire so that they would not come to that place of torment. Abraham tells the rich man that "they have Moses and the Prophets, let them listen to them. Abraham says that if they do not listen to Moses and the Prophets, they would not be convinced even if someone rises from the dead." These are serious words which tell us that the punishment for living outside of God's will is eternal torment. This scares me and motivates me to strive harder each day to live a life pleasing to God. In order to not be separated from God, we must work to be reconciled with Christ, "living holy and blameless, and above reproach in His sight" as it says in Colossians 1:22.

There are two types of fire: the Holy Ghost fire which purifies our hearts; and the hell fire which will destroy us if we fail to live for Christ. Our job is to work to be purified and cleansed from the inside out, so we can help others. We must prepare ourselves to be sensitive to what God is moving us to do, and to be. There will always be a separation unless we reconcile ourselves to Christ and His light. No one can gain salvation by walking in the middle or being lukewarm as Jesus stated to the church of Laodiceans in Revelation 3:14-22. We must be zealous for Christ as Jesus stated. We must have a driven and motivated heart for reconciliation with Christ while we still strive for glory. In this vein, we must make a sincere effort to help bring others to the truth of Jesus Christ which will save them from the hellfire. We don't want to be the one who could have saved a family member or a loved one from going to hell, and failed to help them.

"For this reason we also, since the day we heard it, do not cease to pray for you, and to ask that you may be filled with the knowledge of His will in all wisdom and spiritual understanding; that you may walk worthy of the Lord, fully pleasing Him, being fruitful in every good work and increasing in the knowledge of God; strengthened with al might, according to His glorious power, for all patience and longsuffering with joy; giving thanks to the Father who has qualified us to be partakers of the inheritance of the saints of light. He has delivered us from the power of darkness and conveyed us into the kingdom of the Son of His love (Colossians 1:9-13)." The above verses of scripture are so rich in wisdom. We are encouraged to be filled with the knowledge of God's will so we can know what pleases God. There are many who fail to understand this critical point and the ramifications of not living a life pleasing to God.

"All things were created through Him and for Him (Colossians 1:16)." We were created for God's pleasure, to serve Him and to glorify Him through our actions. I don't believe any believer in Christ wants to be separated from God for eternity. I don't want anyone separated from God, not even those who don't like me. I want all to be in heaven. This being the case, it's important for all of us to get more serious with our spiritual practices, so we can help others.

God wants none of His creations to burn in the hellfire which is why His word is so clear as to what we all must do. I want everyone to be saved as well. I want others to understand why it's important to live a Godly righteous life; because I want no one to say that I didn't do all I could to help others obtain the prize of the upward call of heaven.

How do we become reconciled with Christ? "If indeed you continue in the faith, grounded and steadfast, and are not moved away from the hope of the Gospel which you heard, which was preached to every creature under heaven... (Colossians 1:23). This verse provides a direction along with the fruits of the Spirit as described in Galatians 5:22-23, "Love, joy, peace, patience, kindness, goodness, faithfulness, gentleness and self-control." The fruit of the Spirit are the Godly qualities that Christ wishes us to love by.

This world is not our home, so why do we continue to try to please those living in this world and who is 'of the world'. "For our citizenship is in heaven, from which we also eagerly wait for the Savior, the Lord Jesus Christ (Philippians 3:20)."

Having the right priorities help us to reconcile towards the will of God. "Therefore be imitators of God as dear children. And walk in love.. (Ephesians 5:1-2)." God wants us to be His children in truth and in spirit. We do this by imitating God through the reading, studying and meditating on His word.

2 Corinthians 13:11, our earthly goal is outlined, "Finally brothers, good-bye. Aim for perfection. Listen to my appeal, be of one mind, live in peace; and the God of love and peace will be with you." We should all aim for perfection, which means that we are constantly striving to be better, growing in the knowledge of the Lord. Once we understand our mission, then we are to help others, as Jesus stated in Mathew 28:19, "Therefore go and make disciples of all nations...and teaching them to obey everything I have commanded you." The great commission is on all believers in Christ.

Being in right relationship with God requires us to get our hearts right and then share what we have learned with those who are lost. We don't have to be perfect to share the knowledge. No one knows how long our love ones or our neighbors have on this planet, so it's imperative to take this moment to share the good news of the Gospel of Jesus Christ with everyone. I hope that no one is separated from the love of God for eternity. As Jesus proclaimed in Galilee in Mark 1:15, "The kingdom of God is near. Repent and believe the good news!" No one knows when our time will come and it would be such a shame if we didn't take this opportunity to preach the Gospels to those nearest to us.

Spiritual Refresher for Day #146

Take this time to spiritually reflect on this point: Being an inheritor!

"He who overcomes shall inherit all things, and I will be his God and he shall be My son. But the cowardly, unbelieving, abominable, murderers, sexually immoral, sorcerers, idolaters and all liars shall have their part in the lake which burns with fire and brimstone, which is the second death (Revelation 21:7-8)."

The above words in Revelation made me think about being an inheritor of God's mighty promises. I want the Lord to be my God and I want to be His son so I decided to make sure I understood what it meant to be a new creation, in truth and in spirit. I looked at different bible translations to gain a better understanding because they helped me to get more Godly insight.

"Therefore, as God's chosen people, holy and dearly loved, clothe yourselves with compassion, kindness, humility, gentleness and patience. Bear with each other and forgive whatever grievances (complaints) you may have against one another. Forgive as the Lord forgave you. And over all these virtues put on love, which binds them all together in perfect unity. Let the peace of Christ rule in your hearts, since as members of one body you were called to peace. And be thankful. Let the Word of Christ dwell in you richly as you teach and admonish one another with all wisdom, and as you sing psalms, hymns, and spiritual songs with gratitude in your hearts to God. And whatever you do, whether in word and deed, do it all in the name of the Lord Jesus, giving thanks to God the Father through Him (Colossians 3:12-17)."

This is such clear guidance on how to live each day and become an inheritor. I decided to meditate on each phrase so I could become an inheritor of God's promises. First, we are God's chosen, the believer and follower of Christ Jesus. In that when we believe and follow the will of God, we set ourselves up to be an overcomer. 1 John 5:4 states, "...for everyone born of God overcomes the world. This is the victory that has overcome the world, even our faith." As a child of God, we have the power within us to overcome the world. The power cannot be connected to or accessed until we clothe ourselves in the concepts of the faith which centers on love, forgiveness and gratitude. We are told to do everything, in word or deed, in the name of Jesus Christ. Imagine how amazing life would be if all Christ-like believers did everything each day in the name of Christ. For example, when someone was mean or hateful to us, we responded like Christ by showing them love and praying for them, "Forgive them Father, help them to understand how much you love them and draw them closer to you." Imagine a world where people who are in Christ, would not respond as the natural world responds but as a true Christ-like follower. This can only happen when we allow the Word of Christ to dwell deeply and richly in us.

I have a new directive each day to say only uplifting, edifying or encouraging words to those around me. I have a new operating life principle which tells me to not get mad at others but to love them and then pray for them. My new life is focused on responding to all people in love, kindness, gentleness, humility and patience regardless of how they treat me because this is Christ's will. I realized that when I started this that I had to bite my tongue and deal with my pride and ego but over time, it got easier as I learned to give those negative emotions to God, and he eased my inner distress from those unGodly emotions and feelings. The Bible states clearly that life as a follower of Christ will be hard, but we are to be of good cheer because Christ overcame. Jesus said in John 16:33, "These things I have spoken to you, that in Me you may have peace. In this world you will have tribulation (trouble); but be of good cheer, I have overcome the world."

Romans 8:16-18 provides more insight, "The Spirit Himself bears witness with our spirit that we are children of God, and if children, then heirs -- heirs of God and joint heirs with Christ, if indeed we suffer with Him, that we may also be glorified together. For I consider that the sufferings of this present time are not worthy to be compared with the glory which shall be revealed in us." We, as believers, must decide what we are aiming for: this world or the Divine world with Christ at the right hand of the Father. Being a follower of Christ and imitating His example is a challenge and will cause us to suffer from time to time but it's for the highest goal possible. Proof of the believer's ultimate faith is that he or she suffers, whether it comes through ridicule, anger, persecution or mockery, because of his Lord.

Anyone can be loving to those who are nice to us but Jesus healed the Roman Centurion's ear which Peter cut off during His arrest (John 18:10-11). We are called to walk in the spirit and we will inherit that which was promised but we must be qualified through faith and love.

"Giving thanks to the Father who has qualified us to be partakers of the inheritance of the saints in the light (Colossians 1:12)." Walking in the spirit is walking in the light and in purity of spirit. God dwells in the realm of truth and purity, and we can only inherit when we walk in this same manner. Now, we will never be perfect but this doesn't mean we don't strive each day to crucify the flesh and love with all our heart. When we fall down, we repent and then do better the next time. Walking in the Spirit allows us to gain strength so the next time we confront the same sin, we are better able to overcome it.

"In Him also we have obtained an inheritance, being predestined according to the purpose of Him who works all things according to the council of His will (Ephesians 1:11)." It's all about God and living in His will, not living in our pride or ego which wants to be recognized, appeased, approved but God has approved us and we need to learn to accept His love completely. As Christ was an overcomer, so are we, when we live in the will of the Father.

"So now, brethren, I command you to God and to the word of His grace which is able to build you up and give you an inheritance among all those who are sanctified (Acts 20:32)." The Holy Spirit gives us the strength to endure the troubles of this world, and our faith and our love connects us to the Holy Spirit.

We need to look past our present troubles and focus on our eternal inheritance. Life, joy, peace, perfection, God's presence, Christ's glorious companionship and all else God has planned is the Christ-like believer's reward and inheritance in heaven. Be encouraged today knowing that you have been set up for success through Christ! Your inheritance is waiting for you to collect it! Don't disqualify yourself, accept God's love and share it with everyone!

Spiritual Refresher for Day #147

Take this time to spiritually reflect on this point: Expanding our vision.

Isaiah 42:18 states, "Hear you deaf; and look, you blind, that you may see."

The devil wishes to keep us blind and unaware of our true nature. Many believers have been blinded by the lies of the world, not realizing who they are in Christ. Isaiah warns of this point in 42:20, "Seeing many things, but you do not observe; opening the ears but do not hear."

I have heard some psychologists say, "perception is reality." This is true because our thoughts and words can bring certain things into existence. What we dwell on in our thought life creates a certain reality for us. When we believe God's Word and His promises for us, we live an uplifted reality. We must learn to expand our vision so that we can align it that our God's. Reading the word of God deeply has many purposes, to including learning how we should see the world around us. We also learn how to discern the truth from the lies of the devil. "By this we know the spirit of truth and the spirit of error (1 john 4:6)."

The devil loves confusion and chaos, and many people continue to be blinded by the devils lies each day. The Bible shows us the right way to view the world. Hosea 4:6, "My people are destroyed from lack of knowledge." Many believers actually attend church and do not have a spirit of truth inside because they continue to allow the devil to blind them. The Bible tells us that "Do not be deceived, God is not to be mocked, for whatever a man sows, that he will also reap (Galatians 6:7)." There is a path which God laid out for us that will lead to an abundant life. We must remove the scales from our eyes and seek at every opportunity to know God's truth.

Jesus explained, "If you continue in my word, you are truly my disciples, and you will know the truth, and the truth will set you free (John 8:31-32)." The spirit of truth helps us to discern the truth from the spirit of error. So many believers are living a life of "operator error" because they allow the spirit of error to influence them and direct their feet.

The only thing separating us from knowing and remaining ignorant is our willingness to truly know. There are two ways to read the Word of God: Exegesis is the proper way and results in knowing the truth that makes us free; and Eisigesis is the improper way which causes us to remain ignorant, misinformed, and stagnant in an area of our faith. When we are faithful to read and study the Scriptures, the Holy Spirit is faithful to teach us. The key to wanting to expand our vision is to read the Word of God with a teachable spirit. Eisigesis is reading into God's Word what we already believe, not having a teachable spirit. Exegesis is reading out of God's Word what it says and applying it to our lives with a teachable spirit.

The Scriptures are supposed to change us. We have all been corrupted by society which is why we must all enlarge our vision to see the world through a Godly lens. Jesus offers us a chance to have a deep and knowing vision. He calls us by name, just as He did His disciples, to come away with Him and give us a larger vision. I learned that when I prayed and read the scriptures asking God to speak to me, I started developing an inner spirit of truth. God wants us to see more clearly so we can share that vision with those around us.

Dave Branon stated in the Daily Bread Devotional on 24 may 2005, "Instead of trying to change God's Word to fit our own ideas, let's allow the Word to change us." I think that this is the essence of having a teachable spirit. Being teachable expands our vision.

I propose that nine things happen when we enlarge our vision:

1) We see the world as it is, corrupt and full of darkness, seeking to lead us away from God.
2) We understand that our true nature is in Christ and we live accordingly.
3) We realize that great power lies within us when we align our vision with God's Word.
4) We are at peace and have an inner joy.
5) We are focused on the right things, right battles and right way to live.
6) We find purpose and meaning through God and His son Jesus Christ, and not from the world.
7) We are empowered and energized to do great things each day, because we know whose we are.
8) We are a light to others, and we add light and order to the world.
9) We stop being self-absorbed and start being God-absorbed which leads to an abundant life.

"Then the Lord answered me and said, 'Write the vision and make it plain on tablets, that he may run who reads it. For the vision is yet for an appointed time; But at the end it will speak, and it will not lie. Though it tarries, wait for it; because it will surely come, it will not tarry. Behold the proud, his soul is not upright in him; But the just shall live by his faith (Habakkuk 2:2-4)."

There was a time when I was so broken, depressed and hopeless but today I rejoice because of my relationship with God and how He has enlarged my vision. "For Your Word has given me life (Psalm 119:50)." Today, I shout for joy and have a praise on the inside I can't keep to myself.

"And Jabez called on the God of Israel saying, 'Oh that You would bless me indeed, and enlarge my territory, that Your hand would be with me indeed, and that You would keep me from evil, that I may not cause pain!' So God granted him what he requested (1 Chronicles 4:10)."

Today, ask God to enlarge your vision so that you can glorify His Holy name. Ask the Lord to take you to a place where you can see what He is calling you to be.

Spiritual Refresher for Day #148

Take this time to spiritually reflect on this point: Being a seeker for God's heart.

God is Love! God is Omnipresent, Omnipotent and Omniscient! God is Light! God is Perfect! God is Longsuffering! God is Holy! God is Faithful! God is Merciful! God is Pure! God is Gracious! God is Generous! God is Steadfast! God is Eternal! God is Hope! God is Abundant! God is Compassionate! God is Righteous! God is Just! God is Forgiving! God is True! These are just a few adjectives of His nature. I could write all day about His Ways and Characteristics. I wanted to share a few of these because they also comprise the Lord's heart. This refresher is about being a seeker of God's heart so that we can move our nature closer to His nature.

The Bible speaks of King David being a man after God's own heart. "The Lord has sought for Himself a man after His own heart (1 Samuel 13:14)." Instead of Saul, God was going to chose one whose heart was like His own. This is also mentioned again in Acts 13:22, "I have found David, son of Jesse, a man after My own heart, who will do all My will." No person seeking after God's own heart is perfect, yet he will recognize sin and repent as David did. David sought to know God's heart and this is the goal of this tip to help us to always be seekers of God's heart. David made mistakes, slept with Bathsheba and had her husband sent to the battlefront where he was killed, but David repented (2 Samuel 11 and 12). David stated, "I have sinned against the Lord (2 Samuel 12:13)." David was a true worshipper whom God seeks, one who pursued the truth and the light even after making bad decisions. We can't escape punishment; for example, David's son with Bathsheba died but David turned away from his sin and God forgave him. Even when we fall short or into the abyss, God is still routing for and loving us. In the second part of 2 Samuel 12:13, "Nathan said to David, 'The Lord also has put away your sin and you shall not die.'" The Lord graciously forgave David and He will forgive us but we must always be mindful that there are consequences of our sinful actions. While we can't escape punishment, we also can't escape God's awesome love! Because of God's amazing grace and mercy, every sinner has another opportunity to live an upright life in order to gain the promises of the Lord.

Seeking after God's heart is about being on a quest for fellowship with God. When we stay focused on our quest to know God's heart, we overcome the challenges that come in life. It enables us to believe that God will bless all that we attempt for His glory, to believe that we will have success. Success is defined as being at peace and having inner joy despite the unexpected sorrow which may come from time to time.

When we give our hearts in total trust and loving surrender to God, the Lord awakens a type of faith that allows us to flourish during the storms of life. Giving God our whole heart means trusting Him completely and fully, relying on His goodness, grace and love while believing He is faithful to His promises. The heart is the foundation of our faith and the source of our physical strength as well.

I wanted to highlight some verses which discuss the heart:

"How my heart yearns within me (Job 19:27)." Our goal should be to yearn for God.

"My heart is steadfast, O God, my Heart is steadfast; I will sing and give praise (Psalm 57:7)." Giving God praise in the dark times shows our faith.

"I will praise the Lord with my whole heart (Psalm 111:1)." Jesus might have had this in mind when He said, "You shall love the Lord with your all your heart... (Mathew 22:37)."

"Then I will give them a heart to know Me, that I am the Lord and they shall be My people, and I will be their God, for they shall turn to Me with their whole heart (Jeremiah 24:7)." God is telling us what He desires us to do, to turn our whole heart towards Him.

"Then I will give them one heart, and I will put a new spirit within them, and take the stony heart out of their flesh, and give them a heart of flesh (Ezekiel 11:19)." When we seek God with our whole heart, He provides everything we will need to live a new life.

"Blessed are the pure in heart, for they shall see God (Mathew 5:8)." If we want to see God, then we must become a seeker of God's heart.

"For with the heart one believes, unto righteousness... (Romans 10:10)." Our heart is the doorway which leads to all things of God.

"Let me have joy from you in the Lord; refresh my heart in the Lord (Philemon 20)." Joy comes from the Lord and through our hearts which spreads through our bodies.

"Do not let your heart faint, do not be afraid, and do not tremble or be terrified because of them; for the Lord your God is He who goes with you, to fight for you against your enemies, to save you (Deuteronomy 20:3-4)." When our heart is steadfast, we tell the Lord that we are trusting Him completely and He will save us. Each day we should seek to guard, protect, cleanse, fortify and edify our hearts so that it is aligned with God's heart.

We must all take great care to work to continually cleanse our hearts because, "the Lord does not see as man sees; for man looks at the outward appearance, but the Lord looks at the heart (1 Samuel 16:7)." The Hebrew concept of heart embodies emotions, will, intellect and desires. Our lives will reflect our hearts as Jesus explained in Mathew 12:34-35, "For out of the abundance of the heart the mouth speaks. A good man out of the good treasure of his heart brings forth good things, and an evil man out of the evil treasure brings forth evil things." Too many believers think that evil is the great horrible acts that some do, which they are, but evil is also things which is not 'of God', those things which doesn't please Him. Evil can be as simple as lying or stealing or not forgiving or not loving. There are many things which is not 'of God' and when we becomes seekers of God's heart, we learn what pleases God so that we do those things which please the Lord, those loving and Godly things! God blesses those who seek after the things that He loves!

Spiritual Refresher for Day #149

Take this time to spiritually reflect on this point: Saving faith.

Saving faith is about being in relationship with Jesus Christ whereby we trust Him for the forgiveness of our sins and eternal life, along with believing that He is living inside us through the Holy Spirit. With saving faith, we develop an intimate personal relationship with Christ Jesus. It's about believing in Jesus' Lordship. In the Gospel, Jesus is addressed as "Lord" 185 times. Saving faith urges us to make Jesus the Lord of our life. Saving faith allows us to accept Jesus as the one who paid our sin debt and is now the only way to the Father.

If we believe that Jesus took our sins away on the cross then we don't continue to relive our sins in our mind, wallowing in the shame of the past. We must not just have an intellectual faith, the belief that we understand only with our mind, but a saving faith where our hearts and faith are aligned and intertwined with an intimate relationship with Jesus Christ. Our faith must be centered on how Christ saved us through His sacrifice on the cross, and then that very same faith inspires us to change. We are saved by grace but that doesn't mean we can continue living in rebellion to God's will. If our lives remain unchanged, we don't truly believe the truth we claim to believe. It's more than just saying Halleluiah (Praise be to God) but showing our praise through a commitment of our whole self to God.

I wanted to provide a few verses on faith:

"For we maintain that a man is justified by faith apart from works of the law (Romans 3:28)." Faith eliminates the pride of human effort, because faith is not a deed or a work we can do. Faith is based on our relationship with Christ.

"For we walk by faith (2 Corinthians 5:7)." Faith inspires us to live an upright life.

"For by grace you have been saved through faith; and that not of yourselves, it is the gift of God; not as a result of works, so that no one can boast (Ephesians 2:8-9)." Because of this amazing gift, we should live with love, gratitude, praise and joy. We are motivated to live a changed life by serving God and others with an eagerness that represents a new loving heart.

"One Lord, one faith... (Ephesians 4:5)." Our singular commitment to Christ as our Lord and Savior. Honoring Jesus with our faith becomes our goal each day.

"I know that I will remain and continue with you all for your progress and joy in the faith (Philippians 1:25)." Jesus Christ was humble, willing to obey and serve God with a servant's attitude. Our faith should produce a joyful servant's attitude as well. Faith and joy should go together in our hearts.

"Even so faith, if it has no works, is dead, being by itself (James 2:17)." While we cannot earn salvation by serving and obeying God but such actions show our commitment to God is real. Works of loving service are not a substitute for, but rather a verification of, our faith in Christ (Commentary from the Life Application Study Bible page 2189).

Jesus mentions four types of faith in the Gospels: 1) no faith; 2) little faith; 3) great faith; and 4) failing faith.

No faith: When the disciples were in the boat with Jesus traveling from the western shore to the eastern shore on the sea of Galilee, the wind rose and waves started pounding the boat. Jesus was asleep and his disciples awoke him saying, "Teacher, do You not care that we are perishing?" Jesus arose and rebuked the wind and said to the sea, "Peace, be still! and the wind ceased. Jesus told His disciples, "Why are you so fearful? How is it that you have no faith? (Mark 4:35-41)."

Little faith: Jesus was teaching about not worrying and said, "Do not worry about your life, what you will eat or what you will drink; nor about your body, what you will put on..." Jesus goes on to say, O you of little faith? (Mathew 6:25-30)." In Mathew 6:33, Jesus explains a guiding principle of our faith, "But seek first the kingdom of God and His righteousness, and all these things will be added to you." Faith is about knowing the truth even when we don't see it.

Great faith: Jesus was met by a centurion in Mathew 8:5-10 who ask Jesus to heal his servant who was paralyzed. Jesus offered to come and heal the man's servant but the centurion explained, "Lord, I am not worthy that You should come under my roof. But only speak a word, and my servant will be healed..." When Jesus heard it, He marveled, and said to those who followed, Assuredly, I say to you I have not found such great faith, not even in Israel." This is the goal of all believers, to be person of great faith. I have heard 'great faith' as described as seeing the light in our hearts, even when our eyes only see darkness.

Failing faith: After our Lord and Savior was crucified and resurrected, He appeared to his disciples but Thomas was not there. When the disciples told Thomas that that they had seen the Lord, Thomas said, "Unless I see in His hands the print of the nails, and put my finger into the print of the nails, and put my hand into His side, I will not believe (John 20:25)." Eight days later, Jesus appeared to his disciples and Thomas was there. Jesus showed Thomas his wounds and said, "Do not be unbelieving but believing." Thomas answered and said, "My Lord, my God!" Jesus said to him, Thomas, because you have seen Me, you have believed. Blessed are those who have not seen and yet have believed (John 20:29)." Although Thomas saw all the miracles of Jesus, his faith failed him and he needed to see with his natural eyes.

Saving faith is about focusing on what Christ did for us on the cross. Saving faith is centered on the (F)orgiveness we were given through Christ; the (A)vailability of God's grace for anyone; the (I)mpossibility of sin being allowed in heaven; (T)urning away from our sins and repenting; in order to receive our reward, (H)eaven. F-A-I-T-H.

When we have saving faith, we say, "Forsaking All, I Trust Him." F-A-I-T-H!

Now, I used to have no faith, and then developed a little faith, and I must admit that still sometimes have a failing faith but the difference is that I now constantly seek each day to develop and build my relationship with Christ so that I can grow into a believer of great faith. I recognize my weaknesses only so that I don't fall prey to the tricks and traps of satan. I don't dwell on my weaknesses; I dwell on my Savior and my Awesome God! I dwell on becoming a light in a dark world. I dwell on uplifting and edifying others so I can glorify God!

"No one who is born of God will continue to sin, because God's seed remains in him; he cannot go on sinning, because he is born of God (1 John 3:9)." Later in 1 John 4:11-12, Jesus tells us, "Dear friends, since God so loved us, we also ought to love one another. No one has ever seen God; but if we love one another, God lives in us and His love is made complete in us." When Jesus comes to be in us, with us and upon us; we eagerly seek to please Him, not hold on to old attitudes and beliefs. Trust Jesus Christ right now in truth and spirit; be a person of Godly love today! Be a Christ-like example to others, this day!

We serve a great God! I now understand that my walk in the Lord is based on a 'saving faith' that I must live day by day, hour by hour, and minute by minute based on my love for God and His Son, Jesus Christ.

Today, let us focus on growing an abundance of 'saving faith' so that we can be a light to others!

Spiritual Refresher for Day #150

Take this time to spiritually reflect on this point: Desiring and developing purity.

This refresher is focused on purifying our spirits, hearts, thoughts, words and actions through the Holy Spirit. One night recently, I was asking God to show me areas where I needed to work on and 'purity' came to my heart. I have so much to be thankful for because God has liberated me from so much but there were times when my thought life wasn't as pleasing to God as it should've been. I had changed my words and actions so that I glorified God but there were just times when I judged others or had other unGodly thoughts. The Holy Spirit explained that I had to burn off all those unGodly thoughts even if no one else knew what I was thinking. I felt empowered because I knew the Lord was showing me a new area where to serve Him. I started watching my thought life even more closely so that I could put every thought into captivity which did not glorify God. I posit that when we start to develop purity of thought, the quality of our lives will improve and blessings will more freely enter our lives.

In 1 Corinthians 10:31, we learn our supreme purpose, to glorify God. "Therefore whatever you eat or drink, or whatever you do, do all to the glory of God." We are told to glorify God but we can't do that with darkness in our heart. Purity is about the light and being steadfastly positive despite whatever we encounter or see. God placed on my heart that if I had any negative thoughts then I wasn't glorifying Him. If I had any bad thoughts about anyone, judging thoughts, vengeful thoughts, unloving thoughts then I was glorifying satan, the prince of darkness and illusions. I often speak to people about not fighting the wrong battles in their mind and being negative in one of the ways people fight the wrong battles.

We are done or undone by our appetites. What I mean is that some people give in to every thought or whim which comes into their mind without any true Godly discernment. Our appetites or desires can lead us in the wrong direction. Having an appetite for the Word of God is great and healthy, while having an appetite for not being good to ourselves is not healthy. There are some people who are addicted to a certain kind of sadness, shame or unloving behavior and that becomes their world and limits them. We should not let our appetites rule over us especially if they are unhealthy appetites. Purity of thought leads to a new type of abundance that is 'of God'. God is Pure, and so should we strive to imitate Him!

The Bible discusses how not everything that is permissible or lawful is good for us. The world is all about "having it our way", not a Godly way. There are always enablers who will say "that's okay to do" because everyone else is doing it. As Christians, we are guided to be separate, holy, righteous and just; which is purity.

I came to a new understanding about how I needed to honor God in all I thought and did. It wasn't just avoiding sinful behaviors but understanding how my thoughts could be sinful too. We all have specific areas which are harder for us than others. "Do you not know that you are the temple of God and that the Spirit of God dwells in you? If anyone defiles the temple of God, God will destroy him. For the temple of God is holy, which temple you are (1 Corinthians 3:16-17)." One way to honor God's temple is by maintaining focused thoughts which are of the light, and not the darkness. Whenever we allow ourselves to succumb to the darkness, we are pleasing satan.

I love the following verse, "For the wisdom of this world is foolishness with God (1 Corinthians 4:19)." We are called to grow in all righteousness which is about being pure. Moving closer to the mind of God can only be done by purifying every part within us. I believe that some believers are not receiving the blessings in their lives because they still have not put their thought life into captivity. Purity of heart and spirit is about dwelling on what is good, loving, kind and uplifting. So there is two parts of being pure: eradicating the unGodly thoughts, and dwelling on the Godly thoughts. I started studying the scriptures on purity. Below are a few of the ones that specifically address this topic.

"So God, who knows the heart, acknowledged them by giving then the Holy Spirit, just as He did to us, and made no distinction between us and them, purifying their hearts by faith (Acts 15:9)." Since God knows our hearts, I decided that I need to burn off the impurities even the unseen impurities that no other person knew about. I realized that I had the power through the Holy Spirit to choose what I dwelled on in my spirit and heart.

"By purity, by knowledge, by longsuffering, by kindness, by the Holy Spirit, by sincere love, by the word of truth, by the power of God... (2 Corinthians 6:6-7)." God has given us a direction and it's in sincere love but we can't be love if we are not pure of heart, mind and spirit.

"Let no one despise your youth, but be an example to the believers in word, in conduct, in love, in spirit, in faith, in purity (1 Timothy 4:16)." Although my youth was full of mistakes, those mistakes were also my greatest teachers. If I want to live for Christ then I had to be like Christ and not like I used to be when I lived outside the will of Christ.

"Therefore submit to God. Resist the devil and he will flee from you. Draw near to God and He will draw near to you. Cleanse your hands, you sinners; and purify your hearts, you double-minded (James 4:7-8)."

"And everyone who has this hope in Him purifies himself, just as He (Jesus) is pure (1 John 3:3)."

"He who loves purity of heart and has grace on his lips, the king will be his friend (Proverbs 22:11)."

Desiring and developing purity are two separate concepts because the intent or desire must come first. After we become intentional, then we start purifying ourselves, and continue to do so. Philippians 4:8-9 provides all the guidance that the Christ-like believer needs, "Finally, brethren, whatever things are true, whatever things are noble, whatever things are just, whatever things are PURE, whatever things are lovely, whatever things are of good report, if there is any virtue and if there is anything praiseworthy -- meditate on these things." Wow! This was exactly what I needed to recalibrate my thoughts. When I started this new way of conduct, I found that it was hard to meditate on these things at first because my mind was used to having its own way. I started to train my spirit and now I catch myself in order to stay focused on purity. At first it was a challenge but I allowed the Holy Spirit to move within me and I found it easier after a time to work this spiritual concept.

The Apostle Paul writes one of the most beautifully insightful lines, "Only let your conduct be worthy of the Gospel of Christ (Philippians 1:27)." I will end on this verse because it speaks more about purity than I can even imagine or write.

Be encouraged today, knowing that you have the power to craft the type of future you wish to live!

Spiritual Refresher for Day #151

Take this time to spiritually reflect on this point: Living within the will of God.

Years ago, I knew nothing about living within the will of God. I knew very little about what was actually pleasing to God outside of the 10 Commandments, although I never took those very seriously either. I had to suffer a great "life quake" in order to understand what was truly important, God! The purpose of these refreshers is help myself stay focused and perhaps helps others gain some insight. I hope that others may not have to go through all that I went through to in order to gain a measure of inner peace. Today, I have a new reverence for God's Words, commandments and living within His will.

The will of God was really clear once I opened up my heart and allowed my spirit to connect with the Spirit of God. King David stated in Psalm 19:14, "Let the words of my mouth and meditation of my heart be acceptable in Your sight, O Lord, strength and Redeemer." David sought after God and wanted to do what was pleasing to the Lord. Although David would make mistakes, he was a man after God's own heart because he repented and then strived harder to live within God's will. We all make mistakes but we don't have to live in willful sin. Proverbs 14:12 states, "There is a way that seems right to a man but in the end is the way of death." We must understand what the will of God is by reading and meditating on His word each day.

There is such great wisdom in the Bible. For example, "That we may live peaceful and quiet lives in all Godliness and holiness. For this is good, and pleases God our Savior, who wants all men to be saved and to come to a knowledge of the truth. For there is one God and one mediator between God and Men, the man Jesus Christ, who gave Himself for a ransom for all men (1 Timothy 2:2-6)." God's Word provides guidance so that we will not stay in the darkness nor remain lost in this world.

Living in a way to please God was such a foreign concept for me when I started reading the Bible but overtime I grow in discernment. I never understood how living in a certain manner really mattered because I thought I was a good person overall but I never comprehended that "being a good person overall" was not anywhere near good enough for God. I was judging myself based on my peers and those around me but most of those around me were just as lost as myself. I had no concept of God inside of me nor did I understand who I was in Christ. I thought that I was better than most, although a little worse than others, but that is not the standard that God tells us in His word.

"Do not love the world or anything in the world. If anyone loves the world, the love of the Father is not in him. For everything in the world -- the cravings of sinful man, the lust of his eyes and the boasting of what he has or does -- comes not from the Father but from the world. The world and its desires pass away but the man who does the will of the God lives forever (1 John 2:15-17)."

The above verse would not have had any real meaning to me when I lived in the darkness and when I sought to please the world. I went to church and heard some sermons but nothing touched my heart for any real amount of time because I had my heart closed off to the truth. The eyes of my heart were closed and the ears of my soul were shut because I was seeking the wrong rewards and wrong treasures. I never connected the dots knowing that spiritual health was connected to my own inner well-being. I used to be ill at ease (not at peace), swayed by the things of the world, unhappy and full of stress until I allowed Jesus Christ to be revealed to my heart; from that I changed from the inside out

"Therefore, prepare your minds for actions; be self-controlled; set your hope fully on the grace to be given you when Jesus Christ is revealed. As obedient children, do not conform to the evil desires you had when you lived in ignorance. But just as He who called you is holy, so be holy in all you do; for it is written: Be holy, because I am holy (1 Peter 1: 13-16)." My journey has been one of continuing progress and growth in understanding God's will and what's pleasing to Him. The more my heart was receptive, the more I came to understand about such subjects as love, forgiveness, kindness, charity, joy, etc.

"But is anyone obeys His word, God's love is truly made complete in him. This is how we know we are in Him: Whoever claims to live in Him must walk as Jesus did (1 John 2:5-6)." More truth started to be revealed to my heart when I started seeking Him. The benefits of living within God's will is heaven now and eternal life when we die. "For God gives wisdom and knowledge and joy to a man who is good in His sight (Ecclesiastes 2:26)." I love this verse because it's a promise from God that if we seek to please Him, we will have the things we need in this world.

My journey has been amazing and I want to share it with the world because the joy of the Gospel is also in sharing it with others. I want all to know the joy that I now have because I have different goals and strive for different rewards now.

Be uplifted today knowing that God has told us that, "Fear not, for I am with you (Isaiah 41:10.)."

Spiritual Refresher for Day #152

Take this time to spiritually reflect on this point: Is Jesus enough?

This is a question that many Christians need to ask themselves. I asked myself this very question many days. When I answered this question affirmatively, then the quality of my life changed dramatically.

The Gospel according to John characterize Jesus as God's own light in human form, and believe that Jesus alone brings light to a world otherwise living in darkness. John explains that we can experience God only through the divine light embodied in Jesus. John 1:9 states, "That was the true Light which gives light to every man coming into the world." When I was at my lowest, most broken, depressed and suicidal frame of mind, Jesus gave me light. I came to understand that I may have lost everything but discovered that Jesus was all I needed. I started to trust Jesus regardless of what I saw or experienced, and the scales from my eyes slowly started to fall off.

I read John 3:17 which told me that, "For God did not send His Son into the world to condemn the world, but that the world through Him might be saved."

I had felt condemned to a life of brokenness but when I read the Gospel of John I started to grasp something so profound and beautiful that my thinking was forever changed. Jesus said, "Most assuredly, I say to you, he who believes in Me has everlasting life (John 6:47)."

Was it possible? To have everlasting life... I decided to read the scriptures in search of some comfort. Jesus later stated, "And you shall know the truth, and the truth shall make you free (John 8:32)." I read a few verses later when Jesus stated, "Therefore if the Son makes you free, you shall be free indeed." Overtime as I allowed the verses to enter my heart, I started to understand that freedom was truly about.

I started to read John chapter 10 when Jesus stated, "I am the door. If anyone enters by Me, he will be saved, and will go in and out and find pasture....I have come that they may have live, and that they may have it more abundantly (John 10:9-10)."

I continued to gain knowledge through the Gospel and something touched my heart. When Jesus said, "As the Father loved Me, I also have loved you; abide in My love (John 15:9)." My heart opened up and I felt at that moment that Jesus did love me. I considered myself a sinful and utterly broken human being, but Jesus said that He loved me. Something stirred in me as I read the words, "These things I have spoken to you, that My joy may remain in you, and that your joy may be full." Understanding started to dawn in me, Jesus didn't only come so that I may have everlasting life but that I may have joy in this world despite whatever condition I was in at any present moment. I came to understand that His assurance was a promise I could count on. I developed a faith in Jesus which allowed me to have peace regardless of what was going on around me.

"Peace be with you (John 20:19)." Jesus' words to His apostles before He gave them the Holy Spirit and commissioned them to go out and preach the Gospel, gave me comfort. The peace of Jesus was the goal and His words gave me this peace.

I was led to the verse in Philippians 4:11 when Paul wrote from a Roman prison, "For I have learned in whatever state I am, to be content." If Paul learned to be content, then I could learn to be content. For me it was all about changing my focus. If my ultimate reward was to get to heaven then I needed to believe that Jesus was enough. Either we are going to live a life that tells the world that Jesus is enough or not enough. Some Christians have heard the truth over and over but still live a life not believing that the promise of Jesus is theirs as well. Each day, this type of person chooses to live a life saying that 'Jesus is not enough.' But I learned, how through God's Word, to live a life which says that Jesus is enough.

Joel Osteen explains that, "Our enjoyment of life shouldn't be based on our circumstances. Enjoying life should be an attitude of the heart." An 'attitude of the heart' is a beautiful phrase and it made sense because the Bible talks about loving with our whole heart. Jesus being enough is about the condition of our heart, and what we allow in our hearts. The Gospel was meant to change our heart, mind and soul so that we would be ready when we die to go to our real home. The Bible tells us that this natural world is not our home. Jesus explains in John 14:3 that, "I am going to prepare a place for you..." In Philippians 3:20-21, we read, "For our citizenship is in heaven, from which we eagerly wait for the Savior, the Lord Jesus Christ, who will transform our lowly body that it may be conformed to His glorious body..."

Is Jesus enough? Do you believe that He loves you unconditionally? Do you believe that you have a partner in the Holy Spirit which Jesus promised to send to you? Jesus promised that He would not leave us as orphans in John 14:18. Each day, the believer has a job to do, to believe that Jesus is enough. If you don't believe this simple fact then you crucify Him again and invalidate His work on the cross.

When we believe Jesus is enough, we are no longer fooled by the tricks of the devils. We stop judging others and start loving others as Jesus commanded us. When we believe that Jesus is enough then we trust that the glorious promises written to us in the Bible are true and waiting for us; love becomes our path and we seek to embody love in all we do.

Is Jesus' love enough? If His love is enough then it doesn't matter how others treat us because it's all about Jesus and not our ego or pride. If matters not what others do but it greatly matters what we do each day. We become less self-absorbed and become more Jesus absorbed. If Jesus is enough, then we need to match our words with our belief. Stop living a life less than what Jesus desired for us. There are so many believers who constantly forget how much Jesus loves them.

Today, demonstrate to our Lord and Savior that He is enough through a steadfast demonstration of faith-filled thoughts, words and actions. It's time to stop living a 'less than' life. Get up each day, looking for opportunities to show others that Jesus is enough.

Too many 'believers' still live a life which says that Jesus is not enough as they look to find comfort in alcohol or drugs or smoking or food or sex or other people or beautiful things or cars or other material objects. These people will never find comfort in things because we each have a unique sized space inside which can only be filled with Jesus. I used to chase comfort in many non-spiritual things and always wondered why I was never comforted or at peace.

Until we align our words with our faith, we will keep getting the same results. Too many believers praise and worship too infrequently but when we have Jesus in our hearts, we want to praise and worship Him at all times. I praise Jesus throughout the day and with my whole being. Everyone in my circle knows that I am a follower of Christ through my countenance and my attitude each day. I encourage you to let your faith be clearly known by your attitude each day, and by taking every opportunity to let Jesus know, 'He is enough'. I have a steadfast joy and inner peace because Jesus is enough for me. I dance and have comfort knowing that Jesus is preparing a place for me. I believe and that faith has infected and affected every aspect of my life. I am no longer stressed out by the storms of life and am at peace because I know Jesus didn't leave me as an orphan. As Paul stated, I too have learned to be content in whatever state I am in.

If you get down or sad, tell yourself, "Jesus is enough!" I can testify today that He is enough, He is my everything! He is more than enough! I've got victory in Jesus Christ! And so do you!!

Be uplifted today knowing that Jesus loves you with an unconditional love and that He has prepared a place for you. Today is the perfect time to start living a life where you tell Jesus and the world that, "He is enough." As Jesus was the light to a world of darkness, you can be a light to those around you. Let everyone see a faith in you which says, "I trust You Lord Jesus regardless of what I see or experience." This is how we say, "Jesus is enough!"

When we live a life which says, "Jesus is enough," abundance flows freely into our lives from all sides.

Spiritual Refresher for Day #153

Take this time to spiritually reflect on this point: Building ourselves up.

The anchor verse for this spiritual point is as follows: "But ye, beloved, building up yourselves on your most holy faith, praying in the Holy Ghost, Keep yourselves in the love of God, looking for the mercy of our Lord Jesus Christ unto eternal life (Jude 1:20-21)."

There are many verses in the Bible about how each believer is responsible to build themselves up spiritually. Colossians 2:6-7 states, "As you therefore have received Christ Jesus the Lord, so walk in Him, rooted and built up in Him and established in the faith, as you have been taught, abounding in it with thanksgiving." Once we have heard the truth, then it's on us to build our faith up. We must strive to grow and move towards our God given destiny which was promised to us but this will not happen without work on our part.

Dr Wayne Dyer asks us in his book, *The Power of Intention*, to ponder the meaning behind Anthony de Mello's observation in One Minute Wisdom:"

Why is everyone here so happy except me?
"Because they have learned to see goodness and beauty everywhere," said the Master.

Why don't I see goodness and beauty everywhere?
"Because you cannot see outside of you what you fail to see inside."

Dr. Dyer explains, "What you may fail to see inside is a result of how you choose to process everything and everyone in your world. You project onto the world what you see inside, and you fail to project into the world what you fail to see inside." When we build ourselves up, our whole world changes. By building our inner person, we start to perceive the world differently, in more beautiful and loving ways.

Isaiah 55:8-9 states, "For My thoughts are not your thoughts nor are your ways My Ways, says the Lord. For as the heavens are higher than the earth so are My ways higher than your ways. and My thoughts than your thoughts." We each have a responsibility to God to build ourselves up so that we may break out of the old way of thinking, and old way of doing things. We can ask the Holy Spirit to help us, but the heavy lifting is on us. It's so easy to blame others for our weaknesses and shortcomings without ever taking responsibility for our own salvation.

Life can be as beautiful or as challenging as we think it is. "I love those who love me, and those who seek me diligently will find me (Proverbs 8:17)." This is a promise but it requires us to love and seek God with a sincere heart. Those who love God will happily do His will and not their own will. Too many believers make excuses why they can't follow the commandments of God, or why they can't show love or forgive that unlovable person. Excuses will not get any of us to heaven. This is why we must continue to build ourselves up so that we become more Christ-like each day. Preparation for heaven begins today.

Building ourselves up involves a process of edifying and purifying ourselves, and living a life of love where the ego and pride is set aside so the Holy Spirit can infuse our hearts with love. We each have a responsibility to build our faith to prepare our hearts and spirits so that we can show others the light. When a person builds a house, a foundation is first laid before the floors and walls are then built. This is a good example because it's the same with our spiritual nature which must have a firm foundation in the word of God. The Bible is the foundation for spiritual truth. We build ourselves up by exercising good spiritual habits such as reading the Bible, prayer, fellowshipping with other believers, serving others, ministering and evangelizing, volunteering and listening to God's voice daily. "But God's truth stands firm like a foundation stone with this inscription: The Lord knows those who are His, and 'all who belong to the Lord must turn away from evil' (2 Timothy 2:19)." A building cannot stand with a weak foundation.

Each day, make building a strong spiritual foundation a priority.

"To those who listen to My teaching, more understanding will be given, and they will have an abundance of knowledge. But those who are not listening, even what little understanding they have will be taken away from them (Mathew 13:12)." God is a rewarder to those who seek Him in truth, and by building ourselves each day, we move closer to the upward prize each day.

"I will bless the Lord who guides me; even at night my heart instructs me (Psalm 16:7)." When we build ourselves into the image of Christ, our will begin to show us the way. We will no longer wander aimlessly in the world but the Spirit will show us the way. "So my dear brothers and sisters, be strong and immovable. Always work enthusiastically for the Lord, for you know that nothing you do for the Lord is ever useless (1 Corinthians 15:58)." True success is found in seeking God with our whole heart, mind, soul and strength.

Rumi, a 13th century Sufi poet, wrote a poem which I found insightful:

"You were born with potential.
You were born with goodness and truth.
You were born with ideas and dreams.
You were born with greatness.
You were born with wings.
You are not meant for crawling, so don't.
You have wings.
Learn to use them and fly."

When we build ourselves up on the inside, we are learning how to use our wings. God has given us all we need but we must develop and nurture our inner being because the devil is trying to steal our destiny. We please God when we work to build ourselves up in Godly knowledge and faith. "Finally dear brothers and sisters, We urge you in the name of the Lord Jesus to live in a way that pleases God, as we have taught you (1 Thessalonians 4:1)." We can only hope to build ourselves up through the perfect model of Jesus Christ. Building ourselves up each day to being Christ-like must be our goal. Today, ask God to speak to your heart when you read the scriptures. Ask God to show you in which areas you need to build up. When we build ourselves up, we are able to better deal with hardships in the future and can help others build their foundations as well.

Spiritual refresher for Day #154

Take this time to spiritually reflect on this point: Being fearfully and wonderfully made!

We have so much to be thankful for each day but there are many times that we allow the devil to confuse us and clouds our thinking so that we aren't as grateful as we should be. We continue to want, desire and need 'things' which blind us from who God intends us to be. We were created to praise and worship God who created us to thrive! The greatest blessing that God has given us this day, is life. People want proof of God, just see yourself breathing and living, and that's proof. We could never thank God enough for all He has done for us just yesterday, let alone all throughout our life.

King David wrote in Psalm 139:14, "I will give thanks to You, for I am fearfully and wonderfully made; wonderful are Your works, and my soul knows it very well."

My soul knows this verse, not in an arrogant way but in Divine love where I understand whose I am and why I am here on this planet. This verse is so comforting because it says that we were wonderfully made. God loves us and created us to serve and represent Him on this plane of existence. God's comforting presence is always with us but it's up to us to perceive Him. God is all-knowing, all-seeing, all-powerful and all-present. God knows us and still loves us unconditionally. God's greatest gift is that we can know Him through His word.

Let's break down Psalm 139:114 together.

--The verse starts with thanksgiving; this is a so important because when we give thanks, we take our minds off our issues and focus it on where it should be, on God. Focusing on God keeps our earthly vision clear from the illusions and obstructions the devil wishes us to see. Thanking God throughout the day connects us to the Kingdom of God. Seeking the kingdom of God must be our purpose as Jesus stated in Mathew 6:33 when He said, "But first seek His kingdom and His righteousness, and all these things will be added to you." When we are steadfastly thankful, we are less stressed and anxious because we understand that God is in charge; and as long as we do our job, all will be well. This point includes controlling our thoughts so that we focus on God, goodness, and bringing glory to God. An important point to having an abundant life is being thankful.

--'Being fearfully and wonderfully made' is centered on understanding we are a part of God's great handiwork. 'Being fearfully made' is an interesting phrase because it tells me that we were created in an intricate, specific and intentional manner so that every part of us was put together in the best and most perfect manner. While we were made wonderful, the world seeks to poison us and it's on us to return back to how the Lord created us.

--'Wonderful are your works', we are a part of God's works so we are wonderful as well. Psalm 126:3 says, "The Lord has done great things for us, and we are glad." We must understand that God intended us to be happy and have inner joy. This is a part of how we were made so when we allow sadness or bitterness to rule our hearts, it's not how God meant us to be. The greatest thing about the scriptures is that it shows us how to get back on the path when we get off. This very verse was rolling in my head for days after I heard Joyce Meyer state it in a sermon. The stories of the prophets and the people in the Bible are instructional for us because the same went through the same things we go through today.

--'My soul knows it well' is so beautiful because it tells me that there are things which occur inside of me which is part of God's perfect plan. If I keep reading God's word and allow the indwelling Holy Spirit to connect to God's mind, then my soul will know it well. Inside of us is a Divine spark which was given to us by God. Jesus stated in Luke 17:21, "For indeed, the kingdom of God is within you." I love the phrase, "fully equipped" because truly each of us has been fully equipped for every good work. Romans 8:28 states, "And we know all things work together for good to those who love God, to those who are called to His purpose." Hallelujah, our God is awesome!

Tell yourself right now out loud, "I am fearfully and wonderfully made." This verse resonates in my heart and in my soul! I am uplifted and inspired! I hope this verse helps you to believe in yourself, fully engage and wake up to who they are. Once we awake, we are excited and are inspired to reach higher spiritual levels in life. We live purposeful and with intention.

Our birthright is to reach our full potential but it's up to us to unfold our inner potential so we become the embodiment of the Divine love within us. Our destiny and the will of God are intertwined, and can't be separated. When we understand the essential basic truth that we were created by a perfect God who created us to flourish so we could glorify Him. God wants our potential unleashed and reading this simple verse empowered me to be more than I was, for Christ!

As Shashi Singh wrote in a meditation on the thought of J. Krishnamurti, "cultivate the inner potential and improve our power to control our desires of the body, and not be governed by it, (which) leads us closer to ourselves and God."

Today, understand how you were made! Rejoice and start living up to your full potential this day!

Spiritual Refresher for Day #155

Take this time to spiritually reflect on this point: Spiritual Faithfulness.

"Let us draw near with a true heart in full assurance of faith, having our hearts sprinkled from an evil conscience and our bodies washed with pure water. Let us hold fast the confession of our hope without wavering for He who promised is faithful (Hebrews 10:22-23)."

The above verse sings out to my heart because it's so rich and uplifting. Having a true heart is the first part of this verse. We all know that Jesus told us that the truth shall set us free (John 8:32). Having a true heart leads us to deeper faith. I felt these words speak to me because my faith gives me hope that God will do what He says He will do based on His word.

The Life Application Study Bible provides some great insight in spiritual faithfulness. It says it's critical because, "when we break God's law in full awareness of what we're doing, our hearts become hardened to the sin and our relationship with God is broken. The diverting of our affection is the first step in the blinding process that leads to sin (page 1455)." When we are blind, sin is allowed to reign over us and then our connection between us and God is severed. God is pure and cannot tolerate any sin. So when we live in willful sin, our relationship with our Creator is broken. "For all have sinned and fall short of the glory of God (Romans 3:23)." Now, we all sin but we don't have to continue to live with sinful behavior. The Holy Spirit empowers us to turn away from sin. We are overcomers; we are more than conquerors; we are victors; and we have power through Christ!

What is sin? One must know what it is to fight against it. Sin is missing the mark (God's standard) or turning away from God. The wages of sin is death according to the Bible. There are many types of death, with spiritual death being the most lethal because of the dire eternal consequences. In the New Testament, Jesus explains that sin is not only actions that also evil or unGodly thoughts, such as unfounded anger towards others. I never even knew all the sins I was engaged in until I started absorbing the word of God. Sin is so dangerous because it cools out love for God. Because God is pure, sin doesn't please to God. We can't get the promises without doing what is pleasing.

The following verses provided me more insight into sin so I could know what to avoid:

"Now the works of the flesh are evident, which are adultery, fornication, uncleanness, lewdness, idolatry, sorcery, hatred, contentions, jealousies, outbursts of wrath, selfish ambitions, dissensions, heresies, envy, murders, drunkenness, revelries, and the like, of which I tell you beforehand, just as I also told you in time past, that those who practice such things will not inherit the kingdom of God (Galatians 5:19-22)." These verses were an eye opener for me because I do want to inherit the kingdom of God.

"Let all bitterness, wrath, anger, clamor and evil speaking be put away from you, with all malice (Ephesians 4:31)."

"Avoid the profane and idle babblings and contradictions of what is falsely called knowledge (1 Timothy 6:20)."

"Flee also youthful lusts, but pursue righteousness, faith, love, peace with those who call on the Lord out of a pure heart. But avoid foolish and ignorant disputes, knowing that they generate strife (2 Timothy 2:22-23)."

"For men will be lovers of themselves, lovers of money, boasters, proud, blasphemers, disobedient to parents, unthankful, unholy, unloving, unforgiving, slanderers without self-control, brutal, despisers of good, traitors, headstrong, haughty, lovers of pleasure rather than lovers of God, having a form of godliness but denying its power (2 Timothy 3:2-5)." This is perhaps the strongest verse on what to avoid in order to please God. I constantly have to keep these in mind so that I live a life pleasing to God. It may be a challenge from time to time but "I can do all things through Christ, who strengthens me (Philippians 4:13)."

I constantly need a refresher on 'Spiritual Faithfulness' so this tip is for me, and maybe it will inspire you as well. The below offers a template on behaving like a Christian:

"Let love be without hypocrisy. Abhor what is evil. Cling to what is good. Be kindly affectionate to one another with brotherly love, in honor giving preference to one another; not lagging in diligence, fervent in spirit, serving the Lord; rejoicing in hope, patient in tribulation, continuing steadfastly in prayer; distributing to the needs of the saints, giving to hospitality. Bless those who persecute you; bless and do not curse. rejoice with those who rejoice, and weep with those who weep. be of the same mind toward one another. Do not set your mind on high things, but associate with the humble. Do not be wise in your own opinion. Repay no one evil for evil. Have regard for good things in the sight of all men. If it is possible, as much as depends on you, live peaceably with all men. Beloved, do not avenge yourselves, but rather give place to wrath; for it is written, 'Vengeance is Mine. I will repay says the Lord. Therefore, 'If you enemy is hungry, feed him; If he is thirsty, give him a drink; For in so doing you will heap coals of fire on his head.' Do not be overcome by evil, but overcome evil with good (Romans 12:9-21)." I really needed the above verses today because the world always seeks to lead me away from the Lord.

Remember, how much God loves you and wants you to live an upright life so that we can be true inheritors. We can't get the promises, if we fail to please the Lord.

Spiritual Refresher for Day #156

Take this time to spiritually reflect on this point: Advancing in faith!

"Let us hold fast the confession of our hope without wavering, for he who promised is faithful. And let us consider one another in order to stir up love and good works... (Hebrew 10:23-25)."

Advancing in faith is a lifelong process. Our physical body grows as we get older. Plants grow as it ages, so does animals. All things grow when they are nurtured and fed in the right manners. It should be the same with our faith, in that we should consciously and intentionally grow our faith by feeding it in the right way as we get older.

Faith is the confident conviction that God will do what He promised. Faith doesn't come naturally so we must learn how to walk in faith. The Apostle Paul explained in Colossians 2:6, "As you therefore have received Christ Jesus the Lord, so walk in Him..." We must walk with Jesus, in faith. We must believe with a steadfastness that God is who He says He is, and can do what He says He can do without doubt regardless of what we see. We can only advance in faith when we trust Him on a daily basis because God wants us to grow. No one is born with great faith but we grow our faith as we grow in Christ. The Christian walk is a growing walk, not a stagnant one. This growth doesn't occur only on Sundays but every day where we push those ingrained limits to believe in new radical Godly ways.

Charles Stanley stated in a recent sermon 10 ways to advance our faith:

1) Face and overcome obstacles, tests, trials and temptations. We must have confidence and assurance that God will answer our prayers. It's through challenges that we grow spiritually. Unless we are pushed, pressured or challenged, it's difficult to move the next levels of faith. Understanding the purpose of God's tests.

2) Understanding the very nature of God. God is Holy, Righteous, Kind, Just, Merciful, Forgiving and Loving! He has all power and understanding. Through the Word of God, we understand who God is, and what He can do.

3) Meditating on the word of God. We can't ignore the reading of God's word. God gives direction and guidance through His word. God unfolds His purpose for our lives through the Word. The Bible is the fuel for our faith.

4) Applying the principles of God's word. We reap what we sow. Asking God how we can apply His words to our lives.

5) Observing the ways of the Lord. God uses suffering to bring us to new levels of faith. God tests us and our hearts. There are times when God will allow us to fall to our knees so that we can look up. We increase our faith by leaning on Him completely. Sometimes

God makes us wait because He wants our faith to grow through patience. The ways of God are not our ways, so we must understand how He works.

6) Observing God's work in the lives of other people. Believing that if God could work in other's lives then He can work in our lives. [I look at my father and mother who both have great faith. God healed my mother when she had a health crisis and helped my father after a business crisis. I saw God's handiwork from when He took care of my parents.]

7) Obey God and leave all the consequences to Him. When we obey God, He honors us. Faith allows us to watch God work without any concerns or anxieties.

8) Through answered prayer. Praying with expectation and trust grows and advances our faith. Often times, we continue to limit God. Pray with boldness and assurance.

9) Worship. Confessing with words, songs, hymns and our total being each day, not just on Sunday.

10) Confess your faith failures to God directly. Deal with your issues openly with God by asking God to forgive your lack of faith. God will never fail us, and will always forgive us.

I thought these ten points from Charles Stanley were amazing reminders to how we can advance our faith. God wants to use us for His maximum glory. Ask God to help you build your faith today.

"Be anxious for nothing, but in everything by prayer and supplication, with thanksgiving, let your request be made known to God; and the peace of God, which surpasses all understanding, will guard your hearts and minds through Christ Jesus (Philippians 4:6)." When we advance our faith, we learn to live without being anxious. Following this above verse guarantees us the peace of God. We can only obtain His holy gifts through faith.

Elijah's prayer in the Old Testament was one of faith. "Elias (the New testament name for Elijah) was a man subject to like passions as we are, and he prayed earnestly that it might not rain: and it rained not on the earth by the space of three years and six months. and he prayed again, and the heavens gave rain, and the earth brought forth her fruit (James 5:17-18)." As James stated in 1:6, "ask in faith, never wavering." Also faith must be expressed by actions for "faith without works is dead (James 2:20)." Growing our faith must be an intentional action for us each day especially those days where our faith banks are at its lowest. The ten steps above is an excellent refresher for all of us.

"(God's) righteousness is given through faith in Jesus Christ to all who believe (Romans 3:22)." Through Christ we can come to the Father in confidence, knowing that instead of our sinfulness, God sees the righteousness of Jesus Christ in us. Often times, we lose faith and don't see ourselves as God sees us. Advancing in faith is a constant effort even when our faith is tested.

I read a story about people living in the Middle East where people traveling in the desert to drink lots of water before they went on a trip because this kept them hydrated (and their inner reserves high). Once the people actually felt themselves getting thirsty, it was too late because that was the body telling them that they were dehydrated. Often, those who ignored the advice of drinking lots of water passed out from dehydration during their trip. This is the same with faith; we should advance our faith each day so that when trials or temptations come, we are hydrated in the Spirit. Too many Christians still put so many other things before their spiritual health and then wonder why they are so unsteady, suffering through life. Faith can move mountains and it's through our advancing faith over time which allows us to move that mountain.

"Sow for yourselves righteousness, reap in mercy; break up your fallow ground, For it's time to seek the Lord, till he comes and rains righteousness on you (Hosea 10:12)." We always reap what we sow. If we sow bold seeds of faith each day, this is what we shall reap. If we have half-hearted faith, always looking for natural solutions then we will get a half-hearted result. Reaping what we sow is a Divine Law. In Galatians 6:6, we learn, "Do not be deceived, God is not mocked; for whatever is man sows, that he shall also reap." If our thoughts are faithless, then we will reap the reward of the faithless. If our words are without love, then we will reap a loveless result. If we are unforgiving, then God will be unforgiving to us (Mathew 6:14-15)." These above verses are all a part of God's nature, His unchangeable nature. God is perfect and pure; The Lord doesn't need to change, we do.

Today and every day, work to advance your faith!

Know that God loves you and wants the very best for you so that your testimony can glorify Him!

Spiritual Refresher for Day #157

Take this time to spiritually reflect on this point: What does it mean to be saved?

I posit that being saved means that the Spirit of God lives within us and that we have fully submitted our lives to Jesus. When I was born again, the Spirit of God begin to show me real truth and wisdom. I begin to understand how much more powerful and stronger in spirit I became, after I submitted to Christ because I gained a clarity I never had before.

"There was a man of the Pharisees named Nicodemus, a ruler of the Jews. This man came to Jesus by night and said to Him, "Rabbi, we know that You are a teacher come from God; for no one can do these signs that You do unless God is with him." Jesus answered and said to him, 'Most assuredly, I say to you, unless one is born again (literally - born from above), he cannot see the kingdom of God.' Nicodemus said to Him, 'How can a man be born when he is old? Can he enter a second time into his mother's womb and be born?' Jesus answered, 'Most assuredly, I say to you, unless one is born of water and the Spirit, he cannot enter the kingdom of God. That which is born of the flesh is flesh, and that which is born of the Spirit is spirit. Do not marvel that I said to you, you must be born again (John 3:1-7)." We are saved when we are born again in Spirit, and in our hearts. New birth is an act of God whereby eternal life is imparted to the believer and it's demonstrated by faith in Jesus Christ whereby we are inspired (living with the indwelling Holy Spirit) to live an upright and holy life because we love Him. It's all about love.

Romans 12:1-2 states, "I beseech you therefore, brethren, by the mercies of God, that you present your bodies a living sacrifice, holy, acceptable to God, which is your reasonable service. And do not be conformed to this world, but be transformed by the renewing of your mind, that you may prove what is good and acceptable and perfect will of God." This above passage is what it's all about when we are born again and are saved. The Macarthur Study Bible NKJV states on page 1716 in the commentary section, "Renewing of the mind: this kind of transformation can occur only as the Holy Spirit changes our thinking through consistent study and meditation of Scripture. The renewed mind is saturated with and controlled by the Word of God."

On page 2057, the Macarthur Study Bible lists many Characteristics of believers, and I choose the following in alphabetical order:

Attentive to Christ's voice (John 10:3, 4)
Blameless and harmless (Philippians 2:15)
Bold (Proverbs 28:1, Romans 13:3)
Contrite (Isaiah 57:15, 66:2)
Devout (Acts 8:2, 22:12)
Faithful (Revelations 17:14)
Follow Christ (John 10:4, 27)
Generous (Isaiah 32:8, 2 Corinthians 9:13)
Godly (Psalm 4:3, Mathew 3:16, Acts 10:2, 2 Peter 2:9)

Without deceit (John 1:47)
Holy (Deuteronomy 7:6, 14:2, Colossians 3:12)
Humble (Psalm 34:12, 1 Peter 5:5)
Hunger after righteousness (Mathew 5:6)
Just (Genesis 6:9, Habakkuk 2:4, Luke 2:25)
Led by the Spirit (Romans 8:14)
Loving (Colossians 1:4, 1 Thessalonians 4:9)
Lowly (Proverbs 16:19)
Meek (Isaiah 29:19, Mathew 5:5)
Merciful (Psalm 37:26, Mathew 5:7)
New creatures (2 Corinthians 5:17, Ephesians 2:10)
Obedient (Romans 16:19, 1 Peter 1:14)
Poor in spirit (Psalm 51:17, Mathew 5:3)
Prudent (Proverbs 16:21)
Pure in heart (Mathew 5:8, 1 John 3:3)
Righteous (Isaiah 60:12, Luke 1:6)
Sincere (2 Corinthians 1:12, 2:17)
Steadfast (Acts 2:42, Colossians 2:5)
Taught by God (Isaiah 54:13, 1 John 2:27)
True (2 Corinthians 6:8)
Undefiled (Psalm 119:1)
Upright (1 kings 3:6, Psalm 15:2)
Watchful (Luke 12:37)
Zealous of good works (Titus 2:14, 3:8)

I wanted to list the above so that I can also continue to study them and the attached verses. When we surrender and submit our lives to Christ, the above characteristics are our goal. We are saved through God's grace and we delight in seeking a different way to think, speak, act and live because we love Him. We can do anything because we have the Holy Spirit indwelling in us and guiding us.

Psalm 34:18 says, "The Lord is near to those who have a broken heart, and SAVES such as have a contrite heart." My heart and spirit were broken; I lived in the darkness and got that as a reward. I testify today that God healed my heart and spirit, and today I have a new song on my lips.

We can choose who we want to serve: Jesus or the evil one. Living as we lived before we were saved says we are serving the evil one. Being saved means that Christ is on our minds all the time. A tree will be known by its fruit says the Word of God. When we submit fully to God and an unGodly thought enters our mind, we can drive that thought out when our mind is stayed on Christ. I constantly think on, talk to, praise, worship, and confide in Jesus Christ throughout the day.

Joyce Meyer in her 'Power Thought Devotional' for May 26 states, "...Ask God to open your mind to new ways of doing and seeing things. If He shows you something, then do it, and if He doesn't, then remain peaceful and trust that He will work for you and so what you cannot do...Stay peaceful and stand firmly in Christ, trusting Him to guide you." I love reading her devotional daily as it inspires me to know more of God.

There are Christians out here who still walk around in a fog, not understanding who they are or how much power they have in them through Christ or who they are truly serving through their actions. The poet George Santayana once said, "Those who cannot learn from history are doomed to repeat it." I want to learn from my history because I never want to live as I did when I wasn't saved. I constantly ask myself, am I doing something different or am I thinking in the same way. One can't serve God in truth and spirit when one is self-absorbed, ego driven and worldly focused. This is what I mean when I say I have gained clarity because I now see the world through a God-conscious lens, i.e. God is always close to my heart, mind and spirit. I still have such a long, long way to go but I know the path - Praise Him! I see so much more now because I now view the world through a God conscious lens. I am so happy because I see the Way, the Truth and the Life. I never even knew that there was a way. I used to seek comfort by buying expensive jewelry or clothes because I saw my identity through these things instead of something higher. But now, I have very few material objects but am rich in spirit! My identity is in Christ and that comforts me and brings me peace.

Our goal is to gain wisdom and Godly insight so that we can share it with the world. "Blessed be the God and Father of our Lord Jesus Christ, the Father of mercies and God of all comfort, who comforts us in all our tribulation, that we may be able to comfort those who are in trouble, with the comfort with which we ourselves are comforted by God (2 Corinthians 1:3-4)."

I never knew joy like this before because I have been born again and saved. I know what it means to be saved because the Holy Spirit speaks to my heart and guides me. Our Lord, Jesus Christ, provides such comfort and inner peace - I want to share my experiences to the world so that God is glorified! If you don't know if you are saved this day, seek Him out through the Scriptures, and He will guide you.

The greatest wisdom God ever put on my heart what this: "God always loved me, but the only different is that now I love Him." Jesus stated in John 14:15, "You you love me, keep my commandments."

Be encouraged today knowing there is an easier path, a higher path which brings true peace and inner joy. It's all about Jesus; try Him - trust Him, He's awesome!

100 percent guarantee, Jesus saves!

Spiritual Refresher for Day #158

Take this time to spiritually reflecting on this point: Seeing the world through eyes of radical faith.

I decided to write about faith again today because it's one of the key points in the Christian faith. Faith is a spiritual force. When our faith grows we no longer see our problems as we think they are but as God sees them, just a bump in the road of life. When we are able to change our natural vision to a faith centered vision, the things we saw as difficult in the past are now simple. Faith is the force which make mountains into molehills. Faith can energize and empower like no other force in the universe other that love. Faith is about the present and being fully engaged in whom our God is, and who we are through His Son, Jesus Christ.

"Behold the proud, his soul is not upright in him; but the just shall live by faith (Habakkuk 2:4)."

In this world, it's so easy for our faith to be shaken at times, thus we must constantly keep faith at the forefronts of our hearts and minds. Our pride and ego often leads us in the wrong direction so we must constantly remind ourselves how we should view God and the world around us.

Faith is not a one-time act but a way of life. Does your life show that you live by faith? I pose this question for the reader and for myself. Faith is about radically changing how we see God and how we see the world. Faith is not a feeling. "For we walk by faith, not by sight (2 Corinthians 5:7)." There are times when I am anxious and then I think about the faith question. I immediately get back in the Word of God and put my faith into action.

Billy Joe Daugherty discusses faith in 'This New Life'. He explains that "Sometimes people base their spiritual experiences on their feelings and emotions. Problems arise when the feeling and emotions change. If they have not been grounded in the Word of God, doubt will arise as to whether or not the experience was genuine. For faith to be consistent, it must be based on something with more stability that your feelings...Your faith must be controlled by God's Word, not by what you feel, not by what circumstances looks like, and not by what others tell you." This sums up how we should live.

Faith should propel us even when we are tired, disappointed, sad or depressed because faith is an inner force which connects us to the Spirit of God. Our faith can be tapped in to, on demand, through God's mighty Word. Many people discount the power of faith. For example, a person is losing their house and they first call the bank before calling on God - this is not an example of deep faith. Another example is a person who is ill and first calls the doctor instead of giving it to God in prayer. Faith warriors lean on God first, seeking guidance from the Master. It's not about denying that a problem exists but denying satan the right to steal what the blood of Jesus has done for us. Jesus stated that

He came so that we may have life and life more abundantly. Faith allows us to know this fact even though we may not feel this way or see things opening up for us.

We can't become people of deep faith without aggressively striving to grow our faith each day. Scott Peck, the bestselling author of 'The Road Less Traveled', stated that "he felt most Western people were just spiritually lazy. And when we are lazy we stay on the path we are already on, even if it is going nowhere." I believe that spiritual laziness is a faith problem because people who lack faith also lack the desire to seek to build their faith.

Another quote that I think speaks to faith is from the late American Monk Thomas Merton who pointed out that we may spend our whole life climbing the ladder of success, only to find when we get to the top that our ladder is leaning against the wrong wall. I believe that he is saying when we engage our faith through God's word; we will stay on track and focused.

In the late John Osteen's book, *Becoming a Man of Unwavering Faith*, he lays out ten points about people of deep faith. His son, Joel Osteen, provides commentary throughout the book. In one section about renewing our minds, Joel Osteen reflected that "When you dwell on God's word and start seeing the best in situations, little by little, one thought at a time, you will transform your thinking. God will help you. Stay full of faith. Stay full of joy. Stay full of hope. God will transform your life." The ten points discussed in the book are as follows:

A man of faith can change his destiny.
A man of faith believes the word of God.
A man of faith sees and hears what the world cannot see and hear.
A man of faith prays earnestly even though he has heard the answer.
A man of faith is strong when there is no evidence of the answer.
A man of faith never gives up.
A man of faith goes on when there's just a little evidence.
A man of faith believes for the big when he sees the little.
A man of faith begins with nothing but ends up doing mighty things.

There were three additional points I wanted to highlight from the book: "Regardless of our circumstances, rejoice in the Lord;" "No matter how difficult the situation, thanksgiving and praise, touch the heart of God;" and "Many people admire the Word, study the Word and defend the Word, but they will not act on it as truth."

Albert Einstein stated that "No problem can be solved by the same consciousness that caused it in the first place."

Our goal is to go from no faith, to little faith to a person of great faith. This begins and ends with the Word of God. Each day, by reading more of the Bible, we grow our faith. When we memorize faith verses of the Bible, our faith grows. When we help to show others what the Word of God says, our faith grows. When we volunteer to help others with no expectation of reward, our faith grows. When we love unconditionally as Christ commands us, our faith grows. When we forgive as Jesus requires us to do, our faith grows. Our faith grows with all these things because it tells God we are trusting Him.

Having complete faith in God is one of the most important jobs we can do each day by making sure our words align with the Word of God. Today, be a fully engaged faith warrior!

Spiritual Refresher for Day #159

Take this time to spiritually reflect on this point: Seeking the right things, Godly wisdom.

"Let the wise listen and add to their learning (Proverbs 1:5)."

I used to see God as a far away God but I had a life-quake (like an earth quake which devastates an area of land, my life quake destroyed my life as I knew it) and I was forced to look at life differently. Because of my life quake, I started to view God differently; as a God who loved me, and who was with me and in me. Each person has a part to play in God's plan. It's never too late to become the person who God wants us to become. That said, sometimes it's very difficult for those who are lost, to see the light. The Bible equates God with light. "God is light; in Him there is no darkness at all (1 John 1:5)." I now understand God as light because He shows the way in a dark world. Because of our blindness, spiritual blindness, we stumble around and are cut off from God. The part we play in our own destiny cannot be overstated. I never knew that I had a role in my own destiny other than with work. I didn't realize how my spirit and soul was influenced by what I thought, said and did each day.

Proverbs contains great wisdom but before my life quake, I never viewed the guidance or wisdom as something I needed to rely on. I read one great verse which started my thinking in a new direction: "Trust in the Lord with all your heart, and lean not on your own understanding. In all your ways acknowledge Him, and He shall direct your paths (Proverbs 3:5-6)." I used to live my life in this exact opposite manner. I was one of those people living for the wrong things each day while I neglected my spirit and soul. In hindsight, how could I ever have been a balanced person if I ignored my spiritual well-being? I lived in the darkness of chasing after the carnal pleasures of life. I wasn't fully engaged with life. I lived a dualistic life where I was fully engaged with work but not engaged with my spiritual health.

The Bible states in Hebrew 11:6, "He (God) rewards those who earnestly seek Him." I never sought Him but instead my lifestyle said that I actually sought the evil one. I lived in a world of illusions and I loved it at the time. I sowed chaos and was rewarded with more chaos. We have an enemy; he is real and wants to lead us to a dual hell: hell on earth and eternal damnation of hellfire in the afterlife. I used to be influenced by the devil's tricks because I believed that life was about having fun. I never knew my true nature was a divine one and the beautiful rewards of loving a loving God.

I never pursued anything on the spiritual plane but today I seek after the right things: Godly wisdom. I value Godly wisdom today because I want a different result and a different life. I decided that if I wanted more of the same then I would do the same things. In the past before the life quake, I hated who I had become. It took an earth shattering event in my life to get me to see beyond myself. I now know that God didn't want me to be that man. It's a truism that says if a person wants a different result, then they must do things differently.

Psychologists say that people will not change until they cease to tolerate what they are currently getting in their life. Jesus stated in Mark 5:36, "...Do not be afraid; only believe." I decided to believe that through Jesus I could have a better life. I had nothing to lose, I was just sick of myself and my selfish desires which had led me for so many years. I told myself, "enough is enough!" I was disgusted with the path of my life and called on the Lord to show me a different path. I had to surrender my pride and ego to God so that I start doing things differently. My pride told me that I was not 'that bad' and I just needed to self-correct a little. Once I started reading the Bible, I knew that I needed to completely rewire my inner hard drive. I started listening to what others had suggested who I respected and who had a spiritual foundation. I came to realize that I didn't have all the answers and needed help, a lot of help. The truth which came to me was that only God could provide the answers I needed. It was necessary to rewire myself along a whole and healthy path. All those bible-thumpers had tried for years to bring me to God but it was my fall from earthly grace that inspired me to seek God. I didn't come to the Lord until I had no other place to go.

Have you ever just decided to be a new person, well I learned that it's possible through Jesus Christ. I was able to cast of the past illusions and delusions through the teachings of Christ once I surrendered. I just had to get fed up with the dysfunction of what I called my life. How much pain can a person take? I discovered that the real enemy was myself. The devil never needed to really do that much to get me to run to the darkness. I never want to be that person I was, and with the grace of God I will continue on this Godly path. One thing I can say is that at least now, I strive for a different outcome each day with all my heart, mind and soul.

Proverbs 5:4:25-27 states, "Let your eyes look straight ahead, and your eyelids look right before you. Ponder the path of your feet, and let all your ways be established. Do not turn to the right or the left, remove your foot from evil." This is my new direction in life, a Godly direction whereby I ponder my path each day. I will seek after Godly wisdom each day as I read the Scriptures. I must testify when I now read the verses in the Bible with an open heart, God speaks to me through His word. I hear verses speak to my heart and direct my path.

Today, I know that God still has a plan for me and its working for my good. I have more peace in my life now than ever before and it's because I now seek after the right things.

Spiritual Refresher for Day #160

Take this time to spiritually reflect on this point: Humility.

There is probably a reason that it's taken me 160 tips to get to this spiritual principle. I have always been arrogant and prideful although I would have characterized it as being confident. I believe one of the keys to the Christ-like walk is introspection and self-assessment so that we can get our minds off ourselves and put our minds on God. Humility is one of those overlooked concepts which helps us to keep our minds on God. The devil is in a battle for our hearts and minds, humility helps to keep the evil one in his place, under our foot.

I provide three core verses below which discuss this principle of humility:

"To be ready for every good work, to speak evil of no one, to be peaceable, gentle, showing all humility to all men (Titus 3:2)."

"and be clothed with humility for God resists the proud, but gives grace to the humble (1 Peter 5:5)."

"Therefore, as the elect of God, holy and beloved, put on tender mercies, kindness, humility, meekness, longsuffering; bearing with one another and forgiving one another, if anyone has a complaint against another; even as Christ forgave you, so you also must do (Colossians 3:12-13)."

The key to humility is love because if we are loving then we will be humble and show humility to all. I provide six ways to will help us to build and maintain a humble nature:

1) Be quick to forgive.
2) Be slow to get upset.
3) Be patient with each other.
4) Be kind and gentle with each other.
5) Be humble in spirit.
6) Show love to everyone, at every opportunity.

I think the following verse also describes a humble spirit. "For I say to you, through the grace given to me, to everyone who is among you, not to think of himself more highly than he ought to think, but to think soberly, as God has dealt to each one a measure of faith (Romans 12:3)." When we exercise sound judgment, by thinking soberly, it will lead us to recognize that we are nothing without Christ and will yield the fruit of humility. If we are proud, arrogant, egotistical then we are not following the teachings of Jesus Christ. I used to think I was better than others but I am the exact same as everyone else in the eyes of God. We are all loved by God in the same unconditional way. How we live matters because it either pleases or displeases God. Humility is one of those virtues which please our Lord.

Pride and ego only keeps us from our destiny because we cease to challenge ourselves in Godly ways. If I have a humble spirit then I will continue to strive to allow the Spirit of God to flow through me. This concept allows me to be confident in who I am in Christ because I no longer am trying to impress anyone but am trying to impress the only Being that matters, God. The devil is called the adversary and he wants you to be prideful and egotistical. Pride and ego are two of the devil's greatest weapons. Pride influenced satan to think that he could take the place of God and consequently he was cast out of heaven. The ego pushes us away from God because it disconnects us from God's love in favor of self-love. The ego loves to judge and label everyone which separates us from God. It's difficult to have love and compassion for others when we are allowing our ego and pride to run wild or lead the way. The ego is so dangerous because it feeds on negative emotions and feelings such as fear, anxiety, envy, jealousy, resentment and anger. Pride and ego loves confrontation. All of these negative emotions are in direct opposition to what Jesus preached in the Gospel.

The Bible states in Ephesians 5:17, "Don't live carelessly, unthinkingly. Make sure you know what the Master wants (what God's will is)." If anyone believes that God likes pride or the ego then they have not read the Bible. Humility could be considered the opposite of pride. I realized that when I decided to live for Christ, I needed to understand all my negative unGodly attributes in order to make sure that I didn't succumb to them. I believe that one must know the positive and negative aspects of a concept in order to fully follow the positive aspects of the Gospel.

I love the fifth chapter in Mathew which discusses the Beatitudes. I equate this word 'beatitudes' with having a "beautiful attitude." I just wanted to highlight a few verses (5-8), "Blessed are the meek, for they shall inherit the earth. Blessed are those who hunger and thirst for righteousness, for they shall be filled. Blessed are the merciful, for they shall obtain mercy. Blessed are the pure in heart for they shall see God..." These are qualities of humility and the humble heart.

The MacArthur Study Bible says on page 1399, "Meekness is the opposite of being in control. It is not weakness but supreme self-control empowered by the Spirit." To me, meekness means a Christ-like spirit in opposition to pride, arrogance or ego-driven behavior.

I wanted to provide five more verses to anchor this spiritual principle:

"The Lord lifts up the humble (Psalm 147:6)."

"I dwell in the high and holy place, with him who has a contrite and humble spirit, to revive the spirit of the humble, and to revive the heart of contrite ones (Isaiah 57:15)."

"Seek the Lord, all you meek of the earth, who have upheld His justice. Seek righteousness, seek humility (Zephaniah 2:3)."

"Do not set your mind on high things, but associate with the humble. Do not be wise in your own opinion (Romans 12:16)."

"Humble yourselves in the sight of the Lord and He will lift you up (James 4:10)."

I have heard that the word "EGO" stands for easing God out. This is accurate because too many people allow their ego to rule their lives which blocks out God completely. We will never be able to glorify God without a spirit of humbleness. Jesus' life was an example of humility as he washed His disciples' feet or as he dined with sinners or when he said, "Ye without sin cast the first stone."

A Christ-like walk is a path of humility. I have to remind myself of this daily so that I don't think more highly of myself as the Bible says. Galatians 6:3-5 states, "If anyone thinks he is something when he is nothing, he deceives himself. Each one should test his own actions. Then he can take pride in himself, without comparing himself to somebody else, for each one should carry his own load." If we tend to our own gardens, then the world would be such a better place. I have come to realize that when I work on my side of the street, the quality of my life improves. Many people forget that they have a responsibility to themselves to serve God in truth and spirit. Part of that spirit, is based on having a spirit of humility.

Sometimes the only God people will see, is the God in us. This is why no Christian ever has an excuse for not spreading the Gospel because our conduct can spread the Gospel just as much as preaching a sermon. A life lived in an upright manner can be the greatest testimony anyone could show others. We have a duty as believers to help others come to the truth but we can't do that when we are self-absorbed. A spirit of humility seeks to be focused on God at all times.

Spiritual Refresher for Day #161

Take this time to spiritually reflect on this point: Obedience.

"If you are willing and obedient, you will eat the best from the land (Isaiah 1:19)."

This is a promise from God; and this will set the tone for our lives. 1 John 3:11 states, "Beloved, do not imitate what is evil, but what is good. He who does good is of God, but he who does evil has not seen God." I lived for so many years in the darkness of my own desires. My definition of good was just that, "my definition" and not God's definition of what is good. once I started reading the Bible, God's definition became clear. In the past, my feet were quick to run to evil and I lived a life without any spiritual introspection.

If someone had mentioned obedience to me before the eyes of my heart opened, I would have laughed because I had no spiritual discernment. I had no Godly clarity in my vision. I did things according to the world and didn't eat the best from the land. My own desires were allowed to run wild and obedience to God was not a part of the equation. The greatest gift I ever received was God's unconditional love, with that I gained a spiritual clarity to see the world as it is. We reap what we sow; this is a certainty which many different religions believe in addition to Christians. The world is trying to lead people to hell.

Surrendering to God's will is obedience. The Bible states, "Not my will, but Thy will be done." When we start to see with a spiritual clarity, we no longer allow our sinful nature to lead us. I tried to do it my way for so many years and only received pain and suffering. I thought I knew better but God's wisdom reigns supreme. 1 Corinthians 6:12 states, "Everything is permissible for me...but not everything is beneficial." I had to let go and let God because I was sick and tired of living the way I did. My greatest calamity became my greatest teacher because it forces me to challenge my existing beliefs and attitudes. Without which, I would still be living in the darkness of sin. I had to let go of the trash, to get the treasure.

The biggest difference between me yesterday and today is that I now seek after God. The Lord loves those who seek after Him. If we seeking God then we are striving to obey the Lord. "Come near to God and He will come near to you... (James 4:8)." Too many Christians are still trying to hold on to their old life, while seeking the new life in Christ but we must let go of the old to embrace the new. The Bible says that a man can't serve two masters. I can honestly say that I never would have let go of my old life if not forced. I pray that anyone who reads understand that what they are holding on is part of the illusion. I now understand that I can't live in willful sin (committing willful acts of sin) and expect to live a different type of life. I always tell people that if you are happy and content with your life, keep doing what you're doing but if you want more then the new life starts with a change.

Psychologists state that we will never change what we tolerate. I just became so fed up with how I lived that I decided I could not live what the things that I formally tolerated.

When I started reading the Scriptures in the Bible, God spoke to my heart and explained that He couldn't tolerate my behavior. I was a stink in His nostrils but I was led to a better way. My brokenness was not a permanent state, God could heal me. I was healed and I now know that there is a better way. Desperation can lead to many things and in my case it led to my surrender to something greater than myself. I was desperate at my lowest point and wanted to end my life but God wants none of his precious creations to live like this. The verses in the Bible came alive when I told myself, "just try it because you've got nothing to lose." I just decided to believe. With my belief, I exhaled and decided that I had to obey, not because I was afraid of God but because I started to understand the concept of Godly love. I started to understand how much God loved me and that He wanted the best for me. To eat of the best of the land, I had to stop being hard-headed or obstinate in order to be truly good to myself. I had lived such a self-destructive life previously that I had to trust in Godly wisdom, and not my own. I started reading everything I could in the Bible about how to do God's will.

I never knew how a believer in Christ should live. There was so much more to loving God than just going to church once a week, I learned that it was important HOW a believer lived each day. I stopped looking at other Christians and started deeply reading the Word of God. I stopped looking around the church during the services and started focusing on looking up. I came to see obedience as a great gift because it allowed me to focus on other more important things such as developing my inner talents. Once I fully surrendered to God, I could then live in peace and inner joy came into my heart.

Today, I urge all believers to start looking at obedience in a different light. George Eliot stated, "It's never too late to be who you've might have become." I think this is what the Gospels are trying to tell us. We can live the life that we were meant to live through Jesus Christ, and by loving obedience. Obeying God's word frees us from the worldly limits and opens up new horizons. Today, I strive each day to learn what God wants for my life and the quality of my life has improved greatly.

If we love God then we will obey His commandments. "I love those who love Me; those who look for Me, find Me (Proverbs 8:17)." What a beautiful promise we have from God. Why should we seek to obey because, "Eye has not seen, nor ear heard, nor have entered into the heart of man the things which God has prepared for those who love Him (1 Corinthians 2:9)." Wow!

Remember, "Strength for today; and Bright hope for tomorrow!"

Spiritual Refresher for Day #162

Take this time to spiritually reflect on this point: Praise!

Psalm 148:1 starts by the words, "Praise the Lord!" There is no greater thing we can do each day then praise our Lord and Savior. I love the Psalms because they provide much Godly advice about praise. One of my favorite verses is Psalm 142:7 which says, "Bring my soul out of prison, that I may praise Your name; the righteous shall surround me, for You shall deal bountifully with me."

Before I opened my heart to God, I was in a prison of my own making. My soul was bound by the illusions of life. I lived in a prison of my own desires and my own ego. I believed that my happiness was dependent on external things such as material possessions but now I know that all I need is Jesus. I wanted a lot of things and actually thought I needed those things for my own happiness. I lived by wanting, needing and desiring, totally focused on the wrong things but I came to realize that I had the conditions for my own happiness within me. I already had all I needed. I sought after the wrong things. When I was feeling down or depressed, I would go out and buy something to make me feel better but the feeling I obtained from buying an expensive or pretty thing only lasted for a short time. Over and over I lived this pattern of seeking happiness in the wrong things when I should have been seeking my happiness through Christ.

When God healed my heart and guided me towards spiritual enlightenment, I decided that I would praise the Lord in order to honor Him. All of my tips are based on the premise that we were created to serve God and bring glory to Him. If we believe that it's our job as a Christian to serve God then we need to consider the concept of 'praise'. We can praise God in many ways and this refresher is focused on these many ways.

Outward praise shows our love for God for all to see because praise is a tangible representation of our faith. Psalm 145:2-6 states, "...And I will praise Your name forever and ever. Great is the Lord, and greatly to be praised; and His greatness is unsearchable. One generation shall praise Your works to another, and shall declare Your might acts. I will meditate on the glorious splendor of Your majesty, and on Your wondrous works. Men shall speak of the might of Your awesome acts, and I shall declare your greatness."

Life question: Do our lives say that we are praising God each day?

This is the question I asked myself. Did those around me recognize that I was a praiser of my Lord and Savior? Did my life say that I was thankful for all the God put in my life? I decided that the answers to these questions were no. My life said that I was self-absorbed. I lived in such a way which didn't show anyone anything uplifting. I lived a broken life; broken off from who God was and is. Over these last few years, the quality of my life has improved so much because now I praise God at all times. The greatness of the Lord is on my lips and I seek Him each day, throughout the day. I am quick to mention the Lord to everyone who will listen. I praise God through my smile as well as my words. There are many people around me each day who are down and depressed, but

I praise the Lord through a Godly attitude despite my individual circumstances. I understand now how my life can either lead those around me to God or away from God.

Who would buy a car from a salesman who drove a vehicle which was constantly breaking down and full of defects? I don't know about you but I prefer to buy a car from a salesman who drove a reliable, steady and outstanding vehicle. Okay, this is the analogy for our belief because if we call ourselves Christians and are not praising God then why would anyone be drawn to consider our God. If we are trying to lead others to Christ, then it started with praise. If we are constantly unsteady, wavering and speaking in broken ways, we will actually be leading people away from the God we say we worship. Our conduct and character speaks more volumes about our God than any other thing we do.

We can praise God through our conduct and character each day. Our attitude can praise God, and our smile can praise God. Each day, I get to choose my attitude because I believe that as an ambassador of Christ, it's my duty to show others a different way. God freed me from my inner prison and it's my job to now show others how to be freed.

I often tell people, "Don't let your situation affect your praise; let your praise affect your situation." Lady Julian put it in a better way: "First there is the fall, and then we recover from the fall. Both are the mercy of God!" Life is filled with peaks and valleys but our praise of our God should be constant and steadfast.

In the book, Falling Upward, by Richard Rohr, the author summarizes some great thoughts on pages 94-95 that I relate to changing our view so that praise becomes a new operating directive each day:

"--We are created with an inner drive and necessity that sends all of us looking for our True Self, whether we know it or not. This journey is spiral and never a straight line.

--We are created with an inner restlessness and call that urges us to the risks and promises of a second half of our life. There is a God-sized hole in all of us, waiting to be filled. God creates the very dissatisfaction that only grace and finally divine love can satisfy.

--We dare not try to fill our souls and minds with numbing addictions, diversionary tactics, or mindless distractions. The shape of evil is much more superficiality and blindness than usually listed "hot sins." God hides, and is found, precisely in the depths of everything, even holy things, like Bible, sacrament, or church.

--If we go to the depths of anything, we will begin to knock upon something substantial, "real," and with a timeless quality to it. We will move from the starter kit of "belief" to an actual inner knowing. This is most especially true if we have ever (1) loved deeply, (2) accompanied someone through the mystery of dying, (3) or stood in genuine life-changing awe before mystery, time, or beauty.

--This "something real" is what all the world religions were pointing to when they spoke of heaven, nirvana, bliss, or enlightenment. They were not wrong at all; their only mistake was that they pushed it off into the next world. 'If heaven is later, it is because it is first of all now'.

--These vents become the pledge, guarantee, hint, and promise of an eternal something. Once you touch upon the Real, there is an inner insistence that the Real, if it is the Real, has to be forever. Call it wishful thinking, if you will, but this insistence has been a constant intuition since the beginnings of humanity. Jesus made it into a promise, as when he tells the Samaritan woman that "the spring within her will well up unto eternal life (John 4:14)." In other words, heaven/union/love now emerge from within us, much more than from a mere belief system or any belonging system, which largely remains on the outside of self."

There are many reasons to praise God but I wanted to list a few why we should praise the Lord: 1) We praise God because we feel His presence and are thankful for what Jesus has done for us on the cross; and 2) We are training ourselves to feel God's presence during the times when He seems distant and to show more gratitude for Jesus' sacrifice. Praise is about trusting God to give us what we need. We praise because we have faith in who God is and what Jesus did for us. When we praise God during the difficult periods, we show God that we are trusting Him. It's easy to praise when you win the lottery but the key to the Christian walk is to praise God at all times.

Psalm 147:1 states, "PRAISE the Lord! For it is good to sing praises to out God; For it is pleasant, and praise is beautiful." I love this verse because it exactly what I am trying to speak on in this refresher.

Today do everything with praise in your heart. Imagine if all believers lived with a constant praise on their lips, the world would be a more beautiful place. Work, eat, sleep, exercise, read, walk, speak and live with a 'praise mentality' constantly; and watch God work mightily in your life!!

Today, tell yourself, "Praise is what I do!"

Spiritual Refresher for Day #163

Take this time to spiritually reflect on this point: The anointing on each of us.

Anointing is the supernatural favor which is already over our lives. In the Bible, anointing is equated with blessings. We are already empowered to do every good work but many people disqualify themselves through their lack of faith or their negative thoughts and feelings. There is great power within each of us!

"These things I have written to you concerning those who try to deceive you. But the anointing which you have received from Him abides in you, and you do not need that anyone teach you; but as the same anointing teaches you concerning all things, and is true, and is not a lie, and just as it has taught you, you will abide in Him (1 John 2:27)."

Anointing is the divine empowering force over our life. Isaiah stated in 10:27, "...And the yoke will be destroyed because of the anointing oil." A yoke is a stronghold which keeps us from being who God intended us to be such as an addiction, tragedy, physical pain, injury or illness. God can remove any yoke of bondage as long as we believe. In Mark 9:23, Jesus stated, "If you can believe, ALL things are possible to him who believes." Stop limiting yourselves. The problem is that we doubt so easily when the smallest impediment comes our way. I used to allow the negative thoughts into my mind which took away my blessings but today I strive to put every unGodly thought into captivity. It's a daily challenge to maintain focus but the Godly life is a focused life. I am worth the effort because God created me to great, and He created you to be great. Today, after leaning on the Holy Spirit, I am able to control my thought life much easier.

Don't accept any yokes in your life because God can destroy every yoke over your life. You must just believe. No little faith but great faith is the way forward. We must continue to understand who we are in Christ because we can't do it by ourselves because with faith we can do all things. The anointing doesn't do any good with negative thinking.

There are seeds of greatness inside of each one of us, and they are watered with faith. Faith activates the anointing over our lives. We must each take responsibility to stir up the anointing in us. God never allows us to be in a situation without giving us the tools we need to overcome that situation.

Today tell yourself, "I am anointed and I declare that I can do all things through Christ." We were born to live an abundant life, full of inner peace and joy. Jesus didn't come so that we live broken lives. Jesus did what he did on the cross to put those pieces back together. Anointing is about staying in faith.

The anointing provides the power we need to do mighty things for the Lord. As believers in Christ, we are his heir and children. There are no limits, so why are you putting limits on your life. God is well-able, either you believe it or not. "Why not you?"

Tell yourself today, "Why not me?" Actually Jesus specifically said in His word that He came so that we may life and that we may have it more abundantly (John 10:10). Who are we to argue with Jesus? He wants us to live an abundant life, full of joy! This why I say tell yourself, "Why not me?" Too many times, we ask why or how without truly believing with a steady faith. We have the anointing of Jesus on us, we need to stop living less than we were created to be. We need to have larger, greater visions. Ask yourself today: Why can't I write a best seller? Or Why can't I get that promotion? or Why can't I meet that right person? or Why can't I get that job? The truth is there is no reason why you can't do these things and even more. The anointing has already been put on and in you to live a great life.

We were made for more. David stated in the 23rd Psalm, "You (God) anoints my head with oil, my cup runs over." "Our cup running over is abundance. With God for us, who can be against us; just our own self-imposed negative thinking.

Proverbs 16:7 states, "When a man's way pleases the Lord, He (God) makes even his enemies to be at peace with him." Our greatest enemy is ourselves and our unGodly desires. When we trust God to be God, we are able to live at peace; which leads us to be happier and more productive in all we do. God has already given us His unmerited favor, we have already been anointed, isn't it about time to start to stop struggling and start seeing yourself as God views you.

God can and will do exceeding abundant in your life, if you only believe. Trust God's timing and ask for a fresh anointing from God today. Humble yourself before God and "allow Him to work in your life". Many believers disqualify themselves from God's goodness through their very own negative thought life. We must allow God to work in our lives and that happens through faith.

We must live with expecting faith. The anointing will lead you to your destiny. "Examine yourselves as to whether you are in faith. Test yourselves. Do you not know yourselves, that Jesus Christ is in you? -- unless indeed you are disqualified (2 Corinthians 13:5)." Don't allow doubt to disqualify you from your blessings. Don't allow naysayers keep you from reaching towards your destiny and grasping it. We are already empowered because of the anointing from Christ. Stop accepting mediocrity and seize your destiny today!

We get what we aim for out of life. Aim for the moon! Aim for greatness because it's already in you! We were created for victory and greatness! Be your best, knowing that the Lord has already set you up for a great success! Focus on the anointing already on your life and not your problems. Focus on how great your God is this day and how He has set you up for an abundant life!

Spiritual Refresher for Day #164

Take this to spiritually reflect on this point: Knowing what is acceptable to the Lord.

"For you were once darkness, but now you are light in the Lord. Walk as children of light (for the fruit of the spirit is all goodness, righteousness, and truth), finding out what is acceptable to the Lord (Ephesians 5:8-10)."

I never knew what was acceptable with the Lord before I started reading the Bible with an inner spirit of truth. Before I gave my life to Jesus, I would read verses of Scripture and do mental gymnastics in order to not apply God's words to my life. I read about concepts like love, forgiveness, kindness, generosity, joy, peace, longsuffering and somehow believed that it should apply to other people but not myself. I was the poster boy for the psychological concept of transference because I thought you should conduct yourself like that but believed I was exempt. I thought I was special in that I didn't need to know what was acceptable to God and I never sought to know. Although I am special in God's eyes, this doesn't mean that I'm not exempt from needing to know what is pleasing to the Lord, and then doing it. I never knew that if I loved God then I should willingly do what is acceptable in His eyes.

When I came to the Lord in truth and spirit, and had a personal encounter with God's love, my old world shattered and a new wondrous path opened up before me. I never connected the dots how we get what we aim for out of life. I had to take one hundred steps back and look at my life honestly with God as the judge in order to start the new process of learning how to walk as a Christian.

"See that you walk circumspectly, not as fools but as wise, redeeming the time because the days are evil, therefore do not be unwise , but understand what the will of the Lord is (Ephesians 5:15-17)." Our walk is so important and when I decided to live a true Christian life, I started seeing things I never saw before. I saw the world differently and I started getting a different outcome. Life became sweeter, better and richer when I started walking circumspectly for God. I noticed that blessings started to fall in my lap. I didn't change my thoughts, words and actions for blessings but it came as a by-product. I started to value each day as a gift from God. I read how God wished us in the above verse to redeem the time. Understanding came to me that I could honor God through how I used my time.

I heard a man once say, "Today is tomorrow's yesterday. If we strive to be great today and make the most out of today for a month then we will have a month of greatness. But if we do nothing and waste today then after a month we will have a month of nothing." I would have never completely understood this principle before but as I write this 164th tip aiming to honor God because that's what the Lord wants us all to do: glorify Him!

We should be very careful how we live. I didn't walk circumspectly, and I wasn't careful how I lived. I didn't walk with Jesus, just my ego and I got what the ego wanted; inner chaos. Our goal is to be imitators of God but that can't happen without knowing the will of God. Ephesians 5:1 states, "Therefore be imitators of God as dear children." God is forgiving so when we decide to live in an unforgiving manner then we are not living in an acceptable way to God; and we will reap what that type of behavior sows. When we live in an unloving manner, then we will reap the benefits of that type of life. I lived in a self-imposed prison of my own desires and inner demons for many years. When we live outside the will of God, we are setting ourselves up for a reward of the hell-fire, cut-off from God for eternity, after we die. This had no meaning to me before and when I started to gain wisdom, it motivated me. The thought of being cut-off from God for eternity was the very definition of hell to me.

I believed it was the big things which only mattered but the little things matter just as much, and even more at times. We can all do great things but we must be cognizant of doing the little things in a manner acceptable to God. It's all about God but I used to live in a manner that said it was all about me. It was all about Philip and what he wanted. I had it so backwards. I acted as if God owed me something but it was I that owed God everything. I was so lost that I didn't even know where I was. I didn't know how to get back on God's path but I thank Him for He is merciful because the Lord never gave up on me. I have a God-consciousness today because God's loved me enough to continue speaking to me.

There is such a better way to live. My worse day unemployed with my hand in God's Hand was better than my best day without God in my life making lots of money. I started to truly live when I opened my heart up to God's love. What that meant was that when I started to love everyone regardless of what they may have done to me, my heart started to sing. When I forgave everyone in my life, my soul was regenerated. Life became a daily symphony when I fell in love with Jesus. I was motivated to live for Him and it started with striving to be acceptable in His sight. I learned all I could about living within God's will to get closer to Him each day and the darkness started to subside inside me.

Jesus stated in Mark 3:35, "For whoever does the will of God is My brother and My sister and mother." I want Jesus as my brother. This can only happen when we surrender our will to His will. Jesus stated in Luke 6:32-35, "But if you love those who love you, what credit is that to you? For even sinners love those who love them. And if you do good to those who do good to you, what credit is that to you? For even sinners do the same...But love your enemies, do good and lend, hoping for nothing in return; and your reward will be great, and you will be sons of the Most High..." When we decide to live for Christ, the world will start to see a clear change within us. The test of being a Christian and living within God's will is based how we treat those who mistreat us. Do you want Jesus as your brother? Do you want a great reward from God? Then allow the love of God to flow through you to those around you; this pleases God and makes us His inheritors.

Today take time to know what is acceptable to the Lord. Let's all examine ourselves today to see where we can do more to show God that we love Him. Let's live today and everyday as the song says, "they will know we are Christians by our love."

Spiritual Refresher for Day #165

Take this time to spiritually reflect on this point: Spiritual excellence!

There are many things we strive for each day but today I wanted to challenge all of us to strive for spiritual excellence.

"Therefore, since all these things will be dissolved, what manner of person ought you to be in holy conduct and Godliness (2 Peter 3:11). What are you choosing today? Everything is temporary so the point of today's tip is excellence for Christ! Don't our Lord and Savior deserve our very best each day, not just a few hours on Sunday?

It can be a challenge to live the Christ but the more we strive to not conform to this world, the more empowered we will become. I was blind before I decided to live a different way. Isaiah 42:18 states, "Hear you deaf; and look, you blind, that you may see." God is the only one who can restore the correct spiritual vision we should be seeing with each day.

When we strive for excellence, we build our faith. God honors faith because faith honors God. We are God's property and God will always protect His property.

Edward Everett Hale stated, "Never bear more than one kind of trouble at a time. Some people bear three kinds; all they've had, all they have now, and all they expect to have." This is not spiritual excellence. Spiritual excellence is focused on strengthening the inner person. We must build spiritual strength each day. Building our spiritual strength allows us to get out of our own way. Too many good people can't see beyond their own pain. They continue to view their world through their defective and dysfunctional lens but God wants to change our vision so that we can see ourselves as He sees us. God wants the ears of our heart to hear His voice and the eyes of our spirit to see His plan for us.

Stop living the hurts of yesterday. Joyce Meyer stated in one of her sermons that she met a woman at her conference one day who stated that she felt as if she had been hit by a bus. Joyce replied that she knew exactly how the woman felt because she had felt like she had been hit by a bus too in the past but she decided to climb out from under the bus and drive it away. satan will continue to take advantage of us as long as we allow him.

Jesus states in Mathew 7:21-23, "Not everyone who says to Me, 'Lord, Lord,' shall enter the kingdom of heaven, but he who does the will of My Father in heaven. Many will say to ME in that day, 'Lord, Lord have we not prophesied in Your name, cast out demons in Your name, and done wonders in Your name? And I will declare to them, 'I never knew you; depart from Me, you who practice lawlessness!" Lawlessness is disobedience, those who choose to refuse to obey God's commandments. This verse really got my attention when I opened the eyes of my heart. I decided that I wanted to change from the inside out. I didn't want the same things I had been getting in life. I wanted something different, more than I wanted the same type of life. I am not motivated by fear to serve

God but by love because He loved me first. It's through God's great unmerited favor known as grace that my heart became receptive to the truth.

I used to run from the truth, I deceived myself but I say no more. Devil get behind me, because I'm taking back what's mine. I am striving for spiritual excellence. The devil put up a great fight but now I have the tools to fight him. I can now love the unlovable because Christ loved me even when I was unlovable. Joyce Meyers tells of the love she showed her father after the unspeakable things he had done. Her great love for him, motivated him to accept Christ before he died. I want my faith to grow like hers.

It's all about giving our hearts freely and lovingly to God so that He can change it. "I will bring the blind by a way they did not know; I will lead them in paths they have not known. I will make darkness light before them, and crooked places straight. These things I will do for them, and not forsake them (Isaiah 42:16)."

God is faithful to His word. We should strive for spiritual excellence because we love Him. God will strengthen us when we do those challenging actions for Christ. God wants to change us from the inside out so that we can glorify Him. Excellence in Christ means that we start to focus on things above instead of in the world. People strive for work excellence or physical excellence without focusing on the most important thing in their life, spiritual excellence.

Spiritual excellence means doing more for Christ, learning more and living more for Christ than for our own selfish desires. Our pride will always tell us that we don't need to be loving to that person. When I opened the eyes of my heart I realized that satan loves pride because it got him expelled from heaven, and he longs to keep us from heaven.

Today, I intend to strive even more to take back what the devil has taken from me. You've been robbed and now it's time to get it back from the evil one. Your destiny is waiting for you to take back. Your destiny is intertwined with seeing spiritual excellence!

Today, make a plan for spiritual excellence. Isn't your eternal soul worth it?

Remember: Excellence for Christ!

Spiritual Refresher for Day #166

Take this time to spiritually reflect on this point: Looking for something real.

"But God has revealed then to us through His Spirit. For the Spirit searches all things, yes, the deep things of God (1 Corinthians 2:10)."

There are many people looking for various things, but are they looking for something real. God is 'Real', and He will do what He promised He will do. Some people will follow the doctor's directions to the letter, even giving the medicine the time necessary but they will fail to follow God's directions. I was always seeking but never really looking for something real. Today, I equate real with truth, and the only real truth is from God. "The fear of the Lord is the beginning of knowledge; fools despise wisdom and instruction (Proverbs 1:7)."

God's word is real. Are you looking for it? Are you looking to apply God's words to your life? Or are you looking for a loophole? "For the word of God is living and active, sharper than any double-edged sword, it penetrates even to diving soul and spirit, joints and marrow it judges the thoughts and attitudes of the heart." When I opened my heart to the Word of God, I started hearing that small still voice of the Lord. I found the 'real' through God's word. My job daily is to stay focused on the 'real' so that each day I put in the effort to maintain my eyes on the kingdom of God. Jesus stated that we first must seek the Kingdom of God in Mathew 6:33.

For years, my ego and pride prevented me from knowing the 'real' because I arrogantly thought I was the 'real'. "Ha!" This is laughable now as I think about how lost I was in the past. When I started reading God's Word with expectancy, diligence and faith, I found that there was something more out here. As I put it to others, I came to understand that there was more of God to find. I came to see that I was looking for all the wrong things, in all the wrong places. When we start looking for something real, God starts to pour our His Heart, in order to heal our hearts. God will show us His mind and His thoughts when we start to seek Him out diligently.

"Listen carefully to Me, and eat what is good. And let your soul delight itself in abundance. Incline your ear, and come to Me. Hear and your soul shall live; and I will make an everlasting covenant with you... (Isaiah 55:2-3). Later we learn, "Seek the Lord while He may be found, call upon Him while He is near. Let the wicked forsake his way, and the unrighteous man his thoughts; let him return to the Lord, and He will have mercy on him; and to our God, for He will abundantly pardon (Isaiah 55:6-7)."

God is faithful. If only His children were 25 percent as faithful as He is to us, we would reap great blessings. There is nothing greater than looking for something real, than in the Lord. As the verse above states, we must return to the Lord. Sometimes this return takes daily effort because the world seeks to pull us away from God, or the "Real". The world is one of illusions and deceptions where some Christians make excuses or are just lazy in seeking the Lord. When we give God less than our very best then we get "less than" from God. Lazy Christians will not reap the best from the Lord.

For example, 2 hours a week on Sunday for our Lord and Savior is not giving God our very best. Oh, I forgot, you're too busy. You have more important things to do instead of giving more time with God. Well, I just pray that when you call on the Lord that He doesn't tell you that He's too busy for you. We get out of life what we put in it. If you want miracles to occur in your life, then be a miracle for someone else. If you want more love in your life, then love God more and in deeper ways. If you want to be forgiven, then forgive more. What you seek is at your fingertips, but you must be real. The young people today say, "keep it real." Your spiritual practice must be real, sincere and genuine.

If we were to keep it real vis-a-vis our worship practices, we would see that we haven't been looking for something real many days. We have neglected our spiritual development on a daily basis. Cognitive therapists state that balance is key to an abundant life whereby we strive in three areas daily: Self-maintenance, self-development and fun.

--Self-maintenance is our work to earn a living. This is so that we may pay the bills or take care of the other daily needs to maintain a certain lifestyle.
--Self-development is our habits and our passions. This is practice of building up our inner person as well as our outer person. This is focused on the spiritual, physical and intellectual aspects of our being.
--Fun is our release. This is the time we spend playing a sport because we love it or playing a board game for fun.

Of course, the three areas sometimes cross over but the main idea is that we live a balanced life. We must strive for a balanced existence because each area needs to be worked and challenged.

God wants us to have an abundant life. This is why we have the Bible which provides guidance on how to live in a Godly manner. Jesus told us that He came that we may have life, and has it more abundantly. It's time to start looking for more of God each day! Look for the real! Learn to discern the 'real' from the illusion.

Perhaps this tip will motivate someone to seek more of the Lord each day. "So shall My Word be that goes forth from My mouth; it shall not return to Me void, but it shall accomplish what I please, and it shall prosper in the thing for which I sent it (Isaiah 55:11)." When we seek more of the Lord, we ignite God's favor over our lives. For those who say they don't have the time, God will provide for all your needs when you start giving Him more of your time. When we put more effort in serving God, the Lord puts more efforts in helping us achieve our goals. For example, we start attending weekly Bible studies and we will then be given more clarity to be more efficient and productive at work thereby freeing us of spending longer hours at work. When we start to look for something real, in truth and spirit, then we start to long to spend more time with God and His word.

I can say that today I am happier and have more joy because I sought out something real, God! Strive each day to emote good, think good, and do good everywhere you go knowing that you are aligning your life with what is real, true and Godly by doing this. If we want God to work more powerfully in our lives, then all we need to do is to give more of ourselves to Him each day!

Spiritual Refresher for Day #167

Take this time to spiritually reflect on this point: Making our thought life work for us.

"Casting down imaginations, and every high thing that exalts itself against the knowledge of God, and bringing into captivity every thought to the obedience of Christ... (2 Corinthians 10:5)."

In her 'Power Thoughts Devotional', Joyce Meyer states that the above scripture means, "when you become aware of a wrong thought in your mind, you can choose immediately not to think it....Thank God that He has given us the ability to think for ourselves and not merely be stuck with whatever comes into our minds from some random or outside source. We can learn to think according to God's Word, and when we do, we experience the kind of lives that Jesus dies for us to have."

Joyce Meyer is one of my favorite ministers of God's word because she explains the Scriptures in a way that touches my heart. I fully believe that any one can put their thoughts into captivity by using the Word of God as an anchor. The moment before I read this verse, I was having some unGodly thoughts in my mind and I asked God to take these thoughts away. I then opened Joyce's Devotional and it was on controlling our thoughts. If was as if God was reminding me that I have the power. It was a clear example of how the Scriptures can speak to our hearts when we are open to correction. After I read the verse and the devotional I immediately had peace and changed the internal channel to God's channel instead of Drew's channel.

The Lord gives us a choice each day on how to live. The choice of free will is one of the greatest gifts that God has given us but for some it's also the greatest curse because they choose the wrong thoughts.

Key point: Thoughts --- leads to --- feelings --- which leads to --- behaviors according to cognitive therapists. This is also true for the Christian because Godly thoughts lead to Godly feelings which lead to Godly behaviors.

"And do not be conformed to this world: but be transformed by the renewing of your mind, that you may prove what is that good, and acceptable, and perfect, will of God (Romans 12:2)." Too many "so called Christians" respond in the same unGodly manner as the unGodly. When people are mean or hurtful or hateful to us, we are CALLED to be loving to them. Does the Gospel change you? Have it motivated you to change.

Jesus said, "Whoever desires to come after Me, let him deny himself, and take up his cross, and follow Me (Mark 8:34)." We should be motivated to deny our fleshly desires and needs for revenge or to get back at others if we want to follow Jesus. We must deny our pride and ego. Too many Christians are still carrying negative baggage from the past with them each day. For example, just mention that person that they dislike and see them make that face. Their Christian beliefs disappear quickly as they want to discuss how bad that person is. Instead of responding in the same old unGodly ways, look for new ways to show love. Don't continue to harbor grudges and unGodly feelings. Jesus stated in Mathew 6:20, For where your treasure is, there will your heart be also." To me, if our treasure is focused on Godly and Christ-like love, then our heart will be steeped in the same.

"Let us therefore, as many as perfect, be thus minded: and if any things you be otherwise minded, God shall reveal even this to you (Philippians 3:15).

The more we seek to put those unGodly thoughts into captivity, the more God will help to be transformed closer to His image. Living a Godly life allows us to have Heaven on earth and in the after-life when we live according to His.

Anyone who knows me now, know that I love Proverbs 23:7, "As a man thinks in his heart, so is he."

Godly thoughts lead to Godly feelings which lead to Godly behavior. If you start practicing today at putting your thoughts into captivity, you will start to notice the quality of your life improve. Proverbs 19:8 states, "He who gets wisdom loves his own soul; He who keeps understanding will find good." I'm convinced that there are still Christians walking around here with so much self-hate on the inside that they allow their thought life to lead them to down deep, dark wells of negative feelings which lead to negative behaviors. God wants us to live an upright life where we glorify Him.

Proverbs 30:5 states that, "Every word of God is pure; He is a shield to those who put their trust in Him." I believe this and it has helped me. I created a list of verses which I wrote on a note card that I carry in my pocket each day. When I have the slightest unGodly thought, I refer to that note card and am uplifted.

The Christian walk is as easy or as hard you we wish to make it. "The law of the Lord is perfect, converting the soul; the testimony of the Lord is sure, making the wise the simple; the statutes of the Lord are right, rejoicing the heart; the commandment of the Lord is pure, enlightening the eyes (Psalm 19:7-8)." Allow God to open your eyes today so that you see the old in a new God conscious manner.

Too many Christians are not allowing God to fight their battles because they feel the need to respond back to the negative. Remember the Bible tells us to respond to evil with good. Respond to evil with God, by allowing God to handle it. we just must do our part and reach out to hurting people by showing them the love of God through our behaviors. Too many Christians are striving too little each day. They are not believing God's words in their daily walk. Please remember this verse, "Be you therefore perfect, even as your Father which is in heaven is perfect (Mathew 5:48)." Strive to do great things today for God, and it starts with our thought life.

Remember the following great promise from God in Psalm 18:39, "For You have armed me with strength for the battle..." I carry this in my pocket because it reminds me of who I am in Christ.

Spiritual Refresher for Day #168

Take this time to spiritually reflect on this point: The beautiful struggle forward.

One day a person stopped me in my gym and asked me why I always had a smile on my face. I explained that my smile is because of what Jesus did inside my heart, He transformed it. The man responded by asking, "So that means your life is now easy that you're a Christian?" I explained that life as a Christian is still a struggle, but it's a faith based struggle now. I informed him that although I gave my life to Christ, I feel more empowered and loved than ever before. I described how my soul sang each day and I danced daily because of what I gained through a faith in, a hope in and a love of Jesus Christ. He argued that I was still unemployed and that God didn't give me a job. I answered that it was true I wasn't working or that I didn't received great blessings each day but that I did obtain the gift of developing real spiritual discernment. For example, I informed him how I could decide my attitude each day. I told him that Jesus said, "These things I have spoken to you, that in Me you may have peace. In the world you will have tribulation; but be of good cheer, I have overcome the word (John 16:33). Jesus didn't promise that life would be easy, but he stated that it would be abundant. Jesus also explained, "I have come that they may have life, and that they may have it more abundantly (John 10:10)."

I informed him that through Christ I had started to develop spiritual discernment. For example, I came to know that the things which pleased God was actually good for me as well. There was no longer a war between what I wanted in life, an abundantly peaceful and joyous life, and what God wanted. God and I wanted the same things now, and it made my life easier. "Be perfect, be of good comfort, be of one mind, live in peace; and the God is love and peace shall be with you (2 Corinthians 13:11)." I asked him to consider if he was pleased with how he life currently was; and if he wasn't what would he lose in trying a different path. He thanked me and went on his way. I continued to think about his question and decided to devote this refresher to the beautiful struggle forward.

Each day as a Christian is still hard but I learned through reading the Bible that I actually had more choices than I knew I had. I could choose my attitude each day as well as what things meant to me. I could view events and people through a God-conscious lens. I became empowered through the knowledge of understanding Who created me, and why I was created. While I wasn't transformed into a perfect person, I made real progress each day. It was and is still work each day to turn myself into something pleasing to God. Each day I still struggle with unloving thoughts, impure thoughts and even bad thoughts but there is a difference. I now notice these thoughts for what they are and change the channel to Godly thoughts. It's my choice. At first, I still was attracted to things which displeased God but I noticed that over time it got easier to turn away from those things. I asked God to change my heart and in turn I became stronger at fighting against what my flesh wanted because I had higher goals.

The Apostle Paul provides Godly guidance on this issue. "Finally brethren, be strong in the Lord and in the power of His might, Put on the whole armor of God, that you may be able to stand against the wiles of the devil. For we do not wrestle against flesh and blood, but against principalities, against powers, against the rulers of the darkness of this age against spiritual hosts of wickedness in the heavenly places. Therefore take up the whole armor of God, that you may be able to withstand in the evil day, and having done all, to stand. Stand therefore, having girded your waist with truth, having put on the breastplate of righteousness, and having shod your feet with the preparation of the gospel of peace; above all, taking the shield of faith with which you will be able to quench all the fiery darts of the wicked one. And take up the helmet of salvation, and the sword of the Spirit, which is the word of God... (Ephesians 6:10-17)." This is the template for how to enjoy the beautiful struggle. Meditate on the above passage asking God to show you the deeper meaning of the passage.

The difference today is that I have faith in God; that He would do what He promised even if I couldn't see things happening in the natural. I have hope that my life will get better because I now know that peaks and valleys are an integral part of life. I realized that I learn more in the valleys than on the peaks. I have love for God, a sincere and genuine love, which I didn't have before. My love for God has motivated me to do things that my flesh still rebels against, I seek to obey. The beautiful struggle is what I call it today because the Bible says that trials will enter our lives, and the trials are good for us because they allow us to build our faith and get closer to God. I love what the Apostle Paul wrote in, "being confident on this very things, that He who has begun a good work in you will complete it until the day of Jesus Christ (Philippians 1:6)."

My struggles allowed me to become more loving to even those who cursed me because with faith I decided to let God deal with that person. I learned to let God handle my problems while I prayed for those who bothered me the most. I worked to have love for those people who upset me. It wasn't easy and still isn't because it's a struggle each day, a beautiful struggle each day. But today, I have faith, hope and love as my fundamental belief. I seek love and hope today diligently. I seek higher things and choose to focus my mind on those things each day.

My father, who is a minister, once told me, "either your heart is transformed by Jesus or not." I never knew what this meant until I started reading the Words of Jesus' through the open eyes of my heart. I allowed Jesus to unquestioningly change my heart. It Jesus said it, I now believe. No more discussion. No more debate. I sought to apply it to my life regardless of what it said. Slap my cheek and I will give you the other cheek. Now, I hope you don't slap me but I am prepared. I heard people in my church say, "I'm not there yet, if you hit me, I'll respond." I've surrendered to the point of letting God handle my battles. I am prepared to take that hit, and turn my other cheek because I trust and have faith in Jesus. I am prepared to follow Jesus in truth and spirit.

To follow Jesus I must move forward, away from who I was so that I can become who Christ wants me to be. "Not that I have already attained, or am already perfected; but I press on, that I may lay hold of that for which Christ Jesus has also laid hold of me. Brethren, I do not count myself to have apprehended; but one thing I do, forgetting those things which are behind and reaching forward to those things which are ahead, I press towards the goal for the prize of the upward call of God in Christ Jesus (Philippians 3:12-14)." These words touch my spirit and give me the template of how I must live.

I surrendered to a new way, with the belief that I had no other options, it was either death or Jesus. I can't play this game any longer; there has been too much pain to continue to play mental games with God's word. Many Christians are still struggling in negative and painful ways because they are looking for the loopholes. God's word is not a hustle; we can't hustle God. Many Christians are still trying to have it their way; they make every excuse to not conform to what Jesus has asked us to do. I quit doing the mental aikido of trying to put a little bit of spirituality inside my heart while living how I want to live. It didn't work; I have to give it over to God completely. Now, this never meant that I never doubted anymore, but just when I doubt I know where to go to be recharged, the Bible.

The Christian walk is hard, freaking really hard at times, because my flesh wishes to lash out or my ego wishes to act out or my desires wish to be fed or my pride wishes to tell others that I'm fixed and am perfect. But I'm still a freaking mess but I have given my mess to Jesus and that has given me great comfort. I decided that I was going to follow Christ in truth and spirit or give up. I just don't want to be one of those newly minted Christians who still lived a broken 'less than' life. I asked God to teach me and God told me that all I needed to do is to surrender to His will. God informed me that I needed to learn what was pleasing to him with the same fervor I did other things in my life and then I needed to live differently, radically for Christ. The need to live differently had to be centered on loving the things that God loved and loving Jesus in truth and in spirit. God told me that I would make mistakes but I had to stop planning to sin. I had to stop seeking to do wrong, anticipating God's mercy and kindness because if I died in willful sin then I would be lost forever in the fires of hell. I had to want to do what's right because of love, the same love which led Jesus to the cross for us. I still fail but the difference is how I view God and my life. I see God as my Father who imparts wisdom for my good who is not trying to keep me from having fun.

Now, I can say that I have more fun without alcohol, drugs or sex because of the joy of having Christ in my heart than when I had all the worldly goods. I now understand more and have a deeper understanding then when I lived in the world. My vision is clearer but I must maintain diligence each day so that my focus doesn't veer off the Godly path. I can now feel when I haven't given enough to God. When I allow my Bible study to get cut short or my meditation on God's word to be decreased, I feel the world encroaching over my inner peace.

I became open to a different path because I grew sick of my life after losing my job. My calamity allowed me to see things in a different light and challenge existing beliefs. My struggles saved me because I came to see that Jesus was all I needed to live a great life. I am thankful for my struggles because I learn more when I struggle than when everything goes smoothly. My struggle has been beautiful because it freed me. I say 'long live the struggle' because the struggles allow me to feel alive as I put into practice what Jesus preached about. I don't look for tomorrow to be a Christian but at right now in the present moment. Now is when I need to act Christ-like, not tomorrow because tomorrow's not promised to us. I need to show love now to everyone especially those close to me as Jesus commanded. I need to be in a state where if glory came, I would be ready. I need to make sure my heart is pure without anger or malice so that I can allow Jesus to flow through me.

It's a struggle each day, and I thank God for this because this keeps me sharp. I live with the thought that God is rooting for me to be more and more like Him. 'Imitating God' is now something I strive for. 'Imitating the Apostle Paul, just as he imitates Jesus' is a mantra now. These are goals of mine, every minute of the day as I put my thoughts under captivity. It's a struggle, a beautiful struggle. I understand what's at stake and why its' important to understand the battle. But the great thing is that the battle is not mine alone, the battle is the Lord's and one day I hope to say that it's not a struggle anymore.

Today, I am thankful for my struggles because without which I would not have found the Good News of the Jesus Christ. Because of Jesus, I am not bitter but am better. I understand that there will always be struggles and in those tough times, Jesus will be there holding my hand. I am content and have inner peace because of my faith, hope and love. I have hope for a better understanding each day to make better, healthier choices in order to glorify God. I believe, that's the difference today. I have hope in an upward prize. I am thankful for all that has come into my life! I am on my way and believe in the deep recesses of my heart.

Marcel Proust stated, "The true journey of discovery consists not is seeking new landscapes but in having fresh eyes." Becoming a follower of Christ in truth and spirit gave me new eyes to see the world and myself; and it restored my broken heart which gave me hope and allowed love to flow freely.

Today, embrace the beautiful struggle which is called life knowing that you are not alone! God loves you and is with you each step on the journey!

Spiritual Refresher for Day #169

Take this time to spiritually reflect on this point: Choosing whom we will serve, and working on our sides of the street.

Today's refresher is focused on two points which go together. God put these topics on my heart this morning and I wanted to share them with you. I wanted to start with Joshua, a mighty man of faith. In the exodus from Egypt, Joshua understood who God was and who he was. Joshua focused on serving God in truth and in spirit while being a steadfast supporter of Moses. Joshua was focused on working his side of the street and in the role he was given. He started out as a follower of God and then became the leader of the displaced Israelites. As the new leader, Joshua did what God told him and informed them on what God told Him what God put on his heart.

"Now therefore, fear the Lord, serve Him in sincerity and in truth, and put away the gods which your fathers served on the other side of the River and in Egypt. Serve the Lord. And if it seems evil to you to serve the Lord, choose for yourselves this day whom you will serve, whether the gods which your fathers served that were on the other side of the River, or the gods of the Amorites, in whose land you dwell. But as for me and my house, we will serve the Lord."

Joshua ministered to the Hebrews as he was taught by Moses and God, explaining to them that they should strive to be a true servant of the Lord. He informed them of what they needed to do while understanding that he still had to focus on his side of the street. Joshua's responsibility was to make sure that he served the Lord sincerely and all those in his house. He wasn't distracted by what those around were doing because he was committed to the Lord. Joshua chooses whom he would serve without being swayed by the crowd. This is a great lesson for us because we must decide whom we will serve each day. Once we decide whom we will serve then it's important for us to first work on the inner person so that we can be a light to the world.

Many Christians today want a show at church, or they want to be entertained but growth should occur on the inside. We must believe and make our faith a part of us. Many Christians know what they should do without taking action on that knowledge. Some believers know it, but don't live it. "It" being Christ. When we have faith, we are moved to worship correctly which influences us to make the right choices in thoughts, feelings and behaviors. I have heard some believers say I'm not religious, I'm spiritual but what spirits are they following? Are they following Jesus in truth and spirit?

Today is the most important day in your life because you can decide whom you will serve. Serving the Lord in truth and in spirit is not a one-time decision but a minute by minute step by step process which affects the follow-on moments.

The Apostle Paul wrote to the Thessalonians in 4:11-12, "that you also aspire to lead a quiet life, to mind your own business, and to work with your own hands, as we commanded you, that you may walk properly toward those who are outside, and that you may lack nothing." I think this is such a powerful verse of scripture. First, we must aspire. Aspire for more, more of Christ by allowing His message to be flow through us. Second, we should live a quiet life with a light Godly footprint, not living with inner and outer chaos. Our quiet confidence is in Christ and we don't have to act out or yell or scream because we are changed and are now living in Christ. Our identity is in Christ, not our ego. When it says 'Working with our own hands', I believe this is about focusing on our issues without pointing fingers at others; this is about tending to our own garden. Too many Christians are so focused on others instead of just following Jesus. Just do your part by loving others and trusting God, to be God. It doesn't matter what that person did to you because it's about whom you will serve today. The best way to honor Christ is to live radically as Christ lived. Christ was a radical because everything He taught went against our sinful nature. Christ taught love, deep and radical love.

If Christ lives in you, then the above passage should inspire you to make that first step to the unlovable. And if your first attempt doesn't work then take a second step for Christ, and a third step because you love Christ and you are doing your part for Christ. Being a radical follower of Christ may require you to make numerous attempts until you succeed in touching someone's heart. Show that person that you worship an awesome God! The last verse says, "that we may walk properly (or Godly) towards those who are outside (or still lost and living in the darkness) and we will lack nothing. It's about doing our God-inspired mission each day.

Life Question: Does your behavior say that you have encountered Jesus and now focus your head and heart, mind, body and soul on Jesus Christ. Or does your thoughts and behavior say that Christianity is a hobby for you. Today is the day; it can all change for you by deciding whom you will serve.

Key point: The walk of the believer is centered on moving from being self-centered to being God-centered.

It's on us whom we will serve. No one will force love into your heart. "...work out your own salvation with fear and trembling, for it is God who works in you both to will and to do for His good pleasure (Philippians 2:12-13)." When we bring a receptive heart to Christ, the Holy Spirit enters us and empowers us to change. How we carry our burden each day shows others whom we serve. Our attitude and our outward spirit speak volumes of whom we serve. We can minister to those around us just through the way we walk each day.

Too many Christians still have a victim mentality or a poverty mentality but our Lord Jesus came to bring life. Love brings life. When we live with and in love, we will live abundantly. God wants His divine nature of love to flow through us, in order to change us. If we are still holding on to the same beliefs, grudges, fears, resentments then we are not changed, and we will be a stink in God's nostrils. Aspire to be a believer in truth and spirit today! Each believer must be on fire for Christ. We must first surrender and then work on our own issues so we can be a light to others in the darkness. Too many of my

fellow believers worship themselves instead of God. I was like this until I opened the eyes of my heart to Jesus.
Worship God first. Put Jesus first! When we get on fire for Jesus, then we'll start to see the Lord work mightily in our lives.

Spiritual Refresher for Day #170

Take this time to spiritually reflect on this point: Combating a wavering faith.

Too many Christians are living in the house of fear, instead of the house of faith. Faith leads to faith. The Bible tells us that we are justified by grace through faith. I have heard FAITH described through its letters as [Forsaking All I Trust Him].

Faith is something we can build and it starts with viewing the world differently through a God-conscious lens. James 1:1-8 states, "My Brethren, count it in all joy when you fall into various trials, knowing that the testing of your faith produces patience, But let patience have its perfect work, that you may be perfect and complete, lacking nothing. If any of you lack wisdom, let him ask of God, who gives to all liberally and without reproach, and it will be given to him. But let him ask in faith, with no doubting, for he who doubts is like a wave of the sea driven and tosses by the wind. For let not that man suppose that he will receive anything from the Lord, he is a double-minded man, unstable in all his ways."

I can never write enough about faith because when I do, I minster to myself too. The world and those in it will always seek to weaken our faith. The devil's little lies whispered into our ear make us lose confidence in the dreams God has put on our heart. Faith is the cornerstone of being able to love, forgive and walk in the spirit each day because this is how we express our trust in God, through our faith. Faith is the confident conviction that God is who He is says He is, and can do what He says He can do.

James, Jesus' half-brother, wrote about how doubt can invalidate our faith. We must have an unwavering faith each day regardless of what we see in the natural. Living a Godly life is rooted in having inner joy, happiness, peace, contentment where our faith is steady despite what's going on in our lives. This is a challenge because if you are like me, our doubt has been allowed to run wild without restraint for years. We have to retrain ourselves to recognize doubt when it comes on and tries to take hold. Our thought life can be faith-filled or doubt-filled. The first step is to start to monitor our thoughts, words, tweets, written words, emails to make sure that we are not speaking about our problems but about our God and how great He is. People with wavering faith love to discuss their problems. "Oh, let me tell you how unfair Mary is at my work..." or "Let me tell you how sick I feel today, I can't..." or "I can never get that job because I'm too...." This is how one recognizes a person with wavering faith. Recognition is the first key to empowerment. We will never change what we tolerate.

There are so many Christians who never step out in faith. We have been set up by God to be blessed but we shouldn't resist God's great plans for us by having a negative thoughts life. Many Christians actually call God a liar each day through their very words or their lack of trust in Him and what His word says. "I can't" or "I'm trying" or "I'm not sure" or it could just be a general attitude of "less then" which demonstrates to God our wavering faith. These faith deficient people fight their battles each day, not even thinking that God should have their backs. Go to God first and often is my new first thought. The Bible says, "you have not because you ask not."

Charles Stanley explained in his sermon called "wavering faith" why some Christians faith wavers:

1) When our trust in God conflicts with human reason. We start to put human traits and weaknesses on God but what is too difficult for the Lord?
2) We allow feelings to overcome our faith. We doubt our worthiness. God knows what will happen and when we walk in faith, we know that God will bless us. Always remember that we are more than worthy. I call this principle 'learned worthlessness'.
3) We fail to see God at work in our circumstances. God is always ready, willing and able to answer our prayers, but in His time. We tell ourselves that we have to have it now, which is not a walk of faith.
4) We focus on our circumstances rather than our great God. The more we focus on our pains, the more bigger they will get. Our faith is usually where our focus is. Faith is intricately tied to our focus. Focus = faith. This is why I always say that we must focus on the glory of God instead of our troubles. Daniel knew this principle in the lion's den. Where is your focus?
5) We are ignorance of God's ways. God always is true to His principles such as we reap what we sow. We need to focus on obeying God and leave the consequences to God. Obedience leads to a blessed life. We must know God's ways which can only occur by reading and meditating on God's word.
6) We have guilt over past or current sin. Sin short circuits the power of God in our lives because God is holy and cannot tolerate sin. Sin is a life destroyer, and I can attest to this point. We must allow ourselves to be forgiven by God and then move on focusing on not living in willful sin. Mark 11:22 states, "Have faith in God..." We must trust that once God forgives us, that the sin is gone. Some people refuse to allow God to forgive them.
7) We listen to the lies of the devil. Lust, unforgiveness, hate, greed and other sins comes from satan. The devil is full of lies and is the reason we don't have peace because we allow him to influence our thoughts.

Charles Stanley provides questions to ask ourselves when our faith wavers:

1) Where do these doubts come from? Does it come from God?
2) Has God ever failed me in the past?
3) Has not God provided for my needs in the past?
4) Did the Lord not give me the Holy Spirit to enable me?
5) Did He not promise to never leave or forsake me?
6) Is there anything too hard for God?
7) Where should my focus be?
8) Is this one of the forks in the road which will cost me my future?

We combat wavering faith by meditating on the Word of God; daily, prayerfully, unhurriedly, privately and carefully. We must courageously choose to trust and obey God's Word. Don't allow the devil to steal your Godly inheritance. We must fight the good fight of faith every hour of the day because our efforts will not be in vain according to the Bible.

Remember what Jesus said in Mark 11:24, "Therefore I say to you, whatever things you ask when you pray, believe that you receive them and you will have them." It's all about faith! Please don't allow your doubt to invalidate your blessings. Faith will jump start and enable an abundant life for you and your family!

Spiritual Refresher for Day #171

Take this time to spiritually reflect on this point: Godly self-correction.

Godly self-correction comes from the indwelling Holy Spirit when we put God's word deeply in our hearts. Godly self-correction is a process in which the believer allows the Holy Spirit to guide them and when they fall; they repent and continue walking in God's ways. This principle is based on understanding how to correct ourselves as we are convicted by the Holy Spirit. It's all about learning to listen to the voice of the Lord. When we surrender and attune our ears to God's voice, we get it and seek to live it. I know the way now because I can feel the Holy Spirit guiding me, speaking to me.

Let me paint a picture. It's like traveling from Philadelphia to Washington D.C. I know the way because I have read and trust the map. I have complete confidence that the direction my car is going will lead me to DC. I may get lost along the way but it's easy to find the way back to the path (which is interstate 95 south). It's the same with God's word; I know the way and trust His way fully. I know that it's all about Jesus and letting Him into my heart. I still mess up, make mistakes and get lost but I know the way now, and am committed to His way. I may even move at times in the wrong direction but through Godly self-correction I willingly seek to stay on the path. I have stopped rebelling.

The Apostle Paul wrote to the church at Ephesians about the new man. This is also written for us so we know how to live. "This I say, therefore, and testify in the Lord, that you should no longer walk as the rest of the Gentiles walk, in the futility of their mind, having their understanding darkened, being alienated from the life of God, because of the ignorance that is in them, because of the blindness of their heart; who, being past feeling, have given themselves over to lewdness, to work all cleanness with greediness. But you have so learned Christ, if indeed you have heard Him and have been taught by Him, as the truth is in Jesus: that you put off, concerning your former conduct, the old man which grows corrupt according to the deceitful lusts, and be renewed in the spirit of your mind, and that you put on the new man which was created according to God, in true righteousness and holiness (Ephesians 4:17-24)." There are five points I wanted to bring out from the above verse:

1) We must walk differently. Paul is explaining how as believers in Christ, we are to put off our former conduct. It's incompatible to think we are serving Christ when we are still living in the same old manner. The Gospel of Jesus Christ should compel each of us to change. We can't continue to hold the same old grudges and resentments from the past. We must allow the Holy Spirit to work in us and through us.
2) Learning to see in new ways instead of continuing to allow the blindness of our hearts leads us. The love of Christ should fill our hearts so much that we have love as the foundation of our life. We are compelled to act in the new ways, filled with love so we self-correct when we veer off a Godly path.
3) Internalizing the lessons taught by Christ in the Gospel. We no longer seek to do as the world do but seek to rise above in order to gain a greater prize.

4) Renewed in the spirit of the mind. This is what we should strive for each day as we read and meditate on the Word of God. The Holy Spirit can renew our minds as long as we open the eyes of our hearts and allow our minds to be receptive.
5) Live upright and holy so that others may see us as a guide in a dark world.

Godly self-correction is what I call total surrender to God. When we totally surrender then we are happy to self-correct because we love God and want to please Him. God wants us to get it and has sent us 66 love letters (chapters in the Bible) which shows us the way. The difference between me in the past and now is that I now self-correct along a Godly framework. I challenge myself to obey and seek more truth in God's word each day. I am no longer afraid to read the Bible for being forced to obey God. I get it today because I love God; freely and willingly following what He asked me to do without question. I used to question what the word was saying but when I opened my heart, eyes and mind, God prepared my heart. Let God prepare your heart. You matter to God. You can be the greatest example to someone by living a Godly life. Make Jesus the Lord of your life by living for Him.

I seek to get better each day by following God in spirit in truth. I used to resist, looking for ways to do it my way but it lead to pain. Today, my life isn't perfect but there is peace. I feel something in my heart leading me to the truth. When the devil seeks to influence me, I now recognize his voice for the Holy Spirit. I know the framework in which to work each day. I can recognize the devil's voice from God's beautiful voice. I came to understand how God will never ask me to do something inconsistent with His word. All I needed to do was to check in the scripture to the spiritual principle to back us what the Holy Spirit is telling me.

I understand why it's about love because that's what the worlds lack. From love, all other Godly traits emerge. My journey is now about love. I understand why I can't harbor grudges or hatred anymore because that is not 'of God', and I can't say I am living for God when I voluntarily decide to allow unGodly emotions or feelings invade my spirit. I understand this today.

I understand how faith provides the strength and power for my spirit to soar. Love is the current which allows us to love, forgive, be kind and stay hopeful. When we follow the principle of self-correcting ourselves in a Godly manner, we show love to ourselves by understanding that God wants us to live righteously. We speak positively to ourselves and have our thought life under control. We start to think about what we are thinking about. When we get off the path of God, we immediately repent and then move back to that Godly path. This is how God will use us.

Today, ask God to help you "self-correct" so that He can use you. God wants to use each of us, to glorify Him. Let faith lead you thought life. Fully trust God each day. Train yourself to hear the Lord's voice so that you may self-correct and move to a path acceptable to the Lord. We must nor serve our will but God's will. It's our choice and we have the power to decide whom we will serve. Stop being comfortable and seek more of God. Get used to hearing God's voice. Jesus said, "My sheep hear my voice." We must seek to listen for His voice. Get to learn the voice of God instead of the voice of confusion. Know which way to walk because satan wants us to continue living as we have been. I know the way to go now even when I fall down, God is there waiting to pick me back up.

We must stop being blind and start having a blind faith in God. We can't move to higher levels of abundance until we walk differently, and get rid of the old person to become a true new creation in Christ!

Spiritual Refresher for Day #172

Take this time to spiritually reflect on this point: The creative power of words.

"Let the redeemed of the Lord say so, whom He has redeemed from the hand of the enemy (Psalm 107:2)."

There is such great power in words. If God has saved us, we need to say so. I declare that God has blessed me so greatly; I can't keep it to myself! I write all these tips for myself and others because I want everyone to praise God! Our words can glorify God or minimize God. What are your words doing this day? When we use our words to praise and glorify God, we ignite favor over our lives. When our words focus on how great our God is, instead of our problems, we honor the Lord in truth and spirit.

Today, take your faith further and say how good God is. We can take our faith further through our spoken and written words, which show God that we trust Him. In Genesis 1:3, "Then God said, 'Let there be light' and there was light." The Lord's word set it all in motion. Many times in life, nothing will happen until we speak it into existence.

Too many Christians think, speak and feel defeated before the battle is even fought. Every day, it's our choice how we choose to speak. Activate your faith so that you show the devil that you're not believing his lies.

The Lord said, "So shall My word be that goes forth from My mouth; it shall not return to Me void, But it shall accomplish what I please, and it shall prosper in the thing for which I sent it (Isaiah 55:11)." The word has great power! I'm repeating this phrase because it's so important.

1 John 4:4 says, "You are of God, little children, and have overcome them, because He who is in you is greater than he who is in the world." 1 John 4:6 states, "You are of God..." It's like the Lord knew we would have trouble believing it the first time so He told us again. We, you and I, are of God. So if God's words will prosper in what He sent it to do, then our words can do the same.

Our faith must be sure and true whereby we just can't doubt. We must speak it, claim it and act as if it will come to pass. David said in Psalm 142:5, "I cried out to You, O Lord: I said, 'You are my refuge, My portion in the land of the living...'" David knew how powerful the spoken word is.

When you read the bible today, read it out loud. Speak God's word to empower you. David stated in Psalm 145:18, "The Lord is near to all who call upon Him, to all who call upon Him in truth." We need to speak God's word throughout the day. Say it, declare victory each day.

We are well-able, proclaim it!

Speak only about how amazing your God is each day. Refuse to discuss your problems or grumble about other people. Speak about the life you wish God to help you achieve. Nothing will happen until you declare it. Talk to yourself out loud with Scripture.

Declare favor over your life each morning. Use your words to bless yourself and those around you. Don't focus on your problems but on your God. Change the way you communicate each day by being consistently being positive and expectant.
Romans 4:17 states, "God, who gives life to the dead and calls those things which do not exist as though they did; who, contrary to hope believed..." Call things as you see them with expectant hope as opposed to how your natural eyes see them. Put your faith into action through your spoken words.

Tell yourself each day, throughout the day, how your dreams are coming to pass, how you're getting healthier, stronger, more prosperous, and so on. Use your words to change your situation. Don't speak defeat over your life. Every day declare that you are getting better and better. Remember the song which says, 'let the weak say they are strong.' Only speak about the way you want to be, and don't focus on your infirmities.

Proverbs 6:2 states, "You are snared by the words of your mouth; you are taken by the words of your mouth." This is a warning from God telling us to be careful about our speech. Declare in words today, the life you want. Declare the victory! Tell yourself that, "I'm blessed and highly favored." Today, choose a different path, and start thinking about what you say each day, in order to change it.

God has promised us beauty for ashes. There are many promises in the Bible and one of my favorites is, "Instead of your shame you shall have double honor, and instead of confusion, they shall rejoice in their portion. Therefore in their land they shall possess double; everlasting joy shall be theirs (Isaiah 61:7)." Today, tell yourself that the rest of your life will be the best part of your life. Our words have great power and each believer should only use positive affirmations each day.

I wish you an abundant and highly blessed life; the same wish, I pray for myself!!

Spiritual Refresher for Day #173

Take this time to spiritually reflect on this point: Accepting God's mighty grace.

When we allow Christ into our hearts, we see the world differently. Our circumstances don't change, we do. We see the world through the love of God. We know that we are loved and we no longer seek the approval of others. We can live the life that God intended us to live. We know that God's love, includes His acceptance, when we come to have faith. We can accept ourselves because we believe that our Creator has accepted us and created a masterpiece when we formed us. We love ourselves for who we are but also as the person God intends us to be. We have faith that our Lord will do His job while we do our job to serve Him in truth and spirit. The late Christian monk Thomas Merton stated, "This is His call to us -- simply to be people who are content to live close to Him and to renew the kind of life in which the closeness is felt and experienced." These are such deeply personal words which touch my heart. If I live a life which always strives to get closer to God, I will feel Him and be transformed. When I allowed Christ to enter my heart and accepted God's grace, a new understanding came to me.

God is enough, and I now strive to live this revelation. Before, I never tried to live this way because I believed I needed things to be happy. When we learn to live by this notion of God's love being enough instead of seeking shiny things, the quality of our lives improves greatly. I used to believe that my identity was tied to my profession, the clothes I wore, the cars I drove, the jewelry I wore and the other things I purchased. I thought things made me happy. That was an illusion because a human can never find his or her identity or happiness in things. It's actually ridiculous to think how I lived in the past, chasing those things that everyone else chased. Now with Christ in my heart, I see and actually believe that Jesus is enough.

Too many Christians worship a little god, a small god. Their thoughts, words and actions say they believe god is like them with human characteristics. These christians (lower case to emphasize how they view the world) don't live as if their god is God. When we are changed, our lives will reflect this change through a steadfast faith. We believe in the greatness and boldness of God. We view God as the greatest thing in our lives instead of focusing on our problems. When we understand that God is great and that He has our best interest at heart, we can have great difficulties in our lives but praise the Lord each day. With God at our core, we can live for the first time in our lives with confidence and assurance. Today, my focus is on helping others and trusting God to help me.

Every believer must come to understand that God wants to change our hearts, desires, fears, weaknesses, thoughts in order to conform to His mind. Too many christians have transformed god into a being which is weak and small. God tells us in 1 Timothy 2:4 that He, "wants everyone to be saved." Faith must be the operating principle; not a weak and wavering, far off concept, which doesn't rule over their lives. When we understand how great our God is, then we understand the power in ourselves.

When we live each day knowing that God is God then we start to understand things differently. For example:

Nothing is too great for God (full stop).
God loves us without conditions (full stop).
God wants the best for us (full stop).
God wants us to whole and healthy (full stop).
God wants our minds renewed each day so that we see the world as it is, wicked and lost.
God wants us to have a God-consciousness which rules over our lives (full stop).

Understanding God's grace is important to having a renewed mind and a loving heart. The following verses discuss grace:

"God bestows His glorious grace on us in His Son (Ephesians 1:6)."
"The grace of our Lord has overflowed with the faith and love which are in Christ Jesus (1 Timothy 1:14)."
"The grace of God has abounded more than sin (Romans 5:15, 20-21; 6:1)."
"Grace is a store to which we have access through Christ (Romans 5:2)"
"Grace is given us in Christ (1 Corinthians 1:4)."
"It is received in abundance (Romans 5:17)."
"The Christian is not under the law under grace (Romans 6:14)."
"The gospel itself, which is the good news of grace, can be called grace (Acts 20:24)."
"Grace stands in opposition to the law. Both Jews and Gentiles are saved through the grace of the Lord Jesus (Acts 5:11)."

Grace is the active expression of God's great love. The English mystic Julian of Norwich stated, "The greatest honor we can give Almighty God is to live gladly because of the knowledge of His love." I am happy today with very little with a smile on my face because I know God loves me. I do not focus on what I have materially, but where I want to go (heaven). I know whose I am, and my identity is through Christ, who strengthens me.

I'm convinced that many Christians don't understand the gospel of grace. I know that I went to church for many years and never understood much about it. I was a christian who didn't understand the gospel of grace. Even now, I don't suggest I still understand all the complexities of the gospel of grace but my eyes are opened to it and my heart is receptive. I strive to learn more each day. I just know that I am unworthy but yet still receive it from God. The gospel of grace is the gospel of love. God loved us so much that He gave His son so that we may have eternal life. Many Christians still resist God's great love for them because they internalize feelings of low self-esteem and worthlessness. The free gift of God's grace is available for all, but we each must accept it.

Thomas Merton also stated, "A saint is not someone who is good but who experiences the goodness of God." These powerful words provide clarity to the Christian. Too few Christians actually feel the deep love that Jesus Christ has for each of us. God is love and

He wants us to love Him with our whole being. The Lord gave us the free, unmerited gift of grace and it should motivate us to live for Him. God wants us to glorify Him but that can't happen when we experience feelings of low self-esteem or even arrogance because both of those feelings do not glorify the Lord.

I discovered that when I started to fully accept God's love, real joy entered my life. I opened my heart and allowed Christ to enter and change it because I had nowhere else to turn. I decided that I wanted something more out of life instead of the same old stuff I had been getting. My life may not look outstanding to anyone looking from the outside in, but on the inside my heart sings. I have much work to do but I know whose I am, and what I must do each day: live a life which glorifies and honors the gospel of grace.

Today, start studying about the grace of God so that you may allow it to fully envelop you. Accept the grace of God. God's grace allows us to move beyond the hurts of the past so that we may become the masterpieces that we were intended to be in order to glorify God.

Thank the Lord today for your amazing grace!

Spiritual Refresher for Day #174

Take this time to spiritually reflect on this point: Living with Gratitude.

David states in Psalm 30:11-12, "You have turned for me my mourning into dancing; You have put off my sackcloth and clothe me with gladness; To the end that my glory may sing to You and not be silent. O Lord my God, I will give thanks to You Forever." I can relate to this scripture because I feel as though the Lord has turned my depression into happiness. I wasn't seeking happiness but it was just a by-product of seeking the Lord, praising the Lord and thanking God. Gratitude opens up doors of infinite power inside of us. Being thankful gets us focused on God instead of our troubles. Thankfulness also opens up a wave or positive energy into our lives as opposed to the negative energy which complaining brings.

Many spiritual traditions including Judaism, Islam and Christianity all express the benefit of being grateful. The Prophet Muhammad, founder of Islam, explained, "Gratitude for abundance you have received is the best insurance that the abundance will continue." There is another verse in the Qur'an 7:144 which states, "So hold that which I have given you and be of the grateful." Gratitude channels positive energy into the universe which will bring more joy into your life.

The Apostle Paul wrote much about gratitude a lot including, "Be anxious for nothing, but in everything by prayer and supplication, with thanksgiving, let your request be made known to God (Philippians 4:6)." Gratitude is a spiritual principle which brings a more positive attitude.

"In everything, give thanks (1 Thessalonians 5:18)." When we praise God and are thankful, we are telling God that we trust Him. The opposite of being grateful is complaining. Complaining and gratitude are opposite muscle groups. Complaining and grumbling puts negative energy into the universe. When we complain, it's like we are spitting in God's face for what He has given us. After I lost my job, I started to thank God a hundred times a day because I realized who I was through Christ. My spirit was free to love God and to praise Him. I learned that when I thanked God throughout the more challenging days, I felt better.

Albert Einstein had a great quote, "A hundred times a day I remind myself that my inner and outer life depends on the labors of other men, living and dead, and that I must exert myself in order to give in the same measure as I have received and am still receiving." I started says thank you to God a hundred times a day after reading this quote. We should all be thankful throughout the day as we acknowledge the great blessings in our lives.

Refresher exercise: Each day, make a list of ten things you're grateful for. Say thank you 100 times a day.

We can never be thankful enough. Too many Christians are ungrateful for what they already have. At one point in my life, I had nothing but thanked God each day as if I was man of great wealth. I praised and thanked God because I was rich in spirit. Gratitude is a powerful, positive emotion/feeling. It creates a powerful force inside of us which vibrates out into the world. The Apostle Paul also stated, "Giving thanks always for things to God the Father in the name of our Lord Jesus Christ (Ephesians 5:20)."

David praise and thanked God throughout the Psalms. Whenever I was down, all I had to do was to read the Psalms and was immediately uplifted. Psalm 100, A psalm of thanksgiving.

"Make a joyful shout to the Lord, all you lands!
Serve the Lord with gladness;
Come before His presence with singing.
Know that the Lord, His is God;
It is He who has made us, and not we ourselves;
We are His people and the sheep of His pasture.
Enter into His gates with thanksgiving,
And into His courts with praise.
Be thankful to Him, and bless His name.
For the Lord is good.
His mercy is everlasting,
And His truth endures to all generations."

This is one of my favorite Psalms. Praise opens the door for gratitude. Being grateful for what we already have received, helps to change our heart to have a Godly perspective. There is another Psalm I love 126:3 which says, "The Lord has done great things for us; whereof we are glad."

When I started writing this tip the night before, I meditated on it over night, and in the morning a song came on my heart. The song is called "Give Thanks" and it was written by Henry Smith. I have sung the hymn in church and it came to me as I was praying. The song goes like this: "Give thanks with a grateful heart; Give thanks to the Holy One; Give thanks because He's given Jesus Christ, His Son. Give thanks with a grateful heart; Give thanks to the Holy One; Give thanks because He's given Jesus Christ, His Son. And now let the weak say, I am strong," Let the Poor say, "I am rich," because of what the Lord has done - for us. Give thanks!" This song is beautiful and is available for download so that you can be reminded to be grateful. In the world, it can be a challenge at times to be grateful so we need to stay focused on the Godly things that matter.

God has laid out a plan for us to have an abundant life and gratitude helps us to stay on track and ensures that our hearts remain in the right state. I can say that I have been the cause of my own problems and troubles, just me; and I give God the glory for showing me a way out. I focused each day on the blessings instead of the things I couldn't control. I focused on thinking good thoughts and showing God I was content with all that I had instead of all that I didn't have. Sometimes I am so thankful, I want to be like David in 2 Samuel 6:14, "And Davis dances with all of his might before the Lord." David danced for the Lord because he was grateful. God is awesome and has amazing plans for each of our lives, being thankful shows the Lord that we trust Him.

I wanted to end this section with a general thanksgiving from the Book of Common Prayer:

"Almighty God, Father of all mercies, we, Your unworthy servants, give you humble thanks for all Your goodness and loving-kindness to us and to all men; We bless You for our creation, preservation, and all the blessings of this life; but above all for Your incomparable love in redemption of the world by our Lord Jesus Christ; for the means of grace, and for the hope of glory. And we pray, give us such an awareness of Your mercies, that with truly thankful hearts we may make known Your praise, not only with our lips, but in our lives, by giving up ourselves to Your service, and by walking before You in holiness and righteousness all out days through Jesus Christ our Lord, to whom with You and the Holy Spirit, be the honor and glory through the ages, Amen."

Take the above prayer and write it down. Carry it with you, read it out loud throughout the week, and watch favor and blessings come into your life.

Spiritual Refresher for Day #175

Take this time to reflect on this spiritual point: The God effect.

Doctors have confirmed the placebo effect in medicine. Placebo in Latin means, "I shall please." A placebo is an inert pill which can alter patient's expectations for healing which triggers powerful effects in the brain and the body. This phenomena has been called the placebo effect. This is in contrast to the effect of a nocebo. In Latin, Nocebo means, "I shall harm." A nocebo has the opposite effect of a placebo in that it causes patients to expect symptoms to worsen which can stimulate physiological effects. Both of these effects has been tested and proven to be effective in some patients.

Erik Vance wrote in the July/August 2014 issue of Discovery Magazine in his article, "Why nothing works," about the placebo effect. He explains that the placebo has been proven to trigger the brain's inner pharmacy which is like a perpetually stocked warehouse able to deliver real and active drugs to itself. He explains how the placebo's effectiveness is not based on some neurosis but the brain medicating itself like an inner pharmacy. The article goes on to say that placebos has been shown to improve the symptoms of Parkinson's as well as improving the conditions of general pain, depression, irritable bowel syndrome, anxiety, schizophrenia and other ailments. The article states that imaged studies of the brain has confirmed this fact.

Today, I wanted to discuss the God effect. Placebos work for some people because they believe it will work. For some people it doesn't work because they resist any efforts to be healed. These people who resist being healed never expect to get better. This is the same with the God effect. The God effect is based on faith. Jesus stated that anything is possible to those who believe. The same is true for those who doubt because anything is possible for those who believe that the worse will happen to them. The God effect will work in positive ways for those believers who complete faith in God's system.

Some people resist healing because they never expect to get better. Blaise Pascal reminds us that our achievements of today are but a sum total of our thoughts of yesterday. Messed up minds, leads to messed up lives. But God can take a mess and make a masterpiece out of it but one must believe in the God effect for it to work. The devil is content to let us profess Christianity as long as we do not practice it. Cicero stated, "Any man may make a mistake; none but a fool will persists in it." I decided that I needed to try a different path because the path I was on didn't work for me anymore. I didn't like the path on which my decisions took me so I decided to let go and let God. This may sound like a platitude but I learned that God is real because He touched my heart. God was able to change my thinking and heal the pain in my heart.

I wanted to use the placebo effect to show a dimension of the greatness of God and how we are already fully equipped for every good work. Romans 8:28 states, "And we know that all things God works for the good of those who love Him, who has been called according to His purpose." Do you know this in your heart and in your mind? This is where our belief meets the decisions we make each day because we can walk by faith or by fear. It's our choice every hour on how we choose to live.

There is great power within us but many refuse to accept it, rather they accept the limits that others put on them. Many people are their own worst enemy and put the greatest limits on themselves. The Dhammapada, a Buddhist text, states, "All that we are is the result of what we have thought: all that we are is founded on our thoughts and formed of our thoughts."

Too many Christians actually do not fully believe in the God which is described in the Bible. Their life testifies to a different belief, a broken sort of belief based on how they view the world instead of how God views the world. These Christians are more closely aligned to what the devil is saying than what God is saying.

Proverbs 23:7 states, "So as a man thinks in his heart, so as he is." This is one of my favorite verses in the Old Testament because it puts the responsibly where it should be, on us. Many people get used to living in a cycle of discontent. They speak and/or think defeat into their lives each day.

The most powerful Scripture I can quote is the words of the Son of God; Jesus stated in Mark 9:23, "All things are possible to the one who believes." If we believe then we can benefit from the God effect. God created us so that we would have everything we needed from within. Jesus also stated in Luke 17:21, "The Kingdom of God is within you." All Christians probably know this verse but too few actually believe it deep down. When sick, their first action is to call the doctor instead of calling the Great Physician, God. Jesus said to the leper in Luke 17:19, "Rise and go; your faith has made you well."

The Apostle Paul wrote in 1 Corinthians 3:16, "Don't you know that you yourselves are God's temple and that God's Spirit lives in you?" I want everyone reading this tip to understand that the God effect is already in you, waiting on you to ignite that inner fire. The placebo effect uses a pill to tell the brain to fix the body. The God effect uses the Words of the Lord from the Bible to tell our hearts, spirits, souls, and brains to ignite that internal fire so that we can glorify God through our actions.

God has given us all the tools we need each day to live an abundant life. I propose that if we eliminated all the doubt and other negative thoughts, we could literally achieve any goal we ever dreamed. The battle is in our mind, and we must put every unGodly thought into captivity. This refresher is to remind us that God created a masterpiece when He made us. If you are not operating at peak capacity then all you need to do is to fuel your faith through the reading of God's word, trust in God and take action believing that God had already fully equipped you. Stop speaking about or thinking about your weaknesses and start moving forward in faith. Take action to bring about the dream on your heart.

I realized that I was my own worst enemy but God revealed that I was also my own solution because He had fully equipped me to self-correct through His word, being empowered by the Holy Spirit. The Lord created us to operate perfectly and whatever we need for an abundant life is available through our faith in Christ Jesus.

For the placebo effect to take place, the patient must have faith in the doctor who proscribes the medicine to be healed. For the God effect to come to pass, the believer must have complete and total faith in the Lord. It's that simple. When we put our complete faith, trust and belief in Jesus Christ then mighty things will happen in our lives. There are times when the Lord will not change our circumstances but wants to change us instead so our circumstances no longer bothers us. It's then when we find joy in our circumstances that God may change those circumstances because we are ready to move to the next level.

The God effect is about changing our thinking and our hearts so that we move closer to the mind of the Lord. We can reap blessings and favor in our lives when continue to nourish and cultivate our faith each day knowing that we are God greatest creation!

Spiritual Refresher for Day #176

Take this time to spiritually reflect on this point: Genuineness of our faith.

"In this you greatly rejoice, though now for a little while, if need be, you have been grieved by various trials, that the genuineness of your faith, being much more precious than gold that perishes, though it is tested by fire, may be found to praise, honor, and glory at the revelation of Jesus Christ, whom having not seen you love (1 Peter 1:6-9)."

The above verse of Scripture is insightful because it tells us that our faith may be tested but that we should continue to praise, honor and glorify God despite the circumstances surrounding us. The Macarthur Study Bible states in the commentary section on this verse that, "God's purpose in allowing troubles is to test the reality of one's faith. But the benefit of such as testing or fire is immediately for the Christian, not God. When a believer comes through a trial trusting the Lord, he is assured that his faith is genuine (page 1940)."

The genuineness of our faith is demonstrated through a steadfast internal spirit where we are not moved to doubt. Genuineness of faith leads to having an abundant life and demonstrated our trust in God. There are times when some Christians ask themselves 'where is Jesus' when they start going through troubles or trials. It's during these times when believers think that they should always feel Jesus but with a genuineness of faith, we know He is there even when we don't see it or feel it.

Our genuineness of faith comes from inside. We must allow Jesus to fill that empty space inside. Jesus said, "Seek and you will find, ask and it shall be given, and knock and the door will be open." Jesus is waiting on us to allow Him into our heart. Allowing Jesus to touch our hearts will always bring us peace and contentment. Jesus wants to enter the hearts of all of us. So many believers are looking for joy, happiness, meaning or purpose in life but it can only come through a genuine commitment to Jesus Christ. Jesus lives within the heart of the believer with genuine faith. That faith should be nurtured and cultivated each day.

"That He would grant you, according to the riches of His glory, to be strengthened with might through His Spirit in the inner man, that Christ may dwell in your hearts through faith; that you, being rooted and grounded in love, may be able to comprehend with all the saints what is the width and length and depth and height -- to know the love of Christ which passes knowledge; that you may be filled with all the fullness of God (Ephesians 3:16-19)."

A Christian with genuine faith believes the above verses in spirit and truth. Christ strengthens the believer through His Spirit. The Spirit of Jesus is rooted and grounded in love. One cannot be a genuine believer if one doesn't have love in their heart. Some Christians will raise their hand and say, "I have love in my heart," but once you mention the name of an enemy, they crinkle their nose and their demeanor changes away from love. Love can't be turned on and off if one wants to be a true believer. I had to wrestle with the feelings of resentment towards those who I thought wronged me but I gave it to Christ and He cleaned my heart from those feelings. I trusted Jesus to help me to change the beliefs in my heart, and He did. I now pray for my enemies and if you ask me about them, my nose no longer crinkles up and I bless them.

When we come to know the love of Jesus Christ, we are changed and then want to share the love with everyone else. It starts with allowing Jesus into our hearts. When we seek to embrace Christian values, it's demonstrated by the sincerity of our faith. I seek out opportunities each day to demonstrate the spiritual fruit in my heart. I often meditate on the concept of genuineness of faith which allows me to move closer to Christ even where I can feel the heat of the flames around me. It's a struggle sometimes because the devil tries to whisper in my ear but I just take it boldly to the throne of grace for strength, and I am never disappointed.

"Now unto him that is able to do exceeding abundantly above all that we ask or think, according to the power that works in us (Ephesians 3:20)." I want all Christians to understand the power within them to combat any issue or problem. The remarkable power of God is imparted in us and energized in us by the Holy Spirit. We must believe and have a sincere faith in Jesus. With the power in us which comes from the genuineness of our faith, we can accomplish far more that we can ever imagine on our own.

When we have a genuineness of faith, no one can take our joy. John 16:22 says, "No one will take away your joy." With a genuineness of belief, no one can take our enthusiasm or our peace. This is why it's so important to build a genuine reservoir of faith on the inside.

Don't be a little christian; Be a BOLD Christian! Be a light to others who are struggling even if you are still struggling. The best way to get out of our own minds and egos, and focused on Christ is to help others. When we help others with no expectation of benefiting, we become the hands and feet of Christ. This is genuine faith. Some Christians are waiting to be blessed or for their circumstances to change before they start their ministry, but God wants us to show our faith today. When we seek to serve the Lord with genuine faith; favor and blessings will come into our lives. Step out boldly in faith and watch the Lord work.

Today is the day to drawn near to the Lord, and watch God draw near to you (James 4:8). We are in charge of our thought life and faith life. No one can tell you what to believe. Create faith by reading more of the Bible each day. If your faith is wavering, turn to the concordance in the back of your Bible to look up the verses which discusses faith. This will help to renew and build up your faith. I can't write enough about faith because it's so important to keep this spiritual principle fresh in our minds.

I love the verse in Isaiah 43:19 which says, "Behold, I will do a new thing, Now it shall spring forth; shall you not know it?" Today is a great opportunity to start doing new things in order to glorify the Lord. Plan for victory in your life, not defeat. If we help others with their faith then it helps us with our faith. Life becomes joy-filled when we seek to improve our faith each day.

Regardless of what anyone does or says to us, we have the power within us to decide if we will allow it to affects us or not. Joel Osteen states in his book, *'Every Day a Friday'*, "What a person says about you does not define who you are. His or her opinion of you does not determine your self-worth." We must continue focusing on serving the Lord through a genuineness of faith regardless of what is happening around us. Our identity must be steadfast in Christ. A genuineness of faith is easily recognized in those who have allowed Jesus to touch their hearts.

Be a Bold Christian today! It's time to make the dreams of your heart a reality but it won't happen to until you boldly step out in genuine faith!!

Spiritual Refresher for Day #177

Take this time to spiritually reflect on this point: Worshiping the Lord.

"Therefore, since we are receiving a kingdom that cannot be shaken, let us be thankful, and so worship God acceptably with reverence and awe, for our God is a consuming fire (Hebrews 12:28-29)."

Our God is a consuming fire and we should have a passion to serve and worship Him in the same manner. Too many believers have allowed their fire to go out. It's time to get your fire back for God, which glories Him. The way we carry ourselves often tell a more truthful picture of who we worship. There are so many people who mark the box "Christian" for their religious preference but their thoughts, attitude and words don't say this because they have no fire for God.

"But those who seek the Lord shall not lack any good thing (Psalm 34:10)." When we seek after the Lord with the same passion that we go after worldly ambitions, we are rewarded in many amazing ways. No matter what happens to us, we must always remember that we are never alone because Jesus is always with us, we may just not perceive it. One of the greatest promises in the Bible is, "Who shall separate us from the love of Christ (Romans 8:35)?"

No one nor anything can separate us from the love of Christ Jesus, and this is reason alone to worship Him every day and throughout the day. I never realized that the condition of my heart prevented me from hearing the Lord. Today, I hear the Lord because I changed how I worship. I no longer seek the things of the world first but seek His face, the Lord Jesus Christ first. When we change our focus, pivoting from a life of ambition to a life of meaning, the world as we see it transforms. I see beauty where others see ashes. This is a direct result of having a passion to worship the Lord.

"God is spirit, and his worshipers must worship in spirit and truth (John 4:24)." When we worship in this manner, our ability to discern what pleases God improves and we start to hear that small still voice of God. It's an amazing thing when we start to worship God in spirit and truth, because we will start to see a mirror effect in our lives whereby the quality of our lives improves. By focusing on the spirit of God, we start to transform on the inside. "We ... are being transformed into His image with ever-increasing glory, which comes from the Lord, who is Spirit (2 Corinthians 3:18)." This is the gift that we are promised. When we pursue the Lord as we have pursued things of the world, the great awakening occurs, our spirit awakes and we can begin the work the Lord intended us to do for Him.

"You must worship no other gods, but only the Lord, for He is a God who is passionate about His relationship with you (Exodus 34:12)." I love love love this verse! God is passionate about having a relationship with us! It's only reasonable that we are passionate about Him in return. I try to invite new people to come worship with me at church weekly, and sometimes I am blessed when they come because we are all commissioned to bring people to Christ. But there are sometimes, they tell me that they are too busy but it's all of our jobs as Christians to share the message of the Gospel. No one knows how much time they have before judgment comes, so it's vital that all of the house of faith be ready in season and out. The Ten Commandments has six commandments about our relationship to others and four commandments are about our relationship with God.

There are some Christians who put some many things before God. We are commanded by God to put no idols or gods before the Lord. There are some who make every excuse to do other things instead of spending time with the Lord in order to grow closer with Him. We will never grow closer to God if we don't spend time with His word. Bible study, worshiping in church with other believers and doing volunteer work are all a part of serving and worshiping the Lord. When I started leading a prayer group and teaching others for free, I felt better. We can worship God in many ways to include by being His hands and feet to help others. God is love and when we show love to others, we are worshiping the Lord. "Take your everyday, ordinary life -- your sleeping, eating, going-to-work, and walking-around life - and place it before God as an offering. Embracing what God does for you is the best thing you can do for Him (Romans 12:1)."

God wants us to voluntarily love Him, to come to Him in spirit and truth. In Deuteronomy, God tell the Hebrews to choose life. Worship is choosing life. When I am most down, I start a praise party and focus on the goodness, the greatness, the awesomeness of my Lord Jesus Christ and my mood brightens instantly. Worship is a great way to improve our mood and fight depression. When we change our focus from our problems and to worship, life gets better.

Life gets better, when we get better. A minister told me this statement and I haven't forgotten this point. Whenever I get sad or down, I start worshiping and singing songs to the Lord, and everything gets better. "Give honor to the Lord for the glory of His name. Worship the Lord in the splendor of His holiness (Psalm 29:2)." When we live to give honor and glory to God, favor and blessings rain down on us. I'm not attempting to explain how this mystery works but it does. When our focus is on the great love God has for us and what He has done for us, we are more positive. Having a positive attitude brings more positive things into our lives.

"Great is the Lord! He is most worthy praise! He is to be revered above all the gods (Psalm 96:4)." Reverence for God has been forgotten by many in the church. I never understood how important it was until I read the Bible with an open heart. I still have my struggles each day but my days are better when I put God first and worship Him throughout the day.

Today's tip is focused on getting our fire back to passionately worship the Lord in spirit and truth! Take this time to design a plan to incorporate more worship into your life, and watch God work!!

Spiritual Refresher for Day #178

Take this time to spiritually reflect on this topic: Smiling as praise.

You may wonder why I say to spiritually reflect on smiling. I smile because of what Jesus did on the cross for me. A smile is an expression of inner joy and contentment. Each morning when I get up, I thank God for another day and put a smile on my day because I know it will be a great day. A smile can be a form of praise.

"This is the day the Lord has made, we will rejoice and be glad in it (Psalm 118:29)."

I love this verse because it about recognizing what God has done immediately and then leaving no doubt as to what we will do, rejoice and be glad. Too many people leave room for doubt which allows the devil to enter. "I guess I'm..." or "Maybe I feel this way because ...." These people are already factoring in defeat but Jesus didn't die on the cross for defeat. Jesus defeated death on the cross so that we would live in victory. Too many Christians fail to understand that we must transform our thoughts and words so that they reflect the God we worship, an amazing awesome God!

'We will rejoice and be glad in it', is a declarative statement without doubt. Take the doubt out of your vocabulary. After I wake up and thank God for the day, I put a smile on my face to show God that I am trusting Him. My smile shows that I expect goodness to enter my life. I smile because I am happy for everything that has come into my life and for everything about to come. Jesus explained that, "In the world you will have tribulation and trials and distress and frustration; but be of good cheer ... (John 16:33)." I smile because there is good cheer on the inside. My life is still full of trials but my perspective has changed.

Sometimes we can smile at others and that can be the greatest gift we can give them, especially someone who is hurting. Jesus stated in John 14:27, "stop allowing yourselves to be agitated and disturbed (or not let your heart be troubled)." Smile more, smile brighter and see how things start to look more positive. I was called "smiley" at my gym and in my neighborhood because I smiled so much. I was constantly asked, "why are you always smiling?" I would use that as an opportunity to testify and say, "I smile because of what Jesus has done in my life. I can't speak about He has done for others but I can testify to what He has given me." It became a testimony for me. I would declare that God has given me ability to choose my attitude each day and how I choose to glorify God through my countenance and smile.

I refuse to let anyone steal my joy. Psalm 16:11, "In (God's) presence is fullness of joy." When I allowed God to enter my heart, I experienced true joy for the first time in my life. My smile represents my faith; I want the world to see what God has done in my life. When life gets difficult, that's the time to smile even more because our smile will let the devil know whose child we are, and whose promises we are standing on.

Smiling has become a habit for me now. I rarely smiled before I gave my life to Christ but now I smile always because of what Jesus has done in my heart. Smiling is good for our health and we must constantly remember how it can help our mood. Researchers have found out that wearing a smile brings about certain benefits like slowing down the heart and reducing stress. The very act of smiling can help you feel better, happier. By putting a smile on my face each morning before I climbed out of my bed, I set the tone for the day.

Some research has suggested that only a full genuine smile provides benefits while other studies show that even a polite smile many be beneficial. You can influence your mental health by what you do with your face whether you smile a lot or frown. Frowning also has a health effect, a negative one. So many Americans suffer from anxiety disorders, mood disorders, and depression. I was one of them who suffered from major depressive disorder and I can attest how the simple act of smiling helped me.

We must participate in our own rescue. So many people walk around defeated before the battle has already started. Pindar stated in 500 B.C., "The best of healers is good cheer." Smiling seems to have so many positive benefits over our health even science can not quantify the exact benefits. Smiling also opens up so many other doors in our lives. I learned that my smiles elicited more positive reactions from people because it connects us and draws out a positive reaction. Science has shown that people who smile more tend to elicit more positive connections with other people.

I love the beginning of Psalm 126: "When the Lord brought back the captive ones of Zion, we were like those who dream. Then our mouth was filled with laughter and our tongue with joyful shouting; then they said among the nations. The Lord has done great things for them. The Lord has done great things for us; we are glad." If we put forward an effort to smile, it becomes an outward expression of our faith because we demonstrate our gratitude to God. We have the power inside of us to reach higher levels of spiritual attainment but we need to do things differently. Too many Christians allow their circumstances to effect their praise. A smile can be praise. Don't carry around your worries, give those to God; instead carry around a ready smile. Give someone the gift of a smile today.

Smiling creates positive energy and a positive vibration in the world. We improve our mood and energy levels with smiles. Smiling opens up waves of positive energy and blessings in your life. Start your day with a smile as a way to praise God.

Jesus stated, "Let you light so shine before men, that they may see your good works and glorify your Father in heaven (Mathew 5:16)." We can let our light shine through our smile. A smile is a clear demonstration and testimony to the saving power of God. As believers we can use our smile to glorify God and lead others to Him.

Today, tell yourself:

I smile because of God's unconditional love.

I smile because of God's great grace!
I smile because of Jesus' victory on the cross!
I smile because He loved me first!
I smile because He has fully equipped me for every good work!
I smile because Jesus left me a Comforter, the Holy Spirit, which empowers me!

Many people have internalized such negative habits each day and this draws in more negativity. I was like this but now I focus on healthier habits such as monitoring what my face is doing throughout the day. I work on smiling and it has become a routine positive habit now. Kirk Franklin has a beautiful song called "I Smile" which goes like this: "I smile even though I hurt, see I smile. I know God is working, so I smile. Even though I've been here for a while, I smile...I smile. It's so hard to look up when you've been down. Sho would hate to see you give up now, you look much better when you smile..." These are a few of the lyrics. The fact is that it's harder to be depressed when you smile.

Smile today and trust God to be God. Show the world your light through your smile!

Just smile! It's beautiful and so are you!

Spiritual Refresher for Day #179

Take this time to spiritually reflect on this point: Truth and honesty.

Jesus stated in John 16:13, "However, when He, the Spirit of truth, has come, He will guide you into all truth..."

Truth and honesty leads to living in a Godly manner which pleases God. This refresher is focus on burning off the old spirit of lies and self-deception in order to serve God in spirit and truth. The greatest threat to a deep spiritual life is self-deception. Too many Christian are deceiving themselves because their hearts are far from what Jesus taught, and they are content with not changing. I am not content with living in self-deception. I wrote this refresher to help myself to continue to live in an honest manner. Jesus stated, "And you shall know the truth, and the truth shall make you free (John 8:32)."

Until I allowed Christ to enter my heart, I was constantly lying to myself. I told myself that I was a good Christian because I believed in Christ and I was baptized as a child. I told myself that I lived a pretty good life. I was living in self-created framework instead of walking in truth as Jesus spoke about. "I have no greater joy than to hear that my children walk in truth (3 John 4)." I didn't even understand what truth was because I wasn't seeking it, it wasn't a priority. I wanted to live the way I wanted to live instead of living for Christ. This is rebellion when we decide to do what we want instead of what God tells us. The laws of God are not suggestions. When we rebel against God, there are consequences. God is faithful to forgive our sins but that doesn't exempt us from the consequences of that sin.

There are so many Christian who lie routinely. They speak straight lies, lies of omission and lies of deceit. You could ask some Christians about their belief life and they will think nothing of shading the truth in order to look better. Lying has become such a large part of our culture, we do it without thinking. I know I did, and perhaps I'm just preaching to myself now. Telling the truth seems to have lost its importance in our society.

"Do not lie to one another, since you have put off the old man with his deeds, and have put on the new man who is renewed in knowledge according to the image of Him who created him (Colossians 3:9-10)." Whatever we do for a long time, it becomes a part of our life.

We must focus on being truthful to ourselves and to God about our spiritual practices. If we were honest, we would all be convicted of not serving God in spirit and truth to the best if our ability. In today's society, we think nothing of telling little lies to "protect someone's ego" or "to not be cruel" but we can tell the truth in love without being cruel. Lies come so quickly from some that they don't think nothing of it because truth is not longer valued in our culture. For example, ask a believer who doesn't go to church regularly to come to church with you and watch the truth disappear.

"We know that we are of God, and the whole world lies under the sway of the wicked one (1 John 5:14)." I used to find every excuse to not attend the House of the Lord regularly. My feet were quick to run to wickedness. "People with integrity have firm footing, but those who follow crooked paths will slip and fall (Proverbs 10:9)." I compromised my integrity and I fell but when I gave my life to Christ and got saved, I started a new beautiful journey. I knew that it would take a lot of work in order to move away from the world to get closer to God, but the difference is that I am willing and open to change for God.

The reason we should strive for honesty and truthfulness in all we do is because it's what God expects. Truth pleases God. "He keeps His eye on all who live honestly, and pays special attention to His loyally committed ones (Proverbs 2:8)."

We need to retrain ourselves so our default will be the truth. "My little children, let us not love in word or in tongue, but in deed and truth. And this we know that we are of the truth, and shall assure our hearts before Him (1 John 3:18-19)." There are many Christians who have a difficult time to love in truth. Dysfunction has been allowed to run wild for so long that they no longer recognize the truth. Self-deception clouds their judgment and there is no discernment. A great thing happens when we start serving God in truth, we develop an ability to discern God's voice. The Holy Spirit will show us the truth when we open our hearts to love and Good News of the Gospel.

I begin reading the Bible with an open heart and the truth came upon my heart; and I was freed as Jesus said I would be. "Always learning and never able to come to the knowledge of the truth (2 Timothy 3:7)." There are still Christians today who are living in the fog of sin which blinds them to the knowledge of the truth. The ability to hear God's small still voice is blocked because of the conditions of their hearts.

"Now the Spirit expressly says that in latter time some will depart from the faith, giving heed to deceiving spirits and doctrines of demons, speaking lies in hypocrisy, having their own conscience seared with a hot iron...(1 Timothy 4:1-2)."

Some believers are so good at lying to themselves that it's become such a habit that they do it routinely without thinking. This tip is to remind us all to think about, what we are thinking about and speaking about. It's time to get serious about God because He cannot lie. "In the hope of eternal life which God, who cannot lie, promised before time began... (Titus 1:2-3)." Since God cannot lie, He cannot tolerate those who lie. Developing a deep spiritual practice starts with getting honest with ourselves. We must maintain rigorous honesty with ourselves and with God. Growth and maturity comes when we seek to know the truth so that we can become the people who God intended us to be. "Therefore let us keep the feast, not with old leaven, nor with the leaven of malice and wickedness, but with the unleavened bread of sincerity and truth (1 Corinthians 5:8)."

Psalm 91:4 states, "His truth shall be your shield." Today, I still have challenges of being honest with myself but it's on my spiritual priority list each day. I work on being honest each day, in order to get even more honest. This is what this refresher is about, being better so that we may all be saved. "The coming of the lawless one is according to the working of satan, with all power, signs, and lying wonders, and with all unrighteous deception among those who perish, because they did not receive the love of the truth, that they might be saved (2 Thessalonians 2:9-10)."

We must have a passion for, and love of the truth. Truth is of God. God is love, light and truth. These are the qualities that we should all strive for. "Because God from the beginning chose you for salvation through sanctification by the Spirit and belief in the truth, to which He called you by our Gospel, for the obtaining of the glory of our Lord Jesus Christ (2 Thessalonians 2:13-14)."

Ask God to change your heart so that you can live in a more Godly manner each day. This is what I do every day, I ask God to help me because I know I can't do it alone. It's through the Holy Spirit that our nature can be changed but it starts with surrendering. I had a hard time with this principle because I loved to rebel. When I started to meditate on God's word, insight came to my heart. I saw how my lifestyle had brought certain consequences. My lies were tangible demonstrations of rebelling to God. I know this now and have made a change. I give God my weaknesses in an honest manner, admitting all my sinful thoughts or deeds, so that He may give me His righteousness. God wants the best for you and me. When we align our lives with how God wants us to live, then favor and blessings comes our way.

Satan is called the prince of lies. We can either serve him or serve the Lord. God has promised us that He would never leave nor forsake us. "Call to Me, and I will answer you, and show you great and mighty things, which you do not know (Jeremiah 33:3)." My life changed when I went to God with a receptive heart asking Him to cleanse it and to show me where I needed to change so I could live a life pleasing to Him.

Jesus stated, I am the way, the truth and the life (John 14:6)." We must seek, pursue and be lovers of the truth so that we may all gain the upward prize.

Spiritual Refresher for Day #180

Take this time to spiritually reflect on this point: Fulfilling our ministry.

This refresher has two parts: Fulfilling our unique purpose or ministry that God has given us; and to spread the Good News of Jesus Christ as He commanded us to do.

"Let no one despise your youth, but be an example to the believers in word, in conduct, in love, in spirit, in faith, in purity. Till I come, given attention to reading, to exhortation, to doctrine. Do not neglect the gift that is in you, which was given to you by prophecy with the laying on of hands of the eldership. Meditate on these things; give yourself entirely to them, that your progress may be evident to all. Take heed to yourself and to the doctrine. Continue in them, for doing this you will save both yourself and those who hear you (1 Timothy 4:12-16)." We were created to not just exist, but to serve and glorify the Lord. There are so many Christians just barely making it. God said in His word that we are His masterpieces. Masterpieces are meant to shine and to thrive. There are too many Christians who aren't thriving. I propose that when we start to focus on fulfilling our ministry, we will begin to thrive, and our wings will allow us to soar!

The word "ministry' can be exchanged with the phrase "serving God". We were created by God for a purpose. Everything that God has created has a purpose. We matter to God and it's our job to serve Him and to bring glory to His name. Our purpose or ministry is connected to why God created us. We must want more out of life, because God wants more for us. The Lord wants us to have an abundant life, not an average life. Why are you accepting a "less than" life?

"And He Himself gave some to be apostles, some prophets, some evangelists, and some pastors and teachers, for equipping of the saints for the work of ministry, for the edifying of the body of Christ, till we all come to the unity of the faith and the knowledge of the Son of God, to a perfect man, to the measure of the stature of the fullness of Christ; that we should no longer be children, tossed to and fro and carried about with every wind of doctrine, by the trickery of men, in cunning craftiness of deceitful plotting, but, speaking the truth in love, may grow up in all things into Him is the head -- Christ -- from who the whole body, joined and knit together by what every joint supplies, according to the effective working by which every part does its share, causes growth of the body for the edifying of itself in love (Ephesians 4:11-16)."

Some Christians may be working in their field of specialty but are not living up to their potential. Even though they may be working in their right field, they are not fulfilling their ministry. God wants us to be great, to magnify His name, to bring others to Him. Our ministry must be based on love and serving God with our talents. Being content and settling with where we are in life, is a trick of the devil. There are too many Christians who are still babes in Christ after a lifetime to going to church, because there has been no real growth. The evil one wants us to settle, to tell ourselves that we are done enough. The devil wants to trick us into doing less for Christ.

When we accept Christ into our hearts, then it's time to go to work because we are given a second chance. It's our choice what we want to do with that second choice. I am writing this work because I wish to help others be who God intended them to be. I would have never thought of writing 180 tips to bring glory to God but Jesus saved me and I must shout to the world that if He could touch my broken and wretched heart, then He can do the same for you! I was depressed; He saved me and gave me a second chance, what a glorious Savior! Now, it's my job to serve Him in spirit and truth.

What will you do with you second chance? I want to challenge us today to keep pushing forward in Christ in order to fulfill our ministry. Pray to God to show you in which direction you should. Scour the Scriptures to see which verses speak to your heart.

When we look for opportunities to bless or help others, this helps to point us in the right direction. "All who are led by the Spirit of God are children of God (Romans 8:14)." God's system is so amazing; I never knew this because I was too self-absorbed. This tip is about being Christ-absorbed. Break out of the old way of doing things. For example, start to attend church during the week to reenergize your talents and seek to hear God's voice in different places. Start volunteering at a soup kitchen or the homeless shelter looking for new places God can use you. God wants us to be His hands and feet, it's through these things that we find ourselves. I found myself, through helping others. It's when we are focused on God, that many times He speaks the most clearly to us.

"All things work together for good to those who love God, to those who are called according to His purpose (Romans 8:28)." We are all called to bring others to Christ. We are all meant to be ministers of Christ. Peter tells us that we were chosen by God "to do His work and speak out for Him, to tell others of the night and day difference He made for you (1 Peter 2:9)."

To show this point even clearer, Jesus stated in Mathew 28:18-20, "...All Authority has been given to Me in heaven and earth. 'Go therefore and make disciples of all nations, baptizing them in the name of the Father, and of the Son and of the Holy Spirit, teaching them to observe all things that I have commanded you; and lo, I am with you always, even to the end of this age.' Amen." This is called the great commission and it was given by Jesus to His disciples but it's also His commission to us. The commission is reiterated in the Gospel of Mark 16:15-18. The commission is spoken about also in Luke 24:47. In John 15:16-17, Jesus stated, "You did not choose Me, but I choose you and appointed you that you should go and bear fruit, and that your fruit should remain, that whatever you ask the Father in My name, He may give you. These things I commanded you, that you love one another." Living with love and serving with love, will ignite the fire within!

We are to bear fruit with the gifts and talents God gave us. We, as Christians, are known by our love, a love of truth inspired by the Holy Spirit. When we have love, we want to spread the message which saved us. We long to know the great love of God. We should seek to fulfill our ministry knowing that God has empowered us. "But you are a chosen generation, a royal priesthood, a holy nation, His own special people, that you may proclaim the praises of Him who called you out of darkness into His marvelous light (1

Peter 2:9)." God has given me so much that I want to proclaim it to the world! God wants us to be passionate about Him because He is passionate about us.

Our purpose, our ministry is centered on serving God in spirit and truth. We each have unique ministry based on the God given set of skills and talents we were given at birth. We were all fearfully and wonderfully made. "Therefore, since we have this ministry, as we have received mercy, we do not lose heart. But we have renounced the hidden things of shame, not walking in craftiness nor handling the word of God deceitfully, but by manifestation of the truth commending ourselves to every man's conscience in the sight of God. But even if our gospel is veiled, it is veiled to those who are perishing, whose minds the god of this age has blinded, who do not believe, lest the light of the gospel of the glory of Christ, who is the image of God, should shine on them. For we do not preach ourselves but Christ Jesus the Lord, and ourselves your bondservants for Jesus sake. For it is the God who commanded light to shine out of darkness, who has shone in our hearts to give the light of the knowledge of the glory of God in the face of Jesus Christ (2 Corinthians 4:1-6)."

Each believer has a unique narrative or story which can help others. "Those who believe in the Son of God have a testimony of God in them (1 John 5:10a)." Pastor Rick Warren states in his greatly inspired work, "The Purpose Driven Life," that 'God has given you a Life Message to share. When you became a believer, you also became God's messenger. God wants to speak to the world through you. Paul said, "We speak the truth before God, as messengers of God" (2 Corinthians 2:17b).'

Our testimony shows others how God touched our hearts and moved us to serve Him. Jesus said in Acts 1:8, "You will be my witness." When we start looking for ways to fulfill our unique ministry, we demonstrate our faith in God as a true servant. When others see us, as believers, walking in love, we send a powerful message which leads others to go after the same salvation that we sought.

Be encouraged to share the great love the Lord has shown you today!

All my hope and love! Philip Allan Turner

Learning To Discern God's Voice - 180 Day Devotional for walking in the Spirit by Philip Allan Turner. The author's goal of writing this daily devotional was to help himself to be more devoted to Christ Jesus, and hope it helps the reader in the same manner. These motivational/inspirational tips are meant to inspire and refresh the spirit. He wants to motivate and inspire you to be all that God created you to be. The author invites you to start a 180 day journey to walk in the Spirit in order to change your life for the better. Each daily study builds on the previous lesson. This work is different than your average daily devotional; it's a study in how to discern God's voice in your everyday life. The author wants to ignite that fire within you to live passionately for God!

We are God's greatest masterpiece! "For God has not given us the spirit of fear; but of power, and of love, and of a sound mind (2 Timothy 1:7)." The power is in us, we just have to stir up the gifts within us. The author wants everyone to understand the great love that God has for us.

We have all have the conditions for our own happiness right now. What God has taught the author:

--Failure is not final and God can use me even now to bring others to Christ.
--God provides for all our needs and when once our perspective changes, our needs changes.
--God taught him that a clean and merry heart can heal a multitude of diseases, even a dis-ease of the soul.
--The tests which comes in our lives, only makes us stronger.
--Change always comes but hope is eternal.
--No one is beyond redemption, even the hardest of hearts can be touched by the love of God.
--If we are intentional and purposeful, we can learn to discern the voice of God and walk in the Spirit each day.
--God is the Great Motivator and Inspirer, just lean on Him and watch Him go to work in your life!

He wrote this work to show others who are still in mental bondage that they can be free in spirit regardless of external circumstances. The author's life message is based on these three main points: Pray Big, Hope Big and Love Big!

####

Philip Allan Turner has written two other books: *Know Better, Do Better; How To Lean Into The Light and How To Be Your Best SELF!* and *Know Better, Do Better – 20 Steps to Empowerment and Love*. He has held many jobs to include being a fitness instructor, a carpenter and a real estate agent, but now is focused on serving the Lord full-time. He writes spiritual non-fiction, devotionals and historical fiction books. He is studying to be an ordained minister. He is from Philadelphia originally, but now calls Newark, N.J. home.

www.ingramcontent.com/pod-product-compliance
Lightning Source LLC
LaVergne TN
LVHW061302060426
835510LV00014B/1844